Tolstoy on Education

Tolstoy on Education

Tolstoy's educational writings 1861–62

selected and edited by Alan Pinch *and*
Michael Armstrong
and translated by Alan Pinch

Rutherford • Madison • Teaneck
Fairleigh Dickinson University Press

Associated University Presses, Inc.
4 Cornwall Drive
East Brunswick, NJ 08816

Library of Congress Cataloging in Publication Data

Tolstoy, Leo, graf, 1828-1910.
Tolstoy on education.

Bibliography: p.
Contents: Introduction—On the education of the people—The Yasnaya Polyana school in the months of November and December—[etc.]
1. Tolstoy, Leo, graf, 1828-1910. 2. Education—Philosophy—Addresses, essays, lectures.
3. IAsnopolianskaia shkola imeni L.N. Tolstogo—Addresses, essays, lectures. I. Pinch, Alan. II. Armstrong, Michael, B.Phil. III. Title.
LB675.T6 1982 370'.1 81-65867
ISBN 0-8386-3121-5 AACR2

Printed in the United States of America

Contents

Preface

In the autumn of 1859 Lev Tolstoy started an experimental school for peasant children on his estate, Yasnaya Polyana. The school was a brilliant success, and it remained Tolstoy's principal occupation until he began work upon *War and Peace* in the latter part of 1862. However, the series of articles which he wrote about the school and his educational theories attracted little attention at the time. To this day this episode has remained a relatively neglected aspect of Tolstoy's work, even in Russia.

We first became interested in Yasnaya Polyana school after reading Sir Isaiah Berlin's article 'Tolstoy and Enlightenment' (*Encounter* 16, no. 2, and later included in *Russian Thinkers,* Hogarth Press, 1978), which still remains the most stimulating discussion of the subject in English. On reading Tolstoy's articles and other documents about the school we felt sure that they would interest many English-speaking educationists and admirers of Tolstoy. Since only poor translations existed, or in some cases none at all, we set about repairing the omission.

We wish to express our gratitude for kind assistance and advice to Professor J. C. Dumbreck, Professor Brian Simon, Mrs Joan Simon, Mr Peter Smith, Mr Vladimir Vishniak and Mrs Nesta Williams. We thank the John Rylands University Library of the University of Manchester for permission to read there. We are particularly indebted to the London Library, where we first had access to the Jubilee Edition of Tolstoy's works and discovered a copy of the memoirs of V. S. Morozov. Mrs Pat McMunn was our patient and accurate typist.

The responsibility for any errors and defects remains, of course, solely ours.

An extract from our version of 'The Yasnaya Polyana school in the months of November and December' was published previously in *Outlook,* the magazine of the Mountain View Center for Environmental Education, Colorado.

An English translation of most of the essays appeared in 1904 as volume 4 of *The Complete Works of Count Tolstoy,* published by J. M. Dent & Co (of 29 & 30 Bedford Street, London W. C.). The translator was Leo Wiener, at that time an assistant professor of Slavic languages at Harvard University, but not a native English speaker. Aylmer Maude discusses Wiener's translations in an appendix to the first volume of his biography of Tolstoy in which he evaluates various English translators of Tolstoy's works (*The Life of Tolstoy,* vol. 1, pp. 456–67, O.U.P., 1929). Maude comments that Wiener, 'despite a number of curious slips, understands the Russian he is translating, but the pity is that when he made this version he had no literary command of our language.' The first of Maude's examples of Wiener's curious use of English is, as it happens, taken from the translation of the educational essays. Wiener's translation of what he called the 'Pedagogical Articles' is indeed scarcely readable. Nevertheless a photographic reprint of this translation, though not acknowledged as such, was published by the University of Chicago Press in 1967, with a short general introduction by Reginald D. Archambault, as *Tolstoy on Education*. Not surprisingly, the reprint of an inferior sixty-year-old translation has done little to promote an interest in Tolstoy's educational writings.

A.H.P.
M.A.

Introduction

I The Historical Background: Alan Pinch

The documents collected in this book deal with Lev Tolstoy's educational activities over a period of about three years, 1859–62. This is only a small fragment of Tolstoy's long career and, as we shall show later, not the only time which he devoted to education. There are three reasons that we have chosen to concentrate on these three years. First, they are the richest years of his career in education. In 1859 Tolstoy was thirty-one. He was mature and yet young; his physical and mental energy was vast; he believed he had found his life-work. Although later on (notably when composing his textbook for elementary schools) Tolstoy was to give long and devoted work to education, he was never again to find the same passion and consuming fury for pedagogical studies, never again to give a large proportion of his time to practical classroom teaching. While it lasted it was what the Russians call an *uvlechenie*—a subject of exclusive absorption which draws us away from other work and play—an intellectual *grande passion*. All his original educational thought derives from this period. Later he was to produce some brilliant reading matter for peasant readers and some repetition of his theories (forceful and excusable). But the great days never returned.

Secondly, the documentation for the years 1859–62 is most curious and varied. A glance at the contents will show that we have added to Tolstoy's own descriptions two stories written by his pupils, the reminiscences of one of those pupils, and a brief reminiscence by one of his assistant teachers. We think these additions very valuable. So many great teachers of the past are known only by their own account of themselves. Where else can we find a double account, by teacher and pupil, of the same lesson given over a hundred years ago? And in that lesson a great writer is seeking to teach the art of writing.

Our third reason is the neglect of Tolstoy's educational writings in Britain. They are here translated for the first time by an English-speaking writer (as far as we know). We believe that there is much in them which is relevant to current educational controversy, and much to delight and instruct the admirer of Tolstoy the novelist. There is, indeed, no precise boundary between his literary and his pedagogical activities. For Tolstoy, to write well is above all to tell the truth; to understand children and lead them to the discovery of life is to share with them an experience which has a profound aesthetic dimension. As some Russian critics have recognized, the walk towards the wood in 'The Yasnaya Polyana school in the months of November and December' is a scene unsurpassed even in Tolstoy's fiction. We may doubt whether 'Fyedka' was a greater writer than Shakespeare or Goethe, remarkable though his story is. We should not doubt that Tolstoy learnt from Fyedka as much as he taught him. Fyedka's real literary glory is that he gave Tolstoy a revelation of a new fictional ideal—stories which were to combine moral insight with objective narration and an austere, lucid, classical manner. It was not Fyedka who realized that ideal, but Tolstoy many years later.

The documents which we are presenting are rich, but not very explicit. They do not tell very clearly the external history of the school at Yasnaya Polyana, and of course the school has roots in Tolstoy's earlier experiences. So perhaps it is worth giving the reader a compilation of relevant points from the copious biographical literature on Tolstoy.

Tolstoy never attended a school. His own education was conducted by tutors at home, the usual solution for aristocratic Russian families in his day. We can gather from the portraits of tutors in 'Childhood' and 'Boyhood' something of his relations with them. They do not appear to have had great learning to impart—an important qualification was foreign birth. Tolstoy certainly owed to them his mastery of French and German. He could afford to dismiss foreign languages as a subject of study later on; personally, he never experienced any *technical* barrier to understanding Europe. Perhaps he also derived from his private education something of his feeling for warm personal contact between teacher and taught, uninhibited by the rules of a collective discipline. Tolstoy was never a member of a school *class*. It is clear that all his thinking about village schools assumes a small scale and a generous teacher-pupil ratio. A tutor, however capricious, in charge of a small group, seemed to him more tolerable than a mass which had to be governed by rules, however reasonable. The sight of a child in a large class holding up its hand to ask to go to the lavatory provoked him to a very characteristic fury.

At the age of fifteen Tolstoy prepared, ably but without distinction, a public entrance examination and proceeded to the University of Kazan, situated on the Volga east of Moscow. Kazan was chosen because Tolstoy's guardian had moved there, and because of its special reputation for Oriental languages. Tolstoy had some idea of becoming a diplomat, and began by studying Arabic and Turco-Tartar. These studies appear to have left no trace whatever upon his thought as a mature man. It is clear, however, that the first-year course was a general one with several subsidiary subjects. Tolstoy failed the examination at the end of his freshman year, and decided to take up law instead. He fared little better, however, leaving Kazan University without a degree in 1847. (Tolstoy a lawyer: what a grotesque idea!) A desultory attempt to complete his legal studies later at St Petersburg came to nothing. His private studies during his university years were definitely more significant than his official ones. Institutionalized education did not suit Tolstoy, and the chief reflection of those years in his educational works is a series of contemptuous attacks on universities.

An unsympathetic critic might say that Tolstoy's harsh dismissal of universities and the academic establishment was a case of sour grapes. Aristocratic dilettantes do not like being ploughed, especially if the professors are social nobodies. There is perhaps a grain of truth in this view. The adolescent Tolstoy certainly went through a stage of callow snobbery, and his accusation that the professors were unfair to him sounds a little hysterical. He seems to have failed for reasons perfectly familiar to our university lecturers today.

Nevertheless, to be fair to Tolstoy, the University of Kazan was a mediocre and restrictive institution. The Russian universities in the 1840s played a very much more modest role in the national life than did Oxford and Cambridge in Victorian England. They were not the heirs of an ancient tradition. Kazan had been founded in 1805 as a modest senior extension of the local gimnaziya (or grammar school). It had been quietly neglected for a couple of decades, until it began to be reanimated by a vigorous and dedicated local scholar, who became rector in 1827. This was the great geometer Lobachevsky. Tolstoy's sojourn in Kazan coincides with the close of Lobachevsky's patient struggle to animate and organize a true centre of higher learning. By European standards it was neither large nor prestigious. The students, about four hundred in number, were often more like our sixth-formers in age. They wore uniforms and were subject to detailed rules of behaviour. For being late at a lecture Tolstoy was once confined for some hours in a detention-room with a fellow-student. To complete one's education at a university was only just becoming usual for sons of wealthy families. Many of the finest minds in the older generation had done without. A far more pressing obligation in the eyes of old-fashioned families was a period of state service, military or civil. The universities remained semi-plebeian institutions, more prized by the lower gentry than by Tolstoy's own social stratum.

Tolstoy never came to understand what a really good university can give. At Kazan he observed, perhaps by bad luck, mainly the backward aspects of an institution still suffering from growing pains.

The formal and organized elements in Tolstoy's own education were therefore remarkably slight. In future years he was to regard Russian education, with some justification, as a tabula rasa upon which the common people should be allowed to write. After all, what was there in his own education likely to inspire a reverence for tradition or academic learning? A spacious aristocratic individualism had done him no harm.

The twelve years which elapsed between his leaving Kazan University and the opening of Yasnaya Polyana school were spent in the same spirit. There is no need to give a detailed narrative of them here. The story features much dilettantism, a little dissipation, gambling and flirtation, patches of Victorian moral self-improvement, two important periods of exotic adventure, in the barbaric Caucasus and as an officer in the Crimean War, and his first literary successes. There appears to be very little indeed here which hints at the teacher in Tolstoy. True, his early stories 'Childhood', 'Boyhood' and 'Youth' are delicate studies of adolescence, with numerous analyses of school-room and college situations. But this is in the nature of the *Bildungsroman*.

Tolstoy first opened a school for village children at some point in the years 1847–49, but unfortunately we know extremely little about this first experiment. On leaving the university he had received his share of his dead parents' estate, consisting principally of the village of Yasnaya Polyana. He now owned the village, as we say in speaking of nineteenth-century Russia. That is to say, he possessed land and a manor-house there, and held the entire population as his serfs. Russian serfdom, which Marc Bloch[1] considered to be a far more onerous condition than that of the medieval West, conferred upon the serf-owner vast rights over the peasants' personal lives. He could make them his personal servants or send them into the army, permit or forbid their marriages, flog them within an inch of their lives. The nineteen-year-old master, alone on the estate, discovered an enthusiasm for paternalist philanthropy. (He describes the results, not without irony, in his story 'A Landlord's Morning', written in 1856). The first Yasnaya Polyana school was part of his programme of improvements. We know that he employed a servant, one Foka Demidovich (surname unknown), as a teacher, and the school seems to have survived for some time, until Tolstoy left for Moscow and the Caucasus in 1851. Whether Tolstoy ever taught in it personally is uncertain, but it is clear that he did so very little, if at all. We know of far too many other preoccupations at that time. His silence on the subject suggests that he was content to play the role of Lord Bountiful. It is a mistake to suppose that in his early youth Tolstoy was as close to the peasants as he tried to be later in life. The reader will see from Vasily Morozov's memoirs that in 1859, Morozov and the other village boys, far from being on familiar terms with the count, had never even set eyes on the house he lived in! Tolstoy himself makes only one reference to his first school, saying that he did not know at the time when he set it up that it should have been legally registered.

We cannot follow in any detail the manner in which Tolstoy matured in his own mind the idea of a second, and much more ambitious, village school. On 23 June 1857, while on a visit abroad, he suddenly jots in his diary: 'Above all, a strong and distinct idea has occurred to me of setting up a school in my village for the whole district and a whole *range of activities* of that kind.' But more than two years elapse before the school is opened, and during that time the 'strong and distinct idea' appears to be forgotten or vaguely shelved. It is easy, however, to see that this is a time of discontent and personal crisis for Tolstoy. He is concerned about his continuing bachelorhood, but his roving eye still finds no permanent object. His literary success, which came as easily to him as to any writer in literary history, is not a source of satisfaction for long; mixing in literary circles brings out all that is fractious and fastidiously aristocratic in him.

His sudden renewal of interest in schools in 1859 may well be due to the stimulus of public events. The whole peasant question was clearly coming to a head. Alexander II had succeeded to the throne in 1855, when it was clear that Russia was losing the Crimean War, and that a number of his father's policies were in ruins. He had the reputation of a new broom. In 1856 he had dropped a clear hint to a meeting of nobles in Moscow that an emancipation of the serfs was not far away. In 1858, after a special commission had been working upon the question in secret, the noble serf-owners were called upon to elect committees which should make concrete proposals for the emancipation of the serfs with land. By 1859 nothing much had been done, but an atmosphere of tense expectation existed. It was clear that the tsar meant to make a profound change in the legal and economic status of many millions of peasants. The hopes of liberals ran very high, and rumours of other reforms were current. The censorship was operated less severely than formerly. Amongst the subjects discussed in the unmuzzled journals was education for the peasant masses.

Organizing schools for the people became a fashionable craze amongst radical students. The syllabus and methods of such schools were naturally a subject of public discussion. Some reactionaries, including the romantic folklorist and lexicographer Vladimir Dahl, even expressed doubts whether the people ought to be taught to read and write.

For years Tolstoy had been repelled by the secularist utilitarian radicalism fashionable among the young intellectuals. He was now to take up one of their pet subjects. His talk of objectivity and empiricism will not deceive us. He was determined to prove the incompetence both of the government and of the intelligentsia.

The date of the school's opening is not certain. V. Morozov gives it as 'early in the autumn' of 1859, 'after the feast of the Intercession of the Virgin' on 1 October. A letter of Tolstoy's in 1860 suggests that it may have been as late as November. At all events, from the opening of the school, which started in a room of his own house with the simplest of equipment, Tolstoy seems to have worked with great intensity for some months. His letters of that period contain several expressions of satisfaction at having found a better vocation than literature. He appears to have been without any regular assistant at first except the priest who taught divinity. Probably he adopted very soon the long and irregular hours which are mentioned by himself and by the two Morozovs. Somehow he still found time for a little speculative writing and even, in spite of his protestations, for one or two literary projects. He was conducting a passionate affair with a peasant woman, and was all too aware of the anomaly. It was evidently a season of almost incredible activity, in which Tolstoy showed his extraordinary power of amassing and assimilating experience at a furious pace. It seems likely that by the summer of 1860 he had already drawn his fundamental conclusions from classroom experience, although they were not yet expressed in writing.

Late in the spring of 1860, shortly before the school closed for the summer, his brother Nikolai Tolstoy left Russia for the West, gravely ill with tuberculosis. Lev Tolstoy was extremely fond of Nikolai, whose imaginative stories and idealistic fantasies had made a profound impression on his mind in childhood. The desire to be with Nikolai and assist with his case was one of the motives behind his journey abroad. A second important motive was a plan to study Western schools, especially schools for the working classes, at first hand. He left on 27 June 1860 for Prussia, via Moscow and St Petersburg, and was not to return to Yasnaya Polyana until the beginning of May 1861. All of the observation of foreign schools to be found in these essays derives from this period. He visited Germany, France, Belgium and England and also took a purely touristic trip to Italy. His school visiting came in intermittent bursts, the countries he saw most of being Germany and France. The vivid impressions of popular 'education' in the streets of Marseilles to be found in his first essay were gathered in a few days. He spent a fortnight in London, full of intensive educational studies. His notes include brief comments upon some dozens of English schoolbooks and works of popularization, not always negative. He could read and understand English, but not very fluently. He visited the Houses of Parliament, but does not appear to have understood what was going on, linguistically or otherwise.

As far as educational ideas are concerned, a remark in a letter of Tolstoy to his brother suggests that he had gone abroad to gather weapons against Europe rather than to be conquered by it. He says his chief aim is to ensure 'that no one in Russia will dare to point to pedagogy in other countries, and so as to be well up in everything which is being done in that respect.' Even if his initial attitude had been more conciliatory we could not expect Tolstoy to see much good in the stern and formal schools he visited. Prussia had the oldest and most celebrated system of education for the masses. Tolstoy did not see the Prussian system in its happiest period; Friedrich Wilhelm was a reactionary who was above all concerned that neither the schoolmaster nor his charges should learn insubordination. 'Horrible, Prayers for the King, beatings, everything learnt by heart, frightened, dispirited children'—this diary note, made in Bad Kissingen before he had been abroad a month, does not sound like mere Tolstoyan exaggeration. Everywhere in Western Europe Tolstoy saw his fundamental principles, freedom and the participation of the common people, violated. Perhaps it helped him to see that these were in fact his fundamental principles. In spite of amicable hobnobbings with some distinguished personalities in the German educational world—the writer Berthold Auerbach, Julius Froebel (brother of *the* Froebel), Diesterweg of the Berlin Teachers' Seminary—Tolstoy did not bring home from Europe a single positive educational idea.

It is fair to add that he was to value much more highly an import of another kind picked up in Germany. Gustav Keller was an amiable young student from Jena whom Tolstoy invited to attempt the curious feat of teaching mathematics and drawing at Yasnaya Polyana while still in the early stages of learning the Russian language. Apparently it worked, but we do not know how.

By no means all of the ten months of Tolstoy's trip abroad were devoted to educational studies. The longest interruption occurred when Nikolai Tolstoy died, at Hyères, near Toulon. This was a blow from which Lev did not quickly recover. He found some solace in putting the ideas which he had gathered in Marseilles and elsewhere into writing. This was the first sketch of his essay 'On the education of the people'.

On his return to Russia Tolstoy spent a final fortnight in Moscow and then resumed teaching almost immediately after returning to Yasnaya Polyana. This was in May, however, and since he repeatedly tells us that a Russian village school, cannot function through the summer, it was clearly very late to be starting. He was adapting a building in the grounds for the school, and for a while classes were held in the apple orchard.

Although his enthusiam for education had not abated, Tolstoy was now embarking upon another, novel kind of social work which was to make considerable claims upon his time. In February 1861, while Tolstoy was in London, Alexander II had published the long-awaited decree emancipating the serfs. Appreciating that it would be no great advance to free the peasants without land, Alexander's advisers had devised a complex plan for dividing the land in each village. One share was to remain the property of the former serf-owner, the other was to be bought, with the aid of a state loan, by the peasants. This was further complicated by the fact that the peasants were not to receive the land as individuals, but were to remain, as before, members of a village commune with collective responsibility for taxation and certain other duties owed to the state. A large number of disinterested men were needed throughout the country to negotiate the details of this intricate piece of social surgery. Tolstoy volunteered, and upon his return from abroad assumed the duties of a *mirovoy posrednik* or Arbiter of the Peace. This involved, naturally, personal visits to every village in his district and discussions with both land-owners and peasants.

Although when the autumn returned, these new duties limited the time Tolstoy could spend in Yasnaya Polyana school, in another way they proved useful to his educational plans. For some time past Tolstoy had been ambitious to start not merely a school, but an educational movement. In the spring of 1860 he had written to his acquaintance Yegor Kovalevsky, who happened to be the brother of the minister of education, asking for permission to found a Society for the Education of the People. From the size of the subscription he proposed (100 roubles) it is certain that members were to be drawn from the educated minority, consisting mainly of nobles. The cautious tsarist bureaucracy presumably refused permission, for the society was never founded. A year later Tolstoy had reached the conclusion that this was in any case the wrong way of going about it. The initiative and control of the schools ought to belong to the common people; the role of their privileged well-wishers should be mainly that of advisers and intermediaries in the appointing of teachers and drawing up of rules. The duties of an Arbiter gave him an ideal opportunity of fulfilling this role in neighbouring villages. Not only this, but Arbiters were officially charged with the supervision of schools for the newly liberated peasant population. Tolstoy was unusually active in fulfilling this duty.

It is impossible to discover just how many schools were founded under Tolstoy's auspices in 1861–62. His official reports, the diocesan records and his claim in one of his magazine articles give different figures. He explains to us, however, that he uses the word 'school' in a very broad sense. A handful of boys visiting a village sexton more or less regularly to learn reading and writing with the aid of a psalter would count as a school. Perhaps he thought fit to use a somewhat more rigorous criterion in some of his reports. But the figure was something like twenty.

Tolstoy's attempts to found a free school movement on behalf of the Russian peasantry must count as an audacious failure. On the subject of school organisation he was a voice crying in the wilderness. The tsarist government, on the one hand, was making cautious moves towards establishing state control of education for the masses. These materialised in a law of 1864, which established official schools councils, just as Tolstoy feared. In any case popular education, whether 'free' or official, was not to make rapid progress in Russia for many years to come. In 1904 (towards the end of Tolstoy's life and over forty years after his school movement) only 38 per cent of boys and 15 per cent of girls of school age in the Russian Empire were in fact attending schools.[2]

Nor did Tolstoy find any more response from public opinion amongst the educated classes. Most of the young liberals were just as paternalistic as the government on this question, even if they wanted a somewhat different syllabus. In the last resort they believed that the people must want what would clearly be good for them; they thought in terms of education *for,* but not *by* the people. They also wanted quick results and, as usual, expected to find them in an adaptation of Western forms. Sunday schools (not, of course, mainly religious) and the Lancaster system were catchwords of the day in the intellectual magazines. In the same year, 1859, as Tolstoy started teaching in Yasnaya Polyana, a fashion for Sunday schools arose amongst liberal students and philanthropic ladies in several Russian cities. In the summer of 1862, when Tolstoy was writing these essays, a government decree closed all Sunday schools upon suspicion of spreading subversion. By that time there were two hundred and seventy-three of them. Tolstoy had long felt estranged from the radicals, and made little impression on them with his programme, which must have seemed to them slavophil and obscurantist.

It is in fact a foretaste of the anarchism of his later years. 'I have just read a project for a general plan of organisation of schools for the people. Reading this has produced in me an impression similar to what a man must experience who has long known and loved a young grove of trees, when he receives the unexpected news that they propose to make the grove into a garden—to fell here, to trim and prune there, and in yet another place to tear up the young saplings by the roots and lay metalled drives in their place'.[3] So begins Tolstoy's attack on the bureaucracy. But the *amateur* bureaucracy of the Moscow 'Committee for Literacy' is even worse; they are mere armchair meddlers, like the flies in the fable who sat on the heads of the cart-horses and believed they were causing the load to move. 'Who has produced these tens of thousands of schools, peasant schools, land-owners' schools, clerical, governmental, students', merchants', Sunday, soldiers', women's, tradesmens' schools, and schools of every possible kind which are appearing recently, if it is not that vast committee for education, unconscious of its own existence, which is composed of the whole Russian population striving to reach an equal level in education, some by imparting and others by receiving it?'[4]

Since the desire to learn and the desire to teach are natural impulses there is no need to use coercion to promote popular education. A compulsory state system of education would be positively harmful, since it would deaden the people's love of learning. It would also certainly result in a crushing education tax, for the government would insist upon erecting special buildings, rationally placed at the centre of each parish. Like all bureaucratic plans this is expensive and inefficient. We should rather permit the people to organise schools for themselves how and where they think fit. These will tend to be small and scattered over the countryside in places which we could not possibly foresee, for we are not in living contact with local conditions. But since there is no compulsion a process of survival of the fittest will choose the best places. Children will not be travelling impossible distances in winter to reach a showy and expensive parish building. Buildings are unimportant anyway. Each tiny hamlet will find something—a spare barn, a cottage or somewhere donated by the landlord—*provided that the spontaneous demand is there*. Teachers will be chosen and paid by the peasants, and therefore responsible to them. In the short run this system will not produce many good schools. But it will give the people a chance to choose freedom in education for themselves. Since freedom is the essential condition of good education it cannot possibly be imposed from above. If the people see a free and enlightened school working alongside the sordid and narrow traditional school, if they are given time to observe results and the teacher explains his methods tactfully, they will choose rightly. Such a choice, once made, will not be lightly abandoned, for the people themselves will have made it.

The only role here for the government or the educated classes is a purely advisory one. For instance, illiterate peasants need advice as to the competence of a would-be teacher. 'When he had examined Mihail Petrov, the proposed teacher, the Acting Arbiter of the Peace came to the conclusion that Mihail Petrov was barely able to read; as for writing, he refused to do any on the grounds that he did not have his glasses; as I subsequently discovered, when he did have his glasses he wrote exceedingly badly. The Acting Arbiter advised the Commune not to accept Mihail Petrov as teacher.'[5] This state of affairs, which Tolstoy describes as occurring in 1861, is in his view as it should be. If the worst came to the worst and the peasants had rejected the advice they would have discovered their own mistake quite soon. Better a Mihail Petrov under peasant control than a schoolmaster licensed by the state.

The campaign to encourage voluntary schools naturally led Tolstoy to a search for teachers. In spite of the tolerance which he extended in theory towards the 'popular' type of teacher (sextons, discharged soldiers and so on), in practice he found university students better material for his purposes. In October 1861 he wrote to the liberal academic Chicherin, asking him to recruit teachers from Moscow University. 'Paragons are not to be had, and I am not exacting. A half-educated student in his second or third year, and not a rascal—that is all I want. I know that out of ten we shall get two usable ones, but for that we shall have to start with ten. If there are no university students I shall have to try my luck with the seminary students, and then the risk will be ten times greater.' The response to this appeal was prompt and better, on the whole, than Tolstoy seems to have expected. In the early stages he does record in his diary moments of disillusion and exasperation with the students in general. 'The teachers are no good. Alexei Ivanovich is stupid. Alexander Pavlovich is morally sick. Ivan Ilyich is the most reliable of them. The teachers are keeping back some sort of disgusting secrets. So long as it's women that's all right' (5 November 1861). Perhaps these troubles were due in part to the social gulf separating Tolstoy from the students. He may have been suspicious of their motives. In 1861 several Russian universities, including Moscow, suffered outbreaks of student unrest following the imposition in May of a new code of student discipline and a reduction in the numbers absolved from paying fees. Some of Tolstoy's recruits had the leisure for an experiment because they had been rusticated for a year. Tolstoy at this period was by no means devoid of aristocratic class-consciousness and professed a rather fastidious reformism. He was relieved when his fears of subversive and antireligious propaganda proved unfounded. 'All of the twelve, except one, have turned out to be excellent people; I was so happy that they all agreed with me and submitted, not so much to my influence as to the influence of the environment and the work. Each one arrived with a Herzen manuscript in his trunk and revolutionary ideas in his head, and *each one,* without exception, burnt his manuscripts a week later, threw the revolutionary ideas out of his head and taught the peasant children sacred history and prayers and gave out the Gospels to be read at home' (letter to A. A. Tolstoy).

In Yasnaya Polyana school itself Tolstoy seems to have had two or three assistants in the 1861–62 season. The rest of the young men were distributed in other hamlets of the district by arrangement with the peasant communes. Often they stayed at Yasnaya Polyana for an induction period of a few weeks, observing and practising. On Sundays and holidays Tolstoy kept open house to the student teachers, spending hours in discussion with them. A few of them were definitely failures, but most of the young men were fired in greater or lesser degree by Tolstoy's personal charm and boundless enthusiasm for his cause. In January 1862 one of the first recruits, Alexander Serdobolsky, reported by letter on behalf of a group in a distant village: 'Tomashevsky has undergone a tremendous change: he is quite carried away by his work and would not go anywhere else for any money . . . We await you with impatience: somehow nothing is quite the same without you. It seems to me that our common cause can only go forward under your personal direction, can only be kindled into flame by your warm love for it. I am not sure that all the teachers here at present love this cause, but I am sure they will love it as I do, and as Tomashevsky has come to do, if they succeed in finding in it that poetry, that delight which shines through in your personality.' Nikolai Peterson was a student teacher who was to become, in later years, a determined opponent of the Tolstoyan concept of non-resistance to evil. But he wrote: 'For Lev Nikolayevich personally I have nothing but gratitude: I do not know what I should have become if Lev Nikolayevich had not drawn me to himself in 1862, and life in Yasnaya Polyana and thereabouts throughout the year 1862 was not only joyful but fruitful too.'

The year 1862 was also the time when Tolstoy's plan to create his own educational magazine was finally realized. He first mentions it specifically in March 1860, but to a confirmed graphomane like Tolstoy action and writing are never far apart, and he may well have been thinking of publications when on that first trip in 1857 he dreamed of 'a school . . . and a whole range of activities of that kind'. Besides obtaining permission of the authorities Tolstoy sought for collaborators in the neighbouring town of Tula, where he knew several teachers at the gymnasium, or grammar school. Amongst those he asked was Vladimir Markov, whose polemical article in another periodical, *The Russian Messenger,* was to provoke Tolstoy to write his important theoretical article 'Progress and the definition of education'. Markov, like the other Tula teachers, declined to take part in the magazine *Yasnaya Polyana* and Tolstoy's own resolve faltered for a moment.

The magazine (in which were published all the articles by Tolstoy which we translate here) was a failure by every worldly criterion. Only twelve numbers appeared, dated January to December 1862. In fact only the first two numbers appeared in the month which is shown on the title page, all the rest being one or several months late. The magazine was coldly received by the Russian public, perhaps because of Tolstoy's awkward posture on the political fence—he was neither liberal nor conservative. The influential radical publicist Chernyshevsky reviewed the first number, giving Tolstoy somewhat patronizing praise for his free discipline, but attacking the assumptions of the article 'On the education of the people' with lofty contempt. The magazine never rose above a miserable circulation (under 400 subscribers, as Tolstoy admits in a valedictory note). It lost money heavily, and Tolstoy would doubtless have closed it sooner but for his obligation to persons who had taken out an annual subscription. With the exception of two articles referring to schools in more distant parts of Russia, the only contributors were Tolstoy and his circle of student teachers in the neighbourhood of Tula. The students' contributions were, with one exception, straightforward descriptions of school practice. The magazine was to be accompanied each month by a 'Yasnaya Polyana booklet' or supplement containing reading material for (and sometimes by) peasant children. Twelve of these booklets eventually appeared, and some of the material (which included works by 'Fyedka') was subsequently reprinted.

The fact was that as the summer of 1862 approached circumstances conspired to distract Tolstoy more and more from educational work. He did not foresee it, but his absorption in teaching was to subside as rapidly as it had appeared. In April and May the strain of constant teaching, travelling, writing and arguing had begun to tell—he felt fatigued and depressed. He decided to take a cure based on kumyss—the fermented milk of mares, obtainable from the nomadic Bashkir tribesmen of the steppes. Leaving the school in the hands of Pyotr Morozov, one of his most devoted assistants, he left on 12 May. He took with him two boys, Vasily Morozov ('Fyedka') being one. They were absent from Yasnaya Polyana for two and a half months. An interesting narrative of this journey may be found in Aylmer Maude's *Life of Tolstoy*. Here it is enough to say that Tolstoy's health improved, and that he found time to work upon 'Training and Education'. He returned at the end of July, by which time the pupils had dispersed for the summer. The school was not to be reopened that autumn, although Tolstoy did not take the decision irrevocably until mid-October.

This abrupt abandoning of the school, and indeed of the whole school movement, in mid-career cannot but seem somewhat irresponsible. At least two of the student teachers felt that they had been let down. Most of the schools quietly petered out in the following eighteen months or so. A few survived. Vasily Morozov says that in any case there was a falling-off of demand among the peasants of Yasnaya. But one cannot help thinking that had the demand been never so great Tolstoy would not have continued to participate personally; he would still have followed the demands of his own nature, and the collapse of the Tolstoyan school movement makes nonsense of Tolstoy's claim that he was merely assisting a great spontaneous effort of self-education on the part of the Russian people. On the contrary, nine-tenths of the schools turned out to be dependent on the inspiration provided by one man.

Tolstoy's withdrawal may have been irresponsible; it is not incomprehensible. We can identify clearly a number of discouraging factors. First in time, but not in importance, came the shock of the search. While he was away drinking kumyss the political police ('gendarmes' as they were called) arrived at Yasnaya to find evidence of subversive activities. They had received a denunciation of Tolstoy and his sinister godless students from a local land-owner who resented Tolstoy's decisions in his recent role of Arbiter of the Peace. The gendarmes turned the entire estate upside down, dragged the pond, frightened his female relations and forced them to listen to extracts from his intimate diaries. Nothing incriminating was found. Tolstoy had been neither loyal nor disloyal to the tsar. It was an irritating aristocratic habit of his to treat all the normal subject-matter of political controversy as an irrelevance. The search therefore came as a shock. His furious protests merely met with a cool assurance that he would not be punished for an offence which he had not committed. The incident did not directly deter Tolstoy from his school work, but it must have shown him the impossibility of promoting a free school system, however innocent of subversive intention, without disturbance from the authorities.

A more important factor was courtship and marriage. His relationship with Sofia Andreevna Behrs had been developing erratically over the past six years. Before and after the journey to the eastern steppes Tolstoy discovered his own mind in the matter, and a rapid engagement followed. They were married on 23 September. Probably Sofia Andreevna had as much sympathy as could be expected with her husband's concern for grubby little urchins from the village. She did not kill the school, but she could not help competing with it. Before his departure for the steppes Tolstoy had been working till any hour that he and the boys chose, pursuing each vein of enthusiasm as far as it would lead. With marriage his mind took a different turn. He had an appetite for personal domestic pleasures, a natural desire to set his house and estate in order. All this would have been compatible with some work in the school, but not with work in the old manner. And Tolstoy always found half measures difficult.

Another major cause of the closure was Tolstoy's renewed urge to literary creation. His mind was like one of those limestone landscapes where a stream may plunge abruptly into invisible depths, or reappear as suddenly in a manner which remains mysterious to the superficial observer. As the year 1862 advanced experiences and reflections which had seemed forgotten and rejected years ago forced their way to the surface again. In 1859–60 Tolstoy had not merely renounced literature; he had almost denounced it. His letters express scathing contempt for the pretentions of *littérateurs*. What a relief it was, after their airs and bickering, to find work of palpable social usefulness! Three years later he is longing for literary work almost as ardently as he had rejected it. On 1 October 1862 he writes in a letter, 'I feel strongly drawn towards an independent work *de longue haleine,* a novel or something of the sort.' It was indeed to be *de longue haleine*. After many trials and errors the new work emerged as *War and Peace*.

How much teaching did Tolstoy really do? This is not an easy question to answer, for a day by day record of the work at Yasnaya Polyana school exists only for a fortnight or so, and even then it does not tell us exactly when Tolstoy was in the school. He seems to have been in Yasnaya Polyana for about seventeen and a half months between the autumn of 1859 and the summer of 1862. But evidently there was never any question of clockwork regularity in the activities of a school like Yasnaya Polyana. In the early period, before his trip abroad, Tolstoy was probably the principal teacher, working nearly every day in the school for varying periods. Later on he was probably struggling with far more interruptions, and had some assistants (Morozov and Keller, for instance) who enjoyed his confidence. During the same period he wrote well over 80,000 words on educational subjects, excluding his correspondence (always voluminous), diaries and a small amount of fiction.

It is possible to identify a second educational period, as it were, in Tolstoy's career. For year after year he struggled with the vast inchoate mass of images and ideas which began to preoccupy him in 1862. At last *War and Peace* took shape. This immense labour was not followed by an aversion to literature such as he had felt in 1859, but he would scarcely have been human if he had not felt a sense of relief and a desire for change of occupation. In the years 1871 to 1875 Tolstoy gave a substantial part of his time to education, but this time it was as a writer and promoter of a cause. He was now widely recognized as the greatest living Russian author, intellectually and morally already a power in the land. He was a man who had reflected maturely on his views, and was concerned to have them widely implemented.

So although in 1872 a school existed once more in Yasnaya Polyana, after a decade's omission, this was the least important educational effort of those years. In that year Tolstoy himself, his wife and even his children (at the tender ages of eight and seven) received village children in their home each afternoon in order to teach them to read. It is said to have worked—that is, the children learned quickly. It was a school only in the broad Tolstoyan sense of the word, and it lasted only a few months.

In 1862 Tolstoy's writings about education had been the natural sequel to an intensive period of practice. The school had come first chronologically and morally. In 1872 the school, or rather the reading lessons, had an ulterior motive. The children were serving to some extent as guinea pigs. For Tolstoy had decided to overcome one of the difficulties which he had pointed out ten years before, the absence of appropriate reading-matter for peasant children. The volume which resulted was Tolstoy's greatest achievement for education after the sixties. He called it by an over-modest title: *Azbuka*—that is, *'Alphabet'* or *'ABC Book.'* It is in fact a complete textbook for the syllabus of elementary education which he had come to approve of, except for sacred history and church singing. It includes reading in Russian and Church Slavonic (the closely related language which was the vehicle of Orthodox devotions) and an arithmetic. But the section which has never grown obsolete is the anthology of readings, fictional and non-fictional. To compile it Tolstoy ransacked world literature and folklore, and engaged in careful background studies to substantiate the articles on nature and general science. His work on this book illustrates as well as any episode of his life Tolstoy's ready intellectual enthusiasm and vast capacity for taking pains. Direct verification whenever possible was a principle with him. Thus for a short item on astronomy he stayed up all night gazing at the stars. Adaptations were based where possible on study of the originals. The style of everything in the book had to be pure, rapid and forceful. The emasculated style which we often serve to our children would have revolted him. His version of stories from sources ranging from the *Arabian Nights* to Maupassant are frequently reprinted for Soviet children today.[6] Best of all, he decided to write original stories himself, and this is the origin of a remarkable series of stories in the 'Fyedka' vein. 'A Prisoner in the Caucasus', 'The Bear-Hunt' and 'God Sees the Truth' were written for the *ABC Book*.

Modern teachers will not be surprised to learn that it was an American, the consul Schuyler, who first interested Tolstoy in the typography of textbooks. The attempt to clarify reading difficulties through the use of different types, plus Tolstoy's habit of making last-minute revisions, made the birth-throes of the *ABC Book* particularly acute and prolonged. In the end Tolstoy appointed his friend Strakhov as midwife.

It is sad to record that in the same period Tolstoy made a fool of himself in a controversy about reading methods. In spite of some passages in his essay of 1862 which shift the emphasis from *method* (a concept he virtually destroys) to the relationship between teacher and taught, Tolstoy is in other passages a partisan of a particular technique of explaining the relationship of letters and sounds. After some controversy, an experiment with two specially formed classes was conducted by the Moscow Literacy Committee. One was taught by an adept of the German 'phonetic method' *(Lautiermethode)* and the other by Tolstoy's disciple Pyotr Morozov. After two months the children were tested, and the results were generally held to go against Tolstoy. He then published a long article in the form of a letter to the chairman of the Literacy Committee, which does not display the empirical detachment which he proclaimed in the first number of *Yasnaya Polyana* magazine. After the event he has discovered a number of flaws in the structure and conduct of the experiment. (He had not pointed them out beforehand.) The children in the sample were too young. (Tolstoy believed, mysteriously, that six was too young for learning to read.) Visitors distracted their attention too much, especially in conditions of Tolstoyan free discipline, and, most brazen argument of all, the other class did not really learn to read by the phonetic method as they were supposed to, but by Tolstoy's method, which slipped in unofficially when the children of the two classes were allowed to mix out of school. The truth is that whereas Tolstoy sincerely believed himself to be empirical in his educational studies in practice he paid close attention to his own experiences, and scant attention to anyone else's. The only influence of practice in other schools upon his views is negative.

The same article contains one of Tolstoy's rare attempts to

enlist the support of enlightened officials. Since 1864 Russia had elected county councils, called zemstvos, which were allowed an indirect say in the control of popular schools. This time, in setting out once more his reasons for encouraging cheap, widespread, rudimentary education, genuinely controlled by the peasants, he allotted a limited role to the authorities. They should make grants to supplement the fees paid by the parents, assist in the selection of teachers and set up a model school in each district, whose teacher would act as an uncoercive inspector and adviser to the teachers in the remote hamlets.

Again there was no official response.

Such a scheme required teachers who, without sharing the ignorance and reaction of the 'Mihail Petrovs', were prepared to accept a peasant level of subsistence, and would not even get their modest fees all the year round. (In Tolstoy's scheme schools were to close from 1 May for the summer, and the teacher would get his living by some other hired work until the autumn.) Besides cheapness Tolstoy was seeking to protect peasants from the corruption of urban civilization. Teachers must not become a petty professional stratum, but must remain peasants in outlook and mores.

So in 1874–75 Tolstoy made moves to set up a college at Yasnaya Polyana for training what we might today call 'barefoot teachers' ('a university in bark sandals' was his phrase). At first he was supported by the local zemstvo (to which he was himself elected in 1873), but in the end only twelve sponsored students applied, and he dropped the scheme.

After 1875 Tolstoy's occasional educational activities are of slight importance.[7] He never renounced his ideas of 1862, but in old age he paid little attention to them. Seek ye first the Kingdom of God and educational wisdom will be added unto you. In a letter of 1901 he modified a little his detestation of *training* (in his sense of the word, that is, the attempt to mould another person's character according to your ideal). Now he will tolerate intervention in another's personality to combat the evil habits which come from contact with corrupt civilization. This is not, however, a total contradiction of his earlier view, since he had always held that religious faith was a firmer basis for such intervention than human reason.

As everyone knows, Tolstoy became Europe's most famous guru, and it is at that point that he ceases to be interesting as a teacher.

II The pedagogy of freedom: Michael Armstrong

Tolstoy concludes the opening essay of his journal, *Yasnaya Polyana,* by announcing his future intentions in the most uncompromising terms.

'We know that our arguments will not convince many. We know that our basic convictions, that the sole method of education is experience and its sole criterion freedom, will sound to some people like a hackneyed piece of vulgarity, to others like an unclear abstraction, to yet others like a dream and an impossibility. We would not have dared to disturb the calm of theoretical pedagogues and to utter such opinions, which are disgusting to all society, were we to confine ourselves to the reasoning of this article, but we feel that there is a possibility of proving the applicability and legitimacy of these wild beliefs of ours step by step and fact by fact, and to this end alone we shall dedicate our publication.'

Tolstoy's ambition is nothing less than a reconstruction, almost a reinvention, of the 'science of education'. This reconstruction is to be effected by means of a systematic 'study of the free child', his intellectual environment, his social relationships, his developing thought and action. It is a study which will embrace the organisation, methods and curricula of schools in their social context, the interrelationships of adults and children, learners and teachers, the nature of knowledge and the means of intellectual growth.

There is an absurd grandeur about the enterprise, which Tolstoy's subsequent essays do nothing to conceal. His achievement is to persuade us of the necessity and plausibility of the task which he has set himself and to demonstrate, at least in part, how to set about it. His failure, which we can scarcely deplore, since otherwise we would have been deprived of the two great novels for whose sake he forsook his two sustained attempts at educational reconstruction in the 1860s and 1870s, is to have abandoned the task almost before it had recorded its first tentative achievements and long before it had been brought to such a point of development that others could successfully carry on where he had left off. By the time that he wrote the essay 'Should we teach the peasant children to write, or should they teach us?', the essay which comes closest to justifying his original intentions, he had already abandoned his school, disappointing the expectations of his pupils and finally more or less turning them out of his house. One year later, he was writing to his confidante, the countess Alexandra Tolstoy: 'the children come to me in the evenings and bring with them memories for me of the teacher that used to be in me and is there no longer. Now I am a writer with *ALL* the strength of my soul.' No wonder that by then his pupils had already concluded with regret that 'we could not get on with Lev Nikolayevich as we used to'.[8]

It is easy, however, to be dismissive of Tolstoy's volatile temperament and to ignore or belittle the extraordinary energy which he expended on his school in the three brief years of its existence and the provocative power of his educational theory and practice as displayed in his journal. Few of the great issues which Tolstoy raises have yet been resolved and many are little nearer to resolution than when they were when he wrote and taught. Universal literacy, in any but the most mechanical sense that Tolstoy so savagely derided, remains an aspiration rather than an achievement, while the cultural renaissance which he foresaw as the consequence of a genuinely popular education is still no more than a dream. The continuing vitality of these essays lies in the clarity of their concern for what are still the fundamental problems of popular education, and in the boldness of their attempted solutions.

1. Tolstoy's programme

Tolstoy's first essay, 'On the education of the people', opens with a paradox: that 'incomprehensible' contrast, as Tolstoy sees it, between the universal demand of the people for education and the universal failure of popular education as provided in schools. Of the universality of failure, he believes that there can be no doubt. His travels in Europe have served only to confirm his experience of popular education in Russia; everywhere and whatever the extent of society's or the government's commitment, 'all that the greater part of the people carry away from school is . . . a horror of schooling'. Yet neither can he doubt the universality of the demand. 'Every individual personality unconsciously yearns for education' he writes, and again, 'the people love and seek education as they love and seek air to breathe'. This is the unshakeable premise of all his thinking, determining both the form in which he states his problems and the kinds of solution which he proposes to them. The metaphysical language in which he formulates it should not be allowed to obscure its contemporary significance, for this is a premise which has gradually come to dominate the psychology of human growth and learning over the past twenty-five years. Thus a recent summary of research concerning 'the basic skills of thought and language which children already possess when they come to school' concludes, in terms which closely resemble those employed by Tolstoy in these essays, that 'there is a fundamental human urge to be effective, competent and independent, to understand the world and to act with skill.'[9]

How is it that this yearning for education is accompanied by such a profound distaste for schooling? Is it through ignorance or malice that parents and children alike resist the kind of education which schools have to offer? Or is it that what the schools have to offer is itself faulty or inadequate? In the past, says Tolstoy, it is the people who have generally been blamed. Hence the gradual introduction all over Europe of the compulsory school with its characteristic discipline, and its standardised content, methods and assessments: a structure of meaning which it seeks to impose on all its pupils irrespective of circumstance. (In recent times a similar view has often been taken of concepts such as 'compensatory education': 'it serves to direct attention away from the internal organization and the educational context of the school, and focus our attention upon the families and children', implying that 'something is lacking in the family, and so in the child'.[10])

Tolstoy considers a number of attempts to justify the school's traditional 'mode of operation' on philosophical, sociological and historical grounds; not surprisingly he finds them wanting. The more he examines each line of defence, the more inadmissible and even absurd this 'mode of operation' appears. He is overwhelmed by the violence of the contrast between the intellectual vitality of children's lives outside school and the dull passiveness of their schooldays. In a passage that recalls Blake's 'The School Boy' from *Songs of Innocence and Experience* he pictures 'the same child at home or in the street, and at school—in the one case you see a creature full of the joy of life and love of knowledge, with a smile in its eyes and on its lips, seeking instruction in all things as a joy, expressing its own thought clearly and often forcefully in its own language—in the other you see a weary, huddled creature, with an expression of fatigue, terror and boredom, repeating with the lips alone the words of others in the language of others, a creature whose soul has hidden in its shell like a snail'.

The brute fact is that on entering school a child is entering an environment which systematically devalues his personality and background. He is deprived of the physical and intellectual 'freedom of movement' which is 'the chief pleasure and need of childhood days'; he is 'forced to speak not in his own patois but in a foreign language'; he is taught 'things which nobody understands'; he is made aware that neither his parents nor his teachers support each other's authority. The school is indeed doubly perverse, first by virtue of its own 'stultifying influence' so accurately described by the German word *verdummen*—to make stupid—and then again because it tears a child away 'from those essential conditions of development which nature itself has created for him.'. 'We very commonly hear' Tolstoy continues, 'that home conditions, the boorishness of parents, work in the fields, rural games and so on, are the chief obstacles to schooling. Perhaps they do indeed hinder that schooling which the teachers have in mind, but it is time we convinced ourselves that all these conditions are the main foundations of any education . . . its first and principal activators.' For it is from his home that a child acquires 'the ability to express his thoughts', while 'interest in knowing anything whatever and the questions which it is the school's task to answer are aroused only by those home conditions'. Yet strange though it may seem, schools fail to recognise that it is from life *out of* school that children acquire the ability and readiness to respond to the distinctive business of life *in* school. Thus the school disregards the living interests aroused by children's home environments; it neither answers the questions provoked by children's lives nor provokes new questions in its turn. Nor is this really as strange as it seems; it is an inevitable consequence of the school's traditional structure. For centuries the school 'has laid down as an essential condition a discipline which forbids the children to speak, to ask questions, to choose this or that subject of study—in short, every step is taken to deprive the teacher of the possibility of drawing conclusions as to what the pupils need'. Unable to study 'the free child' who is the object of his action—to discover what questions exercise his pupils' minds, what knowledge absorbs them, what experience has shaped them, what intellectual demands life has made upon them—the teacher has no hope of making school learning significant. The greater the school's insistence on its characteristic forms of order, the greater its isolation and the more impossible its task.

To resolve the paradox of popular education we must look, then, to deficiencies in the school rather than in the child or the family. At present 'the coercive structure of the school excludes the possibility of any progress', by preventing teachers from studying and responding to each child's individual life and character, by preventing children from exercising their own independence of mind, and by preventing knowledge from becoming a source of living interest, sustained by mutual collaboration and free enquiry. Our only hope lies in recognizing 'that if the educator is to know what is good and what is bad, the person being educated must have the full power to express his dissatisfaction, or at least to withdraw from that part of education which does not satisfy his instinct, that there is only one criterion of pedagogy—freedom'.

It is worth observing here that although a hundred years and more of popular education have profoundly affected the character of the elementary school since Tolstoy's day, his strictures against the form and content of compulsory schooling are by no means as irrelevant to the contemporary English primary school as might be supposed. The most recent study of English primary classrooms[11] has shown that they are considerably less 'progressive' than critics and apologists alike are inclined to suggest. Neither teaching nor learning are of the 'questing, exploratory character' recommended, for example, by the Plowden Report in 1967; however 'individualized', the teaching is 'overwhelmingly factual and managerial'; subject matter is highly traditional overwhelmingly devoted to the basic skills and far more often to training in skill than to putting the skill to significant use; 'teacher control is all-pervasive'. 'Rather than concurring with the critics that the Plowden approach has failed', the authors conclude, 'we would argue that it has still to be tried. It is not altogether surprising therefore to find that many contemporary teachers' problems still reflect the weaknesses that Tolstoy sought to expose. Determined to control every aspect of their pupils' activity within a severely constrained curriculum which allows little scope for creative exploration of any kind, they find neither the time nor the inclination to study or promote a child's independent thought and action.

Tolstoy's subsequent essays represent a sustained, though incomplete, attempt to elaborate a pedagogy of freedom in opposition to the traditional pedagogy of compulsion. The pedagogy of compulsion, he argues 'regards the human being in the process of education as a creature completely subordinated to the trainer'; by contrast, the pedagogy of freedom is 'the study of the ways in which people form themselves and cooperation with this free process of formation'. Tolstoy's favourite image of free education is of a mother teaching her child to speak. 'Education in the most general sense, including upbringing, is in our belief that activity of man which has as its basis the demand for equality and the immutable law that education must move forward. A mother teaches her child to speak only so that they can understand one another; instinctively the mother tries to come down to his view of things, to his language, but the law of forward movement in education does not permit her to come down to him but obliges him to rise to her knowledge. The same relationship exists between writer and reader, between the school and the pupil, between government and voluntary societies and the people. The activity of the educator, as of the person being educated, has one and the same objective.'

This powerful but obscure passage is central to Tolstoy's theory. The essence of the mother-child relationship, as Tolstoy sees it, is its reciprocity, and the reciprocity which he has in mind is the reciprocity of conversation. Mother and child seek to understand each other: that is to say, to enjoy each other's interests, enter each other's world of thought and feeling. Their relationship is forward looking inasmuch as the mother cannot unlearn what she has already learnt and what her child has yet to learn, so that the child is compelled, as it were, to rise to her knowledge. In this respect education is necessarily a levelling up. Yet there is no pretence in the mother's determination to come down to the level of her child. For conversation depends upon shared meanings, some notion, however tentative, of a common world which can none the less accommodate and give value to a great diversity of utterance. A one sided conversation is not strictly a conversation at all. The mother's readiness to share her child's point of view is thus the essential condition for conversation to take place between them, as is her child's complementary effort.

For Tolstoy this relationship is the model of all genuinely educational relationships. It is through just such a reciprocal interchange of thought and language, whether with mother, teacher, writer, scholar or friend, that children achieve understanding, knowledge and skill. But the process is one which transforms the understanding of both parties though in diverse ways according to the experience of each. The mother's knowledge is no longer the same for conversing with her child, nor the writer's for conversing, as it were, with the reader, nor the teacher's for conversing with the pupil. Many of the most memorable passages in these essays are directed towards showing how Tolstoy himself has been forced to reconsider his own understanding—of art, literature and morality no less than of education—in the light of his conversation with his pupils.

The image of conversation as central to education recurs in contemporary thought in the writings of Michael Oakeshott,[12] but with the crucial difference that Oakeshott is concerned with higher rather than elementary education. It is Tolstoy's most distinctive and extravagant claim that education almost from the start can become conversational. Conversation is not for him an achievement of elementary education so much as the very heart of its method, 'an unrehearsed intellectual adventure', to appropriate Oakeshott's phrase, which begins almost from the moment pupil and teacher meet.

I want now to examine four interconnected aspects of the pedagogy of freedom, announced in Tolstoy's opening essay, as they are developed in subsequent essays: his experimental method, the teacher-pupil relationship, the problem of knowledge or culture, and his final conclusions about the early life of the mind.

2. *The Method of Experience*

In view of the radicalism of Tolstoy's programme it is disconcerting at first to discover how traditional the curriculum at Yasnaya Polyana seems to be, with its set timetable, standardized marks, and conventional subject divisions. But these are no more than provisional arrangements inherited from the traditional school and adopted at Yasnaya Polyana in the absence of immediately clear alternatives. As experience accumulates, Tolstoy's practice begins to conform, if at first only fitfully, to his theory that the curricular requirements of a school for the people can only be determined by study and free experiment.

The study of education and the teaching of children are not, in Tolstoy's view, separable activities. Teaching children effectively depends for its success on observing them in conditions of freedom, that is to say in an intellectual and social environment which is not determined by teachers alone. Conversely, studying children effectively depends for its success on teaching them, or, as Tolstoy would rather say, on cooperating with them in the processes by which they form themselves. By interlocking research and teaching in this way Tolstoy's experimental method runs counter to the practice of most contemporary educational scholarship and offers a radical alternative to its prevailing methodology.

But how is experiment to begin in the absence of that knowledge of children's requirements which only free experiment can bring? Tolstoy's answer is to start from traditional content and methods, with one all-important difference: that children will not be forced to go to school, nor to follow unquestioningly the teacher's commands once they get there. It is this absence of compulsion that allows his experiment to proceed. Tolstoy observes that already at Yasnaya Polyana traditional forms have been eroded. Of marks he notes that they 'are merely a remnant of our old forms of organization and are tending to drop out of use of their own accord'. The timetable seems infinitely flexible: 'according to the timetable there are four lessons before dinner, but it sometimes turns out to be three or two, and sometimes quite different subjects'. Subjects begin to drop out of the curriculum or to change their content in response to new demands; history and geography seem to have no 'living interest' for young children and may best be left for later years; the study of grammar seems to be important to them but not in its traditional guise.

Always it is his pupils' 'right to freedom' which saves Tolstoy from his own worst errors. He is acutely conscious of the way in which a teacher's authority, however well-meaning or legitimate, may impose upon his pupils against their better judgement. Freedom is their only safeguard. It sometimes happens, for instance, that towards the end of a long day one or two children will decide that they have had enough of school for that day and will pick up their caps and run off home with a hasty goodbye to the teacher. 'This kind of thing is repeated once or twice a week. It is insulting and unpleasant for the teacher—who could fail to agree there?—but who will not also agree how much greater the significance of the five, six and sometimes seven lessons a day for each class, all freely and willingly attended each day by the pupils, because of one case of this kind. Only when such cases are repeated can we be assured that the instruction, although inadequate and one-sided, is not altogether bad and harmful.'

The essays are full of examples of the way in which the children's freedom of action and independence of mind has shown Tolstoy how they learn and therefore how better to teach. Consider for instance his account of the teaching of reading. His initial assumption was that 'for the children to learn to read it was necessary for them to acquire a love of reading, and for them to acquire a love of reading it was necessary that what they read should be understandable and interesting'. So the children began by reading words, phrases and sentences composed by themselves and written up on classroom wall or blackboard. The next stage was reading simple folk-tales, and, after that, popular readers and simple stories by famous writers such as Pushkin and Gogol. 'It seemed so rational and clear but this idea was wrong.' The younger children 'found it beyond them to read and understand folk-tales; the simultaneous labour of spelling out the words and understanding the sense was too great for them'. So, too, 'the elder pupils when reading Pushkin . . . could not combine the job of reading with that of understanding what they read, although they understood a fair amount when we read'.

At first it seemed as if the problem might be solved by divorcing 'mechanical skill in reading' from 'reading with understanding'. Thus, after various trials and errors, it was decided, at the suggestion of a new teacher, to introduce 'reading round the class'. The result was disastrous. 'The boys were made to sit on forms and one was to read aloud while the others followed his reading . . . "Ivanov read." Ivanov searches for a little and reads. Everyone is busy, the teacher can be heard, every word is uttered correctly and they are reading fairly fluently. It seems to be a good idea, but scrutinize closely. . . . The reader grows timid when he hears his lonely voice resounding in the silence of the room; all his powers are concentrated on observing the symbols and stress-accents, and he acquires the habit of reading without trying to understand the sense, because he is burdened with other requirements. The ones who are listening do the same, and always hoping to hit on the right place if they are asked, run their fingers along the lines at an even pace, get bored and are distracted by irrelevant amusements. The meaning of what has been read, being a secondary matter, is sometimes grasped and sometimes not, without their being aware of it. But the chief harm consists in that eternal school battle of wits and laying of traps between the pupils and the teacher which develops in such an order of things, and which we never had in our school before.'

Fortunately, 'reading round the class' did not last long. The older pupils 'began to get up to mischief and to drop out of the lesson', the method was abandoned, and the search for fresh approaches began again. It was at this point, while the teachers were wondering how best to proceed, that the pupils began to devise their own particular methods or to adapt the teachers' methods to their own particular purposes. The success of this spontaneous development undermined still further the distinction between 'mechanical reading' and 'reading with understanding', yet without confirming Tolstoy's initial assumption. 'Now . . . every pupil is given the chance to use all the approaches that he finds convenient, and it is a remarkable fact that everyone uses all the approaches that I know of. . . . The *first,* which is used by mothers throughout the world, not at all a scholastic but a domestic device, consists in the pupil's coming and asking the teacher to read with him for a bit; the teacher reads, guiding him over every syllable and word. . . . The *second* device for teaching reading, also a great favourite . . . consists in the pupil's being given a book and being free to spell out syllables and understand just as he pleases . . . in this way he grows used to the outlines of the letters, to the process of forming syllables, the pronunciation of words and even to working out the meaning, and I have satisfied myself by experience over and over again that insistence that the pupil should necessarily understand what he reads has held us back. . . . The *third* method of teaching reading consists in learning by heart prayers, verses, anything on the printed page, in fact, and in pronouncing what has been learnt while following in the book. The *fourth* method consists in that very thing which proved so harmful in the Yasnaya Polyana school—in reading round the class. It arose of its own accord in our school. At first there were not enough books, and two pupils would be seated beside one book;

then they themselves took a liking to this, and when someone says "Reading", friends who are perfectly equal in ability make off in twos, sometimes in threes, and sit down with the same book; one reads and the others follow him and make corrections. And you will upset everything if you separate them. . . . Finally, the *fifth* method, which we still like, is progressive reading, that is, reading of more and more complex books from the point of view of interest and understanding.'

The conclusions which Tolstoy draws from the teaching of reading explain what he means when he declares that 'the sole method of education is experience'. There is 'no best method' for teaching reading, or any other subject, since each and every method depends for its success upon its responsiveness to particular children's particular needs. The only rule is the avoidance of rules. 'Every individual personality, if he is to learn to read as quickly as possible, must be taught quite distinctly from every other, and therefore there must be a special method for everyone. One will find insurmountable difficulty in something which does not hold up the other in the least, and vice versa. One pupil has a good memory, and finds it easier to learn the syllables by heart than to understand that the consonant is pronounced without a vowel sound; another has a bent for tranquil reasoning and will understand the phonetic method, which is the most rational one; a third has a flair, an instinct, and by reading whole words he perceives the law by which words are composed.

'The best teacher will be the one that always has a clarification of what is holding up the pupil ready at hand. Clarifying difficulties in this manner will give the teacher a knowledge of the greatest possible number of methods, and the ability to invent new methods; he has no one method that he follows, but a conviction that all methods are one-sided and that the best method would be one able to settle all possible difficulties that the pupil might encounter—i.e., no method, but an art or talent'.

3. Two concepts of the educational relationship

In his brief memoir of the Yasnaya Polyana school, Peter Morozov, Tolstoy's most dedicated fellow teacher, points out that 'the count did not run things according to the educational handbooks but according to the plan that his own genius had worked out, based on his desire to turn the school into a family'. There were three particular respects in which Tolstoy wished a school to resemble a family: in the immediacy of its concern for children's everyday interests and questions, in providing a free yet supportive environment for children's self-determined intellectual explorations, and in the mutuality of relationship between teacher and pupil.

Tolstoy is not unaware of the educational limitations of family life: he is full of scorn for an 'avaricious farmer' who refuses to send his son to Tolstoy's school, boasting that 'what I need to do most is to fill him full of my own spirit first'; he is plagued by doubts as to whether the artistic and literary yearnings of his pupils are compatible with the environment in which they live. Yet for all its obvious limitations family life aspires to the conditions which are essential to education in a way in which school life, in its present form, neither does nor can aspire. A school that in this respect resembled a family would necessarily be a better school.

A note of caution is necessary however. For Tolstoy, the school is both more and less than an enlarged family: more inasmuch as it has its own distinctive subject matter, less inasmuch as it is more narrowly self-conscious than the family needs to be. Schooling, as Tolstoy defines it, means 'the conscious action of the educator upon the persons who are educating themselves'. A school is one among many more or less self-conscious agencies of education which develop out of family life and lead back into it, supplementing and enriching the less conscious but more all-embracing education provided in the home. 'Such is the learning of reading and writing from one's friends and brothers, such are the traditional children's games, such are the public spectacles, the peep shows and so on, such are pictures and books, such are folk tales and songs, such are jobs, and such, finally, are the efforts of the Yasnaya Polyana school.'

It is above all in the mutuality of its relationship that the school should seek to resemble the family; in Tolstoy's view, as we have seen, the mutuality of mother and child in the child's acquisition of language, is a model of all genuinely educational relationships. Mutuality however is a rare achievement for schools, even schools like Yasnaya Polyana. Far more familiar is the opposite quality: that 'magisterial attitude of teacher to pupil' which in essay after essay Tolstoy satirizes and denounces. Of all his examples of the magisterial relationship—'the invariable error of the Socratic method', he calls it—none is more bizarre or extravagant than his hilarious but only too believable account of a young German teacher, 'trained in the best method', who is teaching from the 'Fish Book', a kind of visual aid to the teaching of reading, and succeeds in reducing his entire class to such a state of bemused incomprehension that they lose 'all hope and self-confidence' and begin desperately to concentrate their 'intellectual powers' on trying to discover what it is that the teacher wants them to say. However, it is the accounts which Tolstoy offers of his own magisterial practice that carry the most conviction.

Here, for example, is how he describes an attempt to get his pupils to explain to him the meaning of a particular passage from one of Gogol's short stories.

> We were reading Gogol's 'Vii', repeating each period in our own words. Everything went well until page three—there we have the following period:
>
> 'The whole of this learned community, the clerical school no less than the seminary (which two nourished a certain hereditary mutual dislike) was uncommonly short of money for its bodily sustenance, and at the same time unusually gluttonous, so that to calculate how many dumplings each one gobbled up at supper would have been a quite impossible job, and thus the benevolent contributions of the prosperous squires could not suffice.'
>
> Teacher: 'Well, what have you read?' (Nearly all these pupils are highly developed children.)
>
> The best pupil: 'In the clerical school the people were all gluttons, and poor, and gobbled up dumplings at supper.'
>
> Teacher: 'What else?'
>
> Pupil (a cheat, and with a good memory, saying whatever comes into his head): 'An impossible job, the benevolent contributed'.
>
> Teacher (annoyed): 'You must think a bit. That's wrong. What was an impossible job?'
>
> Silence.
>
> Teacher: 'Read it through again.'
>
> They read it through. One, with a good memory, added a few more words which he could remember: the seminary, bodily sustenance of the prosperous squires, he could not suffice. Nobody had understood anything. They began to talk utter nonsense. The teacher pressed them.
>
> Teacher: 'But what was an impossible job?'
>
> He wanted them to say that it was impossible to calculate.
>
> Another pupil: 'It was very poor, it was impossible.'

> They read it through once again. They searched for the word that the teacher wanted as if for a needle, and hit upon everything except the word "calculate", and got into a state of hopeless gloom. I—being that very teacher—did not relent and managed to get them to take the whole period apart, but they understood it far worse than when the first pupil had repeated it. Besides, there was nothing for them to understand. A loosely connected, long-winded period, which gives nothing to the reader, the gist of which had been understood straight away: the poor and gluttonous people gobbled up dumplings—there was nothing else that the author had wanted to say. I was hammering away simply because of the form, which was bad, and in doing so I had spoilt the whole class for an entire afternoon, had destroyed and crushed heaven knows how many flowers of complex understanding which were in the course of opening.

It is the last sentence of this extract which suggests the source of the teacher's error. Instead of eliciting his pupils' own intellectual responses to what they have read he had predetermined what is to be understood and how it is to be understood. The explanations which he demands of them are laboured, the questions which he asks them closed. The appropriate model of his aim is not a conversation but a test; indeed his procedure is, as Tolstoy puts it, no more than a 'remnant of the superstition of the mediaeval school' where everything had to be learned by heart. If knowledge no longer has to be memorized 'word for word' that is only because it is now acquired 'proposition by proposition'. In either case the methods are the same: 'forcible explanation, mugging up and repetition'.

To think of learning in this way is to misconstrue the mind's development. 'It is easy to talk of understanding', Tolstoy explains 'but do we not all realize how many disparate things can be simultaneously understood, when the same book is being read? The pupil who does not understand two or three words in the sentence may understand a fine shade of thought or its relation to what went before. You, the teacher, are insisting on one side of understanding, but the pupil has no need whatsoever of what you want to explain to him. Sometimes he has understood, but he does not know how to demonstrate to you that he has understood you, but at the same time he is dimly guessing his way toward and assimilating something different and, for him, extremely useful and important. You keep teasing him to explain, but of course he has to explain to you by means of words the impression that words have produced in him, and he is silent or else starts to talk nonsense, lies, deceives you, tries to discover what it is that you want, to adapt himself to your wishes, or he invents a non-existent difficulty and hammers away at it; the general impression which the book produced, however, the poetical sense which helped him to guess the meaning, is crushed, and has gone into hiding.'

If our aim is to increase a child's cognitive capacity then it is to less direct means that we must turn. 'We must give the pupil opportunities to acquire new concepts and words from the general sense of what is said. He will hear or read an incomprehensible word in an incomprehensible sentence once, then again in another sentence, and a new concept will begin dimly to present itself to him, and at length he will, by chance, feel the necessity of using the word, he will use it once, and word and concept become his property. And there are thousands of other paths. But deliberately to present a pupil with new concepts and forms of language is, according to my conviction, as unnecessary and pointless as to teach a child to walk by means of the laws of equilibrium. Any such attempt carries a pupil not nearer to the appointed goal, but further away from it, as if a man should wish to help a flower to open out with his crude hand, should begin to unfold the petals, and crush everything round about.'

The contrast which Tolstoy draws between mechanizing the mind and exciting its native powers—between the 'mechanical dismemberment' of 'living speech' and 'living thought' and the 'complex, mysterious and tender process of the mind'—is characteristic of progressive thought from Rousseau to the present day. The organic imagery is often taken to imply a rejection of any kind of intervention by the teacher in children's learning, as if his task were simply to set his pupils within an appropriate environment and wait for them to learn. But this interpretation is for the most part mistaken. It is not so much that intervention is wrong in principle as that it is justifiable, and productive, only in a context of mutuality. We may distinguish between 'intervention' and 'interference': to interfere in a child's learning is to seek to impose on him one's own understanding; to intervene is to share one's understanding with the child in a manner which respects and preserves his autonomy.

Tolstoy's finest single example of mutuality in learning is his description, in part one of "Yasnaya Polyana school in the months of November and December", of a walk through nearby woods with three of his pupils, and of the conversation that took place between them. It happened one wintry evening after school, a fact that Tolstoy considers of some importance: 'outside school (in spite of all its freedom), in the open air, new relations are established between teacher and pupil, with more freedom, more simplicity and more trust, the kind of relations that appear to us to be the ideal towards which a school should strive'. He had been reading Gogol's story 'Vii' to his older pupils—the very story which had led to the futile exercise in comprehension; it seems that, for all that, the reading itself had gone well. 'The last scenes had a strong effect and excited their imagination; some of them mimicked the witch and kept on remembering the last night.' Tolstoy, as he often did, was accompanying his pupils part of the way home. 'At the crossroads we stopped, the older ones, who had been at school for three years, came to a halt around me, asking me to go further with them.' One of them suggested walking to a wood just outside the village, an exciting and frightening spot because of the wolves that lived there; 'the others supported him, and we four went over to the wood together'.

Tolstoy goes on to describe, with incomparable detail, how he retold them a story about the Caucasus which they had remembered and how intently they listened as they walked.

> I finished my story by telling how the abrek, having been surrounded, burst out singing and then threw himself upon his dagger. Everyone was silent.
>
> 'But why did he burst out singing when he was surrounded?' asked Syomka.
>
> 'You've been told—he was getting ready to die, of course,' replied Fyedka irritably.
>
> 'I think he started singing a prayer,' added Pronka.
>
> Everyone agreed. Fyedka suddenly stopped.
>
> 'And what did you say about your aunt being murdered?' he asked—he had not had enough of terrors.
>
> 'Tell us! tell us!'
>
> I told them once more that terrible story of the murder of Countess Tolstoy, and they stood around me in silence, looking into my face.
>
> 'That was a brave chap,' said Syomka.
>
> 'It must have been frightening for him walking around at night, with her lying murdered,' said Fyedka, 'I would have

run away!' And he once again grasped my two fingers with his hand.

We stopped in a copse behind the barns, on the very edge of the village. Syomka picked up some brushwood from the snow and hit the frosty bole of a lime-tree with it. Hoar frost showered down from the branches on to his cap, and the noise resounded, solitary, through the woods.

'Lev Nikolayevich,' said Fyedka (I thought he was going to speak about the countess again) 'why do we learn singing? I often think, really, why sing?'

How he had made the leap from the horror of the murder to that question Heaven knows, but everything: the sound of his voice, the seriousness with which he sought an answer, the silence of the other two, made us feel that there was a very vital and legitimate connection between that question and the preceding conversation. Whether the connection was that he was replying to my explanation that crime may be due to lack of education (I had been telling them that) or that he was testing himself by identifying himself with the murderer and remembering his favourite occupation (he has a wonderful voice and an immense talent for music) or whether the connection was that he felt that now was the time for sincere talk and all the questions which were calling for an answer arose in his mind—at any rate none of us was surprised at his question.

'And why drawing? Why write well?' said I, not knowing in the least how to explain to him what art is for.

'Why drawing?' he repeated meditatively. He was in fact asking 'Why art?' I did not dare to explain, I did not know how.

'Why drawing?' said Syomka. 'You put everything down in a drawing—you can make anything from that.'

'No, that's technical drawing,' said Fyedka, 'but why draw figures?'

Syomka's healthy nature saw no difficulty; 'Why a stick, why a lime-tree?' he said, still rapping the lime.

'Well then, what *is* a lime tree for?' said I.

'To make rafters with,' replied Syomka.

'And what else, what is it for in summer, before it's chopped down?'

'Why nothing.'

'No, really,' Fyedka continued obstinately to ask, 'why does a lime-tree grow?'

And we started to talk about the fact that utility is not everything, but there is beauty, and art is beauty, and we understood one another, and Fyedka quite understood why a lime-tree grows and why we sing. Pronka agreed with us, but he understood better moral beauty—goodness. Syomka understood with his great intelligence, but he would not admit beauty without utility. He doubted, as often happens with people of great intelligence who feel that art is a force but who do not feel in their hearts any need of that force; like them he wanted to approach art with his intellect and was trying to light that fire within himself. . . . But Fyedka understood perfectly that a lime-tree in leaf is beautiful, and it is good to look at in summer, and nothing more is needed. Pronka understood that it is a pity to cut it down, because it too is a living thing: 'You know it's just as if it was blood when we drink the sap out of a birch tree.'

Syomka, although he did not say so, evidently thought that it was not much good when it was rotten. I find it strange to repeat what we said then, but I remember that we talked over—as it seems to me—everything that can be said about utility and about physical and moral beauty.

'It is difficult', Tolstoy admits in a later section of this essay, 'to say how and when the flower of understanding burgeoned' in particular children. Part of the beauty of this conversation about art during an evening walk is the way in which Tolstoy has succeeded here in 'catching this burgeoning of understanding' in his three companions. There can be no doubting the significance of his own interventions, however delicate and indirect, in the tender process of development. He has prepared the ground by his readiness to walk home with his pupils; he triggers off the conversation by his story telling; and he takes part in it as one among four voices of equal yet highly individual worth. If we take him at his word, as I think we must, we may infer that the conversation has brought each participant fresh insight into a fundamental intellectual question, Tolstoy no less than his three pupil companions.

The mutuality so finely achieved in this example is however in one respect misleading. 'We were so close that night,' Tolstoy remarks, and yet it is clear from the general drift of his argument, if never made explicit, that for the most part the self-consciousness of a teacher's task leads to an inescapable ambiguity in his relationship with his pupils. Like the anthropologist, a teacher, even in the context of mutuality, is a figure of divided loyalties, observer as well as participant, at once stranger and friend. However deeply the conversation engages him, he can never entirely escape the other side of his obligation: to study and observe his pupils, 'to regulate this flood of cheerful animation,' as Tolstoy puts it, and to lead the conversation into new and, for his pupils, unforeseen areas of experience. And this brings us to what Tolstoy saw as the deeply puzzling problem of knowledge.

4. The problem of knowledge

At the end of his description of walking through woods with Fyedka, Syomka and Pronka, Tolstoy foresees an objection to the vision of popular education which underlies his narrative. 'I can see honourable, good, liberal people . . . who will say, when they read this, "It's a bad thing" and shake their heads—"Why develop them forcibly? Why give them feelings and conceptions which will set them at odds with their environment? Why take them out of their way of life?" they will say. Not to mention those who are outstandingly hard-headed, and who will say, "A fine thing it will be for the organization of the state when everyone wants to be thinkers and artists and nobody will work!" . . . Whether it is a good thing, whether it is a bad thing, whether we ought to bring them out of their environment and so on—who knows? And who can bring them out of their environment? As if this were some sort of mechanical action. Is it good or bad to add sugar to flour or pepper to beer? Fyedka is not bothered by his ragged little kaftan, but Fyedka is tormented by moral questions and doubts, and you want to give him three roubles, a catechism and a little story about how work and humility, which you detest yourselves, are the only things of use to a man. He does not need the three roubles, he will find them and take them when he does need them, and he will learn how to work without you—just as he learnt how to breathe; what he needs is what your life, your ten generations uncrushed by work have led you to. You have the leisure to seek, to think, to suffer—give him what you have won through your suffering—that is the one thing he needs.'

This impassioned appeal to his fellow intellectuals shows us the strength of Tolstoy's commitment to knowledge as the aim of education. His dislike of certain traditional school subjects, and his hostility to the manner in which all school subjects are traditionally taught, in no way implies a general rejection of knowledge of the arts and sciences as the proper foundation for the popular school. Even as he dismisses the teaching of geography, for example, as a time-consuming irrelevance he takes care to reaffirm his commitment to other forms of knowledge: 'I have a whole world of knowledge in mathematics, natural science, language and poetry which I lack time to communicate; there are innumerable questions drawn from the phenomena of the life surrounding me to which the pupil is demanding an answer and to which I must reply before I draw him a picture of the polar ice, the tropical countries, the mountains of Australia and the rivers of America.'

The world of knowledge which it is the teacher's task to communicate to his pupils is of equal significance and value for *all* children's lives. To acknowledge this is doubtless to offend against common sense, for what use can it be to a peasant child 'to learn the arts'? 'He is not going to be an artist, he will have to plough. If he has artistic urges he will not have the strength to sustain that stubborn, unrelenting work which he needs to sustain, which would render the existence of the state unthinkable if he did not sustain it. . . . This is indeed an absurdity, but I rejoice in this absurdity, I do not come to a halt in front of it but try to find its causes. There is another, yet worse absurdity. This same son of the people—every son of the people—has just the same rights, what am I saying? even greater rights to the enjoyment of art than we children of a fortunate social class who are not forced to undertake that unrelenting work and who are surrounded by all the comforts of life. To deprive him of the right to enjoy art, to deprive me, the teacher, of the right to lead him into the sphere of higher enjoyment to which his whole being is striving with all the strength of his soul, is a still greater absurdity.'

Knowledge, then, whether of the arts or the sciences, is a common human profession, universally accessible and appealing. Or so it ought to be; but it is here that the trouble begins. For despite the apparent self-confidence of Tolstoy's appeal to those who have the leisure to seek, think and suffer, to impart to all, without reserve, the knowledge which they have thereby won, he is for the most part profoundly mistrustful of the knowledge of the leisured class to which he belongs, and more than doubtful whether it either can be or deserves to be communicated to peasant children. The source of his anxiety is to be found in the organisation and distribution of knowledge within society, as he views it: in the social distance between the educated elite and the uneducated people, which has distorted and corrupted not only the processes by means of which knowledge is communicated but the very form and content of knowledge itself.

It is in regard to the teaching of the arts that Tolstoy is most conscious of the incapacitating cultural barrier between himself and his pupils, though occasionally he hints at similar problems as regards the sciences. Consider the case of literature. The aim of teaching it is clear enough: to help children to enjoy and understand good books, the wealth of Russian literature. The teaching problem is also apparently clear. Good books are written in a language that is unfamiliar to peasant children and very different from their own vernacular; Tolstoy's way of tackling the problem is to start the children off with folk-tales written in the vernacular and proceed stage by stage, by way of popular readers and other material specifically written 'for the people' in the literary language, towards the simpler works of prominent Russian authors. But this strategy proves unsuccessful. As soon as the children begin to read books written in the literary language they begin to lose interest in reading. It is not the meanings of words that defeat them so much as the style and content of what is written, the mode of thought embodied in the writing; and this is true not only of obviously inferior works but even of the apparently simple and powerful stories of Pushkin or Gogol. It seems that 'the only books which are understood by the common people and to their taste are books written not for the people but by the people, to wit: folk tales, proverbs, collections of songs, legends, verses and riddles. . . . But however much the pupils love books of this kind, the aim which we have, perhaps mistakenly, set ourselves, is not being achieved: between these books and the literary language the same gulf remains."

'Where is the mistake here,' asks Tolstoy, 'and how do we get out of this situation?' and in reply he outlines four possibilities. 'Perhaps there is a transitional literature, which we do not recognize simply for want of knowledge. Perhaps this is a result of our being cut off from the people, and the coercive education of the upper class, and the only thing that will help is time, which will produce not an anthology but a whole transitional literature. . . . It may also be the case that the people do not understand and do not want to understand our literary language because there is nothing for them to understand, because all our literature is of no use to them, and they are working out their own literature for themselves. Finally, a last supposition . . . is that the apparent deficiency lies not in the heart of the matter, but in our preoccupation with the idea that the end of instruction in language is to raise the pupils to the stage of knowing the literary language and especially in our haste to attain that end. It may very well be that the progressive reading we dream of will appear of its own accord, and that the knowledge of the literary language will come to each pupil automatically in its own good time.'

These various explanations are not mutually exclusive and it is clear that Tolstoy subscribes to all of them, though in differing degrees at different times. The search for a transitional literature, for example, which might mediate between the vernacular tales and songs and the literary classics, preoccupied him throughout the period covered by his educational essays and continued to do so long after he had abandoned his school. Indeed the *ABC Book,* which he published in the 1870s, is nothing less than an attempt to create, single-handed, an entire corpus of transitional literary material for peasant children, composed partly of his own stories, partly of adaptations and translations from other literatures. Throughout his essays he is preoccupied, too, with the need for patience in the pursuit of literary understanding: that anxious and expectant vigilance with which the teacher must attend upon his pupils as they work out their own paths to understanding. But the problem of teaching literature cannot be resolved merely by more patient methods, nor by the discovery and invention of a transitional literature. For Tolstoy believes that his pupils' apparent rejection of 'high' literature reflects, in part at least, their critical appreciation of its limited worth; and if this is so then the teaching of literature requires no less than a revaluation of literature itself. Tolstoy's most unequivocal statement to this effect is contained in the prelude to his discussion of drawing and singing in part three of his article 'Yasnaya Polyana School in the months of November and December'. In writing of great violence, which seems to be directed as much at himself as at his readers, he explains how, in his perplexity at his pupils' resistance to what he has hitherto regarded as the best in art, literature and music, he has been forced to question the value to be placed on the artistic achievements of the 'so-called educated class'. The more he questions them, in the light of his teaching experience, the more doubtful they seem, until at last he is driven to acknowledge that they represent not the highest of which art is capable but rather the corrupt taste of 'a spoilt minority'. 'I have made these observations', he concludes, 'concerning the two branches of our arts which I know the best and which I love passionately—music and poetry. And, dreadful to relate, I have arrived at the conviction that all that we have done in these two branches was done in a wrong and exclusive direction, without meaning, without future and trivial in comparison with the requirements and even the products of those same arts of which we find examples amongst the common people. . . . For years I have laboured in vain to impart to children the poetic beauties of Pushkin and all of our literature . . . and could achieve nothing; but we had only to open by chance Rybnikov's collection (of folk-songs) and the poetical demands of the pupils found complete satisfaction, and a satisfaction which, after calmly and dispassionately comparing the first song I came across with Pushkin's best work, I could not but find to be justified.'

The extravagance of Tolstoy's conclusion tempts us to dismiss his argument out of hand. Yet it is naive to discount the connection between the social circumstances in which art is produced and the values to which it gives expression as it is to deny, as Tolstoy sometimes comes close to denying, the value of any art which is not explicitly of the people. The cultural problem which Tolstoy here identifies has dominated each successive phase of popular education throughout the past two centuries; it is, indeed, inseparable from any sustained attempt to teach the arts, or for that matter the sciences, to all. The most common response to the problem is still to deny, as Tolstoy claims his own fellow intellectuals denied, that a majority of people are capable of high artistic understanding. As one contemporary liberal puts it, 'art of integrity is never likely to be popular . . . it is an art of cultivation, not immediately accessible, for not only its appreciation but its simple, casual enjoyment, depends upon a long apprenticeship.'[13] Tolstoy would have refused to accept this dismal conclusion. It contradicts his own experience of teaching peasant children, which had convinced him that 'the urge to enjoy art and to serve art are to be found in every human personality, no matter what breed or environment it may belong to'. The earliest artistic endeavours of his pupils gave ample evidence, for all of their apparent crudity, of the seriousness of the children's artistic intentions and of their will to learn, of the beginnings that is to say, of both appreciation and apprenticeship. It seemed to Tolstoy to follow that 'if there appear inconveniences and inconsistencies in the enjoyment and production of art by everyone, then the cause of these inconveniences lies not in the method of imparting, not in the diffusion or concentration of art amongst the many or the few, but in the character and direction of art of which we should be suspicious both in order not to burden the younger generation with what is false, and in order to render it possible for that younger generation to work out something new in both form and content'.

How then is a teacher to assist his pupils in their reconstructive task? In the discussion of music, which follows the passage that I have just quoted, Tolstoy distinguishes between the teaching of artistic rules and of artistic discrimination, insisting that 'the object of teaching music to the people should be to impart to them the knowledge we possess of the general laws of music, but definitely not to impart the false taste which is developed in our circles'. The distinction seems forced; laws and taste in art are less readily separable than Tolstoy implies, and, in fact, his own practice in teaching the arts is incompatible with his theoretical recommendation. In the end even a sympathetic reader is bound to conclude that Tolstoy simply did not teach long enough to examine the problem which he had set himself with sufficient care and attention to detail. The nearest he comes to resolving it is in an essay devoted to children's own literary compositions, 'Should we teach the peasant children to write, or should they teach us?' Although this essay, the finest of all Tolstoy's educational writings, has little to say directly about the relationship between children's own writings and the 'literary language', it describes a method of teaching composition which might indeed, if sustained for long enough, enable children to discover their own paths to an appreciation of literature, and through their own literary efforts to begin the task of revival and reconstruction. But more than that, this essay comes closer than any other of Tolstoy's writings to elaborating a comprehensive theory of human growth and development on the basis of his all too brief 'study of the free child' in a free educational environment.

5. *The early life of mind*

'Should we teach the peasant children to write, or should they teach us?' is a study in the early life of mind, the most elaborate pedagogical study that Tolstoy ever attempted. It is a study which displays to particularly good effect his chosen method of inquiry; teaching, observation and speculation become the complementary aspects of a single enterprise, here devoted to the task of documenting a critical insight into the nature of intellectual growth. The essay tells the story of two stories written by Tolstoy's pupils. Through careful, though far from impersonal, description of the process of composition, and close analysis of the finished works, Tolstoy brings out the distinctiveness and purposefulness of children's artistic thought, making use of his findings to propose, at the end, a radical hypothesis concerning human development and the native powers of the mind.

In the first part of his essay Tolstoy describes how, 'inadvertently', he 'hit upon the right method' of teaching his pupils the art of writing. Until this moment, whatever the subject or however wide the choice of subject, they had written for the most part, 'trivia'. Their problem was that the act of writing had no significance for them. 'They did not understand the main point: why write? and what is good about writing it down? They did not understand art—the beauty of expressing life in words and the absorbing power of that art.' Without this understanding they lacked the essential condition of literary success for even the youngest of writers, so Tolstoy felt.

The problem was solved, suddenly, when, one day, Tolstoy suggested that they write a story to illustrate a proverb, a project which he himself had often dreamt of undertaking. He offered them the proverb 'He feeds you with a spoon and pokes you in the eye with the handle', outlining a possible plot; but although several children had been excited by the original idea, once the particular proverb was suggested they lost interest, feeling uncertain how to set about their task and convinced that it was beyond their capacity. The turning point came when one of them suggested that Tolstoy should write the story himself. He agreed and began to write. In a few minutes his pupils had deserted their own compositions and were crowding around him to see how he was getting on. He read them what he had written but they were unimpressed. Upset by their reaction he began to describe what he intended to write next and his renewed enthusiasm seemed to inspire them. They began to make suggestions of their own, criticising each other's ideas as well as Tolstoy's, and participating in the composition. Soon Tolstoy had ceased to be the author of his own story and had become a scribe, writing what the children dictated to him as they argued out the story among themselves.

Suddenly, it seemed, they had understood. 'They were all extraordinarily interested. It was evidently new and absorbing for them to be present at the process of composing a story and to participate in it.' Tolstoy was immediately impressed by evidence of their literary skill. It seemed that as soon as they had seen the point of the activity they could at once begin to exercise critical and creative judgement in its pursuit. He cites numerous instances of the 'unfortuitous and precise' demands made by the children as they argued. Tolstoy wanted to preserve a close correspondence between the meaning of the proverb and the course of the narrative and proposed that the peasant who discovers a frozen and starved old man on his door step and takes him in, should repent of his good deed himself. His pupils however found this contrived and instead 'created a shrew of a wife' as a counterpoint to the kindly peasant, although, as Tolstoy points out, the relationship between husband and wife is treated with some subtlety in the finished story. As published in the Yasnaya Polyana booklets, the story suggests that the children were altogether less interested in the relationship of story to proverb than in the correspondence between the narrative and their own understanding of character, place and action.

Throughout the composition the children paid most careful attention to detail: 'they evidently felt for the first time the excitement of fixing an artistic detail by means of language'. This was especially true of Fyedka and Syomka, the two children who took most part in composing the story. Each of them had his own approach to detail. Syomka chose 'predominantly objective images' which for all their vivid realism bore no necessary relationship either with each other or with the general feeling of the story. By contrast, Fyedka chose only such images as were expressive of the inner meaning of the narrative. This concern for detail is of great significance to Tolstoy in establishing the children's artistry. 'Every word of a work of art,' he writes, 'whether it belongs to Goethe or to Fyedka, differs from the non-artistic in that it calls forth a countless multitude of ideas, images and interpretations.' As one example he cites Fyedka's insistence that the fur coat put on by the nervous and small-minded neighbour, whom the wife summons to persuade her husband to abandon the old man, should be a woman's coat. 'I remember that it struck me so much that I asked: "Why a *woman's* fur coat?" Nobody had led Fyedka up to the idea of saying that the neighbour put a fur coat on. He said "That's right, it's like him." When I asked whether we could say that he put a man's fur coat on he said "No, better if it's a woman's." And this touch is indeed extraordinary. . . . The neighbour in a woman's fur coat is bound to be imagined as a puny, narrow-chested peasant, as he obviously ought to be. The woman's fur coat, draped over a bench, the first one he laid his hand on, also conjures up for you the whole life and manners of a peasant on a winter's evening."

In his determination 'to fix the images of his feeling artistically by means of words' Fyedka is concerned not just with language in general but quite specifically with *written* language. He is not telling a story but writing a composition, in which each word must keep its allotted place. The fixity of the individual word on the page is of the utmost importance to him. 'He wanted to speak by himself—and not to speak in the way that people retell stories, but as they write. . . ; he would not permit me, for instance, to rearrange the words; if he said "I've got sores on my feet" then he would not permit me to say "There are sores on my feet".'

Fyedka is very much the hero of the composition in Tolstoy's narrative, above all because of his remarkable 'sense of measure', which causes him to reject many of the ideas suggested by his fellow pupils and even by Tolstoy himself. Early on in the story, for example, when the peasant finds a sealed paper in the old man's bag but cannot read it, Fyedka had decided that he should say to himself "Now if my Seryozha could read he'd jump up sharp, snatch the paper out of my hands and tell me who this old man is". Tolstoy says that he can remember vividly how these words arose in Fyedka's imagination. At a later point in the story Tolstoy suggests to Fyedka that he should recall this moment. 'I remember too that during the time when the peasant is falling asleep I suggested making him think about his son's future and the future relations of his son and the old man, how the old man would teach Seryozha to read and write and so on. Fyedka frowned and said "Yes, yes, that's all right" but you could see that he did not like the suggestion and twice he forgot it.' For Fyedka it was enough that he should already have hinted at the peasant's wish that his son might read, a wish which is to be fulfilled later in the story when the old man does begin to teach him. To underline the hint, or signal the course of the plot more emphatically, would have been too obtrusive a touch, displaying a lack of due proportion in the construction of the narrative.

Tolstoy describes the composition of this story as the opening of a new world for his pupils: 'the world of art'. An unaccountable 'feeling of excitement, joy, fear and almost repentance' comes over him as he contemplates their achievement—'as though I had been prying into something which no-one ever has the right to see, the birth of the mysterious flower of poetry'. His amazement is not so much that his pupils have suddenly understood the beauty of expressing life in words as that from that first moment of understanding they should apparently be capable of the same qualities, if not the same level, of literary judgement as himself, a mature and recognised artist. No initial course of instruction is required before they can begin to express their artistry; no prolonged period of training in basic skill, in advance of significant performance. The exercise of artistic judgement seems to be embedded within the experience of art itself, from these young writers' earliest endeavours.

Tolstoy is overwhelmed by the evidence of conscious intent in his pupils' writing. Over and over again he declares that what they have written was written not by accident but design: 'there was no mistaking it, it was not chance but conscious creativity'. This emphasis upon the purposefulness of his pupils' writing is one of the many characteristics which makes Tolstoy so unusual among progressive theorists of education. It is common to contrast the playful spontaneity of children's art with the earnest deliberateness of the adult artist. In a recent study of primitivism in art,[14] for example, Ernst Gombrich describes the modern artist's attraction to child art as 'the reversal to earlier phases of mental development; indeed the surrender of rationality and control that characterize the adult mind'. 'Child art', according to Gombrich, 'is spontaneous, happy go lucky, even slapdash, especially since modern schools rightly encourage inventiveness and originality at the expense of manual skill. It has often been observed that this carefree stage comes to an end with puberty and the growing self-consciousness of the adult.' Tolstoy acknowledges the unspoilt directness of his pupils' vision but strongly denies that their artistry is less than conscious. It is indeed precisely the 'conscious artistic power' that most excites him about his pupils' work and that gives rise to the theory of human growth which he derives from his experience.

The evidence of design derives from two complementary sources: on the one hand from the study of children's thoughts, words and deeds as they set about the act of composition; on the other hand from a study of their finished compositions. In the first part of his essay Tolstoy has concentrated on the act of composition; now he turns to an analysis of a completed story. The analysis which he offers is almost unique in the history of educational thought. He treats the chosen story with the utmost respect, assuming its intentionality as given and examining it accordingly, that is to say as one might examine a mature artist's work. The result is a study which corroborates in the most striking manner the evidence of skill and judgement already provided through the study of how the earlier story was composed. Each form of analysis complements the other.

The story which Tolstoy chooses to analyse was written by Fyedka during the summer holidays when he and a few other pupils were living with Tolstoy on his estate. 'Having had their fill of bathing and playing they thought of doing a little work.' Tolstoy suggested that they should write a story and gave them several subjects including 'in the form of an autobiography the story of a boy whose poor and dissolute father was sent to be a soldier and to whom the father returned as a reformed and good man'. Fyedka 'was extremely pleased with this subject', having heard Tolstoy outline briefly how he would set about it. This time he wrote the story by himself and in his own handwriting, though Tolstoy as always was ready with suggestions, sometimes, so Tolstoy says, too ready.

Tolstoy's analysis concentrates on the compression of Fyedka's narrative which he regards as its greatest source of strength. He has already indicated how attentive his child authors were to detail. Now he shows how Fyedka's new story, 'The Life of a Soldier's Wife', is constructed out of a whole series of such attentively detailed moments, moments which do not so much invigorate the narrative as embody it. Consider first the second chapter of the story, which describes in some four hundred words the christening and death of the narrator's baby brother. It opens with an account of the baby's christening which captures with great clarity and economy the young child's astonishment and incomprehension at the ceremony. The christening over, it is at once made clear that the baby is weak and ill. 'The boy was thin; he had puny little legs and kept on screaming. Mother said "Lord, when will that brat be dead?"' Tolstoy remarks that it was he who had suggested that the baby should have thin legs but that the mother's complaint was Fyedka's own idea, and it is this one phrase, Tolstoy argues, that 'puts before the reader all the essence of the situation', the angry despair that prepares the way for the death and subsequent grief. The description of the death is all Fyedka's own. 'At midnight mother started crying for some reason. Grandmother got up and said "What's the matter? Christ be with you." Mother said "My son is dead." Grandmother lit a lamp, washed the boy, dressed him in a shirt, girded him up and placed him beneath the ikons. When dawn came . . .' 'All this', Tolstoy comments, 'is so compressed, so simple and so powerful—not a single word can be discarded, not a single one changed or added. There are but five lines in all, and in those five lines the whole picture of that mournful night is drawn for the reader.' The mother's unexplained crying in the night, the simplicity and finality of her words, 'my son is dead', the grandmother's slow ritual (notice that it is the grandmother and not the mother who lays out the body); each image resonates in the mind, each separate detail incorporates a wealth of impressions.

The full significance of Fyedka's style of narrative can only be understood, as Tolstoy puts it at another point in his analysis, 'by reading between the lines of that condensed and powerful description'. Often it is no more than a word or phrase, as in the case of the mother's complaints, that Fyedka narrates. Tolstoy cites a further example from the scene that follows the baby's death. 'The only rejoicing we had was when we gave my sister to be married. A husband called Kondrashka was found for her. So they came courting, and brought a loaf of white bread and a lot of vodka, and all sat down at a table, and mother sat down too. Then old Ivan poured some vodka into a glass and brought it to my mother; mother drank it. Then he sliced some bread and gave it to mother. I was standing by the table, and I did so want a piece of bread. I bent mother down and spoke into her ear. Mother burst out laughing, and old Ivan said "What does he want, a bit of bread?" and went and cut me off a big piece. I took the bread and went off into the store-room.'

Tolstoy draws particular attention to the words 'I bent mother down and spoke into her ear', pointing out how much more they convey than a straightforward 'I asked': 'and this is not said by chance, it is said because he can remember his relationship with his mother at that period of his growth and how his relations with his mother were timid in front of other people and close when they were alone together'. It is surely a further sign of his timidity that on receiving the bread from 'old Ivan', who has guessed the source of his embarrassment—a 'big piece' of bread, as Fyedka is careful to note—he should retire 'into the store-room' to eat it, shyly triumphant.

The climax of Fyedka's story is his description of the father's homecoming and it is here, in the closing scenes, which Fyedka insisted on working out entirely by himself, that Tolstoy finds the surest evidence of his young pupil's control over his narrative material. Tolstoy observes that the emotional impact of the father's return, powerful as it is, is implicit within the narrative details rather than directly stated. 'In the whole of that encounter there is not a single hint that this is touching; it merely relates what went on, but out of all that went on nothing is related except what is essential if the reader is to understand the situation of all the characters.' Consider the moment of return. When the son brings the father back home, having met him outside the village, he is still unaware that this is his father. Even at home the soldier is too shy and nervous to declare himself at once and the following exchange takes place: 'So I took him to our house. He prayed and said "How d'ye do." Then he took his coat off and sat down on the chest and started to look hard at everything. Then he said "Well now, is this all the family you've got?" My mother said "That's all." At that the soldier began to weep and said "Where's my mother then?" Mother ran up to my father [this is the first time that the narrator calls the soldier his father] and said "Your mother died a long time ago."' The apparently simple sequence of words and actions expresses, with a sureness of touch that is at once literary and psychological, the confused mixture of emotions—amazement, reserve, relief and joy—with which the recognition, after six years absence, is effected. It is hard to imagine a greater concentration of meaning in 'such simple, natural words'. Or consider the unobtrusive yet precise way in which Fyedka points out the father's reformed character. The mother sends her daughter out for vodka to celebrate the father's return. 'The liquor was brought in and put on the table. Father said "What's this?" My sister said "It's for you." Father said "No, I've stopped drinking now." Mother said "Now thank heaven that you've stopped".' Nothing else is said, or needs to be. A few sentences later it is revealed in a similarly unobtrusive way that the father has learnt to read, another sign for Fedka of his change of heart. 'Then Father began to rummage in his pack and Mother and I watched. Then Mother caught sight of a book in it and said "Learnt to read, have you?" Father said "That I have."'

Fyedka chooses this moment to reveal that the father has returned home rich. 'Then Father took out a big bundle and gave it to Mother. "What's this?" says Mother. "Money," says Father. My mother was glad, and hastened, she put it away safe. Then my mother came back and said "Where did you get it from?" Father said "I was an officer and had the army money. I gave it out to the soldiers and there was some left, so I took it."' After a lengthy digression on peasant morality, Tolstoy finally acknowledges that the significance of this incident lies in its uninhibited realism rather than its apparent lack of moral scruple. 'What the author wants is to make his hero happy; his return to the family should have been enough for happiness but it was necessary to remove the poverty which had been weighing upon the family for so many years.' There is one 'tiny detail' in this passage which in Tolstoy's view 'illuminates the whole picture, delineates all the characters and their relationships, and it is but one word, and a word used incorrectly, syntactically wrong—it is the word "hastened". "Hastened" requires a continuation—"Hastened to do what?" the teacher is bound to ask. . . . And this is splendid. I wish that I might say a word like that, and I wish that teachers who give instruction in language would say or write down a sentence like that.' Fyedka's ability to turn a grammatical error to creative effect is for Tolstoy yet another indication of his literary skill. It is also worth noting how this hastening, compounded of excitement and prudence, is the mother's first and immediate response to the money her husband hands her. It is only after she has put it away safe that she returns to ask him how he came by it.

The climax of the homecoming is followed by a closing scene which is as striking and unexpected as any part of the narrative. According to Tolstoy, Fyedka was not satisfied with ending the story with the homecoming itself. 'Those imaginary people had evidently established themselves too vividly in his imagination, he still wanted to imagine a picture of how their way of life changed.' This he does by describing what happened on the day after the father's return. The scene opens with the mother waking her husband up and sending him out to chop wood 'with all his might' for the stove. The rest of the day he spends in the village in search of a frame for a new cottage for the family since their present cottage is falling down. In the evening he returns with his frame but it is not until the last words of the story that his wife asks him about it. 'We finished dinner and Mother said, "Well, what about the frame?" Father said, "Fifty silver roubles." Mother said, "That's nothing." Father said, "Yes, there's no doubt about it, it's a first-rate frame."' There the story ends, the new framework, and the father's success in getting it at such a price, symbolising the family's new strength. It is a remarkable ending to a remarkable story.

The conclusions which Tolstoy draws from his analysis of this story, and from his description of how the previous story was composed, are forthright and unqualified. The stories may be exceptional but he insists that they are characteristic, in style, in content and in the manner of their composition, of all his pupils' stories, whatever the children's 'level of talent' and whatever his own 'level of enthusiasm and participation in their work'. (Unfortunately he produces no examples of these less distinguished yet still distinctive compositions, though such examples would have done much to reinforce his argument.) What his pupils' literary activity proves to him is that the power of creative and critical judgement is not simply a product of mental training but is in some sense native to the mind, intrinsic to its activity at every stage of its growth. Casting his argument in a markedly metaphysical form Tolstoy concludes that 'the instincts for truth, beauty and goodness are independent of the level of development'. All of us carry within ourselves an 'image', 'model' or 'idea' of harmony in terms of which we seek to order our experience. This inner principle is perhaps completely satisfied only at the moment of birth before development has begun. Hence the image of childhood innocence, the 'great proposition uttered by Rousseau' that 'Man is born perfect'. But the rapidity and unevenness of human development constantly threaten to disturb our primal harmony. This is the 'necessary law of development', 'the meaning of the tree of the knowledge of good and evil which our first parent tasted'. It is as if our accumulating experience in whatever realm of knowledge, whether empirical, aesthetic or moral, is continually outstripping our capacity to appropriate and control it. The course of learning, or self-development, is thus an unending struggle to reassert the mind's control in the face of new experience and growing knowledge. Time and time again we must strive to restore the harmony that has been destroyed. To succeed is to achieve at higher levels of development that same harmony which we have already realised, however incompletely and fitfully, at lower levels. The educator's task is no more, but then again no less, than to provide each child with 'material with which to complete himself in a harmonious and many-sided manner', that is to say to offer him the intellectual support, whether of people or of things, which can sustain him in his own intellectual struggle. 'Hence,' Tolstoy ends, 'it is my conviction that we must not teach writing and composition, and artistic composition in particular, to children in general and to peasant children especially. All that we can do is to teach them how to set about composition.' And this, though scarcely in itself an answer to the problem of knowledge as posed by Tolstoy in other essays, is perhaps the best place, after all, to begin to look for an answer.

I would like to propose an interpretation of Tolstoy's conclusion which while preserving the essentials of his position sets it in a less metaphysical context. Tolstoy is deeply impressed, as we have seen, by the consciousness of purpose and skillfulness of performance which he detects in children's early writing. More recent studies of children's writings, as of other aspects of their intellectual activity, strongly reinforce, it seems to me, these twin impressions. Of course the skillfulness is limited by the relative poverty of children's present experience, yet the severity of the constraints within which they write, paint, experiment, calculate and speculate, are less fascinating or compelling than their extraordinary capacity to turn these constraints to significant use as they struggle to express in an appropriate form their own particular understanding. It is in this respect that creativity may be said to be a constant in the mind's development, independent of given levels of experience or culture.

Thus, as Tolstoy has shown with such appreciative sympathy, young writers seem almost from the outset to be aware of the critical distinction between the use of language in writing and in speech, between the improvisatory quality of a conversation, for example, and the permanence and isolation of the written word. They do not represent to themselves the problem of writing as a matter of reproducing on the page the expressiveness of their talk, but of recasting their thought and language into a new form that is appropriate to the special character of the written as opposed to the spoken word. The problem is complicated for them by their lack of literary experience, a deficiency all too apparent in their handwriting, spelling, punctuation, syntax, vocabulary, length of composition, linguistic style, choice of theme and so on. But this complication turns out to be the very means by which they manage, with skillful effort, to liberate and control their literary imaginations. So it is with Fyedka. The compression which is so notable a characteristic of his style is forced upon him by the narrowness of his vocabulary, his inability to compose at length, his severely restricted syntax. If he is to write successfully within his limitations he must look for the simple detail that expresses the essence of an elaborate scene, the word that bears a heavy load of meaning, the few short sentences which entice the reader to read between the lines; he must push to the limit and beyond it his own syntactical and semantic knowledge, even at the expense of correctness. And this is precisely what Fyedka manages to do. There could be no more dramatic example of an eleven-year-old child's success in thus realising his own literary vision within the boundaries of his present literary experience.[15]

But children are not imprisoned within their experience. Even as they succeed in turning their constraints into opportunities, those constraints are being loosened by their rapidly accumulating experience. And it is here perhaps that we can best locate Tolstoy's notion of mental growth as an unending effort to restore an inner harmony that is constantly threatened by development. For the first effects of newly acquired knowledge are often to undermine the hard-won control which a child has gained over a particular medium of expression or tradition of thought. For example, children who have mastered the use of simple conjunctions—'and', 'but', 'then', 'so'—as a means of organizing and diversifying their sentences, and are achieving many fine effects in this way, become dissatisfied with their success as new and more complex constructions occur to them in the course of their literary activity. As they begin to experiment with these new forms and devices, as a way of enlarging the scope of their art, they often experience a falling off of skill, their writing becoming weaker, their achievement less controlled. They have to struggle to reassert their mastery over the new material, to reconstruct, as it were, their literary experience in the light of new knowledge and wider interests. Though Tolstoy himself ignores the implication, it is clear that the simple, compressed power of Fyedka's writing, remarkable as it may be, is no more than a temporary resting place on the way towards a still more complex and comprehensive literary mastery. Had

Tolstoy had time to prolong his studies, to follow and assist Fyedka in his further literary development, perhaps he would have come closer to resolving the problem of knowledge that plagued him—the relationship between high culture and folk culture, between the literary purposes of his pupils and the achievements of the literary masters.

Although he was still to write one final article in his journal—an irritable and argumentative reply to one of his critics—this superb essay on the character of children's thought and action effectively brings Tolstoy's educational writing to its close. For the reader who has followed him thus far, and finds his sympathies still engaged on Tolstoy's behalf, the success of his enterprise, however savagely curtailed, can best be judged by the following circumstance: that we feel his richly provocative conclusion to represent no more than a new point of departure.

[1]

On the education of the people

This is the opening article of the first number of Yasnaya Polyana *magazine, and is obviously intended to define the editor's preliminary position. It should not be confused with the long article of 1874, bearing exactly the same title, which arose out of Tolstoy's controversy in the Moscow Literacy Committee.*

There is one feature of the education of the people, in all ages and places, which I find incomprehensible. The people desire education, and every individual personality unconsciously yearns for education. The more educated class—society and the government—strive to communicate their knowledge and educate the less educated class, the common people. It might seem that this coincidence of needs ought to satisfy both the educating class and the class which is being educated. But the opposite occurs. The people constantly resist the efforts which society or the government, representing the more educated stratum, makes to educate them, and for the most part these efforts fail. Not to speak of the schools of ancient times—in India, Egypt, ancient Greece and even Rome, where we know very little about either the structure of these institutions or the people's attitude to them—this phenomenon is a striking feature of European schools from Luther's time to our own day.

Germany, the birthplace of the school, has found two hundred years of struggle too short a time to overcome the common people's resistance to it. In spite of the fact that the Friedrichs appointed time-expired soldiers as schoolmasters, in spite of the strictness of a law which has been in force for two hundred years, in spite of teachers being trained in the latest fashion in the colleges, in spite of the German's submissiveness to law, the coercive character of the school still weighs as heavily upon the people as ever; German governments cannot make up their minds to annul the law which makes schooling compulsory. Germany can take a pride in its popular education only on the level of statistical data; all that the greater part of the people carry away from school is, as before, a horror of schooling. France, in spite of having transferred education from the king's hands to the directory and from the directory to the clergy, has had just as little success in the field of popular education as Germany, or even less, according to educational historians who go by the official reports. In France serious statesmen are still proposing the introduction of compulsion as the only way to overcome the resistance of the people. In free England, where there could never be any question of introducing such a law—which, however, is a matter of regret to many—it is not the government but society that has been struggling till the present day with a popular resistance to schooling which is expressed more strongly than anywhere else. Schools are founded there partly by the government, partly by private societies. The vast extent and activity of these religious and philanthropic societies for education in England is the best possible proof of the strength of the resistance which the educating part of the nation encounters. Even a new polity, the United States of America, has not been able to avoid the difficulty and has made education semi-compulsory. What then shall we say of our native land, where the common people are bitterly opposed to the idea of schooling, where the most educated dream of introducing the German system of compulsory education, and where a condition of the existence of all schools, even of those for the upper class, is the lure of official rank and the advantages which come with it?[1] Everywhere to this day children are forced almost by violence to go to school and parents are forced, by the severity of the law or by cunning—the holding out of advantages—to send their children to school; whereas the common people everywhere study of their own accord and regard education as good.

How can this be? The demand for education is present in every human being; the people love and seek education as they love and seek air to breathe. The government and society have a burning desire to educate the people and, in spite of all the force, the cunning devices and the obstinacy of governments and educated classes, the common people constantly declare that they are not content with the education offered to them and, step by step, give in only to force.

In this, as in any conflict, we have to answer the question:

which is the more justifiable, the resistance or the pressure itself? Should we break down the resistance or change the pressure?

Till now, as far as we can see from history, the answer given to this question has been in favour of the government and the educating élite. The resistance has been regarded as unjustified; we have seen in it a principle of evil implanted in mankind, and the élite, without abandoning its mode of operation, that is, without abandoning the form and content of education which it had at its command, has employed force and cunning to destroy the resistance of the common people. So far the people have slowly and reluctantly submitted to this pressure.

The élite which conducts education must have had some basis whereby it could know that the education which it had mastered in a certain form was a good thing for a particular people in a particular historical period.

What is this basis? What basis does a school have in our day for teaching this and not that, and for teaching it in this way and not otherwise?

Always, in all ages, humanity has been trying to give more or less satisfactory answers to these questions, and in our times this answer is more essential than ever. A Chinese mandarin who has never left Peking can be made to memorize the sayings of Confucius and to drive these sayings into children by means of the stick. One could do this in the Middle Ages too, but where in our day are we to get that strength of conviction as to the indubitable nature of our knowledge which is strong enough to give us the right to educate the people forcibly? Take any medieval school, take the whole of the learned literature of the middle ages, before or after Luther—what a strength of conviction and of firm, indubitable knowledge of what is true and what false we can see in these men. It was easy for them to know that the Greek language was the one essential condition of education, because Aristotle wrote in it, the truth of whose propositions was doubted by no-one centuries later. How could the monks fail to demand the study of Holy Scripture, which stood upon unshakeable foundations? It was all very fine for Luther to demand categorically the study of the Hebrew language, when he knew definitely that in that language God himself had revealed the truth to men. It is understandable that when the critical sense of mankind had not yet awakened the school had to be dogmatic; that it was natural for pupils to learn by heart truths which had been revealed by God and Aristotle, and the poetic beauties of Virgil and Cicero. Centuries later no one could imagine a truer truth or a more beautiful beauty. But what is the situation of the school of our day, which has retained the same dogmatic principles when, next door to the class room where the pupils are learning by heart truths about the immortality of the soul, they try to make the pupil understand that nerves which are common to man and the frog are what was formerly known as the soul; when, after the story of Joshua, which is told him without any explanations, he finds out that the sun never did go around the earth; when, after an exposition of the beauties of Virgil, he finds the beauties of Alexandre Dumas, which are sold him for five centimes, much greater; when the teacher's only faith consists in saying that nothing is true, that everything that exists is rational, that progress is a good and backwardness is evil; when no-one knows what this universal faith in progress amounts to?

After all that, compare the dogmatic school of the middle ages, in which truth is undubitable, with our school, in which no-one knows what truth is, and which we nevertheless force children to attend and force their parents to send them to. But that is not all. In the medieval school it was easy to know what to teach, what to teach first and what afterwards and how to teach it, when there was but one method and when all knowledge was concentrated in the Bible and the books of Augustine and Aristotle. But as for us, with the infinite variety of teaching methods which are proposed on all sides, with the enormous number of sciences and their subdivisions which have been worked out in our age, how are we to choose one out of all the proposed methods, to choose a particular branch of knowledge and, most difficult of all, to choose a sequence of teaching these subjects which shall be reasonable and right. But even that is not all. Another reason why the search for these foundations in our day turns out to be more difficult, by comparison with the medieval school, is because then education was confined to one particular class which was being prepared for life in certain defined conditions; in our time, when the whole nation has declared its right to education, we consider it yet more difficult and yet more essential to find out what is needed for all these various classes.

What are these foundations? Ask any teacher why he teaches in the way he does and why he teaches one thing rather than another and one thing before another. And if he understands you he will answer: because he knows the truth which has been revealed by God and considers it his duty to transmit it to the younger generation, to bring them up in those principles which are indubitably true; concerning subjects other than religious education he won't give you any answer. Another teacher may explain the foundations of his school in terms of the eternal laws of reason expounded by Fichte, Kant and Hegel; a third will base his right to coerce the pupil upon the fact that it has always been so, that schools have always been coercive and that in spite of that the results of these schools are true education; finally, a fourth may say, gathering all these principles together, that the school must be as it is because religion, philosophy and experience have made it so, and what is historical is rational. All these arguments, which include all other possible arguments, can, it seems to me, be divided into four sections: the religious, the philosophical, the argument from experience, and the historical.

Education which has religion as its basis, that is Divine Revelation, the truth and legitimacy of which no-one can doubt, must indisputably be suitable for the people, and in this case, but only in this case, force is legitimate. Missionaries in Africa and China still act in this way. People still act thus in schools throughout the world with regard to the teaching of religions: the Catholic, the Protestant, the Jewish, the Mahometan and so on. But in our day, when religious education comprises only a small part of education, the question, "What basis has the school for forcing the younger generation to study in a particular way?" is not going to be decided on a religious basis.

Perhaps the answer is to be found in philosophy? Has philosophy as firm foundations as religion? What are these foundations? By whom, how and when are these foundations laid down? We do not know. All philosophers seek for the laws of good and evil; having found these laws, when they are concerned with pedagogy (none of them has been able to help concerning himself with pedagogy) they want to have the human race educated in accordance with those laws. But each of these theories, set against other theories, turns out to be incomplete and merely adds a new link to the consciousness of good and evil which is latent in humanity.

Every thinker merely expresses what his age is conscious of, and therefore it is quite superfluous to educate the younger generation in the meaning of that consciousness—it is already possessed by the living generation.

All pedagogical-cum-philosophical theories have as their aim and object the education of virtuous men. But either the concept of virtue remains the same or it is eternally developing, and, whatever any theories may say, the growth and decline of virtue does not depend on education. A virtuous Chinese, a virtuous Greek, Roman and modern Frenchman are either all equally virtuous or all equally far from virtue. Philosophical theories of pedagogy resolve the question of how to educate the best man according to a given theory of ethics which was developed at such and such a time and which is presumed to be indubitable. Plato has no doubt of the truths of his ethics and constructs his education on the basis of it, and his state upon that education. Schleiermacher says that ethics is an unfinished science, and therefore upbringing and education must have as their aim the development of people capable of entering those conditions they will find in life and who will at the same time be capable of vigorously working out improvements as available. Education in general, says Schleiermacher, has the aim of providing the state, the church, public life and science with a prepared member. But only ethics, even if it is an unfinished science, gives an answer as to what kind of member of these four elements of life an educated person ought to be. Like Plato, all the pedagogical philosophers seek the aim and object of education in ethics, some regarding it (ethics) as a known, others regarding it as an element of human consciousness which is eternally developing; but no theory gives a positive answer to the question: what and how should we teach the people? One says one thing, one another, and the further we go the more diverse these propositions become. Different theories, one contradictory of another, appear at one and the same time. The theological line struggles with the scholastic, the scholastic with the classical, the classical with the modern, and all these lines of thought exist at the present time without overcoming one another, and no-one knows what is false and what true. Thousands of diverse, extremely strange, quite unfounded theories appear, such as those of Rousseau, Pestalozzi, Froebel and so on; all existing schools—modern, classical and theological institutions, make their appearance side by side. All are discontented with what exists and do not know just what innovation is necessary and possible.

After tracing the course of the history of philosophical pedagogy you will find no criterion for education in it, but, on the contrary, one common idea which unconsciously underlies the thought of all teachers in spite of their frequent disagreement amongst themselves, an idea which convinces us that there is no such criterion. All of them, from Plato to Kant, are striving for the same thing, to free the school from its historical trammels, they want to guess what man needs and upon their more or less accurate guesses as to these needs, they build their new school. Luther has Holy Scripture taught in the original and not according to the commentaries of the holy fathers. Bacon has us study nature from nature itself, and not from Aristotle's books. Rousseau wants to teach life from life itself as he understands it, and not from past experience. Each step forward in pedagogical philosophy only consists in freeing the school from the idea of teaching the younger generations what the older generations have considered learning to be, and going over to the idea of teaching what the younger generations need. This same common and yet self-contradictory thought is to be felt throughout the history of pedagogy—common because everyone demands a greater measure of freedom for the school, self-contradictory because everyone prescribes laws founded upon his own theory and thereby restricts freedom.

The experience of schools which have existed and now exist? . . . But how can this experience prove to us that the existing method of coercive education is just? We cannot know that there is not another, more legitimate method, since schools up to now have not been free. True, we see that at the highest level of education (universities, public lectures) education is tending to become ever freer. But this is only a supposition. Perhaps education at lower levels should always remain coercive, and experience may have proved to us that such schools are good? Let us look at these schools, not by consulting the statistical tables of education in Germany, but let us try to get to know the schools and their influence on the people in actuality. The actual situation has shown me the following. A father sends his daughter or son to school against his will, cursing the institution which deprives him of his son's work, and counting the days till his son will be *schulfrei*,[2] (this expression alone proves how the common people look upon the schools). The child goes to school convinced that his father's authority (the only one he has known) does not support the authority of the government, which he is obeying when he enrolls at school. The report he hears from old friends who are already at that institution are not calculated to increase his wish to enroll. Schools appear to him to be institutions for torturing children—institutions in which they are deprived of the chief pleasure and need of childhood days—freedom of movement, where *Gehorsam* (obedience) and *Ruhe* (quiet) are the chief conditions, where he needs special permission even to leave the room, where every transgression is punished with the ruler (which is the same thing as the stick, even though in official circles corporal punishment with the ruler is said to be abolished) or by the continuation of a state which the child finds extremely painful—study. The school seems to the child (quite rightly) to be an institution where they teach things which nobody understands, where—for the most part—he is forced to speak not in his own patois or *Mundart*[3] but in a foreign language, where the teacher for the most part sees his pupils as his inveterate enemies who, out of spite on their own parts and that of their parents, refuse to learn what he has learnt himself, and where the pupils on the other hand, look upon the teacher as an enemy who forces them to learn such difficult things purely out of personal spite. In such an institution they are obliged to spend about six years and some six hours a day. We can see what the results must be like once again, not by considering the figures, but by the actual facts. In Germany nine-tenths of those who attend schools for the common people bring away from school a mechanical ability to read and write and such a strong distaste for the paths of learning which they have tried that they never pick up a book again. Let those who disagree with me show me which books the people read; even Hebbel of Baden[4], even almanacks and popular newspapers are read only as rare exceptions. An irrefutable proof that the people are uneducated is the fact that there is no literature of the common people, and, above all, that the tenth generation has to be sent to school by force just as much as the first. Not only does such a school create a disgust for education amongst the common people, but in those six years it accustoms them to hypocrisy and deceit, which arise from the unnatural situation in which the pupils are placed, and that condition of confusion and instability of ideas which is known as literacy. In my journeys through France, Germany and Switzerland for the purpose of discovering what the school-children knew, their views on the school and their moral development, I put the following questions in elementary schools and to former pupils outside the schools: what is the chief town of Prussia? or of Bavaria? How many sons had Jacob in the story of Joseph? Those still in school sometimes answered me with whole tirades learnt by heart from the book, but those who had completed the course—never. I could scarcely ever get an answer which was learnt otherwise than by heart. In mathematics I could find no general rule—sometimes it was good, sometimes very bad. Then I would set an essay on the subject, what had the pupils done the Sunday before? and always without any exception, the boys and the girls wrote the same thing, that on Sunday they had availed themselves of all possible opportunities to pray to God, but they had not played. This is a model of the school's moral influence. On putting to grown men and women the question why did they not study after their schooling? or why they do not read this or that? they all replied that they had undergone the rite of confirmation, had got through the quarantine of schooling and had obtained a certificate of a certain degree of education—literacy.

Besides that stultifying influence of the school, for which the Germans have invented such an accurate name, *verdummen*[5], and which consists, above all, in a long-drawn-out perversion of the intellectual capacities, there is another still more harmful influence which consists in the fact that the child, being stultified by life at school, is, for long hours of work each day (the most precious time at his age) torn away from those essential conditions of development which nature itself has created for him. We very commonly hear and read the view that home conditions, the boorishness of parents, work in the fields, rural games and so on are the chief obstacles to schooling. Perhaps they do indeed hinder that schooling which the teachers have in mind, but it is time we convinced ourselves that all these conditions are the main foundations of any education, that they are, far from being foes or obstacles to the school, rather its first and principal activators. The child could never learn to distinguish the different lines which form different letters or numbers, or acquire the ability to express his thoughts, if it were not for these home conditions. How can it then be the case that this boorish home life can teach the child such difficult things and then suddenly this same home life becomes not only inadequate for teaching the child such easy things as reading, writing etcetera, but even hinders such teaching? The best proof is to compare a peasant boy who has never done any studying with a boy from the governing class who has studied with a tutor for five years or so. The superiority in intelligence and knowledge is always on the side of the former. Not only that, but interest in knowing anything whatsoever and the questions which it is the school's task to answer are aroused only by these home conditions. And any study ought to be simply an answer to a question provoked by life. But far from provoking questions, the school does not even answer those which are provoked by life. It is constantly answering the same questions as were posed by mankind several centuries ago, and then not by children, questions with which the child is not yet concerned. Such are questions about how the world was created? what sort of land is Asia? what shape is the earth? how do you multiply hundreds by thousands? and what will happen after death? and so on. Whereas he receives no reply to the questions which are posed to him by life, all the more so since, owing to the police-like organisation of the school, he does not even have the right to open his mouth for the purpose of asking to be excused but has to do this by signs, so as not to break the silence and hinder the teachers. And the school is run in this way because the object of the government school, which is instituted from above, is for the most part not to educate the people but to educate them according to our method—above all they want schools to exist and a lot of schools. Are there no teachers? Let teachers be made. Are there still not enough teachers? Let us arrange it so that one teacher can teach five hundred children, *mécaniser l'instruction,* the Lancaster method, pupil teachers[6]. Hence schools organized from above and forcibly, not a shepherd for the flock but a flock for the shepherd. The school is arranged not so that the children shall find it convenient to learn, but so that the teacher shall find it convenient to teach. The teacher is inconvenienced by the talking, the movement, the jollity of the children, which comprise for them an essential condition of study, and in schools which are constructed like prison institutions questions, conversations and movements are forbidden. Instead of convincing themselves that in order to act effectively upon any object you have to study it (and in education this object is the free child) they want to teach in the way they know, just as it occurs to them, and if it is unsuccessful they want to change, not their manner of teaching, but the very nature of the child. This approach invariably gives rise (Pestalozzi) to systems which makes it possible to *mécaniser l'instruction*—that perpetual tendency of pedagogy so to arrange things that, no matter what the teacher and pupil are like, the method shall be the same. You need only look at one and the same child at home or in the street, and at school—in the one case you see a creature full of the joy of life and knowledge, with a smile in its eyes and on its lips, seeking instruction in all things as a joy, expressing its own thought clearly and often forcefully in its own language—in the other you see a weary, huddled creature, with an expression of fatigue, terror and boredom, repeating with the lips alone the words of others in the language of others, a creature whose soul has hidden in its shell like a snail. You need only glance at these two states to decide which of the two is the more favourable to the child's development. In that strange psychological state which I shall call the school state of mind, which we all, unfortunately, know so well, all the higher abilities—imagination, creativity, understanding, give place to some sort of other, semi-animal abilities—the ability to pronounce sounds independently of the imagination, to count off numbers in order: 1, 2, 3, 4, 5, to retain words without letting the imagination support them with any images at all; in brief, the ability to crush all abilities in oneself in order to develop only those which correspond with the school state of terror, memory strain and attention. Any pupil constitutes a disparate element in the school until such time as he drops into the rut of this semi-animal condition. As soon as the child has reached this state and has lost all independence and self-reliance, as soon as various symptoms of the disease—hypocrisy, pointless lying, bafflement—make their appearance in him, then he no longer constitutes a disparate element in the school, he has fallen into the rut, and the teacher begins to be pleased with him. Then we also find those cases which are not fortuitous but constantly repeated, in which the stupidest child becomes the best pupil and the cleverest child the worst. This fact would seem to be significant enough for us to give some thought and try to explain it. It seems to me that this fact alone is an evident proof of the false foundation of the coercive school. Not only this, but besides the alienation of children from the unconscious education which they receive at home, at work and in the street, which is a negative evil, these schools are physically harmful to the body which is so inseparable from the spirit at an early age; this evil is particularly serious in view of the one-sidedness of school education, even if it were good. For the farm worker nothing can replace those conditions of work—life in the fields, the old people's talk and so on, which surrounded him; it is just the same for the craftsman and for the townsman in general. It is not by chance, but for a purpose, that nature has surrounded the agriculturist with agricultural conditions and the townsman with urban ones. These conditions are in the highest degree instructive, and only in such conditions can the respective kinds of worker be educated; the school, however, lays down as the first condition of its education alienation from these conditions. Even this is not enough for the school, not only does it drag children away from life for six hours a day during their best years, it would drag three-year-old children away from the mother's influence. Institutions have been invented (*Kleinkinderbewahranstalt,* "infantschools" [*sic*] *salles d'asile*) which we shall have occasion to speak of in more detail later. It only remains to invent a steam-engine to replace the nursing mother. Everyone agrees that schools are imperfect (for my part I am convinced that they are harmful). Everyone agrees that many, many improvements are needed. Everyone agrees that these improvements must be based upon the greater convenience of the pupils. Everyone agrees that the pupils' convenience can only be discovered when we have studied the needs of children of school age in particular. But what is being done to further this difficult and complex study? For centuries every school has been modelled upon another, which in turn was modelled upon a previous one, and each of these schools has laid down as an essential condition a discipline which forbids the children to speak, to ask questions, to choose this or that subject of study—in short, every step is taken to deprive the teacher of the possibility of drawing conclusions as to what the pupils need. The coercive structure of the school excludes the possibility of any progress. Meanwhile, when we reflect how many centuries have been spent telling children the answers to questions which they would never have thought of asking, when we reflect how far the present generations have departed from that ancient form of education which they inculcate, we fail to understand why schools are still maintained. We would have thought that the school should be both an instrument of education and, at the same time, an experiment with the younger generation which constantly yields new conclusions. Only when experiment is the basis of the school, when every school is, so to speak, a pedagogical laboratory, will the school cease to fall behind the general progress, and experiment will be able to lay firm foundations for a science of education.

But perhaps history will give us the reply to our vain question: what is the basis of the right to force education upon parents and pupils? Existing schools, it will say,have evolved out of an historical process, and by just such an historical process must they continue to evolve and change their forms in accordance with the demands of society and the times; the longer we live the better schools become. To this I will reply: in the first place exclusively philosophical arguments are just as one-sided and false as exclusively historical ones. The consciousness of humanity is the chief element in history and therefore if humanity is conscious of the unsoundness of its schools this fact of consciousness will then be the chief historical fact on which the structure of the school should be based. In the second place, the longer we live the worse schools become, not the better—worse in relation to the level of education which society has attained. The school is one of those organic parts of the state which cannot be contemplated or evaluated separately, since its value consists merely in its greater or lesser correspondence to the other parts of the state. The school is good only when it has recognized those basic laws by which the people live. A fine school for a Russian village of the steppes, one which satisfies all the needs of its pupils, will be an extremely bad school for a Parisian, and the best seventeenth-century school would be the worst school of our day; and on the other hand the worst medieval school of its day was better than the best school of our day, for it corresponded more closely to its age and at least was on a level with the general state of education, if it was not ahead of it, whereas our school is lagging behind it. If the task of the school (to put it in the most general terms) is to hand on everything which has been evolved and brought into consciousness by the people and to answer those questions which life poses to a man, then there is no doubt that in the medieval school the traditions were more limited and the questions which life posed were easier to answer, and this task of the school was fulfilled better. The traditions of Greece and Rome according to insufficient and unstudied sources, religious dogmas, grammar and such mathematics as was known—these were far easier to hand on than all the traditions which we have lived through since those days, and which have thrust the traditions of the ancient peoples so far into the background, and than all that knowledge of the natural sciences which is essential for our age as explanations of the everyday phenomena of life. And yet the means of transmission has remained the same, and for this reason the school was bound to fall behind and become not better, but worse. In order to keep the school in the same form as it had been and not let it fall behind the movement of education we should have been more consistent: we should not merely have made laws for the restriction of schools, but should have forbidden education to move forward by other means—by forbidding machines, means of communication and the printing of books.

As far as one can tell from history only the Chinese have been strictly logical in this respect. The atttempts of other nations to restrict printing and the movement of education in general were only temporary and not consistent enough. And therefore at the present time only the Chinese can boast of good schooling and one that entirely corresponds to the general level of education.

If people tell us that schools are perfected by the historical process we will simply reply that the perfection of schools must be understood in a relative sense, and that, on the contrary, schools grow relatively worse and worse with every year and every hour of coercion, that is, they fall further and further behind the general level of education, since their forward movement has not been keeping up with the movement of education ever since the invention of printing.

In the third place, in reply to the historical argument that schools have existed and are therefore good, I will offer another historical argument. A year ago I was in Marseilles and visited all the teaching institutions for the working people of that city. The number of people studying is so large in proportion to the population that, with a few exceptions, all children go to school for three, four or six years. The school syllabuses consist of the catechism learnt by heart, sacred and general history, the four rules of arithmetic, French orthography and bookkeeping. How bookeeping can be a subject of instruction I could not understand and no teacher could explain to me. The only explanation which I could find when I had had a look at how books were kept by pupils who had completed that course was that they did not even know three of the rules of arithmetic, but had learnt operations with figures by heart and therefore had to learn *tenue des livres* by heart too. (One would think it was hardly necessary to demonstrate that *tenue des livres, Buchhaltung,* as taught in Germany and England, is a study which takes four hours of explanation for any pupil who knows the four rules of arithmetic.) Not one boy in these schools knew how to solve, that is how to pose, the simplest problem of addition and subtraction. However, they were able to operate with numbers in the abstract, multiplying thousands with dexterity and speed.[7] They gave good answers by rote to questions about the history of France, but by getting out of sequence I got the reply that Henri IV was killed by Julius Caesar. The same thing in geography and sacred history. The same thing in orthography and reading. The female sex, or more than half of it, cannot read except from the book learnt by heart. Six years of schooling do not enable them to write a word without a mistake. I know that the facts I am citing are so improbable that many people will have their doubts, but I could write whole books about the ignorance which I saw in the schools of France, Switzerland and Germany. However, let anyone who has these matters at heart try, as I did, to study the schools not from the results of the public examinations, but by prolonged visits and chats with teachers and pupils in and out of the schools. In Marseilles I also saw one secular and one convent school for adults. Out of 250,000 inhabitants fewer than 1,000 people, and only 200 of them men, go to these schools. The instruction is the same: mechanical reading, which is mastered in a year or more, bookkeeping without knowledge of arithmetic, religious homilies and so on. After the secular school I saw daily instruction in the churches, I saw the *salles d'asile* in which four-year-old children go through manoeuvres round the benches, like soldiers, to the whistle, raise and fold their hands at the word of command and sing hymns in praise of God and their benefactors in trembling, strange voices, and I became convinced that the teaching institutions of Marseilles are extraordinarily bad. If by some miracle someone could see all these institutions without seeing the people in the streets, the workshops, the cafés and their home life, what opinion would he form about a people educated in such a manner? He would no doubt think that here was an ignorant, coarse, hypocritical people, full of prejudices and almost savage. But you have only to make contact, to have a chat with somebody from the common folk to be convinced that, on the contrary, the French people are almost what they consider themselves to be: quick of understanding, intelligent, sociable, free-thinking and truly civilized. Take a look at an urban workman of about thirty—he can already write a letter without the sort of mistakes he made at school, sometimes perfectly correctly; he has some idea of politics and consequently of recent history and geography; by now he knows some history from novels; he has some knowledge of the natural sciences. He very often draws and he applies mathematical formulae to his craft. Where has he acquired all this?

I found the answer in Marseilles without meaning to, when I began to wander after school through the streets, the *"guinguettes"*[8] the *cafés chantants,* the museums, workshops, quays and bookshops. The same boy who answered me that Henri IV was killed by Julius Caesar knew the story of *The Three Musketeers* and *Monte Cristo* very well. In Marseilles I found twenty-eight cheap editions, from 5 to 10 centimes, with illustrations. For 250,000 inhabitants they have a circulation of 30,000—consequently, if we assume that ten people read and listen to each copy, then everyone reads them. Besides this there is the museum, the public libraries, the theatres. Cafés—there are two big *cafés chantants,* which anyone has the right to enter if he spends 50 centimes, and which are visited by up to 25,000 people a day, not counting the small cafés which accommodate an equal number—in each of these cafés short comedies and scenes are performed and verses are declaimed. Here already, at the lowest reckoning, is a fifth of the population which receives oral instruction every day, just as the Greeks and Romans were instructed in their amphitheatres. Whether this education is good or bad is another matter, but there it is, an unconscious education, so many times stronger than the compulsory one,—there it is, an unconscious school undermining the compulsory one and making its content almost nil. All that remains is the despotic form almost without content. I say almost, excepting the mechanical ability to put letters together and arrive at words, the only knowledge that is acquired in five or six years of study. Moreover, we must note that this same mechanical skill in reading and writing is often acquired outside school in a far shorter time, and that very often even this knowledge is not brought away from the school and is frequently lost when it does not find an application in life, and that where a law of compulsory school attendance exists there is no need to teach the second generation to write, read and count, since it seems that the mother and father would be in a position to do this at home, and much more easily than in school. I saw the same thing in all the other countries as in Marseilles: everywhere the main part of the people's education is acquired not from the school but from life. Where life is instructive, as in London, Paris and big cities in general, the people are educated; where life is not instructive, as in the villages, the people are not educated, in spite of the fact that the schools are absolutely identical in the one place and in the other. It is as if knowledge acquired in the cities remains, knowledge acquired in the villages is lost. The tendency and spirit of the education of the people, in cities and villages alike, is completely independent, and for the most part the opposite, of that spirit which is supposed to be inculcated in schools for the people. Education goes on its own way independently of the schools.

The historical argument against the historical argument is that, when we review the history of education, far from being convinced that schools develop in accordance with the development of peoples, we are convinced that they fall into decay and become an empty formality with the development of peoples, that the further ahead a people has gone in general education, the more education has passed from the school into life and has made the content of the schooling trivial. Not to speak of all the other media of education—the development of trade relations and means of communication, the greater degree of personal freedom and participation in governmental affairs, the meetings, museums, public lectures and so on, one has only to look simply at printing and its development to understand the difference between the situation of the school, past and present. The unconscious education of life and conscious school education have always gone side by side, supplementing one another; but before printing existed what an insignificant measure of education could be given by life in comparison with the school! Learning belonged to the chosen ones who commanded the means of education. And see what a part can now be played by education from life, when there is no human being who does not possess a book, when books are sold for the most insignificant sums, when public libraries are open to all, when a boy walking to school carries, besides his exercise books, a cheap illustrated novel, concealed on his person, when two ABC books are sold for three kopecks, and a peasant of the steppes is quite likely to buy an ABC book, ask a passing soldier for help and pick up all the learning which once was acquired through years of study with the sexton, when the gymnasium pupil gives up school and prepares and passes the university entrance examination by himself from books, when young people give up the university and instead of studying from the professor's notes work directly from the sources, when, to be honest, any serious education is acquired from life and not from school.

The last, and to my mind the most important argument consists in saying that it is all very well for the Germans, on the basis of schools which have existed for two hundred years, to defend them historically; but what basis have we for defending schools for the people which we have not got? What historical right have we to say that our schools must be the same as European schools? We have as yet no history of education for the people. But if we examine the international history of popular education we shall be convinced that it is impossible for us to organise colleges for teachers on the German model, to counterfeit the German phonetic method,[9] the English infant schools, the French *lycées* and specialized schools and to catch up with Europe by these means, and what is more we shall be convinced that we Russians are living in exceptionally happy conditions as regards popular education, that our schools must not, as in medieval Europe, arise out of civic needs, must not serve certain government or religious ends, must not be developed in the dark, outside the control of public opinion and, in the absence of a high degree of education from life, must not once again go through the labour and pain of getting into and breaking out of the same vicious circle that European schools were involved in for such a long time—a vicious circle whereby the school had to set in motion unconscious education, and unconscious education had to set in motion the school. The European peoples have overcome this difficulty, but they could not help losing a great deal in the struggle. Let us be grateful for the labours which it is our lot to profit from, and for that very reason let us not forget that we are called upon to accomplish a new task in this field. Because of what humanity has lived through, and because our activity has not yet begun, we can introduce a greater degree of awareness into our work and are therefore obliged to do so. If we are to borrow devices from the European schools we have a duty to distinguish what is founded upon the eternal laws of reason from what has arisen simply as a result of historical conditions. There is no general law of reason, no criterion, which justifies the violence used by the schools against the people, and therefore any imitation of European schools as regards compulsory schooling would not be a forward, but a backward step for our people, it would be a piece of treachery to our calling. We can understand why France has developed a disciplined school in which the exact sciences predominate—mathematics, geometry and drawing; why Germany has developed a methodical character-training school in which singing and analysis predominate; we can understand why England has developed those innumerable societies which establish philanthropical schools for the proletariat with their strictly moral and yet practical tendency; but we do not know what sort of school ought to be formed in Russia, and never will know unless we let it work itself out freely and at the right time, that is, in accordance with the historical epoch in which it must develop, in accordance with its own history and, still more, with universal history. If we are convinced that popular education in Europe is taking the wrong course, then by doing nothing for our own popular education we shall do more than if we were suddenly to force into it everything that seems good to each one of us.

An uneducated people, then, wishes to educate itself, a more educated class wishes to educate the people, but the people submit to education only under duress. When we searched philosophy, experience and history for those foundations which might give the educating class the right to do this, we found nothing, but, on the contrary, became convinced that humanity's thinking is constantly pressing for the liberation of the people from force in educational affairs. When we searched for a criterion of pedagogics, that is, a knowledge of what and how we should teach, we found nothing but the most contradictory opinions and assertions, and we were convinced that the further forward mankind moves, the more impossible it becomes to have such a criterion; when we sought that criterion in the history of education, we convinced ourselves not only that for us Russians the schools which have developed historically cannot be models, but that these schools fall further and further behind the general level of education with every step forward, and for this reason their coercive character becomes more and more illegitimate, and, finally, that in Europe education itself, like water seeping through a stratum, has chosen another course—has bypassed the schools and trickled into the instruments of education furnished by life.

What then are we Russians to do at the present moment? Are we all to come to an agreement and take as our basis the English, the French, the German or the North American view of education and one or other of their methods? Or by plunging deep into philosophy and psychology are we to discover what in general is required for the development of a human soul and for transforming the younger generation into the best men according to our conceptions? Or are we to profit from the experience of history, not by imitating the forms which history has worked out, but by understanding the laws which mankind in its sufferings has worked out, and shall we say directly and honestly that we do not and cannot know what future generations will need, but that we feel obliged, and wish, to study these needs; we do not wish to accuse the common people who do not accept our education of ignorance, but we will accuse ourselves of ignorance and pride if we take it into our heads to educate the people in our own way. Let us cease to look upon the people's resistance to our education as a force which is hostile to pedagogy, but, on the contrary, let us see in it an expression of the will of the people, by which alone our activity should be guided. Let us, finally, recognize that law which speaks to us so clearly both from the history of educational theory and from the history of education as a whole, that if the educator is to know what is good and what is bad the person being educated must have the full power to express his dissatisfaction, or at least to withdraw from that part of education which does not satisfy his instinct, that there is only one criterion of pedagogy—freedom.

We have chosen the last course in our own pedagogical activity.

The basis for our activity is the conviction that we do not and cannot know what the education of the people ought to consist of, that not only does pedagogy—the science of education and upbringing—not exist, but that its first foundations have not been laid, that the definition of pedagogy and of its aim in the philosophical sense is impossible, useless and harmful.

We do not know what education and upbringing ought to be, we do not recognize the whole philosophy of pedagogy, because we do not recognize the possibility of man's knowing what it is that man ought to know. Education and upbringing present themselves to us as historical facts concerning the action of certain people upon others; therefore the task of the science of education is, in our opinion, simply to search for the laws governing this action of certain people upon others. Not only do we deny that our generation has the knowledge, not only do we deny that one can have the right to know what is needed for the perfection of man, but we are convinced that if mankind did possess this knowledge we would not be able either to impart it or not to impart it to the younger generation. We are convinced that consciousness of good and evil is latent in all mankind independently of whether man wills it, and develops unconsciously together with history, we are sure that it is as impossible to train the younger generation to share our consciousness by means of education as it is to deprive it of our consciousness and of that level of higher consciousness which the next step in history will raise it to. When we think that we know the laws of good and evil and that we are acting upon the younger generation on the basis of them, we are for the most part resisting the development of the new consciousness which our generation has not yet worked out, but which is being worked out in the younger generation—we are providing an obstacle to education, not an assistance to it.

We are convinced that education is history and therefore has no final aim. Education in the most general sense, including upbringing, is in our belief that activity of man which has as its basis the demand for equality and the immutable law that education must move forward. A mother teaches her child to speak only so that they can understand one another, instinctively the mother tries to come down to his view of things, to his language, but the law of forward movement in education does not permit her to come down to him, but obliges him to rise to her knowledge. The same relationship exists between writer and reader, between the school and the pupil, between government and voluntary societies and the people. The activity of the educator, as of the person being educated, has one and the same objective The task of the science of education is simply the study of the conditions in which these two tendencies come together into one common aim, and to indicate which conditions hinder this coming together. Consequently the science of education is becoming on the one hand easier for us, since it no longer puts questions such as 'What is the final end of education for which the younger generation must be prepared?' and so on; on the other hand, it is becoming immeasurably difficult. We have to study all the conditions which have helped to bring the aims of the educator and of the educated together; we need to determine what that freedom is, the absence of which hinders the coincidence of the two aims, and which alone serves us as a criterion for the whole science of education; we must proceed step by step from innumerable facts towards the solution of the questions posed by the science of education.

We know that our arguments will not convince many. We know that our basic convictions, that the sole method of education is experience and its sole criterion freedom, will sound to some people like a hackneyed piece of vulgarity, to others like an unclear abstraction, to yet others like a dream and an impossiblity. We would not have dared to disturb the calm of theoretical pedagogues and to utter such opinions, which are disgusting to all society, were we to confine ourselves to the reasoning of this article, but we feel that there is a possibility of proving the applicability and legitimacy of these wild beliefs of ours step by step and fact by fact, and to this end alone we shall dedicate our publication.

[2]

The Yasnaya Polyana school in the months of November and December

Since the three parts of this article appeared in the January, March and April numbers of Yasnaya Polyana *magazine the title would appear to refer to November and December 1861. But this is of slight importance, for the article gives a discursive account of the school from its inception to the time of writing.*

I General sketch of the character of the school. Mechanical and progressive reading. Grammar and writing.

We have no beginners. The junior class can read, write, do exercises on the first three rules of arithmetic and tell Bible stories—so that the subjects are divided on the timetable in the following manner:

1. Mechanical and progressive reading; 2. Writing; 3. Calligraphy; 4. Grammar; 5. Sacred history; 6. Russian history; 7. Drawing; 8. Technical drawing; 9. Singing; 10. Mathematics; 11. Talks on the natural sciences; 12. Divinity.

Before talking about the lessons I must give a short sketch of what the Yasnaya Polyana school is and what period of its growth it has now reached.

Like any living organism the school not only changes its form year by year, day by day and hour by hour, but is also subject to periodic crises, storms, maladies and bad moods. The Yasnaya Polyana school passed through one such morbid crisis this summer. There were many reasons for this: to begin with, as always in summer all the best pupils were absent, only occasionally would we meet them, at work in field and pasture; secondly new teachers had arrived at the school and new influences had begun to be felt in it; thirdly, throughout the summer each day would bring new visitors—teachers taking advantage of the summer holidays. And nothing is more harmful to the proper running of a school than visitors. In one way or another the teacher ingratiates himself to the visitors.

We have four teachers. The two old ones have been teaching in the school for two years now, and have got used to the pupils, to their work, and to the freedom and outward disorder of the school. The two new teachers—both of them not long out of school themselves—are lovers of outward exactitude, of the timetable, the bell, the syllabus and so on, and have not settled in to the life of the school as the first ones have. What seems to the first ones reasonable, necessary, unable to be otherwise, like the features of a child, well loved but plain, who has grown before one's eyes, to the new teachers looks like a defect which might be corrected.

The school is situated in a two-story stone house. Two rooms are occupied by the school, one by a study and two by the teachers. In the porch under the balcony hangs a bell with a rope fastened to its clapper; in the entrance hall downstairs stand parallel bars (for gymnastics); upstairs over the entrance hall is a carpentry bench. The staircase and entrance hall are trodden with snow or mud; that is where the timetable hangs too.

The teaching routine is as follows: at about eight o'clock a teacher who lives in the school, a lover of outward order and the administrator of the school, sends one of the boys who nearly always spend the night with him to ring the bell.

In the village they get up before daylight. From the school lights have been visible in the windows for some time by now, and half an hour after the bell, in the fog, in the rain or in the slanting rays of the autumn sun small dark figures appear by twos and threes or singly on the hillocks (the village is separated from the school by a ravine). The herd feeling long ago disappeared. A pupil no longer finds it in the least necessary to wait and shout, 'Hey, kids, come to school!'[1] He already knows that school is of the neuter gender, knows a thing or two besides that and, strangely enough, because of this he has no need of the crowd. The time has come, and off he goes. It seems to me that every day personalities are becoming more and more independent and their characters more clear-cut. Hardly ever have I seen pupils playing on the way, except for some of the smallest or new arrivals who had begun at other schools. No one carries anything with him, neither textbooks nor exercise books. No homework is set.

Not only does a pupil carry nothing in his hands, he need carry nothing in his head either. He is not obliged to remember today any lesson or anything that was done yesterday. He is not tormented by the thought of the lesson to come. He brings only himself, his receptive nature and his certainty that school will be as much fun today as it was yesterday. He does not think about the class before the class begins. Nobody is ever told off for being late, and they never are late: unless it is one of the older ones whose fathers keep them back at home now and again for some work or other. And then they will come running into school at a smart trot, out of breath. Before the teacher arrives they gather, some of them around the porch, pushing one another off the steps or sliding on the ice of the curving pathway, others in the school rooms. When it is cold they read, write or scuffle while waiting for the teacher. The girls do not mix with the boys. When the lads think up something which involves the girls they never address one of them, but always all of them at once, 'Hey, girls, why don't you slide?' or 'I reckon the girls are frozen!' or 'Right, girls, all of you against just me!' Only one of the girls, from a house servant's family, with vast and many-sided abilities and about ten years old, is beginning to emerge from the herd of girls. And to this one alone the boys behave as to an equal, as to a boy, only with a subtle nuance of politeness, condescension and reserve.

Let us suppose that on the timetable there is mechanical reading for the first, junior class, progressive reading for the second, mathematics for the third. The teacher arrives in the room and lads are lying squealing on the floor, shouting 'There's enough of you' or 'You're smothering me, kids!' or 'That's enough, let go of my hair!' and so on. 'Pyotr Mikhailovitch!' one voice shouts from under the heap to the teacher as he enters. 'Tell them to stop it!' 'Hallo[2] Pyotr Mikhailovitch' shout the others, continuing their scuffling. The teacher takes some books and gives them out to those who have come to the cupboard with him; out of the heap on the floor where they are lying the top ones demand a book. The heap diminishes, little by little. As soon as the majority have taken books all the rest are running to the cupboard shouting "Me too, me too! Give me the one I had yesterday, and give me the Koltsov[3] book!" and so on. If there are two or three of them who have become carried away by the battle and remain rolling on the floor the ones sitting with their books shout at them: 'What are you interfering for? We can't hear a thing! That's enough!' The ones who were carried away submit, breathlessly take to their books and only for a while, until their excitement has subsided, they go on scraping their feet as they sit reading. The spirit of the war flies away, and the spirit of reading reigns in the room. With the same absorption with which this boy was pulling Mitka's hair he now reads the Koltsov book (that is what Koltsov's works are called in our school), almost grinding his teeth, his little eyes gleaming, and scarcely seeing anything roundabout him except his book. You would need as much force now to tear him away from his book as you would have needed before to tear him from his wrestling.

Each one sits down where he feels inclined, on benches, tables, the windowsill, the floor and the armchair. The girls always sit together. Friends and children from the same village, especially the little ones (there is more comradeship amongst them) always sit side by side. As soon as one decides to sit in a particular corner all his friends, jostling and diving under the desks, scramble over to the same place, sit down side by side and, looking around them, display on their faces such a look of happiness and satisfaction as if sitting in those places were to make them happy all the rest of their lives. The big armchair, which has somehow turned up in the room, is an object of jealousy to the more independent personalities—the girl from the domestic servant's family and others. As soon as one takes it into his head to sit in the armchair another will have discovered the intention from his face and they clash and struggle. One thrusts the other out and the victorious one sprawls with his head far down against the back of the chair, reading as they all are, quite absorbed in his work. In class time I have never known them to whisper and pinch one another and laugh on the quiet, to snort into their hands or complain to the teacher about one another. When one who started school at the sexton's or in the district school comes forward with such a complaint they say to him, 'Why don't you stick up for yourself?'

The two smaller classes are placed in one room, the senior class goes into the other. A teacher comes into the first classroom too; everyone gathers round him by the board, or they lie on the benches or sit on the table around the teacher or the one who is reading. If it is writing they sit down more peacefully, but they are for ever standing up to look at one another's books and show their own to the teacher. According to the timetable there are four lessons before dinner, but it sometimes turns out to be three or two, and sometimes quite different subjects. The teacher may begin with arithmetic and pass on to geometry, he may begin with sacred history and end up with grammar. Sometimes teacher and pupils get carried away, and instead of an hour the lesson goes on for three hours. It may happen that the pupils themselves shout 'No, more, more!' and shout at those who have got fed up. 'If you're fed up push off to the little ones,' they say scornfully. For the divinity class, which is the only one to take place regularly, because the divinity teacher lives two versts away and comes in twice a week, and for the drawing class, all the pupils are gathered together. Before these lessons the animation, the scuffling, the shouts and outward disorder are at their greatest; some drag benches from one room into the other, some fight, some run home (to the servants) to fetch bread, some toast this bread in the stove, some take things away from others, some do gymnastics, and once again, as with the morning scuffles, it is far easier to leave them to calm down of their own accord and bring themselves into their own natural order than to force them to sit down in their places. Given the spirit of the school as it is now, it would be physically impossible to stop them. The louder the teacher shouts (this has happened) the louder they shout; his shout only stimulates theirs. Leave them or, if possible, draw them away in another direction and the squalls in this little sea will become rarer and rarer and it will calm down. For the most part it is not even necessary to say anything. The drawing class, a favourite class with everyone, is at midday, by which time they have grown hungry and have been sitting down for three hours, and then on top of that benches and tables have to be carried through from one room to another, and a terrible racket begins; but in spite of this by the time the teacher is ready the pupils are ready, and anyone who holds up the beginning of the class will catch it from *them*.

I must make one reservation. In presenting a description of the Yasnaya Polyana school I do not think I am presenting a model of what is necessary and good for a school, but merely a real description of a school. I believe that such descriptions can be of use. If in the following numbers I succeed in presenting clearly the history of the school's development the reader will come to understand why the character of the school developed precisely as it did, why I consider such an order of things to be a good one and why it would not be possible for me to change it even if I wanted to. The school developed freely from principles which were introduced to it by the teacher and the pupils. Despite the prevailing influence of the teacher the pupil has always had the right not to go to school and even, when he came, not to listen to the teacher. The teacher had the right not to admit a pupil to his class and had the opportunity of bringing all the force of his influence to bear upon the majority of the pupils, upon the society which schoolchildren always form. The further the pupils go on the more instruction is divided into branches, and the more essential order becomes. Consequently, provided the development of a school is normal and uncoercive, the more the pupils educate themselves the more capable they become of order, the more strongly they themselves feel that order is required, and the stronger the influence of the teacher on them becomes in this respect. In the Yasnaya Polyana school this rule has been constantly confirmed from the day of its foundation. At first it was impossible to make subdivisions either for classes or subjects, for recreation or for lessons; everything fused of its own accord into one, and all attempts at dividing things up remained vain. But now in the oldest class there are pupils who themselves demand that the timetable be followed, who are discontented when they are taken away from a lesson, and who themselves constantly chase away the little ones who come running in to them.

In my opinion this outward disorder is useful and irreplaceable, however strange and inconvenient it may seem for the teacher. I shall often have occasion to speak of the advantages of this arrangement; of the supposed inconveniences I shall say this. In the first place we find this disorder, or free order, frightening only because we have grown used to quite a different one in which were reared ourselves. Secondly, in this as in many similar cases, violence is used only out of haste and a lack of respect for human nature. It seems to us that the disorder is growing, is becoming greater and greater and has no bounds, it seems that there is no means of putting an end to it other than the use of force—but if only we had waited a little the disorder (or animation) would have settled in its own natural way into a much better and securer order than any that we may invent. Schoolchildren are people, small people but people with the same needs as we have and thinking in the same ways; they all want to learn, that is the only reason why they go to school, and therefore they will very readily come to the conclusion that they must submit to certain conditions in order to learn. Not only are they people—they are a society or people united by a single idea. "Where two or three are gathered together in My name, there am I in the midst of them!" Submissive only to laws which are natural and derived from their own nature, they are exasperated and protest when subjected to your premature interference, they do not believe in the legitimacy of your bells and timetables and rules. How many times have I happened to see boys fighting—the teacher rushes to separate them, and the enemies when they are torn apart snarl at one another and even in the presence of the threatening teacher do not stop jabbing one another still more painfully than before; how many times each day I see a boy like Kiryushka, gritting his teeth, hurl himself at Taraska, seize him by the hair, hurl him to the ground and seem to want to disfigure his enemy if he dies in the attempt, and before a minute has passed Taraska is laughing from underneath Kiryushka, the blows they exchange become lighter and lighter, and before five minutes have passed both have become friends and gone to sit down side by side. Not long ago between classes two boys grappled with one another in a corner; one—a remarkable mathematician—about nine years old, in the second class, the other, a close-cropped boy whose parents are domestic servants, a clever but revengeful, tiny, black-eyed boy nicknamed Kiska. Kiska seized the mathematician's long hair and thrust his head back against the wall; the mathematician grabbed in vain at Kiska's close-cropped bristles. Kiska's little black eyes were triumphant, the mathematician could hardly hold back his tears and kept saying 'Hey! Hey! What's up? What's up?' but you could see that he was in a bad way and was only keeping his spirits up. This went on for quite a long time, and I was undecided what to do. 'They're fighting, they're fighting,' cried the lads and crowded around the corner. The little ones laughed, but the big ones, although they did not set about separating them, looked at each other in a serious sort of way, and these looks and the silence did not escape Kiska. He realized that he was doing something bad and began to smile guiltily and let go of the mathematician's hair. The mathematician recovered himself, gave Kiska such a blow that he hit the back of his head against the wall and walked away, satisfied. The little boy began to cry, dashed after his enemy and hit him with all his strength on his fur coat, but didn't hurt him. The mathematician was about to return the blow, but at that moment several disapproving voices rang out. 'Look at him, he's started on the little'un,' shouted the spectators. 'Beat it, Kiska.' With that the affair concluded as if it had never been, except, I dare say, for a dim recognition by both parties that it is unpleasant to fight, because you both get hurt. Here, one might say I had succeeded in noticing the feeling for justice which guides the crowd; but often affairs like this are settled, by what law we do not understand, but settled they are, with both sides satisfied. How arbitrary and unjust in comparison with this are all the pedagogue's approaches in such cases. 'You are both in the wrong, kneel down!'[4] says the pedagogue, and the pedagogue is mistaken, because only one of them is in the wrong, and that one exults as he kneels and chews over all his pent-up spite and the innocent one is doubly punished. Or 'You are in the wrong because you did so-and-so, and you shall be punished', says the pedagogue, and the child who is punished hates his enemy all the more because that enemy has on his side a despotic power which *he* does not recognize as legitimate. Or: 'Forgive him, that is what God commands, and be better than he is,' says the pedagogue. You say to him: be better than he is, but he only wants to be stronger, and does not, cannot understand any other 'better'. Or: 'You are both in the wrong; ask one another's pardon and kiss, children.' This is worst of all, both because of the falsity, the self-consciousness of that kiss, and because the bad feeling which was subsiding then flares up again. But leave them alone (unless you are a father or mother who is simply sorry for your child and who is therefore always right to pull the hair of whoever hit your son) leave them and see how all this is cleared up and settled just as simply and naturally and yet with as much complexity and variety as in all the unself-conscious relations of life. But perhaps teachers who have no experience of such disorder or free order will think that without the intervention of the teacher this disorder may have physically harmful consequences; that they may thrash one another too hard, break one another's bones, and so on. In the Yasnaya Polyana school since last spring there have been only two cases of blows which left marks. One boy was pushed off the porch and cut his leg open to the bone (the wound was healed in two weeks), another had his cheek burnt with a burning rubber and he bore the scar for about two weeks. It is not more than once a week that anyone starts to cry, and then not so much from pain as from indignation or shame. Apart from these two cases we cannot call to mind any brawls, bruises or bumps all through the summer, with thirty or forty pupils left to do entirely as they please.

I am convinced that the school must not intrude upon the matter of moral training which belongs to the family alone, that the school must not and has no right to reward and punish, that the best policing and administration of the school consists in leaving the pupils complete freedom to learn and to conduct their affairs as they wish. I am convinced of this, but nevertheless the old habits of schools which go in for moral training are so strong in us that not infrequently we in the Yasnaya Polyana school depart from this rule. During the last half-year, in November to be precise, there were two cases of punishments.

During the drawing class a teacher who had recently joined noticed a boy who was shouting, not listening to the teacher, and furiously beating his neighbours without any reason. Finding it impossible to calm him with words the teacher led him out of his place and took his slate away from him—that was the punishment. The boy was streaming with tears throughout the lesson. This was a boy that I had not accepted when the Yasnaya Polyana school opened, considering him to be a hopeless idiot. The chief characteristics of the boy are dullness and meekness. His comrades never include him in games, laugh and make fun of him, and themselves recount with astonishment, 'What a funny chap Petka is! You can thump him—even the little ones thump him, and he just shakes himself and goes away.' 'He hasn't got any heart at all,' said one boy to me of him. If such a boy was reduced to such a state of fury as the teacher punished him for, then it is unlikely that the boy who was punished was the one in the wrong. This is the other case. In the summer, when alteratons to the building were being made, a Leyden jar disappeared from the physics room, and several times pencils and books disappeared at a time when there were no longer any joiners or painters working in the building. We asked the boys: the best pupils, the first scholars to enter the school, our old friends, blushed and looked embarassed, and this embarrassment might have seemed to an investigator a certain proof of their guilt. But I knew them and could be as sure of them as I could of myself. I realized that the very thought of being suspected was deeply and painfully insulting to them; a boy, whom I shall call Fyodor, a talented, tender nature, was quite pale, trembling and weeping. They promised that they would tell if they found out, but refused to investigate. After a few days the thief was discovered—a boy from a domestic servant's family in a distant village. He had led astray a peasant boy who came from the same village, and together they hid the stolen things in a little suitcase. This discovery brought out a strange reaction in his schoolfellows, a feeling something like relief, and even rejoicing, and at the same time contempt and pity for the thief. We proposed that they should fix the punishment themselves: some demanded that the thief should be whipped, but this was to be done only by themselves; others said fix a label to him with 'Thief' written on it. To our shame we had used this punishment before, and the very same boy who had a year ago himself worn a label with 'Liar' written on it now demanded a label for the thief more insistently than anyone. We agreed to the label and when a girl had sewn it on all the pupils looked at it with spiteful joy and jeered at those who were suffering punishment. They demanded that the punishment should be increased.

'Have them led through the village, leave the labels on them till the holiday,' they said.

The boys who were being punished wept. The peasant boy who had been led astray by his comrade—a talented story-teller and wag—a fat, white, chubby little fellow, wept quite without reserve, with all his childish strength; the other, the principal offender, hook-nosed, with a dry-featured, clever face, was pale, his lips trembled, his eyes gazed wildly and viciously at his rejoicing schoolfellows, and occasionally his face would be unnaturally distorted by weeping. His cap with its torn peak was perched on the very back of his head, his hair was dishevelled, his clothing covered in chalk. All this now struck me and everyone as though we were seeing it for the first time. Everyone's malicious attention was directed at him. And he felt this painfully. When, without looking round, his head hanging, with a certain special guilty way of walking, as it seemed to me, he set off for home, and the lads running after him in a crowd teased him in a way that was somehow unnatural and strangely cruel, as if an evil spirit were controlling them against their will, something told me that this was wrong. But things stayed as they were, and the thief went around labelled for twenty-four hours. From that time on he began, as I thought, to do worse at his studies, and he was not to be seen joining in games and conversations with his schoolfellows outside classes.

Once I came into the classroom and all the pupils announced to me with a sort of horror that this boy had stolen again. He had carried off 20 kopecks in coppers from the teachers' room and had been caught hiding them under the stairs. Again we hung a label upon him, and the same monstrous scene started again. I began to admonish him in the way that all moral educators do; a boy who was at this time already fullygrown, a garrulous fellow, began to admonish him too, repeating words which he had presumably heard from his father, an innkeeper.

'You've stolen once, you've stolen again,' he said deliberately and weightily, 'it'll become a habit and lead to no good.'

I began to get exasperated. I felt something like rage against the thief. I looked at the face of the boy who had been punished, which was yet paler, more suffering and more cruel, and for some reason I was reminded of convicts, and suddenly I felt so remorseful and disgusted that I tore the stupid label from him, telling him to go where he liked, and suddenly I was convinced, convinced not intellectually but with my whole being, that I had no right to torment that unhappy child, and that I could not make of him what I and the innkeeper's son wanted to make. I became convinced that there are secrets of the heart which are hidden from us, on which life may have an effect, but not moralizings and punishments. And what nonsense! A boy stole a book—a whole long, complex course of feelings, thoughts, mistaken arguments led him to take a book belonging to someone else and for some reason or other lock it in his suitcase—and I fasten to him a piece of paper with the word 'thief' on it, which means something quite different! Why? To punish him through shame, they tell me. To punish him through shame? Why? What is shame? And do we really know that shame destroys a tendency to thieving? Perhaps it encourages it. Perhaps what was expressed on his face was not shame? I even know for certain that it was not shame but something quite different, which would perhaps have slept forever in his soul and which should not have been brought out. Out there, in the world which is called real, in the world of Palmerstons and Cayenne, in the world where it is not what is reasonable that is reasonable, but what is real, there let people who have been punished invent for themselves the right and duty to punish. Our world of children—of simple, independent people—must remain pure, free from self-deception and the criminal belief in the legitimacy of punishment, a belief and a self-deception which holds that the sentiment of revenge becomes just as soon as we call it punishment. . . .

We will continue the description of the daily teaching routine. At about two o'clock the hungry children run home. In spite of their hunger they nevertheless stay a few minutes to find out who has what marks. Marks, which do not at present confer supremacy upon anyone, are terribly interesting to them.

'I've got 5+ and Olgushka's come in for a whacking great nought. And I've got 4!' they shout.

Marks serve as an evaluation of their work for them, and dissatisfaction with marks occurs only when the evaluation is not correctly done. Woe betide us if someone has tried and the teacher, on looking it over, gives him less than he is worth. He gives the teacher no peace and weeps bitter tears if he does not get it changed. Marks which are bad but deserved remain without protest. Marks, by the way, are merely a remnant of our old forms of organization and are tending to drop out of use of their own accord.

For the first lesson after dinner, after being dispersed, they gather just as in the morning and wait for the teacher in just the same way. Generally it is a lesson in sacred or Russian history, for which all the classes are assembled. Usually it is twilight by the time this class begins. The teacher stands or sits in the middle of the room and the crowd is disposed around him amphitheatre-fashion; some on benches, some on tables, some on the windowsills.

All the evening lessons, and especially this first one, have an atmosphere, quite distinct from those of the morning, one of tranquillity, dreaminess and poetry. If you come to the school in the twilight—there is no light at the windows, it is almost quiet, only the newly trodden snow on the stairs, a faint hum and stirring on the other side of the door and some urchin hanging on to the banisters going up the stairs two at a time prove that there are pupils in the school. Enter the room. It is already almost dark behind the frost-covered windows; the oldest and best pupils are pressed right up against the teacher by the others and are looking right at his mouth, with heads flung back. The self-reliant girl with the worried face from the domestic servant's family always sits on a high table, it looks as if she is gulping down every word; the small fry sit further away, rather closer-packed; they listen attentively, even angrily, they behave as the big ones do, but in spite of all their attention we know that they will not retell the story, although they will remember a lot. One is sprawled across another's shoulders, another is standing right up on the table. Occasionally one of them, having wriggled into the very middle of the crowd, occupies himself behind someone's back by tracing some sort of figures on that back with a finger-nail. It is rarely that anyone looks round at you. When a new story is in progress they all freeze and listen. When it is a repetition self-satisfied voices ring out here and there, unable to hold back from supplying the teacher with something. However even when it is an old story, which they love, they ask the teacher to repeat it all in his own words and do not permit anyone to interrupt the teacher.

'Here you, can't you wait? Shut up!' they shout at the upstart.

It hurts them that the character and artistic form of the teacher's narrative should be interrupted. Recently it has been the story of the life of Christ. Each time they demanded that it should all be retold. If they were not told all of it then they themselves would supply the well-loved ending—the story of Peter's denial and the Saviour's passion. Everything seems as quiet as death, nothing stirs—have they perhaps gone to sleep? In the half-darkness you go up to one of the little ones and look at his face; he is sitting with his eyes glued to the teacher, frowning with attention and for the tenth time pushes away his friend's arm which has dropped on to his shoulder. You tickle the back of his neck, he does not even smile, flicks his head as if driving away a fly and once more devotes himself entirely to the mysterious and poetical story: how the veil of the temple was torn of its own accord and darkness covered the earth—he feels mystified but happy. But now the teacher has finished telling the story and everyone gets up from his place and, each one shouting louder than the next, crowding round the teacher, tries to recount everything that he has retained. A terrible shouting begins—the teacher can scarcely manage to follow everybody. Those who have been prevented from speaking, because we are sure they know the story, are not satisfied with this; they approach another teacher, or, if there is not one—a schoolfellow, an onlooker, even the stoker, they walk up and down from corner to corner in twos and threes, asking everyone to listen to them. It is rare for anyone to tell the story alone. They divide themselves up into groups of equal ability and tell the story, one encouraging, monitoring and correcting another.

'Right, let's have a go with you,' says one to another, but the one who is addressed knows that he is not on the same level as the other and sends him away to someone else.

As soon as they have had their say and calmed down candles are brought in, and then another mood comes over the boys.

In the evenings generally and in the following classes there is less scuffling, fewer shouts, more obedience to and trust in the teacher. One notices a particular distaste for mathematics and analysis, and a desire for singing, reading and especially for story-telling.

'Why always mathematics and writing—better if you tell something, about the earth, or else history, and we'll listen,' they say.

By about eight o'clock eyelids are drooping, they begin to yawn, the candles burn lower and are snuffed less often, the older ones hold out, the younger and weaker ones are falling to sleep, leaning on the table, to the pleasant sound of the teacher's voice. Sometimes, when the classes are interesting and there have been a lot of them (sometimes there are up to seven good hours a day) and the children have grown tired, or before a holiday, when the stoves at home have been prepared for a steam bath, suddenly, at the second or third lesson after dinner, two or three boys run into the room and without saying a word hastily pick up their caps.

'What's up?'

'Going home.'

'But what about the lessons? There's singing you know!'

'But the lads say they're going home!' he replies, slipping away with his cap.

'But who says?'

'Come on lads!'

'What's all this? What?' asks the teacher in concern, having prepared his lesson. 'Stop.'

But another boy runs into the room with a flushed, anxious face. 'What are you waiting for?' he turns angrily upon the boy who has been delayed, and is picking at his cap in indecision; 'the lads are way over there by now, up by the smithy, I reckon.'

'Coming?'

'I'm coming.'

And they both run off, shouting from the doorway, 'Goodbye, Ivan Ivanich!'

And who are these lads who have decided to go home? and how did they make the decision? Heaven knows. You have no way of finding out exactly who made the decision. They did not hold a conference, did not make a plot, but it just occurred to the lads to go home. 'The lads are going' and small feet rang out on the steps, somebody tumbled down the steps head over heels and, hopping about and shoving in the snow, running past one another on the narrow pathway, shouting, the lads went running home. This kind of thing is repeated once or twice a week. It is insulting and unpleasant for the teacher—who could fail to agree there?—but who will not also agree how much greater the significance of the five, six and sometimes seven lessons a day for each class, all freely and willingly attended each day by the pupils, because of one case of this kind. Only when such cases are repeated can we be assured that the instruction, although inadequate and one-sided, is not altogether bad and harmful. If the question were put this way; which is better—that there should be no such case in the course of a year, or to have such cases repeated in more than half the lessons—we would choose the latter. At any rate I in the Yasnaya Polyana school have been glad that such events have recurred several times a month. Though I frequently tell the children that they can always go away when they like, the teacher's influence is so strong that I have been afraid lately lest the discipline of classes, timetables and marks might encroach upon their freedom without their noticing it, so that they would submit completely to the cunning net of order we have cast and lose the possibility of choice and protest. If they continue to come willingly in spite of the freedom which is offered to them I do not by any means think that this proves that the Yasnaya Polyana school has special qualities—I think the same thing would be repeated in most schools, and that the wish to learn is so strong in children, that in order to satisfy this wish they will put up with many difficult conditions and forgive many defects. The possibility of running off like this is useful and necessary simply as a means of insuring the teacher against the worst and crudest mistakes and bad practices.

In the evenings we have singing, progressive reading, talks, physics experiments and essay-writing. Of these subjects reading and experiments are the favourites. In reading the seniors stretch themselves on the big table in a star-shape—heads together, feet splayed—one reads and the others recapitulate to one another. The juniors sit down two to a book and, if that book is comprehensible, read as we read—they arrange themselves in a good light and prop themselves up comfortably and evidently enjoy themselves. Some of them, trying to combine two pleasures, sit in front of the stoked-up stove, warming themselves and reading. Not everybody is allowed into the experiments class—in the second class only the eldest, and the best, the most reflective. This lesson, as regards the character it has assumed in our school, is the one best suited to the evening, the most fantastic lesson, entirely appropriate to the mood which is evoked by reading fairy-tales. Here the fairy-tale world passes into reality—they personify everything: the juniper-berry which is repelled by sealing wax, the magnetic needle which repels, the filings scurrying across a piece of paper underneath which a magnet is drawn, all these represent living creatures to them. Even the cleverest boys, who understand the explanation of these phenomena, get carried away and start to mutter at the needle, the berry and the filings 'Hey you! Where are you going? Stop! Hey! On you go!' and so on.

Usually the lessons end at eight or nine, unless carpentry keeps the older boys back longer, and the whole gang runs shouting together as far as the servants' quarters and from there on begins to make off towards various corners of the village in groups that shout across to one another. Sometimes they take it into their heads to coast downhill to the village on a big sledge which is parked by the gate—they tangle with a snowdrift, go slap into the middle and disappear from view with a shriek into the powdered snow, leaving here and there on the road—black patches—boys that have tumbled out. Outside school (in spite of all its freedom), in the open air new relations are established between teacher and pupil with more freedom, more simplicity and more trust, the kind of relations that appear to us to be the ideal towards which a school should strive.

Recently we were reading Gogol's 'Vii'[5] in the first class; the last scenes had a strong effect and excited their imagination; some of them mimicked the witch and kept on remembering the last night.

It was not cold outside—a moonless, cloudy, winter night. At the crossroads we stopped; the older ones who had been at school for three years came to a halt around me, asking me to go further with them; the little ones looked on for a bit—and started sliding downhill. The juniors had started work with a new teacher, and there was not the same trust between me and them as between me and the seniors.

'Well then, let's go to the plantation'[6] (a copse about two hundred paces from the dwelling-houses) said one of them.

Fyedka begged me to hardest of all, a boy about ten years old, a tender, receptive, poetical and dashing nature. It seems that for him danger is the most important condition of enjoyment. In summer it always used to be frightening to watch him swimming out with two other boys into the very middle of the pond, which is about a hundred yards across, and occasionally disappearing altogether in the warm reflections of the summer sunshine, swimming across the deep stretch, turning over on his back, spurting out streams of water and calling out in a thin voice to his friends on the bank to see what a fine fellow he was. Now he knew that there were wolves in the wood; that is why he wanted to go into the plantation. The others supported him, and we four went over to the wood together. Another one—I shall call him Syomka—is healthy both physically and morally; a fellow about twelve years old, nicknamed Vavilo, walked in front and kept shouting and making warbling calls to somebody. Walking beside me was Pronka, a sickly, meek and unusually gifted boy, a son of a poor family, sickly, it seems, mainly from lack of food. Fyedka was walking between me and Syomka and kept on making remarks in a specially soft voice, now telling how he had guarded horses here in summer, now saying that there was nothing to be afraid of, and now asking 'What if one did jump out?' and demanding categorically that I should say something in reply to that.

We did not go into the middle of the wood—that would have been too frightening, but even near the wood it had grown darker: the path could scarcely be seen, the lights of the village had vanished from sight. Syomka stopped and began to listen.

'Stop lads! What's that?' he said suddenly.

We fell silent, but there was nothing to be heard; even so it added to our fear.

'Well, what are we going to do when he jumps out and chases us?' asked Fyedka.

We talked about Caucasian robbers. They remembered a story about the Caucasus which I told them long ago, and I began to tell them again about abreks[7] and cossacks and Hadji

Murat[8]. Syomka was walking in front, striding out in his big boots and swaying his healthy back in rhythm. Pronka was about to try to walk beside me, but Fyedka pushed him off the path, and Pronka, who always gives in to everybody, no doubt on account of his poverty, came running up to one side only in the most interesting parts, even though he sank up to his knees in the snow.

Anyone who knows a little about peasant children will have noticed that they are not used to and cannot bear any sort of caressing, soft words, kissing, stroking with your hand and so on. Once I happened to see a lady in a peasant school, who wanted to make much of a boy, say 'Then I'll give you a kiss, darling!' and kiss him, and I could see the boy who was kissed was shamed, insulted, and unable to understand why *that* had been done to him; even a five-year-old boy is above these caresses—he is already 'a lad'. I was therefore particularly struck when Fyedka, who was walking beside me, suddenly, at the most frightening point of the story, touched me lightly with his sleeve; he then gripped two of my fingers in his whole hand and did not let them drop. As soon as I fell silent Fyedka began demanding that I tell more, and in such an imploring and excited voice that I could not do anything but carry out his wish.

'Here you, get out from under our feet,' he said angrily to Pronka, who had come running forward; he was absorbed to the point of cruelty, he felt so creepy and happy holding on to my finger, and nobody should dare to disturb his pleasure. 'Now some more, some more! It's *fine*!'

We walked through the wood and started to approach the village from the other end.

'Let's go further,' they all said as the lights came in sight 'Let's go through again.'

We walked in silence, stumbling here and there on the unfirm, badly worn pathway; it was as if a white darkness were swaying before our eyes; the clouds were low, as if something were pouring them down upon us; there was no end to that *whiteness* in which we alone were crunching over the snow; the wind roared in the bare tops of the aspens; but for us it was quiet on the other side of the wood. I finished my story by telling how the abrek, having been surrounded, burst out singing and then threw himself upon his dagger.Everyone was silent.

'But why did he burst out singing when he was surrounded?' asked Syomka.

'You've been told—he was getting ready to die, of course,' replied Fyedka irritably.

'I think he started singing a prayer,' added Pronka.

Everyone agreed. Fyedka suddenly stopped.

'And what did you say about your aunt being murdered?' he asked—he had not had enough of terrors.

'Tell us! tell us!'

I told them once more that terrible story of the murder of Countess Tolstoy, and they stood around me in silence, looking into my face.

'That was a brave chap,' said Syomka.

'It must have been frightening for him walking around at night, with her lying murdered,' said Fyedka, 'I would have run away!' And he once again grasped my two fingers in his hand.

We stopped in a copse behind the barns, on the very edge of the village. Syomka picked up some brushwood from the snow and hit the frosty bole of a lime-tree with it. Hoar frost showered down from the branches on to his cap, and the noise resounded, solitary, through the woods.

'Lev Nikolayevich,' said Fyedka (I thought he was going to speak about the countess again) 'why do we learn singing? I often think, really, why sing?'

How he had made the leap from the horror of murder to that question Heaven knows, but everything: the sound of his voice, the seriousness with which he sought an answer, the silence of the other two made us feel that there was a very vital and legitimate connection between that question and the preceding conversation. Whether the connection was that he was replying to my explanation that crime may be due to lack of education (I had been telling them that) or that he was testing himself by identifying himself with the murderer and remembering his favourite occupation (he has a wonderful voice and an immense talent for music) or whether the connection was that he felt that now was the time for sincere talk and all the questions which were calling for an answer arose in his mind—at any rate none of us was surprised at his question.

'And why drawing?' said I, not knowing in the least how to explain to him what art is for.

'Why drawing?' he repeated meditatively. He was in fact asking 'Why art?' I did not dare to explain, I did not know how.

'Why drawing?' said Syomka. 'You put everything down in a drawing—you can make anything from that.'

'No, that's technical drawing,' said Fyedka, 'but why draw figures?'

Syomka's healthy nature saw no difficulty; 'Why a stick, why a lime-tree?' he said, still rapping the lime.

'Well then, what *is* a lime-tree for?' said I.

'To make rafters with,' replied Syomka.

'And what else, what is it for in summer, before it's chopped down?'

'Why nothing.'

'No, really,' Fyedka continued obstinately to ask, 'why does a lime-tree grow?'

And we started to talk about the fact that utility is not everything, but there is beauty, and art is beauty, and we understood one another, and Fyedka quite understood why a lime-tree grows and why we sing. Pronka agreed with us, but he understood better moral beauty—goodness. Syomka understood with his great intelligence, but he would not admit beauty without utility. He doubted, as often happens with people of great intelligence who feel that art is a force but who do not feel in their hearts any need of that force; like them he wanted to approach art with his intellect and was trying to light that fire within himself.

'Tomorrow we're going to sing "Ije",' I can remember by line.'

He has a good ear, but lacks taste and refinement in singing. But Fyedka understood perfectly that a lime-tree in leaf is beautiful, and it is good to look at in summer, and nothing more is needed. Pronka understood that it is a pity to cut it down, because it too is a living thing:

'You know it's just as if it was blood when we drink the sap out of a birch-tree.'

Syomka, although he did not say so, evidently thought that it was not much good when it was rotten. I find it strange to repeat what we said then, but I remember that we talked over—as it seems to me—everything that can be said about utility and about physical and moral beauty.

We walked to the village. Fyedka still did not let go of my hand, out of gratitude now, I thought. We were all so close that night, as we had not been for a long time. Pronka walked beside us along the broad village road.

'Look, there's still a light at the Mazanovs'!' he said. 'As I was walking to school today Gavryukha was riding away from the pot-house' he added 'as dr-r-r-unk as drunk, his horse was all foaming, and he was flogging it. . . . I always feel sorry. Really! what does he want to beat it for?'

'And the other day', said Syomka, 'he gave his horse its head out of Tula and it took him off into a snowdrift, and him asleep drunk.'

'And Gavryukha does whip him across the eyes so . . . and I felt so sorry for it,' said Pronka once more. 'Why was he beating it? There were tears, and he goes on whipping it.'

Syomka suddenly stopped. 'Our folks are asleep by now' he said, peering into the windows of his crooked black cottage. 'Won't you walk some more?'

'No.'

'Goodby-y-ye Lev Nikolayevich,' he suddenly shouted and, as if he were tearing himself away from us with an effort, trotted up to the house, lifted the latch and vanished.

'So you'll see us back, first one and then the other' said Fyedka.

We walked on. There was a light in Pronka's place; we looked in at the window: his mother, a tall, beautiful but worn woman with black brows and eyes, was sitting at the table and peeling potatoes; in the middle of the room a cradle was hanging; the mathematician of the 2nd class, Pronka's other brother, was standing by the table eating a salted potato. The cottage was black, tiny and dirty.

'You've been gone long enough!' shouted his mother to Pronka. 'Where've you been?'

Pronka gave a meek, pained smile, looking at the window. His mother guessed that he was not alone and at once changed to an ugly, false expression. Only Fyedka was left.

'We've got the tailors sitting up in our place, that's why there's a light,' he said in the softened voice he had that evening. 'Goodbye Lev Nikolayevich,' he added quietly and tenderly and began to bang the ring on the locked door. 'Open up!' his thin little voice sounded through the wintry silence of the village.

It was a long time before they opened to him. I looked in at the window: the cottage was a big one; logs could be seen on the stove and benches; his father was playing cards with the tailors; a few copper coins were lying on the table. A woman, the step-mother, was sitting by the light and staring hungrily at the money. The tailor, a young peasant who is a hardened rogue, was holding his cards, which were bent right over, on the table, and gazing in triumph at his partner. Fyedka's father, his collar undone, all frowns from the intellectual tension and vexation, was shuffling his cards and in his indecision waving his workman's hand over them.

'Open up!'

The woman got up and went to unlock the door.

'Goodbye,' Fyedka repeated once more. 'Let's always go walking like that.'

I can see honourable, good, liberal people, members of philanthropic societies, who are ready to give and do give one hundredth part of their property to the poor, who have established and are establishing schools and who will say, when they read this, 'It's a bad thing!' and shake their heads, 'Why develop them forcibly? Why give them feelings and conceptions which will set them at odds with their environment? Why take them out of their way of life?' they will say. Not to mention those who are outstandingly hard-headed, and who will say 'A fine thing it will be for the organization of the state when everyone wants to be thinkers and artists, and nobody will work!' These people are saying straight out that they do not like work, and therefore it is necessary that there should be people, not exactly incapable of other activity, but slaves who will work for others. Whether it is a good thing, whether it is a bad thing, whether we ought to bring them out of their environment and so on—who knows? And who can bring them out of their environment? As if this were some sort of mechanical action. Is it good or bad to add sugar to flour or pepper to beer? Fyedka is not bothered by his ragged little kaftan, but Fyedka is tormented by moral questions and doubts, and you want to give him three roubles, a catechism and a little story about how work and humility, which you detest yourselves, are the only things of use to a man. He does not need the three roubles, he will find them and take them when he does need them, and he will learn how to work without you—just as he learnt how to breathe; what he needs is what your life, your ten generations uncrushed by work, have led you to. You have the leisure to seek, to think, to suffer; give him what you have won through your suffering—that is the one thing he needs; but no, like an Egyptian priest you veil yourself from him in a mantle of mystery, you bury in the earth the talent which history has given you. Never fear: nothing human is harmful to a human being. Do you doubt it? Yield to feeling and it will not deceive you. Have trust in his nature and you will be convinced that he will take only that which history has entrusted to you to impart to him, that which has been worked out in you through suffering.

The school is free and the first pupils in point of time were from the village of Yasnaya Polyana. Many of these pupils left the school because their parents thought the instruction bad; many, having learned to read and write, gave up coming and took jobs at the station[10] (the chief industry of our village). At first children used to be brought in from the poor neighbouring villages, but they were soon removed, either because of the inconvenience of coming or that of boarding them out (our people charge at least two silver roubles a month). The richer peasants from distant villages were tempted by the absence of payment and by the gossip spreading amongst the people that children were well taught at the Yasnaya Polyana school, and they would have sent their children, but this winter, with the opening of schools in the villages, they withdrew them and sent them to fee-paying village schools. There remained in the Yasnaya Polyana school the children of the Yasnaya Polyana peasants, who come in winter and work in the fields in summer from April to the middle of October, and the children of caretakers, estate managers, soldiers, house servants, innkeepers, sextons and rich peasants, who were driven in from thirty to fifty versts around.

The total number of pupils is as high as forty, but there are rarely more than thirty at once. The girls make up from one tenth to one sixth—we have from three to five. For boys the most common, normal age is from six to twelve. Besides this each year we have three or four adults, who attend for a month, sometimes all the winter, and then give up altogether. For the adults who come to the school one by one the school routine is extremely inconvenient. Because of their years and their sense of superiority they cannot join in the animation and life of the school, cannot give up despising the children and remain quite solitary. The animation of the school merely hinders them. For the most part they come to complete their studies, already knowing something, and convinced that study is the same business of learning a book off by heart which they have heard of or even tried before. Before coming to the school the adult student has had to overcome his fear and shyness, and withstand the displeasure of his family and the jeers of his companions 'Look at the girt oaf—he's goin' to school!' Moreover he continually feels that every day lost at school is a day lost for the work which is his sole capital, and therefore all the time in school he is in an exasperated state of hastiness and earnestness which more than anything else vitiates study. During the period of which I am writing there have been three such adults, one of whom is still studying now. An adult in school behaves like a person at a fire; as soon as he has finished writing, at the same moment as he puts down his pen with one hand, he seizes the book with the other and begins to read standing up; as soon as the book is taken away from him he takes to the slate; when that is taken away too he is quite lost. Last autumn there was a workman who studied and did the stoking for the school. He learned to read and write in two weeks, but it was not study, but a sort of illness like a drinking bout. As he walked through the classroom with the firewood in his arms he would stop, and peering over a boy's head, he would spell out s-k-a, ska and walk to his place. When he had not time to do that he would look at the children with envy, almost with malice; on the other hand when he was free you could do nothing with him, he glued himself to a book, repeating b-a,ba r-e,re and so on, and since he was in this state he lost the ability to understand anything else. When it came to singing or drawing or listening to a story from history or watching experiments—you could see that adults were submitting to cruel necessity and, like hungry men torn from their food, were only waiting for the moment when they could once more glue themselves to the ABC book. Adhering faithfully to my rule, just as I did not force a boy to study the reading primer when that was not what he wanted,so also I did not make an adult learn mechanics or technical drawing when he wanted the reading primer. Each took what he wanted.

Generally adults, who have 'swotted' before, have not so far found a place for themselves in the Yasnaya Polyana school, and their studies do not go well: there is something unnatural and feverish in their attitude to the school. In the Sunday schools which I have seen there is the same phenomenon as regards adults, and therefore any information concerning the successful and free education of adults would be a precious acquisition for us.

The people's views about the school have changed a lot since it began. We shall have occasion to speak of an earlier opinion in the history of Yasnaya Polyana school, but now it is said amongst common folk that in the Yasnaya Polyana school they teach them everything and all the branches of knowledge, that they have such cunning teachers you'd never believe it; they do say they can make thunder and lightning! Still, the children understand all right; they have begun to read and write. Some, the rich owners of farmsteads, send their children out of vanity, to have them learn all there is to be learnt, so that they can even do division (division is their ultimate notion of scholastic wisdom); other fathers suppose that learning is very profitable; but the majority send their children unthinkingly, in submission to the spirit of the times. As regards these boys, who make up the majority, the happiest thing we have noticed is that there are some who were sent 'for no reason' but who have taken such a liking to learning that by now the fathers are yielding to the children's wishes, sense unconsciously that something good is happening to their children and cannot bring themselves to take them away from the school. One father told me how he had burnt a whole candle through at one sitting, holding it over his son's book, and warmly praised both his son and the book. It was the Gospels.

'My dad too', reported another scholar, 'now and again he'll listen to a story,[11] and laugh and go off again, but when it's something sacred he'll sit up till midnight listening, and holding the light himself.'

I visited the home of a certain pupil with a new teacher and, so as to boast in front of the teacher, made the pupil solve an algebraical equation. The mother was bustling around the stove, and we forgot about her; as she listened to her son, absorbed and confident, saying as he rearranged the equation, "2ab − c = d, divided by 3", and so on, she kept on covering her face in her hands, scarcely able to contain herself, and at last burst out into fits of laughter and could not tell us what she was laughing at. Another father, a soldier, who had come to fetch his son, came across him in the drawing class and, when he saw his son's skill, started to address him as 'Vy'[12] and could not bring himself to hand over to him in the classroom the water chestnuts which he had brought him as a present. It seems to me that the general opinion is this: they teach them everything (just like gentlefolks' children) and a lot of it is useless, but they teach them reading and writing as well in a short space of time—so you might as well send the children. Malicious rumours go the rounds as well, but by this time they do not carry very much weight. Two splendid boys recently left the school on the grounds that we were supposed not to teach writing. Another soldier wanted to send his son, but, upon examining our best pupil and finding that he could read the Psalter only hesitantly, he decided that the instruction was no good, it was only *talk* to say it was good. One or two of the Yasnaya Polyana peasants still have fears that the rumours which were going about before might turn out to be true; they reckon that we are teaching them for some ulterior purpose, and that as soon as their backs are turned we will have carts drive up and carry the pupils off to Moscow. The dissatisfaction because we do not beat the children and there is no subordination in the school has almost entirely vanished, and I have often had occasion to observe the bafflement of a parent who has driven up to the school to get his son when the running about and scuffling and wrestling started while he was present. He is convinced that softness is harmful and believes that they are being taught well, and how the two go together he cannot understand. Gymnastics still gives rise to rumours sometimes, and the conviction that the stomach is 'all churned up' by it does not pass away. As soon as fasting is over, or in the autumn, when the vegetables are gathered in, gymnastics does the greatest harm, and grandmothers, as they put their cooking-pots on the stove, explain that it is all because of indulgence and bouncing about. For some parents (a small number, however) the spirit of equality in the school is a matter for discontent. In November there were two girls, daughters of a rich innkeeper, dressed in little coats and caps, who kept themselves to themselves at first, but who got used to things and forgot about tea and cleaning their teeth with snuff and had begun to study splendidly. When their father arrived, in a Crimean sheepskin which he wore unfastened, on entering the school he found himself among a crowd of dirty children in bast sandals who were leaning their arms on the girls' caps as they listened to the teacher; the father took offence and removed his daughters from the school, although he did not admit the reason for his dissatisfaction. Lastly, there are pupils who leave the school because their parents, having sent them to school in order to curry favour with someone, take the children away again when the need to curry favour has passed.

So—there are twelve subjects, three classes, forty pupils in all, four teachers, and from five to seven lessons in the course of a day. The teachers keep diaries of their work, which they show one another on Sundays, after which they make their teaching plans for the following week. These plans are not carried out each week, but are altered to suit the pupils' demands.

Mechanical reading. Reading forms part of the instruction in language. The object of such instruction is, in our opinion, to guide the pupils towards an understanding of the contents of books written in the literary language.[13] A knowledge of the literary language is essential, because only in that language do good books exist.

Previously, just after the school was founded, there was no subdivision of reading into mechanical and progressive—the pupils read only what they could understand: their own compositions, words and phrases written on the walls in chalk, then the folk-tales of Hudyakov and Afanasiev.[14] I supposed that for the children to learn to read it was necessary for them to acquire a love of reading, and for them to acquire a love of reading it was necessary that what they read should be understandable and interesting. It seemed so rational and clear, but this idea was wrong. In the first place, in order to go on from reading things on the walls to reading from books one had to work at mechanical reading separately with each pupil from any book. With a small number of pupils and no subdivision of subjects this was possible, and I managed without great difficulty to transfer the first pupils from reading on the wall to reading from a book, but it became impossible with the new pupils. The younger ones found it beyond them to read and understand folk-tales; the simultaneous labour of spelling out the words and understanding the sense was too great for them. Another disadvantage was the fact that progressive reading broke off at these folk-tales, and whatever book we then took, *The People's Reader, The Soldier's Reader,* Pushkin, Gogol, Karamzin[15]—it turned out that the elder pupils when reading Pushkin, like the younger ones when reading folk-tales, could not combine the job of reading with that of understanding what they read, although they understood a fair amount when we read.

At first we thought that the difficulty was only a lack of mechanical skill in reading on the pupils' part, and we hit upon mechanical reading, reading for the sake of the process of reading. The teacher and pupils read alternately, but the work made no progress, and there was the same pointlessness in reading *Robinson Crusoe*. In the summer, when schools are in a transitional stage, we thought of beating the difficulty by the simplest and commonest means. Why not admit it? We gave in to false shame in front of our visitors. (Our pupils were reading much worse than pupils who had studied for the same amount of time with the sexton.) A new teacher proposed to introduce reading round the class, and we agreed. Once having accepted the false idea that the pupils ought certainly to be reading fluently that very year, we wrote on the timetable: mechanical and progressive reading, and made them read for two hours a day out of the same books, and we found it very convenient. But one departure from the rule of freedom for the pupils led to falsehood and one mistake after another. Books were bought (Pushkin's and Yershov's fairy-tales[16]); the boys were made to sit on forms, and one was to read aloud while the others followed his reading; in order to check whether they were really following the teacher was to ask first one then another by turns. For a while this seemed to us a very good idea. When you came into the school they were sitting sedately on their forms, one would be reading and the others following. The reader might pronounce it 'Have mercý my lady fish', the others, or the teacher, would correct it to 'mércy'—everyone was following. 'Ivanov read!' Ivanov searches for a little and reads. Everyone is busy, the teacher can be heard, every word is uttered correctly and they are reading fairly fluently. It seems to be a good idea, but scrutinize closely; the one who is reading has read the same thing before thirty or forty times. (A printer's sheet[17] will not last more than a week; it would be terribly expensive to buy new books all the time, and there *are* only two books which peasant children can understand: the folk-tales of Hudyakov and Afanasiev. Moreover, a book which has been read aloud by one class and is remembered word for word by several of the pupils, is well known by then not only to all the school children, but all the people at home are tired of it too.) The reader grows timid when he hears his lonely voice resounding in the silence of the room, all his powers are concentrated on observing the symbols and stress-accents, and he acquires the habit of reading without trying to understand the sense, because he is burdened with other requirements. The ones who are listening do the same, and, always hoping to hit on the right place if they are asked, run their fingers along the lines at an even pace, get bored and are distracted by irrelevant amusements. The meaning of what has been read, being a secondary matter, is sometimes grasped and sometimes not without their being aware of it. But the chief harm consists in that eternal school battle of wits and laying of traps between the pupils and the teacher which develops in such an order of things, and which we never had in our school before; whereas the sole advantage of this approach to reading, which consists in the correct pronunciation of the words, was of no significance for our pupils. Our pupils had begun by reading from the walls phrases which they had written and pronounced themselves, and they all knew that one writes 'Kogo' but pronounces 'Kavo';[18] learning pauses and modulations of the voice from the punctuation marks I consider to be useless, because any five-year-old child observes punctuation correctly with his voice when he understands what he is saying. It is surely easier to teach him to understand what he is saying out of the book (which he must arrive at sooner or later) than to sing from the punctuation marks as if from a musical score. But how convenient that seems for the teacher!

The teacher is always unconsciously striving to choose the means of instruction which is most convenient for himself. The more convenient a method of instruction is for the teacher the less convenient for the pupils. The only right way of teaching is that which is satisfactory to the pupils.

These three laws of teaching were reflected most clearly in the matter of mechanical reading at the Yasnaya Polyana school.

Thanks to the liveliness of the school spirit, especially when the older pupils returned to it from the work in the fields, this type of reading dropped out of its own accord: they began to get up to mischief and to drop out of the lesson. But above all, reading and retelling the story, which was intended to verify the progress made with mechanical reading, proved that there had been no such progress, that they had not moved a step forward in reading for five weeks, and many had fallen behind. The best mathematician in class I, R., who can work out square roots in his head, had lost so much of his skill in reading in that time that we had to read with him working out syllable after syllable. We abandoned reading round the class and racked our brains, trying to invent a method of mechanical reading. The very simple thought that the time for good mechanical reading has not yet come and that there is no necessity for it at present, that the pupils themselves will find the best method when the need arises, has only recently occurred to us. During that period of searching the following process developed of its own accord. During the reading lessons, which are by now only nominally divided into mechanical and progressive, the worst readers take a book in pairs (sometimes folk-tales, sometimes the gospels, sometimes a collection of songs or a number of 'Readings for the people'[19]) and the two of them read simply for the sake of the process of reading, and when the book is a folk-tale and easy to understand they read with understanding and demand that the teacher hear them, although the class may be called mechanical reading. Sometimes they (generally the worst ones) may take the same book several times running, open it at the same page, read the same tale and commit it to memory not only without being told to, but even in spite of the fact that the teachers told them not to; sometimes these bad readers come to the teacher or to a senior pupil and ask if they can read the book over together with him. Those who are somewhat better at reading, in class two, are less fond of reading in company, read less often for the sake of the process of reading, and, if they commit anything to memory, memorize verses and not a folk-tale in prose. The same thing happens with the seniors, with one special feature which impressed itself upon me in the past month. In their progressive reading class they are given one book of any kind, which they take turns to read and then all retell the story together. This autumn they were joined by an exceptionally talented mind, Ch., who had studied under the sexton for two years and had thereby outstripped all of them in reading; he reads as we do, and therefore in progressive reading the pupils do understand at least a little, but only when Ch. is reading, and yet each of them wants to read himself. But as soon as a bad reader begins to read they all express their dissatisfaction—especially when the story is interesting—they laugh and get angry, the bad reader grows ashamed, and endless arguments break out. Last month one of them announced that at all costs he would manage to read as Ch. does within a week; others also gave a promise, and suddenly mechanical reading became their favourite occupation. They began to sit for an hour to an hour and a half without tearing themselves away from a book which they did not understand; they started taking books home and in fact made such progress in three weeks as we would never have expected.

What happened to them was the exact opposite of what usually happens to people learning to read. It usually happens that a person learns to read and there is nothing for him to read and understand; but here it turned out that the pupils had convinced themselves that there are things worth reading and understanding, and that they lacked the skill to do it, and they began to gain fluency in reading themselves. Now we have dropped mechanical reading altogether, and the work goes on in the way described above—every pupil is given the chance to use all approaches that he finds convenient, and it is a remarkable fact that everyone uses all the approaches that I know of viz: 1) reading with the teacher; 2) reading for the sake of the process of reading; 3) reading and learning by heart; 4) communal reading and 5) reading with understanding of what is read.

The *first,* which is used by mothers throughout the world, not at all a scholastic but a domestic device, consists in the pupil's coming and asking the teacher to read with him for a bit; the teacher reads, guiding him over every syllable and word—the first, the most rational and irreplaceable method, which the pupil himself demands before anything else and which the teacher stumbles upon without meaning to. In spite of all the means which are supposed to mechanise instruction and allegedly lighten the task of the teacher with a large number of pupils, this method remains the best and only one for teaching people to read and read fluently. The *second* device for teaching reading, also a great favourite, which everyone who has learnt to read fluently has used, consists in the pupil's being given a book and being free to spell out syllables and understand just as he pleases. A pupil who has learnt to spell out enough for him not to feel the need to ask the grown-up to read with him, but has confidence in himself, always catches that passion for the process of reading which is mocked so much in Gogol's Petrushka[20], and goes further as a result of that passion. How reading of this kind ever sorts itself out in his head Heaven only knows, but in this way he grows used to the outlines of the letters, to the process of forming syllables, the pronunciation of words and even to working out the meaning, and I have satisfied myself by experience over and over again that insistence that the pupil should necessarily understand what he reads has held us back. There are many autodidacts who have taught themselves to read well by this method, although its defects must be obvious to anyone. The *third* method of teaching reading consists in learning by heart prayers, verses, anything on the printed page, in fact, and in pronouncing what has been learnt while following in the book. The *fourth* method consists in that very thing which proved so harmful in the Yasnaya Polyana school—in reading round the class. It arose of its own accord in our school. At first there were not enough books, and two pupils would be seated beside one book; then they themselves took a liking to this, and when someone says 'Reading!' friends who are perfectly equal in ability make off in twos, sometimes in threes, and sit down with the same book; one reads and the others follow him and make corrections. And you will upset everything if you separate them—they know themselves who is on a level with whom, and Taraska insists on having Dunka: 'Now, you come here and read, and you go to your own people.' However a few do not like this communal reading at all because they have no need of it. The advantage of communal reading of this kind lies in more exact pronunciation and in giving those who are not reading but following elbow-room for understanding; but all the advantage gained by such a method turns sour when this method, or any other, is extended to the whole school. Finally, the *fifth* method, which we still like, is progressive reading, that is reading of more and more complex books from the point of view of interest and understanding. As we have said above all these methods came into use in the school spontaneously, and the work made considerable progress in one month.

The teacher's job is simply to offer a choice of all known and unknown methods which may make the pupil's job of learning easier. True, with a certain method—reading round the class for example—instruction becomes easy and convenient for the teacher and has an air of orderliness and correctness; given our order of things, on the other hand, instruction not only appears to be difficult, but to many people will seem impossible. How, they will say, are we to guess just what each pupil needs and decide whether what each one demands is legitimate? How, they will say, are we to avoid getting lost in this heterogeneous crowd which is not subjected to a general rule? To this I shall reply: the difficulty appears to exist only because we are unable to renounce the old view of the school as a disciplined company of soldiers, which is commanded by one subaltern today and another tomorrow. A teacher who has got used to the school's freedom will see every pupil as a special character exhibiting special needs which only freedom of choice can satisfy. Were it not for the freedom and external disorder, which seems to certain people so strange and impossible, not only should we never have hit upon these five reading methods, but we should never have managed to use them and adapt them to the pupils' needs, and therefore would never have achieved those brilliant results which we have lately achieved in reading. How often we have had occasion to see the bafflement of visitors to our school who in the space of two hours wanted to study a method of instruction, which we have not got, and who in the course of the same two hours recounted *their* method to us; how many times have we heard such visitors advise us to introduce that very method which, though they failed to recognize it, was being used in the school before their very eyes, only not in the form of a despotic rule applied to everyone.

Progressive reading. Although, as we have said mechanical and progressive reading have really combined into one, nevertheless for us those two subjects are still subdivided as regards their aim; as it seems to us, the first aims at knowledge of the literary language. A way of acquainting them with the literary language naturally occurred to us which seems to be the simplest one, but is in fact the most difficult. We supposed that after the pupils had read sentences which they had themselves written on the board they should be given the folk-tales of Hudyakov and Afanasiev, then something a little harder, a little more complex in language, and so on, until they got to the language of Karamzin, Pushkin and the legal code; but this preconception, like the greater part of our preconceptions and of preconceptions in general, was not justified. We succeeded in transferring them from their own language written down on the blackboard to the language of the folk-tales, but there was no intermediate 'something or other' in literature which would transfer them from the language of the folk-tales on to a higher stage. We tried *Robinson Crusoe*—the work did not go well: some pupils were weeping with frustration because they could not understand and retell it; I began to tell them the story in my own words—they began to believe in the possibility of understanding this fount of wisdom, began to fumble towards the sense and read *Robinson Crusoe* through in a month, but with boredom and towards the end almost with disgust. The labour was too great for them. They would rely more on memory and, when they were retelling straight away what had been read in one evening they would recite some passages by heart; no-one had mastered all the content. Unfortunately they remembered only certain words which they did not understand and began to use them in and out of season, as semi-literate people do. I could see that something was wrong, but I did not know what to do about the trouble. In order to check up on myself and satisfy my conscience I began to give them (although I knew beforehand that they would not like them) various imitation folk-tales, such as those of 'uncle Nauma' and 'auntie Natalie',[21] and my presupposition was vindicated. After *Robinson* I tried some Pushkin, 'The Coffin-maker'[22] to be precise; but without help they could retell even less of it than they could of *Robinson,* and the 'Coffin-maker' seemed to them much more boring. The addresses to the reader, the author's flippant attitude to his characters, the mock characterizations, the elliptical mode of narration—all this was so unsuited to their needs that I renounced Pushkin once and for all, whose stories had formerly seemed to me, in my preconceptions, the most correctly constructed, the simplest and therefore the most comprehensible to the common people. Then I tried Gogol: 'Christmas Eve'.[23] When I read it it pleased them at first, especially the mature ones, but as soon as I left them alone they could understand nothing and grew bored. Even when I was reading they did not ask me to go on. The richness of the colour, the fantastic events and the capriciousness of the construction are quite foreign to their needs. I then tried Gniedich's *Iliad,*[24] and this reading only gave rise to a strange sort of bafflement; they supposed that it was written in French, and could understand nothing, until I retold the content to them in my own words, but even the plot of the poem did not sort itself out in their minds. Syomka the sceptic, of a severe logical nature, was struck by the picture of Phoebus, with his arrows sounding at his back, flying down from Olympus, but evidently did not know how he should take this image.

'But how did he fly down from the mountain and not get smashed?' he kept asking me.

'But you see, according them he's a god,' I replied.

'How can he be God! They've got a lot of 'em, haven't they? Can't be a proper god. Wouldn't be very easy to fly down from a mountain like that; therefore he must have been smashed,' he would keep on demonstrating to me, throwing his arms wide.

I have tried *Gribouille*[25] by Georges Sand and the *People's* and the *Soldier's* readers, all in vain. We try everything that we can find and everything that is sent to us, but by now we try almost without hope. You sit in school and break the seal on a pseudo-popular book which has come by post.

'Let me read it, let me!' shout several voices, and they stretch out their hands, 'so long as it's easier to understand!'

You open the book and read 'The life of the great and Venerable Alexis offers us an example of burning faith, piety, tireless activity and ardent love of our Fatherland, for which this holy man performed important services'; or 'The frequent occurrence in Russia of self-educated men of talent has long since been observed but not everyone explains it in an identical way'; or

'Three hundred years have passed since Czechoslovakia became dependent on the German Empire'; or 'The village of Karacharovo, extending along the shoulder of some hills, is situated in one of the most fertile grain-producing provinces of Russia'; or 'Broad it stretched and broad it lay, the road, the pathway'[26] or a popular exposition of a natural science on one printer's sheet, half filled by the author's endearments and manner of addressing a peasant. Give one of the lads a book like that and his eye begins to grow dull, he starts to yawn.

'No, I can't understand it, Lev Nikolayevich,' he says and returns the book.

Who writes these books for the people and for whom remains a mystery to us. Of all the books of that kind which we have read, with the exception of the 'story-telling granfer' Zolotov, who has had a great success in the school and at home, nothing has remained.

Some are simply bad works, written in a bad literary language and incapable of finding readers amongst the ordinary public and therefore dedicated to the common people; others are still worse works, written in a sort of un-Russian, newly invented, would-be popular language, something like the language of Krylov's fables;[27] a third kind are adaptations of foreign books which were directed at the common people but which are *not* popular. The only books, however, which are understood by the common people and to their taste, are books written not for the people but by the people, to wit: folk-tales, proverbs, collections of songs, legends, verses and riddles, recently Vodovozov's collection, and so on. Unless you have experienced it you could not believe the unfailing enthusiasm with which all books of this kind without exception are read—even the 'Tales of the Russian people', byliny[28] and song-books, Snegiryov's Proverbs, chronicles and all the monuments of ancient literature without exception. I have noticed that children are keener than adults to read books of this kind; they reread them several times, learn them by heart, take them off home with satisfaction, and in their games and conversations give one another nicknames out of the old byliny and songs. The adults, whether because they are less natural, or have already acquired a taste for showing off bookish language, or because they unconsciously feel a need to know the literary language, are less inclined towards books of this kind, but prefer those in which half of the words, images and thoughts are incomprehensible to them. But however much the pupils love books of this kind, the aim which we have, perhaps mistakenly, set ourselves, is not being achieved: between these books and the literary language the same gulf remains. So far we see no means of breaking this vicious circle, although we have made and are constantly making new attempts, new suppositions—we try to identify our mistake and ask all those who have this work at heart to inform us of their proposals, experiments and solutions of the question. The question which we have failed to resolve consists in this: for its education the people must have the opportunity and the desire to read good books; good books are written in a language which the people do not understand. In order to learn to understand it one must read a lot; in order to read willingly one must understand. . . . Where is the mistake here, and how do we get out of this situation?

Perhaps there is a transitional literature, which we do not recognize simply for want of knowledge; perhaps the study of books which circulate amongst the common people and of the common people's opinion of those books will reveal to us the paths by which people from the common folk may attain to understanding of the literary language.

We are devoting a special section of the magazine[29] to such a study and we request all those who understand the importance of this matter to send us their articles on this subject.

Perhaps this is a result of our being cut off from the people, and the coercive education of the upper class, and the only thing that will help is time, which will produce not an anthology but a whole transitional literature, consisting of all the books which are now appearing and which will automatically arrange themselves into a course of progressive reading. It may also be the case that the people do not understand and do not want to understand our literary language because there is nothing for them to understand, because all our literature is of no use to them, and they are working out their own literature for themselves. Finally, a last supposition, which seems to us the most probable of all, is that the apparent deficiency lies not in the heart of the matter, but in our preoccupation with the idea that the end of instruction in language is to raise the pupils to the stage of knowing the literary languages and especially in our haste to attain that end. It may very well be that the progressive reading we dream of will come to each pupil automatically in its own good time, as we constantly see in the case of people who read without understanding one after the other the psalms,[30] novels, legal papers and who by this means somehow attain a knowledge of the language of books. Going on this supposition, the only thing we do not understand is why all the books which appear are so bad and not to the people's taste and what schools are to do while they are waiting—for there is just one supposition which we cannot admit, namely, that having made up our minds that a knowledge of the literary language is useful, it should be possible to teach the people the literary language against their will by forcible explanation, mugging up and repetition, as French is taught. We must admit that we have tried this more than once in the past two months and have always met with an insuperable distaste on the part of the pupils which have proved the wrongness of the path we took. In these experiments I merely convinced myself that to explain the meanings of words and of speech is quite impossible, even for gifted teachers, not to speak of those explanations so beloved of ungifted teachers, that 'an assembly is a small Sanhedrin' and so on. In explaining any word, the word 'impression' for example, you either replace the word you explain by another word which is just as incomprehensible, or by a whole series of words, the connection between which is just as incomprehensible as the word itself.

Almost always it is not the word itself which is not understood, but the pupil just does not have the concept which the word expresses. The word is almost always ready when the concept is ready. Moreover the relation of word to thought and the formation of new concepts is such a complex, mysterious and tender process of the mind that any interference becomes a crude, clumsy force which retards the process of development. It is easy to talk of 'understanding', but do we not all realize how many disparate things can be simultaneously understood, when the same book is being read? The pupil who does not understand two or three words in the sentence may understand a fine shade of thought or its relation to what went before. You, the teacher, are insisting on one side of understanding, but the pupil has no need whatsoever of what you want to explain to him. Sometimes he has understood, but he does not know how to demonstrate to you that he has understood you, but at the same time he is himself dimly guessing his way towards and assimilating something different and, for him, extremely useful and important. You keep teasing him to explain, but of course he has to explain to you by means of words the impression that words have produced in him, and he is silent or else starts to talk nonsense, lies, deceives you, tries to discover what it is that you want, to adapt himself to your wishes, or he invents a non-existent difficulty and hammers away at it; the general impression which the book produced, however, the poetical sense which helped him to guess the meaning, is crushed, and has gone into hiding. We are reading Gogol's 'Vii', repeating each period in our own words. Everything went well until page three—there we have the following period:

'The whole of this learned community, the clerical school no less than the seminary (which two nourished a certain hereditary mutual dislike) was uncommonly short of money for its bodily sustenance, and at the same time unusually gluttonous, so that to calculate how many dumplings each one gobbled up at supper would have been a quite impossible job, and thus the benevolent contributions of the prosperous squires could not suffice.'

Teacher: 'Well, what have you read?' (Nearly all these pupils are highly developed children.)

The best pupil: 'In the clerical school the people were all gluttons, and poor, and gobbled up dumplings at supper.'

Teacher: 'What else?'

Pupil (a cheat, and with a good memory, saying whatever comes into his head): 'An impossible job, the benevolent contributed.'

Teacher (annoyed): 'You must think a bit. That's wrong. What was an impossible job?'

Silence.

Teacher: 'Read it through again.'

They read it though. One, with a good memory, added a few more words which he could remember: the seminary, bodily sustenance of the prosperous squires, he could not suffice. Nobody had understood anything. They began to talk utter nonsense. The teacher pressed them.

Teacher: 'But what was an impossible job?'

He wanted them to say it was impossible to calculate.

A pupil: 'The clerical school was an impossible job.'

Another pupil: 'It was very poor, it was impossible.'

They read it through once again. They searched for the word that the teacher wanted as if for a needle, and hit upon everything except the word 'calculate', and got into a state of hopeless gloom. I—being that very teacher—did not relent and managed to get them to take the whole period apart, but they understood it far worse than when the first pupil had repeated it. Besides, there was nothing for them to understand. A loosely connected, long-winded period, which gives nothing to the reader, the gist of which had been understood straight away: the poor and gluttonous people gobbled up dumplings—there was nothing else that the author had wanted to say. I was hammering away simply because of the form, which was bad, and in doing so I had spoilt the whole class for an entire afternoon, had destroyed and crushed heaven knows how many flowers of complex understanding which were in the course of opening. On another occasion I hammered in the same sinful and hideous way at the interpretation of the word 'weapon', and just as vainly. On the same day in the drawing class a pupil, Ch., protested against the teacher's demand that they should write in their books the words 'A drawing by Romashka'. He said we had done the drawing ourselves in our books, but Romashka had only invented the pattern, and therefore we ought to write not a drawing, but a composition by Romashka. How the distinction between these concepts came into his head, just like the question, how do participles and even parentheses occasionally turn up in their compositions—remains to me a mystery into which we had better not pry.

We must give the pupil opportunities to acquire new concepts and words from the general sense of what is said. He will hear or read an incomprehensible word in an incomprehensible sentence once, then again in another sentence, and a new concept will begin dimly to present itself to him, and at length he will, by chance, feel the necessity of using that word, he will use it once, and word and concept become his property. And there are thousands of other paths. But deliberately to present a pupil with new concepts and forms of language is, according to my conviction, as unnecessary and pointless as to teach a child to walk by means of the laws of equilibrium.

Any such attempt carries a pupil not nearer to the appointed goal, but further away from it, as if a man should wish to help a flower to open out with his crude hand, should begin to unfold the petals, and crush everything round about.

Writing, grammar and calligraphy. Writing was conducted in the following manner: the pupils learned simultaneously to recognize and to trace letters, to spell out words by syllables and to write them; to understand what they had read and to write. They would take their places around the wall, marking out sections in chalk, and one of them would dictate whatever came into his head; the others would write. If there were a lot of them they would divide into several groups. Then others would dictate by turns, and they would all read over one another's work. They wrote in printed letter-forms and corrected first mistakes in syllables and divisions of words, then mistakes of 'o' for 'a', and then 'a' for 'e', then confusion between the two kinds of Russian "e",[31] and so on. This class educated itself. Any pupil who has learnt how to write letters is seized with a passion for writing, and at first the doors and outer walls of the school and the cottages where the pupils live are always scrawled over with letters and words. Writing a whole sentence (like 'Today Marfutka had a fight with Olgushka') gives him even greater pleasure. In order to organize this class the teacher had only to teach the children how to carry on the work together, just as an adult may teach the youngsters some children's game. And in fact this class was carried on without changes for two years, and each time with as much joy and liveliness as if it had been a good game. Here we have reading and pronunciation and writing and grammar. In writing like this the most difficult job in the early stages of language study is tackled—belief in the immutability of the form of the word, not just of the printed, but of the spoken word, *his own* word. I think any teacher who gives instruction in language and does not just do so from Vostokov's grammar has come across the first difficulty. You want to direct the pupil's attention to some word or other, let us say it is 'me'. You seize upon his sentence: 'Mikishka shoved me off the porch' he has said.

'Who did he shove off?' you say, asking him to repeat the sentence and hoping to get the word 'me'.

'Us' he replies.

'No, how did you say it just now?' you ask.

'We fell off the porch because of Mikishka,' or 'When he shoved us Praskutka went flying, and I came down after her' he replies.

Here you are looking for your accusative case of the singular number and its ending. But he cannot understand how there can be anything different about the words he has said. If on the other hand you take a book or start to repeat his sentence he will be analysing with you not the living word, but something quite different. But when he is dictating his every word is caught as it flies by the other pupils and written down. 'What did you say?

What?' and now they won't let him alter a single letter. In doing this there are perpetual arguments because one has written one thing and another something else, and very soon the one who is dictating starts pondering how he is to say it, and begins to understand that there are two things in speech: form and content. He starts a sentence thinking only about the content—this sentence flies out of him quickly, like a single word. They start to cross-examine him: what? how did you say it?, and as he repeats himself several times he begins to clarify the form and the parts of speech and underlines them in the spoken word.

This is how they write in class 3, i.e., the lowest—some know how to write in cursive hand, some in print. Not only do we not insist on their writing in cursive, but, if we allowed ourselves to forbid the pupils anything we would not allow them to write in cursive, which spoils their hand and is indistinct. Cursive letters come into their writing of their own accord: one of them learns two or three letters from a senior, the others imitate them and often write words like this: UnclE, and within a week they are all writing in cursive. With calligraphy exactly the same thing happened this summer as with mechanical reading. The pupils were writing very badly, and a new teacher introduced writing according to model copies (another highly sedate and peaceful exercise for the teacher). The pupils began to grow bored, we were obliged to abandon calligraphy and could devise no means of correcting the handwriting. The senior class found a means itself. When they had finished writing sacred history the older pupils began to ask if they could take their exercise books home. The exercise books were blotched, torn and grotesquely written. The meticulous mathematician R. asked for paper and began to copy out his history. This took everyone's fancy. 'I want some paper too', 'I want an exercise book too' and a fashion for calligraphy arose which is still continuing in the senior class. They take an exercise book, put the model alphabet in front of them, copy out each letter and boast to one another, and in two weeks they have made great progress. Almost all of us were forced when little always to eat bread with a meal, and for some reason we did not want to then, but now we want to take bread when we eat. Almost all of us were forced to hold a pen with the fingers extended, and we all held the pen with our fingers bunched up, but now we extend our fingers. The question arises: why did they torment us like that, since the thing came of its own accord when it was required? Will not this desire and demand for knowledge come in just the same way in everything?

In class 2 they write compositions on slates, from an oral story drawn from sacred history, and then copy them on to paper. In the junior class 3 they write whatever comes into their head. Besides this in the evenings they write one at a time sentences which they have all composed together. One writes and the others whisper to one another, noticing his mistakes, and are just waiting for him to finish so that they can catch him writing the letter 'yat' instead of 'ye'[32] or leaving a preposition in the wrong place, and sometimes they make a blunder themselves. Writing correctly and correcting other people's mistakes gives them great pleasure. The seniors seize upon every letter that turns up, practise correcting mistakes, try with all their might to write well, but they cannot bear grammar and the analysis of language and in spite of our former liking for analysis they permit it only in very small doses or else they drop asleep or begin to cut classes.

We have made various attempts to teach grammar and we must admit that none has achieved the object of making such teaching interesting. In the first and second classes a new teacher began explaining parts of speech in the summer, and the children—only some of them and at the beginning—took the same sort of interest in it as they do in charades and riddles. Often, at the end of the lesson, they would hit upon the idea of riddles and amuse themselves with asking one another either 'Where is the predicate?' or 'What sits on a spoon with its legs hanging over?' But there are no applications of this to correct writing whatsoever, and if there were then there would be more false ones than correct. It is just the same thing as happens with the letter 'o' written instead of 'a'. You say that one pronounces 'a' but writes 'o', and he goes and writes robota (instead of the correct rabota[33]) and molina (instead of malina[34]): you say that two predicates are separated by a comma, and he writes: 'I want, to say,' and so on. It is impossible to demand that he should always consider in every proposition which is a noun clause and which is a predicate. If he does consider this, then in the process of searching he will lose all the instinctive feeling he will find essential if he is to write the rest correctly, not to mention that in syntactical analysis the teacher is constantly obliged to cheat and deceive the pupils, which they sense very clearly. For instance, we came across the sentence: 'There were no mountains on the earth'. One said that the subject was 'earth', another that the subject was 'mountains', and we said that it was an impersonal proposition, and we could see quite well that it was merely a sense of decency that made the pupils keep silent, but they have realized perfectly well that our answer was much sillier than their answers, with which view we privately agreed. Having convinced ourselves of the unsuitability of syntactical analysis we also tried parsing—parts of speech, declensions and conjugations, and we posed similar riddles to one another about the dative and the adverb, and as a result we got the same boredom, the same abuse of the influence which we had acquired, and the same inability to apply the knowledge. In the senior class they always put 'yat' in the dative and propositional case[35], but when they correct the same mistake in the juniors' work they are never able to say why, and have to be brought back to the riddles about cases in order to remember correctly that it is 'yat' in the dative. The very youngest ones, who have yet to hear of parts of speech, very often shout out ' "to himself"—must be "yat" ', without knowing why themselves and obviously enjoying having guessed right. Recently I tried out in class 2 an exercise of my own invention, which I had become enthusiastic about, as all inventors do, and which seemed to me extraordinarily convenient and rational until such time as I convinced myself in practice of its ineffectiveness. Without naming the parts of speech in a sentence I would make them write something, sometimes setting them a theme, i.e., the subject, and would make them expand the proposition by adding qualifiers, new predicates, subjects, circumstances and objects. 'The wolves are running.' When? where? how? what sort of wolves are running? who else is running? they are running and what else are they doing? It seemed to me that as they got used to the answers to the questions which required this or that form they would grasp the difference between the parts of a sentence and parts of speech. And they did grasp them, but they were bored and in private asked themselves why? which I should have asked myself and to which I could find no answer. There is no way of getting man or child to give over his living speech to mechanical disemberment and mutilation without a struggle. There is a sort of sense of self-preservation in this living speech. If it has to develop then it strives to develop independently and only in accordance with all the conditions of life. As soon as you want to catch that speech, to screw it to a joiner's bench, hew it into shape and add to it those adornments which in your opinion it needs then you find that that speech with its living thought and content has shrivelled and hidden away, and all that remains in your hands is a husk, upon which you may perform your tricks, neither harming nor enhancing the speech which you set out to form.

Syntactical and grammatical analysis and the exercise in expanding propositions continue in class 2 still, but they proceed desultorily and I dare say they will soon drop out of their own accord. In addition we also use the following as language exercises, although they are not in the least grammatical.

1. We make them construct sentences from set words; for instance, we write 'Nikolai, wood, study,' and one of them will write 'If Nikolai hadn't been cutting wood he would have come to study', and another 'Nikolai is good at cutting wood; we ought to study the way he does it' and so on.
2. We compose verses in a given metre, an exercise which catches the interest of the senior pupils more than all the others. The verses turn out to be something like the following:

   By the window an old man
   Sits; his coat's in rags.
   In the street a countryman
   Is shelling coloured eggs.

3. An exercise which is very popular with the lower class: any word is chosen—at first a noun, then an adjective, an adverb, or proposition. One goes out and each of the remaining ones has to make up a sentence containing the set word. The one who went out has to guess it.

All these exercises—writing sentences with set words, verse composition and word-guessing—have one common aim: to convince the pupil that a word is a word, having its own immutable laws, modifications, endings and relations between those endings—a conviction which for a long time does not occur to him and which is necessary as a prelude to grammar. All these exercises are liked; all grammar exercises produce boredom. What is strangest and most noteworthy is that grammar is boring in spite of the fact that there is nothing easier. As soon as you start to teach it according to the book, starting from definitions, within half an hour a six-year-old child is beginning to decline and conjugate and recognize genders, numbers, tenses, subjects and predicates, and you feel that he knows all this quite as exactly and well as you do yourself. (In our district there is no neuter gender: 'ruzhyo' [gun]; 'syeno' [hay]; 'maslo' [butter]; 'okno' [window][36] are all used with feminine adjectives and pronouns, and here grammar does not help at all. The senior pupils have known all the rules of declension and the gender endings for more than two years now and yet they still write sentences where 'syeno' [hay] appears with a feminine adjective—and they only get out of the habit in so far as you correct them and in so far as they are helped by reading.) What is it I am teaching them, you ask yourself, when they know all this as well as I do? If I ask them what is the feminine genitive plural of 'bol 'shoi'? or what the subject is and what the predicate? or what word 'raspakhnulsva' is derived from [37] the pupil finds nothing difficult but the nomenclature, and he can always use an adjective correctly in any case and number you like. Surely he knows declension. He never makes an utterance without a subject and he does not confuse the subject with the rest. As for 'raspakhnulsya', he feels that it is related to the word 'pakh', and is more aware of the laws for formation of words than you are, because no one invents new words so often as children.

Why then this nomenclature and demand for philosophical definitions which are beyond his capacities? The only explanation of why grammar is needed, apart from its being required in examinations, is that it has an application in the correct expression of thoughts. In my personal experience I have not found this application to exist, I do not find it in the case of people who know no grammar and write correctly, or of people holding the degree of candidate of philosophy who write incorrectly, and I can hardly find a hint that the Yasnaya Polyana school children have put their grammatical knowledge to any use at all. It seems to me that grammar goes its own way, as an intellectual gymnastic exercise not devoid of use, and language—the ability to write, read and understand—goes its own way. Geometry and mathematics in general also appear at first to be merely mental gymnastics, but the difference lies in the fact that every geometrical proposition, every mathematical definition, entails endless further deductions and applications; in grammar, on the other hand, even if we see in it an application to language, there is a very narrow limit to these deductions and applications. As soon as the pupil has by one means or another mastered language all applications of grammar break off and fall away as something dead and outgrown.

We personally are still unable to abandon entirely the tradition that grammar, in the sense of the laws of language, is essential for the correct expression of thoughts; it even seems to us that there is a demand for grammar in the pupils, that the laws of grammar are unconsciously present in them; but we are convinced that the grammar we know is not at all that which the pupils need, and there is some great historical misunderstanding in this custom of giving instruction in grammar. The child recognizes that one must write 'yat' in the word 'syebye' (to himself) not because it is in the dative case, however many times you may have told him that, and not only because he blindly imitates what he has several times seen written—he generalises these examples, only not in the form of the dative case, but in some other way. We have a pupil from another school who has a splendid knowledge of grammar but can never distinguish the third person from the infinitive in the reflexive and another pupil, Fyedka, who has no concept of the infinitive, but never makes a mistake, and who explains the matter to himself and others by means of adding the word 'budet' in its sense of 'enough'. 'I don't want to learn'. He is in doubt and says 'You don't want to learn? Well then that's enough to learn [budet uchit'sya]. Must be spelt with a 'yer'.[38] But if the piece is like this: 'Syomka learns badly' (Syomka durno uchitsya) he says 'he learns badly? So it's enough learns', and that does not work out, he considers, and he does not put 'yer'. We in the Yasnaya Polyana school, just as in the teaching of reading and writing, recognize in the teaching of language that all known methods have a use and employ them in the degree to which they are willingly accepted by the pupils and according to the extent of our knowledge; however, we do not accept any one of these devices exclusively and are constantly trying to seek out new devices.

We are as much in disagreement with Mr. Perevlessky's method, which did not stand up to two days of trial in the Yasnaya Polyana school, as we are with the extremely widespread view that the sole method of studying language is writing, although writing constitutes the chief means of studying language in the Yasnaya Polyana school. We are seeking and hope to find.

Writing essays. In the first and second class the choice of essays is left to the pupils themselves. A favourite essay subject in the first and second class is stories from the Old Testament, which they are writing two months after the teacher told them. The first class recently began to write about the New Testament, but it is far from being as successful as the Old; they have even made more spelling mistakes—they understood it less well. In the first class we have tried essays on set subjects. The first subjects, which occurred to us in the most natural manner, were descriptions of simple objects, such as corn, a cottage, a tree and so on; but, to our extreme surprise, these demands reduced the pupils almost to tears and, in spite of help from the teacher, who subdivided the description of corn into the description of its growth, its production and its use, they absolutely refused to write on subjects of this kind and, if they did write, made incomprehensible, quite dreadful mistakes in spelling, language and sense. We tried setting them a description of events, and they all rejoiced as though we had given them a present. The descriptions so much beloved in schools of what are called simple objects: a pig, a flower pot, a table, turned out to be incomparably harder than whole narratives drawn from memory. The very same mistake was repeated here as in all the other subjects of instruction: to the teacher what is simplest and most general seems easy, and to the pupil only what is complex and alive means easy. All the textbooks of natural sciences begin with general laws, textbooks of language with definitions, of history with divisions into periods, even geometry begins with a definition of the concept of space and of the mathematical point. Nearly all teachers, guided by the same line of reasoning, set as the first essay the definition of a table or a bench and do not want to be convinced that in order to define a table or a bench you have to be at a high level of philosophical and dialectical development, and that the same pupil who sheds tears over the essay on a bench will describe beautifully the feeling of love or hatred, or Joseph's meeting with his brothers, or a fight with his mate. Essay subjects which they chose themselves were descriptions of events, relationships with people and reporting stories which they have heard.

Writing essays is their favourite occupation. Whenever paper and pencil fall into the hands of the older pupils outside school they do not start writing 'Hon. Honoured Sir'[39] but write off the cuff a tale of their own composition. At first I was put off by the inconsequence and lack of proportion in the construction of the essays; I would suggest what I thought was necessary, but they misunderstood me and things went badly; they still did not seem to recognize that anything else was required except not making mistakes. But now the time has come of its own accord, and expressions of dissatisfaction are often to be heard when a composition is long-winded or there are frequent repetitions or jumps from one subject to another. It is hard to define what they require, but those requirements are legitimate.

'It's a muddle!' shout some of them, listening to a classmate's composition; some of them do not want to read their own when the composition read by a classmate has been good; some of them grab the exercise-book from the teacher's hands, discontented, because it is not coming out as they wanted, and read it themselves. Individual characters are beginning to express themselves so sharply that we have tried the experiment of making them guess whose composition we were reading, and in the first class they guess without any mistake.

For lack of space we are postponing a description of the teaching of language and other subjects, and extracts from the pupils' diaries, till another number; however, we append here sample essays by pupils in class one, without changing the spelling and punctuation which they themselves provided. We hope, however, to include their essays from sacred history in the following volume.[40]

Essays by B. (a very bad pupil, but an original and smart boy) on Tula and on studying. The essay on studying enjoyed the greater success amongst the children. B. is eleven years old, it is the third winter of his studies in the Yasnaya Polyana school, but he has studied before. 'On Tula. Last Sunday I went to Tula again. When we got there, then Vladimir Alexandrovich says to me and Vas'ka Zhdanov go to Sunday School. We set off, walked and walked, at last we found it, we arrive and see all the teachers are sitting down. And there I saw a teacher the one that taught us botany. Then I says hallo gentlemen! they say hallo! Then I went up into the class and stood by the table I got bored so I upped and walked round Tula. I walked and walked and I see a woman selling buns. I started to get money out of my pocket, when I took it out and began to buy buns, I bought them and went. And then I saw a man walking about on a tower and looking to see if there isn't a fire somewhere. I've finished about Tula.'

'Essay on how I studied. When I was eight they sent me to Grumy to the cow-woman, I studied well there. And then I got fed up, I began to cry. And the woman would take a stick and ow she would beat me. And I would shout all the more. And after a few days I rode home and told them everything. And they took me away from there and sent me to Dunya's mother. I studied well there and they never beat me there, and I learnt all the alphabet there. Then they sent me to Foka Demidovich. He beat me and it hurt a lot. One day I run away from him and he tould them to catch me. When they caught me and took me to him. He took me, laid me out on a bench and took in his hands a bunch of burches and began to beat me. And I shout for all I'm worth and he floged me and made me read. And he listens and says: oh? you son of a bitch oi how badly he reads! oi what a swine.'

Here are two samples of Fyedka's essays: one on a set subject, on how corn grows; another chosen by himself, on a trip to Tula. (It is Fyedka's third winter of study. He is ten.)

'On corn. Corn grows out of the ground. In the beginning it is green corn. And when it grows up, then the ears grow out of it and the women reap them. There is corn like grass too, the cattle eat it very well.'

With that it was all over. He felt that it was no good, and was chagrined. But on Tula he wrote the following, without corrections.

'On Tula. When I was still little, I, was five year old; and I heard people were going to somewhere called Tula and I didn't know what Tula was like. So I asked dad. Dad! take me with you, I'll have a look at Tula. Dad says well then, come Sunday I'll take you. I was glad began to run about the shop and jump. After these days came Sunday. As soon as I got up in the morning dad was harnessing the horses in the yard, I started putting my boots and clothes on quickly. Soon as I was dressed and come out into the yard dad had already harnessed the horses. I sat in the sleigh and set off. We drove and drove, we went fourteen versts. I caught sight of a tall church and shouted out: daddy! look at that tall church. Daddy says: there's a lower church that's more beautiful, I started to ask him daddy let's go there, I'll say some prayers. Daddy went. When we got there suddenly they struck the bell, I was scared and asked daddy what that was, or were they playing on the chimes. Daddy says: no that's mass starting. Then we went into the church to pray. When we had prayed, then we went to the market. So I walk and walk and I stumble, I'm looking around me all the time. So we came to the bazaar, I saw they were selling buns and wanted to take some without money. But daddy said to me, don't take any or they'll take your cap off. I say what will they take it off for but daddy says, don't take any without money, I say well give me a grivna, I'll buy myself a bun. Dad gave it to me, I bought three buns and ate them and I say: daddy, what nice buns. When we had bought everything we went to the horses and watered them and gave them some hay, when they had eaten, we harnessed the horses and drove home, I went up into the cottage and undressed and began to tell everyone how I had been to Tula, and how daddy and I had been in a church, and prayed. Then I went to sleep and I dream of daddy dryving to Tula again. As soon as I woke up, and see that everyone is asleep, I took and fell asleep.'

II Sacred history, Russian history, geography

Sacred History. From the very foundation of the school and even at present work in the subjects of sacred and Russian history goes like this: the children gather round the teacher, and the teacher, basing himself on the bible alone, and for Russian history upon Pogodin's *The Norman Period*[41] and Vodovozov's compilation, tells a story and then asks questions, and everyone begins to talk all of a sudden. When there are too many voices at once the teacher stops them, getting one of them to speak; as soon as one falters he calls upon the others once more. When the teacher notices that some have understood nothing he makes one of the best ones repeat it for those who did not understand. This was not invented, but came about of its own accord and is repeated with uniform success with five pupils or with thirty, provided that the teacher follows everybody, does not permit shouting out of words that have already been said, does not let the shouting rise to the pitch of fury, and regulates this flood of cheerful animation and rivalry as much as he finds necessary.

In the summer, when there were frequent visits and changes of teachers, this routine was changed, and the teaching of history got on far worse. The new teacher could not understand the general shouting; he thought those who were telling the story in the shouting would not be able to tell it alone; he thought they were shouting just for the sake of shouting; but above all it was hot and he felt cramped in the crowd of pupils who were climbing on to his back and creeping right up to his mouth. (In order to understand as well as possible children need to be near to the person who is speaking, to see every change in the expression of his face and his every movement. I have frequently noticed that they always remember best of all those places where the story-teller managed to make the right gesture or the right intonation.)

The new teacher introduced sitting on benches and answering individually. The child who was called upon would fall silent and was tormented by shame, and the teacher, with a *good-natured* air of submission to his fate or a gentle smile would say 'well, . . . and then? good, very good', and so on, a teacher's approach which we all know so well.

Quite apart from the fact that I have been convinced by experience that there is nothing more harmful to the child's development than this kind of individual questioning and the resulting magisterial attitude of teacher to pupil, for me there is nothing more revolting than such a spectacle. A large human being torments a small one without the least right to do so. The teacher knows that the pupil is in torment, blushing and sweating as he stands before him; he himself is bored and depressed, but he has a rule according to which the pupil must be trained to speak alone.

But why he is to be trained to speak alone, nobody knows. Could it be so that you can have him read a little fable when His or Her Excellency calls? Perhaps I shall be told that without it we shall not be able to assess the level of his knowledge. And I shall reply that it is indeed impossible for a third party to assess what a pupil knows in the space of an hour, but that the teacher, without having the child answer and without examination, can always sense the measure of his knowledge. It seems to me that this device of individual questioning is a remnant of an old superstition. In the old days the teacher who had made them learn everything by heart had no other means of assessing his pupils' knowledge than by ordering them to repeat it all word for word. Then it was discovered that repeating words by heart is not knowledge, and they began to make pupils repeat things in their own words; but the practice of calling upon pupils one by one and demanding that they reply when the teacher chooses was not changed. They quite lost sight of the fact that one can demand from someone who knows them by heart a repetition at any time and in any circumstances of certain words from the psalms or a fable, but in order to be capable of grasping the content of a speech and conveying it in his own way the pupil has to be in a certain appropriate mood.

Not only in elementary and secondary schools, but even in universities I fail to see the point of examinations based on questions[42] unless the material is learned by heart word for word or proposition by proposition. In my time (I went down from the university in '45) I used to mug things up before examinations not word for word but proposition by proposition and I would get a 5[43] only from those professors whose notes I had learnt by heart.

Visitors, who have done so much harm to the teaching in the Yasnaya Polyana school, have done me a great deal of good in one respect. They finally convinced me that repeating of lessons and examinations are a remnant of the superstition of the medieval school, one which (in the present order of things) is quite impossible and can only do harm. Often, carried away by a childish conceit, in the space of one hour, I wanted to show a visitor whom I respected what my pupils knew, and either it turned out that the visitor was persuaded that the pupils knew something they did not know (I had surprised him with some trick or other), or else the visitor supposed that they did not know something which they knew very well. And what a tangle of misunderstandings formed in this time between me and the visitor, who was an intelligent, gifted man and a specialist in the matter, and that with completely free intercourse between us. So what must go on when you have official visits by inspectors and so on, not to speak of the disturbance of the learning process and the confusion of concepts which such examinations produce in the pupils.

By now I have come to the following conviction: to make a résumé of all that a pupil knows for the benefit of the teacher or of a third party is impossible, just as it is impossible to make a résumé of what you or I know on any subject. If you were to subject an educated forty-year-old person to an examination in geography it would be just as stupid and bizarre as when you subject a ten-year-old person to the same examination. Neither would have any choice but to base his answers on rote learning, and their real knowledge could not be discovered in the course of an hour. In order to discover what either of them knows you would have to live with them for months.

Where examinations are introduced (I mean by examinations any demand that questions be answered) a new and useless subject demanding special toil and special capacities makes its appearance, and that subject is called *preparation for examina-*

tions or tests. A pupil in a gymnasium studies history, mathematics and above all *the art of giving answers in examinations.* I do not consider that art to be a useful subject of instruction. I, the teacher, estimate the level of knowledge of my pupils as truly as I can estimate the level of my own knowledge, although I have not made either the pupil or myself recite lessons aloud, and if an outsider wants to assess this level of knowledge let him live with us for a while, and study our result and the application to life of our knowledge. There is no other way, and all attempts at examining are so much deception, lying and hindrance to teaching. In teaching work the only judge who can stand on his own feet is the teacher, and only the pupils themselves can check up on him.

In history teaching the pupils answered all at once not in order to verify their knowledge, but because they feel an urge to reinforce the knowledge they have received by means of the spoken word. In the summer neither the new teacher nor I realised this; we regarded it merely as a check on their knowledge and therefore thought it more convenient to check up on them individually. I had not yet reflected upon the reason why the lesson was boring and wrong, but my faith in the pupils' right to freedom saved me. The majority were beginning to be bored, two or three of the boldest were constantly answering by themselves, two or three of the most timid ones were constantly silent, cried and got noughts. During the summer I neglected the sacred history classes, and the teacher, a lover of order, had complete freedom to arrange the children on benches, torment them one by one and wax indignant about the children's *pig-headedness.* Several times I advised him to let the children leave the benches in the history lesson, but the teacher received my advice as a pleasant and pardonable eccentricity (as, I know in advance, this advice will be received by the majority of my teacher-readers also) and until the old teacher turned up this arrangement was maintained, and in the teacher's diary there appeared observations like the following: 'I can't get a single word out of Savin; Grishin would not retell anything; Pet'kas obstinacy astonishes me: he did not say a single word; Savin is even worse than before' and so on.

Savin is a ruddy-faced, chubby son of a peasant proprietor or a merchant, with liquid eyes and long lashes, who wears a little tanned sheepskin, boots that fit his feet (and not his father's), an Alexander shirt and foot-cloths.[44] The amiable and lovely personality of this boy made a special impression on me through the fact that in the arithmetic class he was first in understanding and joyful animation. He is also not bad at reading and writing. But as soon as he is asked a question he hunches his handsome curly young head to one side, tears emerge on to the long lashes, he seems to want to hide away from everybody and is obviously suffering unbearably. If you make him learn something by heart he will recite it, but he cannot or dare not compose a speech by himself. Whether it is fear produced by his former teacher (he studied before with some person of clerical status) lack of self-confidence, vanity, awkwardness when placed amongst boys who are in his view beneath him, aristocratic feeling or irritation because in this one particular he is lagging behind others, or because he has already shown up badly once before in the teacher's eyes, or whether it is that this young mind was insulted by some inept phrase which slipped off the teacher's tongue, or whether it is all these things at once, Heaven only knows, but this shyness, even if it is a bad quality in itself, is probably inextricably linked with all that is best in this childish mind. It is *possible* to beat all this out of him with a physical or moral rod, but there is a danger that one may at the same time beat out valuable qualities, without which the teacher would be hard put to it to lead him further.

The new teacher listened to my advice, released the pupils from the benches and let them clamber wherever they wanted to, even on to his back, and in that very lesson they all began to retell incomparably better, and it is recorded in the teacher's diary that even 'the pigheaded Savin said a few words'.

In a school there is an undefined something, almost beyond the teacher's control, something quite unknown to the science of pedagogy and yet constituting the essence and the successfulness of the teaching: it is the spirit of the school. This spirit is subject to certain laws and to the negative influence of the teacher, that is, the teacher should avoid certain things in order not to destroy that spirit. . . . The spirit of the school, for instance, always varies inversely with the coercion and orderliness of the school, inversely with the teacher's interference in the pupils' mode of thought, directly with the number of pupils, inversely with the duration of the lesson, and so on. This spirit of the school is something which is quickly communicated from one pupil to another, and which is even communicated to the teacher, something which is expressed, quite obviously, in the sounds of the voice, the eyes, the movements, the intensity of the competition—something very tangible, necessary and precious, and which ought therefore to be the goal of every teacher. Just as saliva in the mouth is essential for digestion, but unpleasant and superfluous without food, so this spririt of intense excitement, which is tedious and unpleasant outside the class, is an essential condition for the reception of intellectual food. It is impossible to invent this mood or to prepare it artificially, and it is unnecessary to do so, for it always appears of its own accord.

I made this sort of mistake in the beginning of the school. As soon as a boy began to understand things badly and unwillingly, and that so common scholastic state of *deadlock* was coming over him, I would say to him: 'Hop about for a bit! Hop about!'—The boy would begin to hop about, other children and he himself would start laughing, and after his hop about the pupil felt different. But after we had tried this hopping about several times it turned that when one said 'Hop about for a bit!' the pupil would be overcome by still greater dismay, and he would begin to cry. He could see that his mental state was not what it ought to have been or what was necessary, but he could not control his mind and did not want to allow anyone else to do so. It is only in a state of agitation that a child or a man is receptive, and it is therefore a gross error, which we all too often commit, to look upon the joyful spirit of the school as an enemy and a hindrance.

But when this animation is so great in a large class that it prevents the teacher from leading the class, so great that the teacher cannot be heard and they are not listening to him, what, it would seem, can he do then but shout at the children and suppress that spirit? If the excitement is about the lesson one could wish for nothing better. But if the excitement has been transferred to some other object it is the teacher's fault for failing to lead the excitement. The teacher's task, which nearly every teacher fulfils unconsciously, is to keep on feeding this excitement and gradually give it freer rein. You ask one child a question, another wants to recite—he knows it, straining towards you he stares at you hard and can hardly keep his words back, he follows the boy who is retelling eagerly and will not let him get away with a single mistake. If you ask him he will recite passionately, and what he is reciting will be engraved on his memory for ever, but if you hold him back, he will start to pass the time by pinching his neighbour.

Another example: go out of the classroom in a district school or a German school, when it has been quiet, ordering the children to go on with their work, and half an hour later listen at the door: the class is excited, but the object of the excitement is something else, the sort of thing people call mischief. We have often tried this experiment with our classes. Having gone out in the middle of the class, when they have already done a good deal of shouting, you go up to the door and hear the boys continuing to recite, correcting and confirming one another, and often, instead of beginning to get up to mischief, when you are not there they quieten down altogether.

Just as in the case where the children are arranged on benches and asked questions individually, so also with this order of things there are certain characteristic methods, not difficult ones, but which must be known and without which a first experiment may turn out unsuccessfully. You must see that there are no hollerers who repeat the last words that have been said simply for the joy of making a noise. This attractiveness of noise must not be their chief aim and occupation. You must check with certain pupils to see that they can recite everything by themselves and that they have grasped the meaning. If there are too many pupils, divide them into several sections and make them recite to one another by sections.

It is nothing to be afraid of if sometimes a new arrival does not open his mouth for a month. One should simply watch to see whether he is attending to the story or to something else. Usually a pupil who is a new arrival grasps at first only the material aspect of the thing and is entirely absorbed in observing how they are sitting or lying, how the teacher's lips move, how everyone suddenly shouts out, and he sits down meticulously in the way the others do, and when he feels bold starts to shout out just as the others do, without remembering anything, merely repeating his neighbours' words. The teacher and his companions stop him and he realizes that something else is required. Some time later he begins to retell a thing or two himself. It is difficult to say how and when the flower of understanding burgeoned in him.

Not long ago I succeeded in catching this burgeoning of understanding in a certain downtrodden little girl who had been silent for a month. Mr. U. was telling the story, and I was supernumerary, looking on and observing. When they all set about retelling the story I noticed Marfutka slipping down from the bench with the gesture that they use to change from the role of listener to that of teller, and drawing nearer. When they had all started shouting I looked round at her; her lips were moving in a scarcely noticeable manner, and her eyes were full of thought and animation. Meeting my gaze, she dropped her eyes. A minute later I looked round once more; she was whispering something to herself again. I asked her to do some retelling; she became quite tongue-tied. Two days later she retold the whole story beautifully.

In our school the best check upon what the pupils remember of such stories is the stories which they write down themselves out of their own heads and with correction of their spelling mistakes only.

An extract from ten-year-old Marfutka's book:

God commanded Abraham to take his son Isaac to be sacrificed. Abraham took two servants, Isaac carried the wood and the fire, and Abraham carried the knife. When they came to Mount Or there Abraham placed his two servants and went up on to the mountain himself with Isaac.

Isaac says, 'Daddy! we've got everything, where's the victim?'

Abraham says, 'God commanded me to take you.' So Abraham lit the fire and laid his son down.

Isaac says, 'Daddy, bind me or else I shall flare up and kill you.'

Abraham took him and bound him. He had just swung the knife up when an Angel flew down from heaven and stayed his hand and says:

'Abraham, do not raise your hand against your stripling son, God sees your faith.' Then the Angel says to him, 'Go to the thicket, a ram is caught there, sacrifice it instead of your son'—and Abraham sacrificed to God.

Then the time came for Abraham to give his son in marriage. They had a workman Eliezer. Abraham summoned the workman and said, 'Swear to me that you will not take a bride in our city, but go where I send you.'

Abraham sent him into the land of Mesopotamia to Nahor. Eliezer took the camels and went. When he came to the well he started to say, 'Lord, give me the bride who shall come first and give me to drink and give my camels to drink, let her be the bride of my master Isaac.'

Hardly had Eliezer said these words when a maiden came. Eliezer began to ask her for something to drink.

She gave him some to drink and says, 'I expect your camels are thirsty.'

Eliezer says, 'Please give them some drink.'

She gave the camels a drink too, then Eliezer gave her a necklace and says, 'Couldn't I spend the night at your house?'

She says, 'Yes.' When they got to the house her relations were having supper and started to ask Eliezer to sit down to supper.

Eliezer says, 'I will not eat until I have told you something.' Eliezer told them.

They said, 'We are willing, what about her?'

They asked her and she was willing. Then her father and mother blessed Rebecca, Eliezer mounted with her and they rode off, and Isaac was walking in the fields. Rebecca saw Isaac and covered herself with a cloth. Isaac went up to her and took her by the hand and led her into the house, and they were married.

From the boy I. F.'s book, on Jacob:

Rebecca was unfruitful for nineteen years, then she bore two twins—Esau and Jacob. Esau worked at hunting, and Jacob used to help his mother. Once Esau went out to catch animals and killed nothing and came home hungry; and Jacob was eating a mess of pottage.

Esau came and said, 'Give me some pottage.'

Jacob said, 'Give me your birthright.'

Esau said, 'Take it.'

'Swear!' Esau swore. Then Jacob gave Esau some pottage.

When Isaac had grown blind he said, 'Esau! Go and kill me some game.' Esau set off.

Rebecca heard this and said to Jacob 'Go and kill two kids.' Jacob went and killed two kids and brought them to his mother. She roasted them and covered Jacob with the skins and Jacob took the food to his father and said, 'I have brought you your favourite dish.'

Isaac said, 'Come nearer to me.' Jacob came up. Isaac began to feel his body and said, 'The voice of Jacob, but the body of Esau.' Then he blessed Jacob.

Jacob had just come out of the door when Esau comes to the door and says, 'Here you are, Dad, your favourite dish.'

Isaac says, 'Esau has been to me.'

'No, Dad, that was Jacob deceiving you,' and for his own part he went through the doors and burst into tears and said, 'When Dad's dead, I'll pay you back then.'

Rebecca said to Jacob, 'Go and ask your father's blessing and then go to Uncle Laban's.'

Isaac blessed Jacob and he set off for his Uncle Laban's.

Then night overtook Jacob. He set about spending the night in the fields; he found a stone, placed his head upon it and fell asleep. Suddenly he dreamed he saw a staircase going from earth to heaven, and Angels going up and down it, and at the top the Lord himself was standing and said, 'Jacob! the land on which you lie I give to you and to your descendants.'

Jacob got up and said, 'How frightening it is here, it must be the house of God here, when I return I shall build a church here.' Then he lit a lamp and walked on and he saw herdsmen watching over stock. Jacob began to ask them where his uncle Laban lived?

The herdsmen said, 'There's his daughter driving sheep to be watered.'

Jacob went up to her; she couldn't push the stone away from the well. Jacob pushed away the stone and watered the sheep and said, 'Whose daughter are you?'

She replied, 'Laban's.'

'I am your cousin.' They kissed each other and went home.

Uncle Laban received him and said, 'Jacob, live with me, I'll give you wages.'

Jacob said, 'I'll not live on wages, but give me your younger daughter Rachel.'

Laban said, 'Live with me for seven years, then I'll give you my daughter Rachel.'

Jacob stayed for seven years and Uncle Laban gave Jacob Leah instead of Rachel. So Jacob said, 'Uncle Laban, why did you deceive me?'

Laban said, 'Live with me for another seven years, then I will give you my younger daughter Rachel, otherwise we have no right to give away the younger daughter first.'

Jacob lived with his uncle for another seven years, then Laban gave him Rachel.

From the book of the eight-year-old boy T. F., on Joseph:

Jacob had twelve sons. He loved Joseph best and made him a coat of many colours. Then Joseph had two dreams and told them to his brothers: 'We were reaping the rye in the field and we reaped twelve sheaves. My sheaf stood up straight and eleven sheaves bowed down to my sheaf.'

And the brothers said, 'Shall we really bow down to you?'

And he had another dream. 'There were eleven stars in the sky and the sun and the moon bowing down to my star.'

And his father and mother said, 'Shall we really bow down to you?'

The brothers went away to look after the cattle, and then their father sent Joseph to take food to his brothers; the brothers caught sight of him and said, 'Here's our dreamer coming; let's put him in a bottomless well.'

Reuben thought to himself, 'As soon as they go away somewhere I will get him out.' And merchants came by. Reuben said, 'Let us all sell him to the Egyptian merchants.'

And they sold Joseph, and the merchants sold him to Potiphar the king's courtier. Potiphar loved him and his wife loved him too. Potiphar went away somewhere and his wife said to Joseph, 'Joseph, let us kill my husband and I will marry you.'

Joseph said, 'If you say that to me again I will tell your husband.

She took him by his clothing and screamed. The servants heard and came to them. Then Potiphar arrived. His wife told him that Joseph wanted to kill him and marry her. Potiphar ordered them to put him in prison. Since Joseph was a good man he served well there too, and he was ordered to look after the prison. One day Joseph was walking through the dungeon and he saw two men sitting sorrowing.

Joseph went up to them and asked, 'Why are you sorrowing?'

And they said, 'We have just dreamed two dreams on the same night and there is no one to interpret them for us.'

Joseph said, 'What is it?'

The butler began to tell: 'I broke off three berries and pressed the juice and gave it to the king.'

Joseph said, 'In three days' time you will be in your own place again.'

Then the baker began to tell. 'I was carrying twelve loaves in a basket and the birds flew around and pecked the bread.'

Joseph said, 'In three days time you will be hanged and the birds will fly around and peck your body.'

And so it turned out. Once king Pharaoh dreamed two dreams on the same night and gathered together all his wise men and no one could interpret them for him.

The butler remembered and said, 'I can think of a man.'

The king sent a carriage for him. When they fetched him the king began to tell. 'I was standing on the river bank and seven fat cows came out and seven thin ones, and the thin ones threw themselves upon the fat ones and ate them and they did not become fat.' And he had another dream. 'Seven full ears of corn grew upon one stalk, and seven empty ones; the empty ones threw themselves upon the full ones and ate them up and they did not become fat.'

Joseph said, 'This is what it is about: there will be seven fruitful years and seven hungry ones.'

The king gave Joseph a gold chain across his shoulder and a ring from his right hand and ordered them to build granaries.

Everything we have said applies to the teaching not only of sacred, but also of Russian history, to natural history, geography and in part to physics, chemistry, zoology and all subjects in fact with the exception of singing, mathematics and drawing. But concerning the teaching of sacred history in particular at that time I must say the following.

In the first place about why we chose the Old Testament to begin with. Quite apart from the fact that a knowledge of sacred history was demanded both by the pupils themselves and by their parents, of all oral reproductions which I have tried out in the course of three years, nothing has been so well suited to the concepts and cast of mind of the boys as the Bible. The same thing has been repeated in all the other schools which I have had occasion to observe. At first I tried the New Testament, I tried Russian history and geography, I tried those *explanations of natural phenomena* which are so beloved nowadays, but all this was forgotten and listened to with reluctance. The Old Testament was remembered at once and retold with passion and delight both in the classroom and at home, and impressed itself so upon their memories that two months after the telling children were writing sacred history in their exercise books out of their own heads with extremely insignificant omissions.

It seems to me that the book of the childhood of the human race will always be the best book for the children of any human being. I think it is impossible to replace this book. To alter and abbreviate the Bible, as is done in the sacred histories of Sonntag, etc., seems to me harmful. Everything, every word in it is truthful as revelation[45] and truthful as art. Read through the creation of the world in the biblical version and in that of a brief sacred history, and the editing of the Bible in the sacred history will appear quite incomprehensible to you; nothing can be done with the sacred history version but learn it by heart; in the Bible version a lively and majestic picture is presented to the child, which he will never forget. The omissions in a sacred history are quite incomprehensible and only destroy the character and beauty of holy scripture. Why, for instance, do all the sacred histories omit that, when nothing was, the spirit of God moved upon the face of the waters, that God, after having created, looks upon his creation and sees that it is good, and that then the morning and evening were such and such a day? Why do they omit to say that God breathed the immortal soul in at the nostrils, that, when he had removed Adam's rib he filled up the place with flesh, and so on? It is necessary to read the Bible to unspoilt children in order to understand how necessary and true all this is. How commonly we hear it said in joke that the Bible is an indecent book and that it should not be placed in the hands of young ladies. Perhaps we should not put the Bible into the hands of corrupted young ladies, but in reading it to peasant children I neither altered nor omitted a single word. And none of them tittered behind each other's backs, and they all listened with a tremor of the heart and natural veneration. The story of Lot and his daughters and the story of the son of Judah arouse horror and and not laughter.

How comprehensible and clear everything is, especially for a child, and at the same time how severe and serious!. . . . I cannot conceive what sort of education would be possible without this book. But it seems we got to know these tales in my childhood only to forget them partly later on—what use are they to us? And would it not have been just the same if we had never known them at all?

So it seems to us until, upon beginning to teach, we are following all the elements of our own development in other children. It seems as though it should be possible to teach children to read, write and count, and give them some notion of history, geography and the phenomena of nature without the Bible and before beginning the Bible, on the other hand, there is nowhere this is done—everywhere the first thing the child gets to know is the Bible, or stories and extracts from it. The first relationship between taught and teacher is based on this book. A phenomenon so universal does not come about by chance. My completely free relationship to the pupils at the beginning of the Yasnaya Polyana school, helped me to elucidate this phenomenon.

A child or a person entering a school (I make no distinction between a ten-year-old person and a thirty- or seventy-year-old) brings with him his own particular view of things, which he has derived from life and which he loves. In order that a person of any age should begin to learn it is necessary for him to come to love learning. In order that he should come to love learning it is necessary for him to recognize the falsity and inadequacy of his view of things and to sense beforehand the new view of the world which learning will open up to him. Not a single man or child would be capable of learning if he imagined his future studies as being merely the art of writing, reading or counting; not a single teacher would be able to teach if he did not have in his power a higher view of the world than that of the pupils. If a pupil is to yield himself up entirely to his teacher it is essential to lift up one edge of the veil which was concealing from him all the delight of that world of thought, of knowledge and of poetry to which learning ought to introduce him. Only when he is constantly under the spell of that light which is gleaming in front of him is the pupil able to work upon himself in the manner we demand of him.

But what means have we got of lifting that edge of the curtain for our pupils? . . . As I was saying, I thought, as many people think, that, since I myself inhabit that world into which I ought to lead the pupils it would be easy for me to do so, and I taught them reading and writing, I explained natural phenomena, I repeated, as in the ABC books, that the fruits of learning are sweet; but the pupils did not believe me and continued to be alienated. I tried reading the Bible to them and had them completely in my power. The edge of the curtain was lifted, and they yielded to me completely. They conceived a love for the book and learning and me. It only remained for me to guide them further. After the Old Testament I told them stories from the New Testament; they loved learning and me more and more. Then I recounted to them world history and Russian and natural history: after the Bible they listened to everything, believed in everything, asked to go further and further and further, and ever before them stretched the perspectives of thought and knowledge and poetry. Perhaps this was chance. Perhaps, with a different method at the beginning, in a different school, the same results have been attained. Perhaps, but this chance has been repeated too uniformly in all schools and all families, and the explanation of this phenomenon is too clear to me, for me to agree to accept it as chance. In order to open up a new world to the pupil and without knowledge to make him conceive a love for knowledge no book will do but the Bible. I speak even for those who do not look upon the Bible as revelation. No, I at least know of no work which unites in itself in such compressed poetic form all the aspects of human thought which are united in the Bible. All questions concerning natural phenomena are explained by this book, all primary relationships amongst people, families, states and religions are perceived for the first time through this book. Generalizations of thought, wisdom, in a form of childlike simplicity, for the first time captivate the pupil's intellect with their charm. The lyricism of the psalms of David is effective not only on the minds of adult pupils but, more than this, everyone recognizes in this book for the first time all the charm of the epic, in inimitable simplicity and power. Who has not wept at the story of Joseph and his meeting with his brothers, who has not told with a tremor of the heart the story of the bound and shorn Samson who perishes himself as he takes revenge upon his enemies under the ruins of a demolished palace, and hundreds of other impressions on which we are reared as on our mothers' milk? . . . Let those who deny the educational importance of the Bible, who say that the Bible is obsolete, let them devise such a book and such stories, explaining the phenomena of nature, or drawn from world history, or from their imagination, such as will be accepted in the way the biblical ones are, and then we will agree that the Bible is obsolete.

Pedagogics serves as a means of verifying many many phenomena of life, and social and abstract questions.

Materialism will be entitled to declare itself the victor only when the Bible of materialism has been written and children are educated from that Bible. Owen's attempt cannot serve as proof of such a possibility any more than the growing of a lemon tree in a Moscow hothouse is a proof that trees can grow without the open sky and the sun.

I reiterate my own conviction, drawn, perhaps, from one-sided experience. The development of child and man is unthinkable without the Bible in our society, just as it would have been unthinkable in Greek society without Homer. The Bible is the only book for beginners' and children's reading. The Bible, in form as in content, must serve as a model for all primers and reading books for children. A translation of the Bible into the language of the common people[46] would be the best book for the people. The appearance of such a translation in our day would constitute an epoch in the history of the Russian people.

Now about the approach to teaching sacred history. I consider all brief sacred histories in the Russian language to be a double crime: against a sacred object and against poetry. All these adaptations, which are meant to facilitate the teaching of sacred history, render it more difficult. The Bible is read for pleasure, at home, with one's head propped upon one's hand. Little stories are learnt by heart, following the words with a pointer. Not only are these little stories boring and hard to understand, but they ruin the ability to understand the Bible's poetry. I have frequently noticed how bad, incomprehensible language destroys the acceptance of the Bible's inner meaning. Words which are not understood, such as 'stripling', 'the deep', 'spurned', etc. force themselves on the memory quite as much as the events, bring the pupils' attention to a halt by their novelty and serve as landmarks, as it were, by which they guide themselves through the story.

Very often a pupil speaks simply in order to use a word which has caught his fancy, and the simplicity with which he imbibed the content alone is already lost. I have also frequently observed that pupils from other schools always felt the charm of Bible stories much less, and sometimes not at all, since it has been destroyed in them by the necessity of learning by heart and the crude teaching methods associated with this. These pupils have even spoilt their junior fellow-pupils, whose manner of recounting has picked up certain vulgar formulae from the brief sacred histories. By means of these harmful booklets such vulgar tales have found their way to the common people too, and often pupils bring with them from home peculiar legends about the creation of the world and of Adam and Joseph the fair. Even these pupils do not have the same experiences as fresh pupils, as they listen to the Bible and seize upon each word with bated breath and think that now, at last, all the wisdom of the world will be revealed to them.

I have taught and still teach sacred history only from the Bible and regard any other teaching as harmful.

The New Testament is told in exactly the same way according to the Gospels and is written in the exercise books afterwards. The New Testament is harder to remember and therefore requires more frequent repetitions.

From the book of I.M., a boy, on the Last Supper:

> Once Jesus Christ sent his disciples to the town of Jerusalem and said to them, 'Whatever man you happen to find with water, you go after him and say to him, "Master, show us an upper room where we can prepare the passover." He will show you, and you prepare it there.'

They went and saw what He had shown them, and prepared it. Towards evening Jesus Himself went there with his disciples. During the supper Christ took off his clothing and girded Himself with a towel. Then he took a basin and filled it full of water and began to go up to each disciple and wash their feet.

When he came up to Peter and wanted to wash his feet Peter said, 'Lord! You shall never wash my feet.'

And Jesus Christ said to him, 'If I do not wash your feet you shall not be with me in the Kingdom of Heaven.'

Then Peter was afraid and said, 'Lord, not just my feet, but my head and all my body.'

And Jesus said to him, 'Only the feet of a pure man need be washed.' Then Jesus Christ dressed and sat down at the table, took some bread, blessed it and broke it and began to give it to his disciples and said, 'Take and eat—this is My body.' They took it and ate.

Then Jesus took a cup of wine, blessed it and began to offer it to his disciples: 'Take and drink, this is my blood of the New Testament.' They took it and drank.

Then Jesus Christ said, 'One of you will betray me.'

And the disciples began to ask, 'Lord! Is it I?'

And Jesus Christ said, 'No.'

Then Judas said, 'Lord! Is it I?'

And Jesus Christ said in a low voice, 'It is you.'

After that Jesus Christ said to his disciples, 'That man will betray me to whom I give a piece of bread.'

Then Jesus Christ gave the bread to Judas. Straight away Satan entered into him, so that he was ashamed and went out of the room.

From the book of R.B., a boy:

Then Jesus Christ went with his disciples to the garden of Gethsemane to pray to God, and said to the disciples, 'You wait for me and don't sleep.'

When Jesus came and saw that his disciples were asleep, He woke them and said, 'You could not wait one hour for me.'

Then he went again to pray to God. He prayed to God and said, 'Lord! May not this cup pass from Me,' and prayed to God until he broke into a bloody sweat.

An Angel flew down from heaven and began to give Jesus strength. Then Jesus returned to the disciples and said 'Why do you sleep? The hour is coming when the Son of Man shall be betrayed into the hands of his enemies.'

And Judas had already said to the High Priest, 'Take the one that I kiss.'

Then the disciples went after Jesus and saw a crowd of people. Judas went up to Jesus and wanted to kiss him.

And Jesus said, 'Do you betray me with a kiss?' And he said to the crowd, 'Whom do you seek?'

They said to Him, 'Jesus of Nazareth.'

Jesus said, 'It is I myself.' After these words they all fell upon him.

History, Geography. Upon finishing the Old Testament I naturally hit upon the idea of teaching history and geography, both because this instruction is still carried on everywhere in schools for children and I had learnt it myself, and because the history of the Jews in the Old Testament led the children naturally, as it seemed to me, to questions about where, when and in what conditions the events they had heard about took place—what was Egypt, the pharaoh, the king of Assyria, etc.?

I started history, as it always is started, from ancient history. But neither Mommsen nor Duncker[47] nor all my efforts helped me to make it interesting. They cared nothing for Sesostris, the pyramids of Egypt and the Phoenicians. . . . I had hoped that such questions as, for example, who were the nations that had to do with the Jews, and where did the Jews live and travel to, ought to interest them, but the pupils had no use at all for such information. A hotch-potch of King Pharaohs and Egypt and Palestine do not give them the slightest satisfaction. The Jews were their heroes, the rest were incidental unnecessary characters. And I failed to make the Egyptians and Phoenicians into heroes in the children's eyes for want of materials. I daresay no one ever has succeeded or will succeed. Neither historical nor fictional materials are lacking. The history of the Egyptians is, I suppose, as thoroughly studied, if not more, as the history of the Jews, but the Egyptians did not leave us a Bible. Though we know in ever so much detail how the pyramids were built, and what were the position and mutual relations of the castes, of what use is that to us? i.e., to us children. In those histories there is no Abraham, Isaac, Jacob, Joseph or Samson. A bit here and there of ancient history was found memorable and pleasing—Semiramis and so on, but it was remembered by chance, not because it explained anything, but because of its artistic, fairy-tale quality. But such bits were rare, the rest was boring and pointless, and I was obliged to abandon instruction in world history.

The same failure occurred in geography as in history. I sometimes tell them whatever occurs to me, something of the geography of Greece, England or Switzerland, without any continuity, but merely as an edifying and artistic fairy-tale.

After world history I was bound to try out Russian history, which is accepted by everyone everywhere and is for us the history of the Fatherland, and I began that Russian history which is sadly familiar to us, which is neither artistic nor edifying, and which has appeared in so many different adaptations, from Ishimova's[48] to Vodovozov's. I began it twice over: the first time before reading all the Bible and the second time after the Bible. Before the Bible pupils absolutely refused to commit to memory the existence of the Igors and Olegs. The same thing is repeated again now with the junior pupils. Those who have not yet learnt from the Bible how to penetrate the material which has been related and reproduce it listen up to five times over and still remember nothing about the Ruriks and Yaroslavs. The senior pupils now remember and write down Russian history, but incomparably worse than they did the Bible, and they require frequent repetitions. We tell it to them on the basis of Vodovozov and Pogodin's *Norman Period*. One of the teachers somehow got carried away and, without listening to my advice, did not omit the period of the apanage princes and drove straight into the meaningless tangle of Mstislavs, Bryachislavs and Boleslavs. I entered the classroom at the time when pupils were supposed to be recounting. It is hard to describe what occurred as a result. Everyone was silent for a long time. At last those that the teacher called upon, the bolder ones and the ones with the best memories, began to speak. All their intellectual powers were concentrated upon remembering the 'funny' names, and who did what was for them a secondary matter.

'Now he, what d'you call him, Bariklav, isn't it?' began one, 'went to war with .— what's it called?'

'Muslav, Lev Nikolayevich,' suggested a girl.

'Mstislav,' I replied.

'And hit him over the head,' said another proudly.

'Wait a minute, there was a river.'

'And his son gathered together an army and thumped—what's his name?—on the head.'

'But what was it about that woman with the awful name?' said a girl with a good memory, blindly.

'And that funny woman or other' said Syomka. 'You know that woman, Mislav, Chislav, whatever it was, drat 'er.'

'Don't you butt in if you don't know it.'

'And of course *you* know, very clever!'

'And what are you squealing about?'

The ones with the best memories tried again and I daresay they would have got it right with a bit of prompting here or there. But all this was so horrible, and it was so pitiful to watch these children; they were all like hens who had formerly had corn thrown to them and who were suddenly thrown sand, they suddenly fell into confusion, rushed hither and thither, fussed about vainly and were ready to peck one another, so that the teacher and I resolved to make no more such mistakes. Leaving out the apanage period, we are continuing with Russian history, and this is what emerges from it in the exercise books of the senior pupils.

From the exercise book of the pupil V.R.:

> Our ancestors were called the Slavs. They had neither kings nor princes. They were divided into clans and used to attack one another and go to war. Once the Normans attacked the Slavs and defeated them and imposed a tribute.
>
> Then they said, 'This is no way to live! let us choose a prince for ourselves, to rule over us.'
>
> Then they chose Rurik and his two brothers—Sineus and Truvor. Rurik settled in Ladoga, Sineus in Izborsk in the land of the Krivichi and Truvor at Byeloozero. Then those brothers died. Rurik took their place.
>
> Then two men went to Greece, Askold and Dir, and they called at Kiev and said, 'Who is ruling here?'
>
> The men of Kiev said, 'There were three men here, Ki, Shchek and Khariv. Now they are dead.'
>
> Askold and Dir said, 'Let us rule you.' The people agreed and began to pay them tribute.
>
> Then Rurik ordered them to build cities and fortresses and sent out boyars to collect the tribute and bring it to him. Then Rurik thought of going to war with Constantinople with two hundred boats. When he rode up to this city at that time there was no emperor. The Greeks sent for him. The people were still praying to God. Then the bishop brought out the robe of the Mother of God and dipped it in the water, and a terrible

storm arose and Rurik's boats were all thrown about. And so there were even very few of them saved. Then Rurik went home and died there. He had one son left, Igor. When he was small then Oleg took his place. He wanted to conquer Kiev; he took Igor with him and went straight down the Dnieper. On the way he conquered the towns of Lyubich and Smolensk. When they came up to Kiev Oleg sent his ambassadors to Askold and Dir to say that merchants had come to see them, and he himself hid half of the army in the boats, and left half behind. When Askold and Dir came out with a small band of warriors Oleg's army jumped out from behind the boats and rushed at them.

Then Oleg lifted up Igor and said, 'You are not a prince and not of a princely line, but this is who the prince is.'

Then Oleg ordered them to be killed and conquered Kiev. Oleg stayed there to live, made that town the capital and called it the mother of all Russian cities. Then he ordered them to build cities and fortresses and sent out boyars to collect the tribute and bring it to him. Afterwards he used to go out to war against the neighbouring tribes—he conquered a lot of them. He did not like fighting meek people, he liked fighting against brave people. Then he prepared to go to war with Greece and went straight down the Dnieper. When he had gone down the Dnieper he went over the Black Sea. When he came up to Greece his army jumped out on to the shore and began to burn everything and rob.

Oleg said to the Greeks, 'Pay us a tribute; A grivnya for every ship.' They were glad and started to pay them the tribute. Then Oleg gathered three hundred poods[49] and set off for home.

From the exercise book of a pupil V.M.:

When Oleg died then Rurik's son Igor took his place. Igor wanted to marry. One day he went for a trip with his warband, he had to cross over the Dnieper. Suddenly he caught sight of a maiden sailing in a boat.

When she had sailed to the shore Igor said, 'Let me get in.'

She let him get in. Then Igor married her. Igor wanted to be distinguished. So he gathered together an army and went to war, straight down the Dnieper, neither to right nor to left. From the Dnieper into the Black Sea, from the Black Sea into the Caspian Sea. Igor sent ambassadors to the Kagan, asking him to let him go through his lands; when he came back from the war he would give him half of his plunder. The Kagan let

> him through. When they were already coming up near to the city Igor ordered his people to get out on to the shore so as to burn everything and chop down and take prisoners. When they had finished destroying everything they began to rest. When they had rested they went home with great joy. They came up to the Kagan's city. Igor sent the Kagan what he had promised. The people heard that Igor was coming back from the war and began to ask the Kagan to order them to be avenged on Igor because Igor had shed the blood of their relations. The Kagan did not order them to, but the people did not obey, and they began to fight—a mighty battle took place. The Russians were overcome and they took away from them everything that they had won.

There is no living interest, as the reader can see from the extracts which we have cited. Russian history goes better than world history only because they have grown used to assimilating and writing down what is related and again because the question 'What is this for?' has less place. The Russian nation is their hero, just as the Jewish one was. In the one case because it was the nation that God loved, and because its history was artistic. In the other case, although it has no artistic right to this, nevertheless national feeling speaks in its favour. But this instruction proceeds dryly, coldly and tediously. Unfortunately the history itself very rarely gives an occasion for national feeling to triumph.

Yesterday I came out of my own classroom into the history class in order to find out what was causing the excitement which I could hear from the other room. It was the battle of Kulikovo[50]. Everyone was excited. 'Now that's a story! Fine!—Listen, Lev Nikolayevich, how he put the wind up the Tartars! Let me tell it! No, me!' shouted the voices.

'How the blood ran like a river.' Almost everyone was able to recount and everyone was in ecstasies. But if we are to do nothing but give satisfaction to nationalist feeling what will be left of our history? The years 1612[51] and 1812 and that is all. You will not get through all of history by responding to nationalist feeling. I can understand that one can use historical tradition in order to develop and satisfy that artistic interest which is always characteristic of children, but that will not be history. A preliminary development of the historical interest in the children is essential for history teaching. How is this to be done?

I have often heard people say that history teaching should be begun not from the beginning but from the end, i.e., not from ancient history but from the most recent. Basically this idea is perfectly correct. How can you relate the beginning of the Russian state to a child and interest him in it when he doesn't know what the Russian state is or what any state is. Anyone who has dealt with children must know that every Russian child is firmly convinced that all the world is a Russia just like the one he lives in; exactly the same applies to a French and a German child. Why is it that all children and even those adults who are childishly naïve always show surprise that German children speak German? . . . The historical interest in the main makes its appearance after the artistic interest. It interests us to know the story of the foundation of Rome because we know what the Roman Empire was in its hey-day, just as we are interested in the childhood of a man whom we acknowledge to be great. The contrast between that greatness and a paltry crowd of refugees makes up the essence of our interest. We follow the development of Rome holding in our imaginations a picture of what is attained. We are interested in the foundation of the tsardom of Moscow because we know what the Russian Empire is. According to my observations and experiences the first germ of an interest in history appears as a result of getting to know contemporary history and sometimes of participating in it, as a result of an interest in politics, of political opinions, arguments and reading the newspapers, and the idea of beginning history from the present day must naturally occur to every thinking teacher.

I made some experiments back in the summer, made notes on them and quote one of them here.

A first lesson in history. I intended to explain in the first lesson how Russia differs from other lands, her frontiers, the characteristics of the state structure, to tell them who is now reigning and when the emperor came to the throne.

Teacher: 'Where do we live, in what land?'

One pupil: 'In Yasnaya Polyana.'

Another pupil: 'In the country.'

Teacher: 'No, what land are Yasnaya Polyana and Tula province in?'

Pupil: 'Tula province is seventeen versts away from us; where's the province?—that's the province.'

Teacher: 'No, that's the provincial capital, but the province is different. Now, what's the land[52] like?'

Pupil (who has previously had geography lessons): 'The world is round, like a ball.'

By means of questions about what country a German whom they knew formerly lived in, and where you would get to if you kept on travelling in the same direction, the pupils were led to answer that they lived in Russia. However some said, in answer to the question, where would you get to if you kept on driving in the same direction?—that you would not get anywhere. Others said that you would get to the end of the world.

Teacher (repeating a pupil's answer): 'You said that you would come to other countries; when would Russia end and the other countries begin?'

Pupil: 'When the Germans started coming.'[53]

Teacher: 'How do you mean, if you met Gustav Ivanovich and Karl Fyodorovich[54] in Tula would you say that the Germans had come and it must be another country?'

Pupil: 'No, when you come to nothing but Germans.'

Teacher: 'No, there are such areas in Russia too, where there are nothing but Germans. Ivan Fomich comes from there, but these lands are Russia just the same. Why is this so?'

(Silence.)

Teacher: 'Because they obey the same law as the Russians.'

Pupil: 'How do you mean, the same law? The Germans don't go to our church and they eat meat.'[55]

Teacher: 'They don't have the same law, but they obey the tsar.'

Pupil (Syomka the sceptic): 'That's funny! Why do they have a different law and obey the tsar?'

The teacher feels it is necessary to explain what law is and asks what it means to obey the same law, to be under the same law.

Pupil (an independent girl from a family of domestics, hastily and timidly): 'To take the law means *to get married.*'

The pupils look questioningly at the teacher—is that right?

The teacher begins to explain that the law is the fact that if somebody steals or murders he is put in prison and punished.

Syomka the sceptic: 'And haven't the Germans got that?'

Teacher: 'The law also consists in the fact that we have got gentry, peasants, merchants and clergy.'[56] (The word 'clergy' gives rise to bafflement.)

Syomka the sceptic: 'And don't they have there?'

Teacher: 'In some countries they do, in others they don't. We have the Russian tsar, and in the German lands there is another one—the German tsar.'

This reply satisfies all the pupils and even Syomka the sceptic.

The teacher, seeing that it is necessary to pass to the explanation of legal classes, asks what classes they know of. The pupils begin to count: gentry, peasants, priests, soldiers.

'Any more?' asks the teacher. Domestics, artisans, samovar-makers.[57] The teacher asks about the difference between these classes.

The pupils: 'The peasants plough, the domestics work for their masters, the merchants trade, the soldiers do service, the samovar-makers make samovars, the priests say masses, the gentry don't do anything.'

The teacher explains the real difference between the legal classes, but tries in vain to explain why soldiers are necessary when they are not fighting anybody, just for the purpose of securing the state against attacks, and the work that the gentry do in state service. The teacher tries to explain the difference between Russia and other states geographically; he says that all the earth is divided into different states. The Russians, the French and the Germans have divided all the earth into states and have said to each other: up to here is mine, up to there is yours, so that Russia, like other nations, has its boundaries.

Teacher: 'Do you know what boundaries are? Somebody give an example of a boundary.'

Pupil (a clever boy): 'Up there on Turkin hill there's a boundary.' (This boundary is a stone pillar which stands on the road between Tula and Yasnaya Polyana, marking the beginning of Tula district.)

All the pupils agree with the definition.

The teacher sees that it is necessary to point out boundaries in a location they know. He draws a plan of two rooms and points out the boundary which divides them, brings a map of the village and the pupils themselves recognize several boundaries. The teacher explains, i.e., it seems to him that he explains, that just as the territory of Yasnaya Polyana has its boundaries, so has Russia. He flatters himself that they have all understood him, but when he asks how we can tell how far it is from our locality to the frontier of Russia the pupils, without the slightest hesitation, reply that it is very easy, you have only to measure with a yardstick from here to the frontier.

Teacher: 'In what direction?'

Pupil: 'Push on straight from here to the frontier and write down how much it comes to.'

We pass once more to sketches, plans and maps. It becomes apparent that the concept of scale is needed, which they lack. The teacher proposes to draw a plan of the village, which is laid out in the form of a street. We begin to draw it on the blackboard, but not all the village can be got in, because we have taken too big a scale. We rub it out and start afresh to draw it on a small scale on a slate. *Scale, plan* and *boundaries* are clarified a little. The teacher repeats everything that has been said and asks what Russia is and where it comes to an end.

Pupil: 'It's the land that we live in and that the Germans and Tartars live in.'

Another pupil: 'It's the land that's under the Russian tsar.'

Teacher: 'Where does it come to an end?'

Girl: 'Where the heathen Germans begin.'

Teacher: 'The Germans are not heathens. The Germans believe in Christ too.' (Explanation of religions and denominations.)

Pupil (zealously, obviously rejoicing at how much he can remember): 'In Russia we have laws, people that do murders are sent to jail, and then there are all sorts of people: *clergies,* soldiers, and gentry.'

Syomka: 'Who feeds the soldiers?'

Teacher: 'The tsar. That's why they collect money from everybody, because they do service for everybody.'

The teacher explains what the exchequer is, and just succeeds in getting them to repeat what has been said about frontiers.

The lesson goes on for a couple of hours; the teacher is sure that the pupils have retained a lot of what was said, and continues succeeding lessons in the same manner, but only afterwards does he come to the concluson that these methods were wrong and that everything that he has been doing is utter nonsense.

I had fallen without meaning to into the invariable error of the Socratic method, which has reached its final stage of perversity in the German *Anschauungsunterricht.* [58] In these lessons I gave the pupils no new concepts, while imagining that I was doing so, and I merely obliged the children by my own moral influence to answer in the way that I wanted. 'Russia' and 'Russian' still remained the same unconscious signs for what is one's own, what is ours, a vacillating, undefined something. 'Law' remained the same incomprehensible word. I made these experiments about six months ago and was at first extremely pleased and proud of them. Those to whom I read them said that it was extremely good and interesting; but after three weeks during which I was unable to work in the school myself I tried to continue what I had begun and came to the conclusion that all that had gone before was trivial and a self-deception. Not a single pupil could tell me what a frontier was, what Russia and Russian meant, what a law was and what were the boundaries of Krapivensk county; they had forgotten everything which they had learnt by heart, and yet they knew all this in their own way. I became convinced that I had made a mistake; the only thing on which I was undecided was whether the mistake consisted in a wrong method of instruction or in the idea itself; perhaps before a certain period of general development and without the aid of newspapers and travel there is no possibility of awakening an interest in history and geography in a child; perhaps we shall find (I am constantly trying and seeking) the device by means of which we shall be able to do this. I know only one thing, that this device will certainly not consist in what people call history and geography, i.e., in study from books, which kills these interests instead of arousing them.

I have made yet other experiments in the teaching of history beginning with the present day, and remarkably successful experiments. I have recounted the history of the Crimean campaign,[59] the reign of the Emperor Nicholas and the history of the year 1812. All this was in an almost fairy-tale tone, which was for the most part historically untrue and grouping the events around one person. As one might expect it was the tale of the war with Napoleon which was the greatest success.

This lesson has remained a memorable hour in our life. I will never forget it. A promise had been made to the children long ago that I would relate things to them from the end and another teacher from the beginning, so that we should meet. My evening pupils had wandered off; I came into the Russian history lesson—the story of Svyatoslav was being told. They were bored. On a high bench, as usual, three peasant girls were sitting side by side, swathed in kerchiefs. One had fallen asleep.

Mishka nudged me: 'Look at our cuckoos sitting there; one

of them has fallen asleep.' And they really were like cuckoos.

'Why don't you tell us from the end!' said someone, and they all joined in.

I sat down and began to tell the story. As always for a couple of minutes there was scuffling and groans and shoving: some came under the table, some on to the table, some under the benches, some on to the shoulders and knees of others, and all fell silent. I hope to place this story in the 'booklets' section, and therefore I shall not repeat it here. I began with Alexander I, told them about the French Revolution, the successes of Napoleon, about his seizure of power and the war which ended with the Peace of Tilsit. As soon as the affair got to us sounds and words of lively sympathy were heard from all sides.

'Is he going to beat us too?'

'I reckon Alexander will show him!' said somebody who knew about Alexander, but I had to disappoint them—the time had not yet come; and they were hurt by the fact that it was proposed to give him the tsar's sister in marriage and that Alexander talked to him as to an equal on the bridge.

'Just you wait!' burst out Petka with a threatening gesture. 'Well, go on, tell us! Go on!'

When Alexander did not give in to him, i.e. declared war, everyone expressed encouragement. When Napoleon and all the nations of the earth marched against us and he raised revolt amongst the Germans and in Poland everyone was frozen with excitement.

A German, a friend of mine, was standing in the room.

'Ah, and you're on to us too,' said Petka (the best story-teller) to him.

'Shut up now,' shouted others.

The retreat of our troops tormented the listeners, so that from all sides they were asking for explanations why, and cursing Kutuzov and Barclay.[60]

'Your Kutuzov's rotten.'

'You wait,' said another.

'But what did he give in for?' asked a third.

When the battle of Borodino came, and when at the end of it I was obliged to say that still we did not win, I felt sorry for them: you could see that I was dealing them all a deadly blow.

'If we didn't get it at least they didn't.'

When Napoleon arrived in Moscow and waited for the keys

and bows of submission they all thundered out their feeling of defiance. The fire of Moscow was of course approved. At last began the triumph—the retreat.

'As soon as he quitted Moscow Kutuzov pursued him and began to strike,' I said.

'Clouted him!' Fyedka, who was sitting opposite me, corrected me, red all over, and twisting his slender black fingers with excitement. It is a habit of his.

Hardly had he said this than the whole room started roaring with proud delight. One of the little ones was smothered at the back, and nobody noticed.

'That's better! There are your keys for you!' and so on.

Then I continued about how we drove the French on. The pupils were pained to hear that someone was too late at the Berezina, and we let him get away.

Petka even grunted: 'I would have shot him, the son of a bitch, for being late!'

Then we felt a little sorry even for the frozen Frenchmen. Then, when we had crossed the frontier and the Germans, who had been against us, came over to our side, somebody remembered the German who was standing in the room.

'Hey, you, so that's how it is! First you come at us, and then, when you're not strong enough, you start being with us?' and suddenly they all got up and started to exclaim at the German, so that you could hear the din in the street. When they calmed down I continued about how we escorted Napoleon to Paris, placed the real king on the throne, triumphed and feasted. Only remembrance of the Crimean War marred the whole affair for us.

'Just wait,' exclaimed Petka shaking his fists, 'just let me grow up and I'll give it to 'em!' If we had been on the Shevardinsky Redoubt or Malakhov hill[61] just then we would have repulsed them.

It was late by the time I finished. Usually the children are asleep by that time. No one was asleep; even the cuckoos' eyes were glowing. As soon as I stood up Taraska, to our great astonishment, crept out from under my chair and looked at me excitedly and yet seriously.

'How did you creep in there?'

'He was there from the very beginning,' someone said.

There was no need to ask whether he had understood; you could see it in his face.

'Well, will you retell it?' I asked.

'Me?' He thought for a bit. 'I shall retell all of it.'

'I shall tell it at home.'

'And so shall I.'

'And me.'

'Won't there be any more?'

'No.'

And they all flew down the stairs, some promising to show the French, some reproaching the German and some repeating how Kutuzov had clouted him.

'Sie haben ganz russisch erzählt' ('You told it in a very Russian way') said the German who had been exclaimed at to me in the evening. 'You should hear how completely differently we tell the story. You didn't say anything about the German struggles for freedom.' ('Sie haben nichts gesagt von den deutschen Freiheitskämpfen.')

I entirely agreed with him that my narrative was not history but a tale which aroused national feeling.

I dare say, *as history teaching* this attempt was even more unsuccessful than the first ones.

In teaching geography I did the same thing. First of all I began with physical geography. I remember the first lesson. I began it and stumbled straightaway. Something which I had completely failed to expect turned up, viz. that I did not know that which I wished ten-year-old peasant children to get to know. I was able to explain day and night, but stumbled in the explanation of summer and winter. Ashamed of my ignorance, I went over it again and then asked a lot of people I knew, educated people, and no one, apart from those who had recently left school or who were teachers, could give me a proper account of it without a globe. I ask all my readers to check this observation. I maintain that *only one in a hundred people knows this, and yet all children learn it*. Having gone over it thoroughly I set about explaining afresh and with the help of candles and a globe explained it, as it seemed to me, splendidly. They listened to me with great attention and interest. (They found it particularly interesting to know something which their fathers did not believe in, and to be able to show off their wisdom when the chance came.)

At the end of my explanation of winter and summer Syomka the sceptic, the quickest of them all to understand, brought me to a halt with the question 'How is it that the earth moves but our cottage still stands in the same place? It ought to be shifted as well.' I saw that I was still 1,000 miles ahead of the cleverest one in my explanation—what then must the slowest ones have understood?

I went back, explained, drew, and brought in all the proofs that the earth is round: journeys round the world, the mast of a ship showing before the deck, and so on, and, comforting myself with the thought that *now* they understood, I made them write the lesson down. They all wrote 'The earth is like a ball: first prufe. . . ; second prufe . . .' and forgot the 'third prufe' and asked me. Evidently in their eyes the main job was to remember the *proofs*. Not once, not ten times but a hundred times I returned to these explanations and always without success. In an examination all the pupils would have answered and they now answer satisfactorily; but I feel that they do not understand, and remembering that I myself did not understand the thing properly until the age of thirty, I excused them their lack of understanding. Like myself in childhood they too believed on the verbal level that the earth is round and so on and understood nothing. I still found it easier to believe what my nurse impressed upon me in early childhood, that at the end of the world the earth and the sky meet, and there the women at the edge of the earth wash their clothes in the sea and lay their beating-sticks[62] down on the sky. Our pupils long ago firmly grasped and continue to possess ideas completely contrary to those which I want to convey to them. It is necessary to spend a long time yet destroying the explanations which they do have and that view of the world which nothing has yet disturbed before they will understand. The laws of physics and mechanics will be the first things that thoroughly eradicate the old conceptions. But they, like me, like everybody, began physical geography before physics.

In the teaching of geography, as in all other subjects, the most usual, grossest and most harmful mistake is haste. It is as though we were so overjoyed that we know that the earth is supposed to be round and move round the sun that we hasten to impart this as soon as possible to the pupil. Yet it is not valuable to know that the earth is round, but it is valuable to know how people arrived at this idea. Very often people tell children that the sun is so many billion versts away from the earth, and this is not at all surprising or interesting to the child. He is interested in knowing how they arrived at this. A person who wants to talk about this will do better to tell them about parallaxes. This is quite possible. I have dwelt upon the roundness of the earth because what has been said about it applies to all of geography. Only one in 1,000 educated people, apart from teachers and pupils, knows properly the reason for winter and summer, and knows where Guadeloupe is; out of 1,000 children not one can understand while still a child the explanations of the roundness of the earth and not one believes that Guadeloupe really exists, yet everybody is taught about both in childhood.

After physical geography I began the continents with their characteristics, and nothing of this has remained except the fact that if you ask them they will vie with one another in shouting out 'Asia, Africa, Australia!' but if you suddenly ask them what continent France is in (when you had told them a moment earlier that England and France are in Europe) somebody will shout that France is in Africa. The question *what for?* is to be seen in every dejected gaze and in every sound of their voices when you begin geography, and there is no answer to this sad question *what for?*

Just as in history the usual idea is to start from the end, so in geography the idea has cropped up and become usual of starting from the schoolroom, from one's own village. I saw these experiments in Germany and I myself, in despair at the failure of ordinary geography, embarked upon a description of the room, the house and the village. As plan-drawing these exercises are not without use, but it is not interesting to know what country lies beyond our village because they all know that Telyatinki is there. And knowing what lies beyond Telyatinki is not interesting because it is probably another village just like Telyatinki, and Telyatinki and its fields are not at all interesting. I tried giving them geographical landmarks such as Moscow and Kiev, but all this was stuffed into their heads with so little connection that they learned it by heart. I tried drawing maps and this engaged their interest and did in fact help their memories, but again the question presented itself, why help their memories? I tried telling them about the polar and equatorial countries; they listened with pleasure and retold the material, but remembered everything in these stories except what was geographical in them. The important point is that drawing plans of the village was drawing plans and not geography; drawing maps was drawing maps and not geography; stories about beasts and forests and lions and cities were wonderful tales and not geography. Geography was just learning things by heart. Of all the new books—Grube, Biernadsky—not one was interesting. One little book similar to a geography and forgotten by everybody read better than all of them, and is in my opinion the best model of what should be done to prepare children for the study of geography, to arouse geographical interests in them. This little book is Parley,[63] the Russian translation of 1837. The book *is* read, but it serves rather as a guiding thread for the teacher, who accordingly tells what he knows about each country and town. The children retell it, but they rarely retain any name or place on the map connected with the event which is being related—for the most part only the events remain. This lesson, however, belongs to a category of talks about which we shall speak in its turn. Just recently, however, in spite of all the skill with which the swotting up of unnecessary names is concealed, in spite of all the care with which we approached it, the children have tumbled to the fact that they are just being lured on with little stories, and have conceived a distinct aversion for this lesson.

I have at last come to the conclusion, as regards history, that not only is it unnecessary to know tedious Russian history, but Cyrus, Alexander of Macedon, Caesar and Luther are also unnecessary for the development of any child whatsoever. All these persons and events interest the pupil not in so far as they are important in history, but in so far as the pattern of their activities possesses artistic attractiveness and its treatment by the historian, and in particular not by the historian but by folk tradition, is artistic.

The story of Romulus and Remus is not interesting because these brothers founded the most powerful state in the world, but because the story of how they were suckled by the she-wolf, etc. is entertaining, wonderful, beautiful. The story of the Gracchi is interesting because it is artistic, and so is the story of Gregory VII and the humiliated emperor, and there is a possibility of arousing interest in it; but the history of the migration of the nations is tedious and lacking in point, because it is inartistic, just as the history of the invention of printing is, try as we may to impress upon the pupil that it is a turning-point in history and that Gutenberg was a great man. Make a good job of telling the story of how matches were invented and the pupil will never agree that the inventor of matches was not so great a man as Gutenberg. To put it briefly, for a child and for any person who is studying and who has not begun to live, the historical interest, i.e. not counting the general human one, does not exist. There is only the artistic interest. People say that with adaptation of the materials it will be possible to have an artistic presentation of all the periods of history—I cannot see this. We are just as much unable to place Macaulay and Thierry[64] in the pupils' hands as Tacitus and Xenophon. To make history popular what we need is not an artistic outward form but personification of historical phenomena, such as is done sometimes by tradition, sometimes by life itself and sometimes by great thinkers and artists. Children like history only when its content is artistic. For them there is not and cannot be any historical interest, consequently there is not and cannot be a history for children. History merely serves sometimes as a material for artistic development, but until the historical interest has developed there cannot be any history. When all is said and done Berte and Kaidanov remain the only texts. It is like the old story—'the history of Medes is obscure and fabulous'. Nothing more can be made out of history for children who do not understand the historical interest. On the other hand attempts to make history and geography artistic and interesting, Grube's biographical essays and Biernadsky, satisfy neither artistic nor historical requirements, they satisfy neither consistency nor the historical interest, and yet with their detail they drag on to an impossible length.

It is the same in geography too. When Mitrofanushka was being urged to study geography his mother said, 'Why teach him all the countries? The coachman will drive him wherever he needs to go.'[65] Nothing more cogent has ever been said against geography, and all the scholars in the world are unable to say anything in reply to this indestructible deduction. I am speaking perfectly seriously. Why did I have to know the position of the river and the city of Barcelona, when, in thirty-three years of life, I have never once needed this knowledge? And as regards the development of my own spiritual powers, as far as I can see the most picturesque description of Barcelona and its inhabitants would not have helped. Why should Syomka and Fyedka know about the Maryinsky Canal and its communications by water if, as we must assume, they will never happen to go there. And if Syomka does happen to go there then it will make no difference whether he learnt it or not, he will get to know those water communications in practice, and to know them well. Whereas how it is going to help the development of his spiritual powers to know that hemp goes down the Volga and tar up, that there is a pier at Dubovka and that a certain subterranean stratum goes as far as such a place, and the Samoyeds ride on reindeer and so on I cannot imagine. I have a whole world of knowledge in mathematics, natural science, language and poetry which I lack time to communicate, there are innumerable questions drawn from the phenomena of the life surrounding me to which the pupil is demanding an answer and to which I must reply before I draw him a picture of the polar ice, the tropical countries, the mountains of Australia and the rivers of America. In history and geography experience says the same thing and everywhere confirms our thoughts. Everywhere the teaching of geography and history goes badly; mountains, cities and rivers, tsars and kings are learnt by heart for examination purposes; Arseniev and Obodovsky, Kaidanov, Smaragdov and Berte remain the only possible textbooks, and everywhere people complain about the teaching of these subjects, look for something new and do not find it. It is funny that everyone recognizes that the requirements of geography are incompatible with the spirit of pupils the world over and therefore they invent thousands of ingenious methods (such as Sidov's method) in order to oblige children to memorize words; whereas the simplest idea, that we do not need this geography, we do not need to know these words, never by any chance occurs to anyone. All the attempts to combine geography with geology, zoology, botany, ethnography and I know not what else, and history with biographies, remain empty dreams which give birth to miserable little books like Grube, which suit neither children, nor youth, nor teachers nor the general public. Indeed, if the compilers of these supposedly new textbooks of geography and history were to ponder what they wanted and tried themselves to apply these books to teaching, they would be convinced of the impossibility of what they had undertaken. In the first place geography in combination with the natural sciences and ethnography would make up a vast branch of knowledge for which life-long study would be insufficient, and it would be a less childish and dryer subject than geography by itself. In the second place sufficient materials for the compilation of such a textbook could scarcely be found in a thousand years. When I am teaching geography in the Krapivensk district I shall be obliged to give the pupils detailed information about the flora, fauna and geological structure of the earth at the North Pole and details about the inhabitants and trade of the Kingdom of Bavaria, because I shall have materials for this information, and I shall hardly be able to say anything about the Belevsk and Yefremovsk districts because I shall have hardly any materials for this. But the children and common sense demand of me a certain harmoniousness and correctness in my teaching. It only remains either to teach them to learn Obodovsky's geography by heart or not to teach it at all. Just as for history the historical interest must be aroused, so for the study of geography the geographical interest must be aroused. But the geographical interest, according to my observations and experience, is aroused either by a knowledge of the natural sciences or by travel, predominantly, in ninety-nine cases out of a hundred, by travel. What reading the newspapers and above all biographies and a feeling for the political life of one's fatherland do for history, travel usually does for geography—it serves as the first step towards the study of the subject. Both have become extremely accessible and easy for everyone nowadays and we have therefore all the less to fear in renouncing the old superstition of teaching history and geography. Life itself has become so instructive nowadays in this respect that if a knowledge of history and geography really was as essential for our general development as we suppose, life would always fill the gap.

And indeed, if we do renounce the old superstition, it is not at all frightening to think that people will grow up without having learnt in childhood that there was a Yaroslav and an Otto and that there is a place called Estramadura and so on. Why, they have stopped teaching astrology, they have stopped teaching rhetoric and poetics, they will stop teaching Latin, and the human race is not growing stupid! New sciences are born, in our day the natural sciences are beginning to be popularized, the old sciences, which are not sciences but those facets of the sciences which become untenable with the birth of new sciences, must be discarded and left behind.

To arouse an interest in knowing how mankind lives, has lived, has been composed and has developed in various states, an interest in knowing the laws by which mankind is eternally moved, to arouse, again, an interest in understanding the laws of natural phenomena over all the globe and the distribution of the human race upon it—this is another matter. *Perhaps* it may also be useful to arouse such an interest, but neither the Segurs,[66] nor the Thierrys, nor the Obodovskys nor the Grubes will lead us to the attainment of this end. I know of only two elements which do that: the artistic feeling for poetry and patriotism. There are as yet no textbooks for the development of either of these; and until there are we need to seek, and not to waste time and effort and ruin the younger generation by making them learn history and geography simply because we were taught history and geography. *Not only do I see no need to teach history and geography before the university stage; I see great harm in it.* Beyond that I do not know.

III Drawing and singing.[67]

In my account of the Yasnaya Polyana school in November and December I now come to two subjects with a character completely distinct from all the others; these are drawing and singing—the arts.

But for the fact that in my view we do not know what we should teach this or that person and why, I should be obliged to ask myself whether it will be of use to peasant children, placed in a situation where they will have to spend their whole lives in concern about their daily bread, to learn the arts, and what they want with them? Ninety-nine out of a hundred would reply to that question and reply in the negative. And no other answer can be given. As soon as this sort of question is posed common sense demands this sort of answer: he is not going to be an artist, he will have to plough. If he has artistic urges he will not have the strength to sustain that stubborn, unrelenting work which he needs to sustain, which would render the existence of the state unthinkable if he did not sustain it. In saying 'he', I mean the child of the people. This is indeed an absurdity, but I rejoice in this absurdity, I do not come to a halt in front of it but try to find its causes. There is another, yet worse absurdity. This same son of the people—every son of the people—has just the same rights, what am I saying? even greater rights to the enjoyment of art than we children of a fortunate social class who are not forced to undertake that unrelenting work and who are surrounded by all the comforts of life.

To deprive him of the right to enjoy art, to deprive me, the teacher, of the right to lead him into that sphere of higher enjoyment towards which his whole being is striving with all the strength of his soul, is a still greater absurdity. How are we to reconcile these two absurdities? This is not lyricism, with which I was reproached à propos of the description of a walk in the first number—it is merely logic. Any reconciliation is impossible and is simply self-deception. People will say and do say: if drawing *is* needed in a school for the people then we can admit only drawing from nature, technical and with an application to life; the drawing of a plough, of a machine, of a building—drawing only as an auxiliary skill for technical drawing. And this common view of drawing is shared by the teacher at Yasnaya Polyana whose account we are presenting. But it is experience of this sort of teaching of drawing that has convinced us of the falsity and unfairness of this technical programme. The majority of pupils, after four months of careful, solely technical drawing, from which all sketching of people, animals and landscapes was excluded, had in the end lost interest to a large extent in the drawing of technical subjects and had so developed in themselves the feeling for and urge towards drawing as an art that they started their own secret sketch-books, in which they draw people and horses with all four legs coming out of the same place.

The same applies to music. The ordinary programme of schools for the common people does not admit of singing beyond choral church singing, and in just the same way either this is a most boring and tormenting from of rote learning for the children, learning to produce particular sounds (i.e., the children become and are regarded as so many throats which replace the pipes of an organ) or else their sense of the beautiful develops and finds satisfaction in the balalaika, the accordion and in frequently hideous song, which the educator does not recognize and in which he does not even think it necessary to guide the pupils. Either one thing or the other: either the arts are altogether harmful and unnecessary, an opinion which is by no means as strange as it seems at first glance, or else everyone, without distinction of classes and occupations, has a right to them and a right to devote himself completely to them on the ground that art will not tolerate mediocrity.

The absurdity is not in this, the absurdity is in the very posing of such a question as 'Do the children of the common people have a right to the arts?' To ask this is just the same as asking 'Do the children of the common people have a right to eat beef?' i.e., 'Do they have a right to satisfy their human demands?' The question is not whether the beef which we are offering or denying to the people is good beef. In just the same way, when offering the people certain knowledge which we have in our possession and observing the bad influence which it produces upon them I conclude, not that the common people are bad because they do not accept this knowledge, not that the people have not yet matured to the point where they will assimilate this knowledge as we do, but that the knowledge is bad and abnormal and we need, with the help of the common people, to work out new knowledge acceptable to us all, to educated society and to the people. I merely conclude that this knowledge and these arts live amongst us and seem harmless to us, but cannot live amongst the people and seem harmful to them only because this knowledge and these arts are not those which are generally needed. We live in the midst of them only because we are corrupted, only for the same reason that people sitting without harm in the poisoned air of a factory or a pot-house do not suffer from the very same air that would kill a fresh man who has just arrived in it.

People will say,'Who said that the knowledge and arts of our educated class are false?' 'Why do you draw conclusions as to their falsity from the fact that the people do not accept them?' All the questions are resolved very simply: *because there are thousands of us, but millions of them.*

I will continue the comparison with a well-known physiological fact. A man comes from the fresh air into a smoke-filled, foul, low-ceilinged room; all his vital functions are still fully exercised, by means of respiration his organism has been fed with a large quantity of oxygen which he has taken from the pure air. Following that same habit of his organism he begins to breathe in the poisonous room; noxious gases pass into his blood in large quantities, the organism grows weak (often a fainting fit occurs, sometimes death). Whereas hundreds of people continue to breathe and live in the same poisonous air simply because all their functions have become less extensive—in other words they live more feebly, live less.

What if people say to me, 'Both lots of people are alive, and who is to decide whose life is more normal and better?' Just as a man coming out of the foul atmosphere into pure air often faints, so also the other way round. For the physiologist and for the man of common sense in general the answer is easy; he will merely say, 'Where do most people live—in the fresh air or in foul prisons?' and he will follow the majority; and the physiologist will make quantitative observations concerning the functions of both and will say that the functions are stronger and nutrition is fuller in the person who lives in the fresh air.

The same relationship exists between the arts of so-called educated society and what the common people demand from art. I am speaking of painting, sculpture, music and poetry. A picture by Ivanov[68] will excite in the people only astonishment at technical mastery, but it will not excite any poetic or religious feeling, whereas this very poetical feeling is excited by the popular print of Ioann of Novgorod and the devil in the pitcher.[69] The Venus de Milo will excite only a proper disgust at nakedness, at the insolence of corruption, the shame of a woman. A Beethoven quartet of the last period will seem to them an unpleasant noise, perhaps interesting merely because one is playing on a big pipe and the other on a big fiddle. The best product of our poetry, a lyrical poem by Pushkin, will seem to them an assemblage of words and its sense as contemptible trifles. Introduce a son of the people to that world—you can do so and are constantly doing so through the hierarchy of educational institutions, academies and art classes—and he will appreciate, and appreciate sincerely, both the picture by Ivanov and the Venus de Milo and the lyric poem by Pushkin. But on entering that world he will no longer be breathing with full lungs, the fresh air will now strike him in a morbid and hostile manner when he happens to go out into it again. Just as in the matter of respiration common sense and physiology give the same reply, so in the matter of the arts the same common sense and pedagogy (not the pedagogy which draws up curricula but the one which tries to study the general directions of education and its laws) reply that it is not the one who lives in the artistic sphere of our educated class who lives better and more fully, and that the demands made upon art and the satisfaction which it gives are fuller and more legitimate amongst the common people than amongst us. Common sense will say this simply because it sees a happy majority, mighty not only in its numbers, living outside this environment; the educationist will make observations concerning the spiritual functions of people who are situated inside and outside this environment, and will make observations when people are led into the foul room, i.e. when our arts are introduced amongst the younger generations, and on the basis of the fainting fits, the revulsion which fresh natures evince when they are led into the artificial atmosphere, on the basis of the restriction of their spiritual functions he will conclude that what is demanded of art by the people is more legitimate than what is demanded by a spoilt minority from the so-called educated class.

I have made these observations concerning the two branches of our arts which I know the best and which I once loved passionately—music and poetry. And, dreadful to relate, I have arrived at the conviction that all that we have done in these two branches was done in a wrong and exclusive direction, without meaning, without future and trivial in comparison with the requirements and even the products of those same arts of which we find examples amongst the common people. I am convinced that a lyric poem like, for instance, 'I remember a wonderful moment'[70] and musical works like Beethoven's last symphony have not such an unqualified and universal beauty as the song of 'Van'ka the caretaker' and the melody of 'Down our Mother the Volga', that Pushkin and Beethoven please us not because they have an absolute beauty but because we are just as corrupt as Pushkin and Beethoven, because Pushkin and Beethoven alike flatter our distorted responses and our weakness. How often we hear that paradox, battered to the point of utter banality, that a certain training is necessary for an understanding of the beautiful—who said this? Why?, by what is it proved? It is only a device, a way of escape from an impasse which the misdirection and the attachment of our art to one class have led us into. Why is it that the beauty of the sun, the beauty of the human face, the beauty of an act of love and self-sacrifice are accessible to everyone and demand no training?

I know that for most people all that I have said will appear to be chatter, mere hot air, but pedagogy—free pedagogy—elucidates many questions by means of experience and by innumerable repetitions of the same phenomena takes questions from the sphere of dreams and speculations into that of propositions which are proved by facts. For years I have laboured in vain to impart to children the poetic beauties of Pushkin and all of our literature, a vast number of teachers are doing the same—and not only in Russia— and, if these teachers observe the results of their efforts, and if they have the desire to be frank, they all admit that the chief result of developing the poetic sentiment was the killing of it, that it was the most poetical natures who showed the greatest revulsion from these interpretations. . . . I have laboured, I say, for years and could achieve nothing; but we had only to open by chance Rybnikov's collection[71] and the poetical demands of the pupils found complete satisfaction, and a satisfaction which, after calmly and dispassionately comparing the first song I came across with Pushkin's best work, I could not but find to be justified.

The same thing happened to me in connection with music too, about which I have now to speak.

I will try to summarize all that I have said above. Faced with the question: do the people need the arts?—educationists are usually embarrassed and grow confused (only Plato decided this question boldly and in the negative). They say: they do need them, but with certain limitations; it is harmful to the social structure to give everyone the opportunity of being artists. They say certain arts and a certain level in them can only exist in a certain class of society; they say the arts must have their own exclusive servants, who are devoted to their work alone; they say that great talents must have the opportunity to emerge from the environment of the common people and devote themselves entirely to the service of art. This is the greatest concession which educational theory makes to the right of each person to be what he wants. It is to the attainment of these ends that all the efforts of educationists concerning the arts are directed. I regard all this as unjust. I assume that the urge to enjoy art and to serve art are to be found in every human personality, no matter what breed and environment it may belong to, and that this urge implies rights and must be satisfied. Assuming this proposition as an axiom, I say that if there appear inconveniences and inconsistencies in the enjoyment and production of art by everyone, then the cause of these inconveniences lies not in the method of imparting, not in the diffusion or concentration of art amongst the many or the few, but in the character and direction of art, of which we should be suspicious, both in order not to burden the younger generation with what is false, and in order to render it possible for that younger generation to work out something new in both form and content.

I present the drawing teacher's report for November and December. It seems to me that the method of this teaching may be considered suitable because of the devices whereby technical difficulties are circumvented in a way that the pupils either do not notice or find amusing. The question of art itself, however, is not touched upon, because when he began teaching the teacher had prejudged the question as to whether it is useless for peasant children to be artists.

Singing. Last summer we were coming back from bathing. We were all feeling very gay. A peasant boy, the same one as had been tempted by the domestic servant's son into stealing books, a thickset boy with wide cheek-bones, covered all over in freckles, with crooked legs turned inwards, having all the mannerisms of an adult peasant of the steppes, but an intelligent, strong and gifted nature, ran forward and took a seat in a cart which was driving in front of us. He took the reins, pushed his hat askew, spat to one side and burst out in some long-drawn-out peasant song—and how he sang!—feelingly, with intermittent pauses and sudden bursts of song. The lads burst out laughing. 'Look at Syomka, look at Syomka, doesn't he play it fine?' Syomka was completely serious. 'Here you, don't interrupt the song,' he said during an interval in a special, deliberately husky voice and gravely continued his singing. Two of the most musical boys took seats on the cart, began to seek harmonies and sang them. One was harmonising now in an eighth, now in a sixth, the other in a third, and it turned out excellently. Then other boys came up and began to sing, 'As under such an apple tree'; they started shouting and the result was noisy but no good. The singing began with that evening; now, after eight months, we sing, 'An angel cried out" and two cherubim pieces—numbers four and seven, all the usual mass and short choral songs. The best pupils (only two of them) write down the melodies of songs that they know and can almost read music. But so far everything they sing is a great deal less good than their song when they were coming back from bathing. I do not say this with some arrière pensée, not so as to prove something, but I am saying what is the case. However, I shall now tell how the teaching, with which I am comparatively pleased, has proceeded.

In the first lesson I divided everyone into three parts, and we sang the following chords:

We very soon succeeded in this. And each one sang what he wanted to, trying the descant and transferring to the tenor and from the tenor to the alto, so that the best ones got to know the whole chord—do-mi-sol, and some of them all three. They pronounced the French names of the notes. One sang: mi-fa-fa-mi, another one: do-do-ré-do, and so on. 'My, doesn't it fit, Lev Nikolayevich,' they would say. 'It even starts buzzing in your ears. Come on, some more, some more. . . .' We sang these chords in the school and in the courtyard, in the garden and on the way home, till late at night, and could not tear ourselves away or get over our joy at our success.

The next day we tried a scale, and the most talented ones went right through it; the worst ones could hardly get up to the third. I wrote the notes upon a stave in the treble clef, the most symmetrical one, and gave them their French names. The next ones and the next ones after that, for about six lessons, proceeded just as gaily; we sang some new chords, minor ones, and transitions to major ones, 'Lord Have mercy', 'Glory to the Father and to the Son' and a song for three voices with piano. One half of the lesson was occupied by this, the other by singing a scale and exercises which the pupils themselves invented: do-mi-ré-fa-mi-sol, or do-ré-ré-mi-mi-fa, or do-mi-ré-do-ré-fa-mi-ré and so on.

Very soon I noticed that the notes on the staves were not visually clear and found it necessary to replace them by figures. Besides figures offer more advantages in the explanation of intervals and the variation of keys. After six lessons some were already taking any intervals I asked for as requested, going up to them on an imagined scale. They found special pleasure in an exercise in fourths: do-fa-ré-sol and so on, downwards and upwards. Fa (of the subdominant) struck everybody particularly by its strength.

'A real lusty one, that fa,' said Syomka. 'It doesn't half whizz!'

The unmusical natures had all dropped out, but with the musical ones our lessons were stretching on to three and four hours. I tried to give them a notion of time according to the accepted method, but the task turned out to be so difficult that I was forced to separate time from melody and write down sounds without bars, analyse them and then write down time, i.e. measure without notes, analyse one bar by rapping and then combine the two processes.

After several lessons, when summing up what I was doing, I came to the conclusion that my teaching approach was almost the same as that of Chevet,[72] whose method I had seen in action in Paris, and which I did not accept at first simply because it was a method. To all concerned with the teaching of singing I cannot recommend too highly this work, which bears on the fly-leaf in large letters *'Repoussé à l'unanimité'*[73] and which now circulates in tens of thousands of copies all over Europe. In Paris I saw astonishing examples of the success of this method with Chevet himself teaching. A hall with five hundred to six hundred men and women, sometimes forty to fifty years old, singing in unison at sight anything the teacher puts before them. In Chevet's method there are many rules, exercises and devices laid down which are of no importance and which any intelligent teacher can make up by the hundreds and thousands on the field of battle, i.e., during the lesson; there is a very comical, and perhaps a useful way of reading the time without notes—for instance, for 4/4 the pupil says: ta-fa-té-fé, for 3/4 the pupil says ta-té-ti,for 8/8 ta-fa-té-fé-té-ré-li-ri. All this is interesting as one of the devices by which music can be taught, interesting as the history of a particular musical school, but these rules are not absolute and cannot constitute a method. It is this which is always the source of error in methods. But Chevet has some ideas remarkable for their simplicity, three of which make up the essence of his method: the first, which is old and was expounded by J.-J. Rousseau in his *Dictionnaire de Musique,* is the idea of expressing musical symbols in figures. Whatever the opponents of this mode of writing may say, any teacher of music can make the experiment and will always be persuaded of the enormous superiority of figures over staves for both reading and writing. I taught from staves for about ten lessons and only once demonstrated in figures, telling them that it was the same thing, and the pupils always ask me to write in figures and always write in figures themselves. The second remarkable idea, which belongs to Chevet exclusively, consists in teaching the notes separately from time and vice versa. Once having used this method of instruction anyone will see that what appeared to be an insuperable difficulty suddenly becomes so easy that one wonders why such a simple idea did not occur to anyone before. How much suffering would have been spared the unfortunate children who learn 'And let Him atone' and so on in the diocesan and other choirs, if the choirmasters would try out this simple thing—make the pupil, without singing, rap out with a stick or a finger the phrase of notes which he is to sing: four times for a whole note, once for a quarter, once for two eighths and so on, then let him sing the same phrase without time, then sing one bar and then again with both together.

For example, in written form:

First the pupil sings (without time), do-re-mi-fa-sol-mi-re-do; then the pupil does not sing, but says—rapping out the note in the first bar—one, two, three, four; then he raps for each note of the second bar and says one, two, three, four; then for the first note of the third bar he raps twice and says one, two, for the second note of the third bar and says three, four, and so on; then he sings the same thing with time and raps, and the other pupils count aloud. This is my routine, which, just like Chevet's, cannot be prescribed, which may be useful but it may be possible to find something still more useful.

But the nub is just a matter of separating the study of the time from the notes, and there can be countless numbers of routines. Finally, the third and great idea of Chevet is to make music and the teaching of it popular. His teaching approach completely fulfils this aim. And this is not merely what Chevet wishes and not merely what I suppose—it is a fact. I have seen in Paris hundreds of workmen with calloused hands sitting on benches with the tool with which they came away from the workshop underneath, singing from music, understanding and taking an interest in the laws of music. Looking at those workmen I found it easy to imagine Russian peasants in their place—if Chevet only spoke Russian they would sing in the same way and would understand just the same everything that he said about the general rules and laws of music. We hope to speak again of Chevet in more detail and above all of the importance of popularized music for raising up an art which is declining.

I pass to the description of how teaching proceeded in our school. After six lessons the goats separated themselves from the sheep, only the musical natures, the amateurs, were left, and we went on to minor scales and the explanation of intervals. The only difficulty was in finding and identifying the minor second as distinct from the major. They had already nicknamed fa 'the lusty one', do turned out to be the same sort of shouter, and thus I did not need to teach them—they sensed themselves what was the note in which the minor second was resolved, therefore they also sensed the second itself. We easily found for ourselves that a major scale consists of a series of two major, one minor, three major and one minor second. Then I showed that it is possible to sing or write down a scale upon any note you like, that if a major or minor second does not appear when it is wanted you can put in a sharp or a flat.

For the sake of convenience I wrote them out a chromatic scale like this:

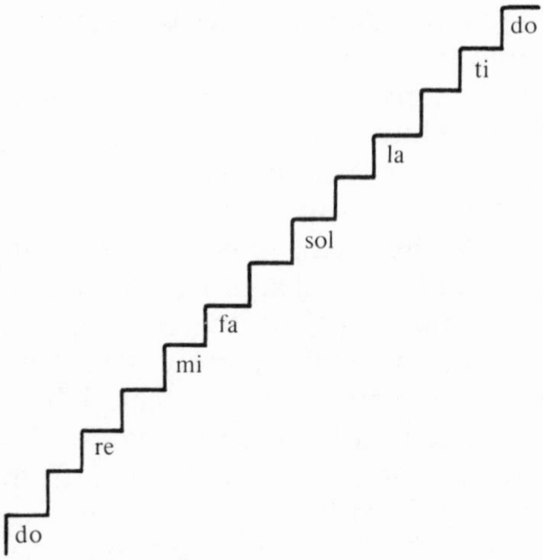

On this scale I made them write all possible major and minor scales, starting from any note they liked. They found these exercises extraordinarily absorbing, and the success was so striking that two of them often amused themselves between lessons with writing out the melodies of songs that they knew. These pupils often hum the airs of some songs or other which they cannot put names to, and they hum them delicately and tenderly and, this is the main thing, they sing them better in two parts and do not like it now when a lot of people yell the song out together formlessly.

Altogether there were scarcely twelve lessons in the whole winter. Our teaching was spoilt by vainglory. The parents, we teachers and the pupils themselves took a fancy to astonish all the village by singing in the church; we began to prepare a mass and Bortnyansky's cherubim pieces. It seemed as though this would be more fun for the children, but it turned out to be the contrary. In spite of the fact that the desire to drive to the choir of the church kept their spirits up, and that they loved music, and that we teachers were insistent about this subject and made it more compulsory than the others, still I often felt sorry as I looked and saw some little mite of a Kiryushka in tattered foot-bands hammering out his part on 'mysteriously for-or-or-or-or-or-ming' and being made to repeat it ten times and he at last losing patience and, jabbing the music with his fingers, argued that he was singing it just like that. We drove to the church once and enjoyed a success; the enthusiasm was enormous, but the singing suffered; they began to get bored with the lessons and stop away, and only by great efforts was the choir reassembled for Easter. Our singers were coming to resemble the diocesan ones, who often sing well, but who have, for the most part, had all their desire to sing killed as a result of this skill and who definitely do not know how to read music, while imagining that they do know. I have often seen people who have gone through that school themselves setting about teaching without having any notion of the notes, and they turn out to be quite unreliable as soon as they start singing something which has never been shouted into their ears.

From the small experience I have had of teaching music to the people I have drawn the following beliefs:

1. That the method of writing down notes in figures is the most convenient method.
2. That to teach time separately from notes is the most convenient method.
3. That if music teaching is to leave some trace and be willingly

accepted it is essential to teach art from the very beginning and not skill in singing or playing. It may be possible to teach young ladies to play Burgmüller's exercises, but children of the people had better not be taught at all than taught mechanically.

4. That nothing is more harmful to music teaching than things that resemble a knowledge of music—performances of choirs at examinations and speech days and in churches.
5. That the object of teaching music to the people should be to impart to them the knowledge we possess of the general laws of music, but definitely not to impart the false taste which is developed in our circles.

[3]

An extract from the reminiscences of a teacher at Yasnaya Polyana school: P. V. Morozov

Morozov is quite a common surname, and Pyotr Morozov the teacher was no relation to the pupil Vasily Morozov ('Fyedka'). The former was educated at the clerical seminary in the neighbouring town of Tula. (The clerical schools offered one of the few chances of extended education for plebeian youths, and in this period a number of their alumni did not become clergy.) He joined the staff of Yasnaya Polyana school early in February 1862, after a short induction at a neighbouring school. Tolstoy came to have a high opinion of him, and he had a long subsequent career as a teacher in a third village school in the same district. In 1874, when Tolstoy was embroiled in controversy over reading method with the Moscow Literacy Committee, it was Morozov whom he asked to give test lessons according to his (Tolstoy's) method.

Extracts from Morozov's memoirs were published posthumously in 1912 by the newspaper Russkoye Slovo.

Near the manor house we met a man in a sheepskin jacket and felt boots. 'We want the count.' 'I am the count.' 'So we can see,' replied my brother derisively. 'Do you work as the count's stoker? I've brought the count a teacher.'

The man in the sheepskin jacket did turn out to be the count. He walked to the school with me. We went in. What struck me was the inconceivable din the children were making. When we entered the boys started to shout.

'Lev Nikolayevich! He's hired a new teacher again! This one'll run away too, y'know, just like I.I. and N.O.! You'd do better to work with us by yourself—we don't need a teacher!'

Afterwards I learned that before me the count had had a succession of five or six teachers in the space of one month, some of whom had left of their own accord, because they could not get on with the pupils, and the others had been dismissed by the count because of coarse behaviour.

Looking around me, I began to examine the work which was going on. There was nothing resembling the school in which I had studied myself, or those I had seen. For the most part the lads were sitting in pairs, occasionally in threes or in big groups of five or so. One pair was reading, another was writing letters or words, a third was writing figures, a fourth was drawing, and so on. In a word, each one was doing whatever was handiest. You could hear nothing but shouts of 'Lev Nikolayevich! Come over here to us, have a look and see if we're reading it right.'

That day the count went away to see his brother Count Sergei Nikolayevich in Pirogovo. I stayed in the school alone. The counting-house clerk arrived and yelled to the lads 'Be off home! Give Pyotr Vasilyevich a chance to rest after his journey, and come back tomorrow.'

The lads went away very unwillingly. Towards evening they came back, but the porter sent them away. . . .

Soon Lev Nikolayevich arrived. I still remember the boys running into the school with excited faces shouting:

'Lev Mikolayevich[1] has come! Lev Mikolayevich has come! He's coming over to us right away!'

The count came into the school, and the lads literally clung to him like a swarm of bees clinging to a bush. It was ten minutes before I had a chance to come up to him and greet him.

The count and I started work together.

You would get up in the morning at six or seven o'clock, never later, and the lads were already right there. Some of them would be snowballing outside or doing gymnastics in the corridor, others would be at work in the school. Sometimes I ended up going to school without finishing my morning tea. At about eight o'clock, sometimes earlier, the count himself would arrive. We would work all day. When, you will ask, did the lads have dinner? They were free to dispose of their time without bothering about any set hours for their work. Some would leave, others would come, and so it went on from early morning until late in the evening. Unless it happened that the count himself had no time for the work in the evening; then the lads were driven out of the school, as it were. And then it was not the count and I who did so, but the porter. We had not the heart to drive them away, even if they went to sleep under the table. Then, after waking up those who had fallen asleep, the count and I would accompany the lads as far as the village. We often had to hear their mothers' grouses. For instance, we would knock on Matryona Kozlova's door:

'Who's there?' Matryona would ask.

'Open up, Matryona! It's us. Let your children in.'

'Drat you, fooling around in the middle of the night. Nothing better to do, I suppose. You just spoil the children and come disturbing honest folk!'

The school did not weary me, thanks to the lack of official discipline. Nobody there ever made anyone else stand to attention. Each person felt at home, in a straightforward atmosphere, and this did not in the least mean that there was no orderliness; on the contrary, the orderliness of the school work consisted precisely in that. The apparent disorders which occurred there were matters of principle, for the count did not run things according to the educational handbooks, but according to the plan that his own genius had worked out, based on his desire to turn the school into a family. The lads would come or go away without asking leave of anyone, they would settle down to work without any compulsion, of their own free will, and, moreover, each one to whatever work he wanted to do.

This was the basis of a false idea which was put about concerning the Yasnaya Polyana school, alleging that Lev Nikolayevich's school was like a gypsy camp or a village meeting. This is all lies; there was never any special mischief to be noticed in the school; perhaps now and then some inveterate scamp would start up some outdoor games in school; in that case the lads themselves would at once eject the scamp without ceremony. We did have a scamp of this kind—Fyedka Rezun, a unique expert in mischief. But as soon as he started his nonsense the lads would start to reason with him:

'Now Fyeddy, if you want to play, go out in the street, and don't get in our way. How would you like it if you were threshing and we came along and started playing about on the threshing floor?'

However there were occasions when no amount of arguments from his comrades had any effect on a boy like Fyedka Rezun. Then a friendly tussle would begin. On such occasions the count would always go out of the school and not interfere with the boys' affairs. But, I repeat, all this was extremely rare.

I grew accustomed to the school, worked in it until the last day of its existence, and left Yasnaya Polyana with regret.

[4]

Extracts from the reminiscences of a pupil at Yasnaya Polyana school: V. S. Morozov

Vasily Morozov was the 'Fyedka' of Tolstoy's articles. Apart from the interest of seeing what sort of writer the mature Fyedka really became, these memoirs are also an invaluable source of social background. In describing a school the pupil's view is so often the hardest bit to get right.

The memoirs were published in 1917, after the death of Morozov. He was in his early sixties when he wrote them, and he had talked over his experiences with Tolstoy later in life, so he may not be presenting absolutely independent testimony.

No one except Tolstoy has ever regarded Morozov as an important author in his own right, but as a mature man he did write at least one short story which was published, not without Tolstoy's patronage. We have read it, and found it undistinguished.

The passages we have omitted are those which shed little light on Tolstoy as a teacher. For instance, there are further descriptions of Tolstoy's romps with the boys, of how he treated them to a beanfeast, and of Morozov's journeys with Tolstoy.

My life

My memories of Lev Nikolayevich often arise in my mind. I often recall the happy years which I spent as a pupil in the school at Yasnaya Polyana. This is how I understood the school: in it you could learn to read and write and make out the psalter,[1] then you could read over the bodies of the dead, earn quarter-roubles and enjoy at the dead man's expense the dinner which was given in his memory. I knew too that after your schooling you could get some income. You would be able to write letters and charge five or ten kopecks apiece for them. Then our villagers would no longer go to the sexton or the deacon to get them to write a letter to Moscow or Petersburg. Then I would have a share of luck, then I would wear boots instead of bark sandals. It was with ideas like these that I entered the school as a ten-year-old boy and burned with enthusiasm, begging God and all the saints I knew or had ever heard of to help me in my studies.

My seventeen-year-old sister burned with no less ardour than myself to have God give me the very thing I needed, the ability to read the Psalter and write letters and thus earn an income, because the conditions in which we lived were very hard. We might as well have been complete orphans, for our mother had died when I was a child of two. In earlier times my father had been a good businesslike husbandman, but after my mother's death he soon married another wife more beautiful than my late mother. His new happiness did nothing to alleviate our situation as orphans. Our stepmother held us in contempt; she hated us as an extra burden. 'Sewing for you, washing for you! What good are you and your children to me?' she used to shout at my father. She was a lot younger than father and used to feel ashamed when we called her 'Mum': 'Hey what the devil! I'm no mother o'yours!' And soon after the marriage my father became sad, gloomy and taciturn, frequently exchanged abuse with my stepmother and once even beat her, and after that we did not see her in the house for three days. Our poor father lost his hopes of domestic happiness with every day that passed. And now he could bear no more and began to drink, and to drink more and more as it went on, and from being a nondrinking, homely man he turned into a thoroughgoing drunkard. From that time onwards our last possessions were borne away on the winds and we came to know poverty—poverty, cold and hunger.

I will never forget or wipe from my heart the memory of my poor sister's sadness, her sudden access of bitterness. It happened like this. On some feast-day or other my good father, concerned to prepare for the feast, raked out the last two poods[2] of flour, took it over to Dvorniki[3] and bought vodka and herrings in honour of the occasion. The table had been scrubbed down. The feast was laid out in its glory on the table: vodka and herrings. My sister and I sat on the stove and suffered agonies of appetite looking at the herrings and whispering to one another, 'What d'you think, will they give us some herring or not? The guests will eat them. Mum must be getting dressed in the punka[3], and Dad has gone to get the guests. There's not much herring, they'll scoff the lot.' Just then the door opened. Unrecognizable, like a boyar's lady, our stepmother came into the cottage all dolled up, her arms bare to the elbows, a lovely silk dress, big beads round her neck, large hollowed-out earrings in her ears and a cashmere apron trimmed with lace and braid before her. I had never seen my stepmother in such finery. My poor sister (she was a young girl by then) peering out from behind the stove, looked Mother and her finery up and down. Suddenly she began to tremble, seized me by the sleeve and began to squeeze me tighter and tighter against herself; her eyes grew dim, not with weeping, but with a sort of suppressed sobbing, and she began to repeat in a low and indistinct voice, 'Vasya, it's all Mummy's, Mummy's. When she died she left it all to me.'

Her arms dropped away from me and she collapsed face downwards. Frightened, I moved away from her into the corner of the stove and gazed at her in terror. Her eyeballs had rolled up and vanished beneath her brows, a mass of froth thrust out of her mouth. She lay motionless, only her leg or arm occasionally twitching.

Through the will of God my sister had suffered a severe fit, she got over it and then everything calmed down again.

Our way of life grew worse and worse. Contempt, drunkenness, hunger, cold—it was real destitution.

Making the acquaintance of Lev Nikolayevich

But now the time came, a happy time. Early in the autumn of 1859 it was announced to us in the village of Yasnaya Polyana that Lev Nikolayevich, ''is lordship' as we used to call him then, desired to open a school in Yasnaya Polyana and that children who wanted to might come and study; the school he was opening would be a free one. I remember what a to-do there was. There began to be meetings in the village and various rumours and opinions started.

'How? Why? Isn't it some sort of trick? It'll be no picnic teaching 'em free. I daresay they'll get about fifty lads, maybe more.'

And some parents even asserted that if they sent their children to be taught, ''is Lordship' would train them and give them to the tsar for soldiers. And there they'd be straight away fighting the Turks.

'That way he wants to curry favour with the tsar along of our lads.'

But some said sagely, 'We've seen what was and we shall see what will be, but we ought to send the kids to be taught since the man's taking it on for nothing, and there's Ivan Fokanov has been going to the sexton for three winters now and hasn't learnt a thing, and that's for a fee of two roubles a month.'

'You do what you please, but I'm sending mine,' said one, and a second and a third after him; some hesitated and then they all agreed, 'So shall I, I shall send mine.'

The matter was left till the Tuesday, as being an easy day. On Tuesday I got up early and glued my nose to the window, looking down the street to see if the children were gathering, and whether they were going. There were no bunches of children in the street; all I could see was friends running to and fro from cottage to cottage. I saw first Danilka going to see Syomka, then Syomka going to see Ignatka, then Taraska going to see Nikishka. They were all dressed already—clean white shirts, new bast sandals, their heads greased with vegetable oil or butter according to what they had got. Then Kiryushka slipped past our window and dashed into our cottage.

'Where's Vas'ka? Why aren't you getting ready?'

Without meaning to I seemed to stand on tiptoe with joy in front of Kiryushka and stare at him. He was dressed up and his head was richly oiled.

'Kiryush,' I said, 'I've got nothing to put on my feet, no sandals.'

'I've got a heel that's done for myself,' he said, 'but I'm going. Do you think the Master's going to look at our feet then? So long as our heads are right.'

And he dived out of the hut again, without even shutting the door, but merely shouting at me

'I'm ready, I'm just going to find a kaftan.'

'Oh the damned urchin, he's stuck the door open!' groused my stepmother.

Heaven helped me and I was soon ready myself. My solicitous sister had had her own sandals and kaftan ready for me for some time, although they were not the right size; the sandals were too big and the kaftan too long, for I was as thin and skinny as a peeled sapling. But I made ready just the same; I hitched up the kaftan, turned up the sleeves and anointed my head with kvass[5]—we had no oil. The children were starting to assemble in the street, some of them being accompanied by mothers and fathers. The procession started moving, and I followed behind them all, accompanied by my sister. A few minutes later we were standing in front of the master's house. The children whispered amongst themselves. Parents gave instructions. 'As soon as 'is Lordship comes out you have to bow and say "Wish you health, y'r honour".'[6]

I stood there like something the dog had left, feeling that I was worse dressed than any of them and even shorter than any of them, poorer than any of them and an orphan. I began to imagine things. 'They'll drive me away in a minute. Stepmother will pitch into me again. My sister will cry again. And how nice it is here! Of course I've never been here before, never seen such a house.[7] My, what big windows, like our gates, you could drive a cart through them! And trees round about, and gardens, and sand scattered by the porch. And who's going to teach us? 'Is lordship? I've never seen him. Is he all right or not? Won't he send me away?' With such timidity I thought about myself as I stood in front of the house. I do not know how it was with my friends, but I was thinking that I was the worst of them all.

Then our fates were settled; from somewhere on the staircase above a virile and yet somehow tender voice was heard. 'Have they been here long?'

'A long time now.'

'Why didn't you tell me before?'

'They were still gathering.' Someone was defending himself, apparently his servant.

One more second and there appeared a man in the porch, ' 'is Lordship', our teacher. Everyone bared their heads and bowed low. With my heart in my mouth I seized hold of my sister, grasping her from behind, and stood behind her as if behind a small fortress.

'Hallo! Have you brought your children?' Lev Nikolayevich addressed the parents.

'Just so,[8] m'lord,' replied the eldest ones with a bow.

'Right then, I'm very glad,' he said, smiling and surveying us all.

And he rapidly pierced the crowd with his gaze, seeking out the little ones who were hiding behind their father or mother. He went into the middle of the crowd and began to question the first boy:

'Do you want to study?'

'Yes.'

'What's your name?'

'Danilka.'

'And your surname?'

'Kozlov.'

'Right then, we shall study.' And he began to address every boy. 'What's your name?'

'Ignatka Makarov.'

'And yours?'

'Taraska Fokanov.'

Turning in another direction, Lev Nikolayevich stumbled upon my sister. 'What's this, have you come to study? You're going to study? Let the girls come too. We shall all study.'

'No, I haven't come to study, you see, I . . .' in her tears and shyness my sister did not finish what she was saying.

It had come to my turn.

'What about you, do you want to study?'

And I was standing face to face with the teacher and trembling like an aspen leaf.

'Yes,' I answered him timidly.

'What's your name?'

'Vas'ka.'

'And do you know your surname?' he asked, and it seemed to me that he was looking at me as if I were a half-starved waif.

'Yes.'

'Tell me.'

'Morozov.'

'Well, I shall remember you. Morozov, Vas'ka the cat.'[9] And he smiled, and his face seemed to me to be encouraging. It was if we had met one another before some time.

'Well, Morozov, come on! Makarov, Kozlov, you all follow me. And you go home, and God be with you. I will show them the school; send some more children. Let the girls come too. We shall all study.'

We went up the long staircase and found ourselves in a large room, as high as the threshing shed in the village. The ceiling was clean, and the floor was nice too, cleaner than our tables, and some sort of pictures were hanging on the walls, just like the gods[10] in our church. Only different. They were shaven, and one of them had a long mane of hair. Some of us were about to cross ourselves, but the teacher noticed and said, 'Those are not gods, but men, my relations and people I know.'

The other room was just as light, with floor and ceiling just as clean, and just as high. There were no pictures. There were long benches and equally long tables in the middle of the room. Two blackboards were hanging on the wall. Beside them on a little shelf lay chalk. In the corner stood a cupboard with various books and papers and slates.

'Right now, our school is going to be here, we shall all study. And if there's not enough room we shall take over here too'—he indicated the room where the 'gods' were hanging. 'I think you are not all here yet, have some of you been left behind?' And he looked us all over, and his questioning gaze halted, with a smile, when he reached me. I lost my tongue, and none of us gave him an answer. Being unable to get an answer out of us, and seeing that we were shy, he took a piece of chalk and said:

'We shan't do any work today, but tomorrow'—and he began to write the letters A, B, V, G, D, Z[11] on the blackboard—'but from tomorrow, then, we shall start studying. And now come along, I'll show you where I live.'

He opened another room, entered and sat down in an armchair. The room was smaller than the ones where we were going to study. But in it were sofas, an armchair, some ordinary chairs, tables, papers, pictures, a sort of figure made out of 'lebaster'[12] which was like a human being, there was a gun hanging up and a sort of woven bag and many odds and ends such as we had never seen in our lives. All this was interesting for me and for all of us.

'This is where I live and sleep.' said our teacher gaily, smiling at us all kindly as if stripping the covering of shyness from us.

It looked as though this one-sided chat placed him in a difficulty; how was he to draw us into conversation? He began to ask us questions individually, first one and then another:

'Kozlov, how old are you?'

'Twelve.'

'And what did you do in the summer?'

'Me?'

'Yes.'

'I ploughed and harrowed.'

'That's good. Were you helping your father?'

'Yes, I was. He did the marking out, and I ploughed.'

'What about you, Makarov?'

'I did ploughing too.'

'And you?'

'I ploughed too, and harrowed, and watched the horses.'

It turned out that they all helped their families.

'Now how old are you, Morozov?'

'I was ten last feast of St Basil of Caesarian.'[13] He smiled and was on the point of bursting out in a guffaw.

'What did you say, Morozov? Last what Caesarian?' and Lev Nikolayevich could hardly restrain his laughter.

'Well, that's when I was born.' But I thought to myself 'What a funny man he is, he doesn't know the saints.'

He did not set about asking me next what I was doing in the summer, I think because I did not look as if I weighed more than one pud, so what work could be got out of me.

'Now I'll write you all down, what you are called and your surnames.' He took a pen and paper. 'Now then, Morozov, Makarov, Kozlov, Fokanov, Vorobyov' and so on. 'I think I've written you all down, twenty-two of you. Now go home and God be with you, and come early tomorrow. We are going to study. Come, I shall be expecting you.'

We left the school, taking leave of our dear teacher and promising to come early tomorrow. Our delight knew no bounds. We related to one another, as though some one of our number had not been there, how he came out, how he asked questions, how he talked and how he smiled.

'And he's nice, you know. My dad was saying that he's still young. He's not thirty yet.[14] And isn't he tough and smooth and ugly. His beard is black like a gypsy's. And his hair's long like ours and his nose is thick. And the way he looked us over! I was scared right away. But when he started asking questions and smiling I got to like him and then I seemed to stop being scared.'

This was how Kiryushka told it, and indeed we all felt in this way.

'But he must weigh ever such a lot!' concluded Makarov.

Chattering like this we seemed in a moment to be united in one community and we did not see that we had drawn near to the village; we then started shouting across to one another.

'You call for me, and you for me, and I'll call for you,' and we ran off in various directions, each to his own cottage.

The first lesson

Next morning we assembled amicably as if at a signal and set off, just as well-groomed as the day before, but our conversation hung fire. Each was thinking to himself, 'How shall I get on with the studying?' We did not wait by the house. Lev Nikolayevich's servant Alexei Stepanovich came out to us and asked:

'Have you all come?'

'Yes.'

'Come into the school, the count will soon come out to you.'

We strung out along the staircase and went up into the room that we knew and passed through into the other one with the blackboards, where yesterday's letters had not yet been rubbed out. We gathered in a little bunch and stood closely around the blackboard looking at the letters. There was dead silence, none of us whispered to one another, each of us was thinking the thoughts God sent him. Suddenly a voice rang out from some distance, sonorously and gaily, 'A, B, V, D'. And rapid steps were heard coming through the first room. And towards us came our acquaintance of yesterday, our teacher, sturdy and dark.

'Hallo!'

'Wish you health, y'r lordship,' replied some scattered voices, those whose parents had taught them beforehand how to behave.

'Have you all come?'

'Yes.' Each of us answered the question on his own behalf in a timid voice.

'Really all? How is it that I can't see Caesar Morozov then?'

I was standing in a bunch of friends, as hemmed in as a match. The front rank opened, they retired to either side and I came into view. His gaily smiling eyes were gazing at me.

'Has Shurayev come too?'

'Yeth, I've come.' This Shurayev was taller and older than any of us, seventeen years old and lisped.

'Well, now we are going to work, we shall start studying.'

He took a piece of chalk and wrote up all the remaining letters.

'Now then, say after me.' Then he took a stick which served as a pointer and prodded the first letter with it.

'Now, say after me: a, b, v.'

Transferring his pointer to the other letters, g, d, e, zhe, he put a comma, and then went back to the first letter again.

'This is a, b . . .' and so on as far as the mark.

We trailed after him in a sing-song, quietly at first, in a whisper, but later we found our voices and repeated it after him louder and louder. Each one wanted his voice to be heard as well, and we warmed to our chanting so much that we lost all formality—at first we had been afraid even to look at ' 'is Lordship', and now we had crept up so far that we were crowding round him and several hands were holding on to his blouse.

'That's fine. Who can repeat it? I shall ask you questions.' said Lev Nikolayevich, jabbing the first letter with his pointer. 'What's this?'

It turned out that we were embarrassed, although we knew the first letter and could remember it, but something had broken, as though we were afraid of our own voices.

'Have you forgotten? Which of you can say it? Who can remember?' And he transferred his gaze to the blackboard. He had understood us, understood that his gaze was hindering us from replying. At that moment I squeaked out rapidly, in a voice that seemed to be not my own, but somebody else's 'A.'

They all joined in joyfully after me.

'Right, good. Next. What's this?'

Again there was a hitch. I let out another yelp, but was wrong. 'Ba.'

Voices were heard behind me: 'Be.'

Being the upstart amongst them all I felt ashamed of my mistake. My shame did not escape that watchful eye. And I was already imagining a punishment, as I had heard before about the sextons and retired soldiers punishing and teaching with the pointing stick.

'Right, right, that's good! Who said it first?' said Lev Nikolayevich half-seriously, looking at me with a kindly smile.

I did not reply, I was too timid. Someone out of the crowd gave me away, Kiryushka, I think.

'That was Morozkin making a mistake.'

'Morozov, what did you say? Splendid, good. Well, and what is the letter after "be" called?'

Again a blank. We were all silent. The letter seemed to be a tough one.

'Well, who will say it? Morozov, can you remember?'

I was silent, fearing a mistake.

'Who can, then?'

Everyone looked dumbly at the letter, no one answered, everyone had forgotten.

'And who knows what you carry water from the well in?'

'A vedro, a bucket,' said Ignatka.

'And what's the letter?'

Memory suddenly seemed to come back to our tongues. We cheerfully replied, 'Ve-e!' And so we went on learning by heart. If we could not manage he would hint at some object, for instance zhelezo, iron, and we would reply 'zhe'.

A week passed by in study, after it another one, a month slipped by. Imperceptibly autumn came to an end. Winter arrived. We had had time to grow quite familiar with the walls of the school, and time for our hearts to grow quite accustomed to Lev Nikolayevich. One day Lev Nikolayevich said to us: 'Don't call me "Your Lordship". I am called Lev Nikolayevich, so you call me that.' And after that we never called him 'Y'r Lordship'.

Before three months had passed our studies were getting on like a house on fire. At three months we were already reading boldly, and from twenty-two our numbers had grown to seventy. There were pupils from every quarter of our county, there were children of townspeople, there were shopkeepers' children, peasants and children of the clergy. The whole group was divided in our school into three classes: the senior one, the intermediate and the junior. The senior class was considered to be the first one with the best pupils; I was enrolled on the list of the senior class. In the senior class we had no more than ten pupils; the rest of the pupils were in the second or third. All seventy pupils would sit round Lev Nikolayevich. One would come up with a question, another one would bring his book up.

'Lev Mikolaich,[15] have I written it right?' one would ask. He would look it over.

'That's right, that's good. Only you've missed something out here, otherwise it's all good. Don't hurry.'

'And have I written it right?' another and a third, and all the class would insist.

He would look through it seriously, offer kindly encouragement and make comments in places:

'You'll have to write it again here. You've missed something out.'

In the other room where class 3 was someone could be heard making a mistake. Learning the three-letter syllable: zhe-re-a he was pronouncing it zra.

'No, no, not like that!' said Lev Nikolayevitch firmly, jumping up from the exercise book straight away. 'Not like that,' and he hurried into class 3, pronouncing as he went 'Zhe-re-a—what does it come to?'

'Zhra' was the amicable reply.

All his bubbling enthusiasm was an encouragement to us, and our morale rose daily.

Misdeeds and punishments

We had fun at school and worked with a will. But Lev Nikolayevich worked with even more of a will than we did. He worked so zealously that he not infrequently went without lunch. In school he assumed a serious air. He required of us cleanliness, care of the school things and truthfulness. He did not like it if one of the pupils got up to some silly tricks, he did not like jokers who laughed at dirty jokes. He liked to have a question answered with the truth, without any embroidery after the event. A certain boy, I cannot remember from what village, but not from ours, once uttered a nasty swearword in my ear, and, tittering at me, covered his face with his hands and turned away from Lev Nikolayevich.

'What's up? What are you laughing at, Glinkin?' asked Lev Nikolayevich.

The boy quietened down and plunged into his work. Again he glanced at me and again tittered into his hands. Lev Nikolayevich came up to him, irritated, and said:

'What is it, Glinkin, what are you laughing like that for?'

'Me! Me! Nothing, Lev Nikolayevich.'

'I am asking what you are laughing at?'

I heard Glinkin starting to lie, telling something quite different from what he had whispered into my ear. There was nothing to laugh at at all in what he was now telling Lev Nikolayevich. I could see that Lev Nikolayevich was displeased by Glinkin's denial and did not mean to break off before getting out of him the truth that he was hiding.

'Morozov, come here! What did Glinkin say in your ear? What was funny?'

My thoughts were divided: should I lie or tell the truth? Lev Nikolayevich was staring fixedly at me as if he could read in my face that he would soon get the truth from me. And after a little hesitation I looked at Glinkin and said to Lev Nikolayevich:

'Glinkin said something bad, I'd be ashamed to tell you.'

'Tell me, what did he say that was bad?'

'He was swearing with a dirty word.'

'Of course that is bad and silly. What made you laugh into your hands at a stupid thing like that?'

'I didn't say it, it's Morozov lying.'

Lev Nikolayevich drew himself up straight, as though he were reflecting upon what he ought to do, and turned to the pupils.

'Do you know what . . .' (Lev Nikolayevich mentioned several people's names) 'let's do like this. If somebody tells lies we'll write a label saying "liar" and stick it on the back of the person who tells lies and we'll lead him through the village. We might do it to Glinkin right now, for instance.'

Everyone agreed. A label was prepared and stuck to Glinkin's back. All the pupils laughed. They came up to him and read it:

'Li-liar, li-'

Glinkin felt himself to be friendless, was embarrassed and blushed to the point of tears. This did not last long. Lev Nikolayevich ordered us to take the label off.

And there was another, more serious case. A weighty matter required investigation. One pupil somehow or other stole a penknife from a classmate. The thief was detected in this larceny. Immediately the whole school under the chairmanship of Lev Nikolayevich determined to punish the thief by sticking a label with the inscription 'thief' on to his back. The label was ready, and it was time to take action. The guilty boy stood there petrified. He would rather die than walk through the village labelled 'thief'. An unexpected twist directed the affair another way. Lev Nikolayevich was standing there and thinking something over, then he turned to us as though he were seeking counsellors to support his own side. He looked at me and said:

'Now what do you think, aren't we doing wrong? We're disgracing a human being and going to lead him through the village with a label on? And everyone is going to jeer and laugh at him. When he grows up they'll still be laughing at him. It's not worth disgracing someone for all his life.'

'Well, we mustn't do it then,' some people agreed.

'And then his father'll kill him,' said Ignatka.

'Lev Nikolayevich, he'll get married and he'll have children. And they'll be jeering at his children too, "Your father was a thief".' I said, and concluded our council.

It ended in forgiveness. The guilty one brought in the penknife and handed it to his classmate who had suffered the loss.

However, I too suffered a punishment. We were sitting working. It was so quiet and serious in the school, even a cough was heard but rarely. It was just our luck that a workman from the master's household, Andryusha, a twenty-five-year-old, happened to come. We nicknamed him 'the blockhead'. He had asked Lev Nikolayevich to let him study in his spare time. He sat down beside me and started to memorize three letter words. Everything was peaceful. Lev Nikolayevich was reading some book or other. Why did I have to take it into my head to tease Andryushka? I tweaked his ear, but he buried himself in his book. I thought it was funny to see a grown-up like that learning his letters. Andryushka said nothing, but he glared at me savagely. As soon as he buried himself in his alphabet, holding his pointer against the A's, I started again, jogging his elbow and whispering softly:

'Blockhead!'

Again he did not say a word to me. Again he glared wrathfully. It seemed to me that he was thinking to himself 'Just you wait! As soon as you go outside I'll have a joke with you.'

I thought of something else. For no reason at all I shouted out:

'Oi! What are you playing at?' and I looked at Andryushka. Lev Nikolayevich looked up from his book and asked:

'What's up?'

I replied, 'Ivushkin is pinching me.'

Ivushkin was nonplussed and did not know how to defend himself; he vowed, 'I've done nothing but breathe, I haven't moved.'

I bent over my book again. Seriously, in a business-like fashion, as if Ivushkin really was annoying me. All was calm; Lev Nikolayevich settled down again to read his book. I burst out again. Again I shouted.

'Lev Nikolayevich! Tell him not to. He's tickling me.'

Lev Nikolayevich put his book aside in irritation and said, 'Ivushkin! come and kneel down for making mischief.'[16]

Not knowing how to defend himself, Ivushkin reluctantly left the bench and nodded his head wrathfully at me, as much as to say, 'Just you wait, I'll break every bone in your body, you little devil!'

Uncontrollable laughter. I burst out in front of the whole class.

'Morozov, you come out too, kneel down next to him.'

We knelt side by side, and it seemed still funnier to me when I remembered about the A's. We had been studying 'big A and little a'. It seemed to me that we were kneeling there like two letters; Ivushkin was big A and I was little a. And I began to tease him again, picking the plaster off and throwing bits of it at him. Out of all patience, Ivushkin rose from his knees. He wanted to get his complaint in first, in case I should shout out too soon, 'Cross my heart, it's not me! It's him that's throwing dirt at me.'

Evidently the fearful thought had crossed his mind, 'Shall I be kneeling here right up till the Feast of the Intercession without any wages?'

And Lev Nikolayevich burst out laughing both at the vast Ivushkin and at my dwarfish self. Lev Nikolayevich had seen the crimes I had committed, child-like, in joke. He said: 'Now go and don't be mischievous again.'

We sat down again and I did not tease Ivushkin any more.

This was the first time that Lev Nikolayevich made us kneel down and that was almost in joke; otherwise we never had any punishments. Lev Nikolayevich never punished anyone for pranks or disobedience or laziness. And if we were very mischievous he would merely say: 'Quieter, please!'

We were a model of orderliness throughout the three years.

If, however, as sometimes happened, a pupil got completely stuck and was either embarrassed or else would not give an answer out of obstinacy, Lev Nikolayevich used to ask him to hop about. If the pupil did not want to, Lev Nikolayevich would urge him on.

'Well, hop about then, hop about!' He would either take the pupil by the hands and start to hop about with him until everybody, including the pupil himself, burst out laughing, or else he would tell one of us to hop with that pupil. We would seize hold of him and hop about like pestles. Everyone would have a good laugh, and the pupil's bad mood would pass.

Chats on the terrace

In the course of joys and celebrations such as these we had grown as close to Lev Nikolayevich as the cobbler's wax is to the wax-end. We were miserable without Lev Nikolayevich, and Lev Nikolayevich without us. We were inseparable from Lev Nikolayevich and were only ever parted from him late at night. For we would spend the day in school, the evening was passed at our games and we would sit on his terrace till midnight. He would tell us some story or other, or tell us about the war, how his aunt in Moscow was murdered by a cook, or how he went hunting and was mauled by a bear, and he would show us the mark around his eye where the bear had torn him with its paw. We would tell him exciting things too, about sorcerers and the demons of the forest. How the demons play jokes on people in the forest and lead them out of their way, and appear in the form of a forester; they pretend to take a man to the forester's lodge out of pity and get him to climb up on to the stove,[17] but as soon as the first cock crows the man sees that he is not on the stove in a forester's lodge, but perched somewhere on the pile of a bridge just above the river.

'That's what the wood-demons of the forest are like!' we would say to Lev Nikolayevich.

Once we told him how old Mother Kopylov the witch, who had long been dead, used at one time to come home again each night at twelve o'clock, all in white. They used to leave her some supper, and it was all locked up round about, no one knew where she got through. She would eat it and be off again before cock-crow.

'Well, she doesn't walk any more. Her son Gerassim put up with it and put up with it, until he lost patience. Even though he was sorry for her—being his mother and all—still he had had enough. He went to Father and asked him to say a mass for her and drove a stake of aspen-wood through her head. From then on she stopped coming.'

'But Lev Nikolayevich, what's the truth, are there any wizards?' I asked.

Lev Nikolayevich said, seriously and with something like annoyance in his voice:

'There aren't any witches, and there aren't any forest demons either. And old Mother Kopylov was no witch. There is nothing like that; it's all nonsense. Silly people have told your fathers; they believed it and told you, and you believe it. It's all silliness and lies, there is nothing. Which of you believes in wizards, then? Bring me one, I'll give one hundred roubles to the person who brings one to me. Let him bewitch me!'

Walking home we were still talking about how fearless Lev Nikolayevich was; he was not afraid of wizards.

One day we were sitting once again with Lev Nikolayevich on the terrace of his house on some holiday, I do not remember which one, but I do remember that it was in the last days of

August, because they had started to bring in the crops from the fields. All of us pupils from Class 1 (i.e. the seniors) were sitting there. We were chatting and joking and just having a good chin-wag, although sometimes the conversation became serious and demanded attention and reflection.

Then Lev Nikolayevich told us of the war,[18] of how there was nothing, nothing at all that he had not seen there and seen his fill of: men killed, the wounded, the sick and doctors sawing off the wounded men's legs and cutting off their arms and gouging out eyes which had been pierced. As a result of such a nauseating story there was hardly one of the pupils who did not shrink into himself.

'Now I'll tell you about the new thing I've thought of,' said Lev Nikolayevich, 'Do you want to hear?'

'Yes! Yes!' we answered all together.

'This is what I have thought of,' said Lev Nikolayevich. 'I want to give up my property and my gentleman's life and go over to being a peasant; I'll build myself a cottage on the edge of the village and I'll marry a girl from the village and work like you, doing mowing and ploughing and all sorts of work.'

'What, be a labourer and a laughing-stock before people,' said Ignat.

'Why a labourer? I shall work for myself on my own farm, and for my family.'

'Well, if it's like that what will you do with all your property then?' we asked.

'What property? The land? We'll measure it all out, yours and ours, and make it common property; we shall be equal owners.'

'And what about if people laugh at you and say: "That's Tolstoy the down and out gentleman, he lost his money and works himself". Won't you feel ashamed?' we asked.

Lev Nikolayevich began to utter his words very crisply, as if he were in adult company.

'What shame do you mean then? At working for yourself? What have your fathers been saying to you then, when did they say that they were ashamed of working? No! Where is the shame then, if a man feeds himself and his family by honest work? And now I deserve to be laughed at precisely because the boot is on the other foot. That is what I think: there is nothing to laugh at in working, but there's a lot to laugh at and to curse at in the fact that I do no work and live better than you do, I am ashamed. I drink and eat and go for drives and play music and somehow it's all a bore. I think to myself: I'm an idler!'

Lev Nikolayevich let his gaze dwell on Ignat, glanced at me and all the others and said:

'Well then, Ignat, shall we settle the matter?'

For us the question was new and astonishing, one that we had never heard before, and very tricky. Ignat might be talkative, but still he did not start off straight away. We all fell silent and were overcome by bafflement and disbelief in Lev Nikolayevich's invention. It was as though everyone were wondering whether Lev Nikolayevich was speaking the truth or joking—how could a gentleman turn himself into a peasant?

The thought of all the work in the fields at harvest-time suddenly came into my head. I was the first to break the silence by saying:

'No, Lev Nikolayevich, it's difficult! It's all very easy to talk about and to look at, but when you're doing it, my word, you just try!'

I rose and stooped over, placed a hand on my waist and demonstrated how my father used to suffer as he rubbed his waist with horseradish juice. Lev Nikolayevich smiled and said:

'Well, and after he's rubbed it, does he feel better?'

'Why he just gives it a rub and he's a new man!'

Lev Nikolayevich smiled and jotted something down in pencil in his notebook.

At last everyone's tongues were loosened and we began to discuss the knotty problems of how to find a wife for Lev Nikolayevich, how to make the arrangements, what would be the best and hardest-working girl to pick; if there turned out to be none in our village we should look around in another one, in Kaznacheevka or Baburino. 'Marry in haste and repent at leisure; it's not a sandal that you can shake off!' And we instructed him in the minutest details.

He sat looking at us all, smiled, questioned some of us and noted things down in his book.

Somehow or other our conversation was curtailed at what one might say was the most interesting point. Our conversation was disturbed by Ivan Rodionich, an old man with a stutter, a Yasnaya Polyana peasant with no land of his own. He stood for a long time beside the lime-tree without being noticed, waiting for the end of our conversation. He was growing impatient: he took off his cap, spat on his hands, ruffled his hair so that it stood on end and trotted up to the terrace in short steps like a horse that has been watered, fell on his knees, thrust his head to the ground and muttered, stammering:

'You-you-you-your Lordship! K-k-k-kind man that you are, par-pardon me.'

Lev Nikolayevich left our circle, went down three steps and asked, 'Wait a minute, what are you asking me about?'

Ivan Rodionich made no reply, he only uttered this entreaty:

'You-your Lordship! K-kind m-man that you are, pardon me!'

Lev Nikolayevich asked again, 'Pardon you what? Perhaps I am in the wrong? Get up, Ivan Rodionich, you and I will have a talk.'

But Ivan Rodionich had evidently determined beforehand that he would obtain Lev Nikolayevich's forgiveness and therefore he still did not get up. Lev Nikolayevich, irritated and not knowing how to get sense out of Ivan Rodionich, went down the last step, knelt down facing Ivan Rodionich, laid his head on the ground also and said:

'Ivan Rodionich, you forgive me too for God's sake, let us stand up and have a talk.'

Ivan Rodionich, seeing that without meaning to he had upset the count, rose with difficulty to his feet; Lev Nikolayevich also got up.

'Well, now let's talk. What are you asking about?'

'I-I'm so-sorry, Y-Your Lordship,' he began to drag out the words which had got stuck in his throat.

When a person stares straight at a stutterer he stutters still worse, I have tried this out myself; but Lev Nikolayevich was always easy to talk to—he never embarrassed anybody with his gaze, he talked to such people holding his head to the side and listened with his ears.

Ivan Rodionich's petition amounted to the fact that the steward had impounded his two horses from out of the master's garden and imposed a fine of a rouble per horse.

Lev Nikolayevich said, 'Take the horses, I don't want any fine, and tell the steward that if he cares about my property he should drive things out, and not in.'

'Th-th-thank you, Y'r—Lordship, y-yr very kind.'

We all rose and began to say good-bye to Lev Nikolayevich; we asked him to come to the village to take part in round-dances and watch Grishka Lokhmachev dancing.

Lev Nikolayevich's journey abroad

Our school was still growing and growing. By now it had become famous not only in our province but even in Moscow and Petersburg. What am I saying? It had become famous abroad, not to speak of Russia. Even then I realized what a centre and meeting-point Yasnaya Polyana had become.

For the third winter or after nearly three years Lev Nikolayevich was not alone with us. We had teachers, five or six teachers. Each one knew his own subject. All the teachers were kind and gay, cut to the pattern of Lev Nikolayevich, as it were, with only one exception. I do not remember his surname, but he was called Vladimir Alexandrovich. I think he was a retired soldier. Heaven knows how he turned up amongst our flock! It seems Lev Nikolayevich was away at the time and Vladimir Alexandrovich took his place for arithmetic. Perhaps he begged for a job and a crust of bread. He was a stern character. He used to ask things of us which he did not understand himself. He would set us problems which he could not solve himself. In his irritation at not understanding he would take it out on our cheeks with the palm of his hand or a ruler. With a teacher like that we were becoming stupider. He did not so much provide us with food for the spirit as stifle what was in us. But by God's will he was soon dismissed without any denunciation from us.

During the period of our studies Lev Nikolayevich twice went away from Yasnaya Polyana; once was for a couple of weeks, I do not know where. But the second time Lev Nikolayevich meant to travel abroad.

For some reason we once carried on our work into the evening. The junior classes had gone home, but we seniors were wrestling with a difficult problem. Apparently Lev Nikolayevich had to rack his brains along with us. We finished it with some difficulty and were about to go home; we had begun to say goodbye to Lev Nikolayevich, but he stopped us, told us to wait and said:

'I am going away tomorrow, but you keep on coming to school as you have been doing. Pyotr Vasilyevich[19] and Vladimir Alexandrovich are going to work with you.'

The questions came from us in showers.

'Lev Nikolayevich, are you going away for long? Where to?'

He said: 'I shall come back soon.'

'But how soon?'

'Well, I shall be there for a week or two.'

'And are you going far?'

'To another country.'

We were bitterly cast down that Lev Nikolayevich should be going so far and for such a long time. Two weeks seemed a very long time to us. After all, if we had been parted from him for a single hour we felt as though we had not seen him all day. If he had said that he was going away for months I do not know what would have become of us. Probably our whole school would have disintegrated. We began to implore Lev Nikolayevich not to go; we told him that he could go at some later time. But Lev Nikolayevich said that he had to go.

'We shan't come to school. Studying won't be studying without you,' we said to him.

But Lev Nikolayevich consoled us by saying that two weeks would soon go by without our noticing and said that if anyone did not come to school he would fall behind in his studies and would have to be transferred to the junior class.

We were grieved at Lev Nikolayevich's departure, but what could we do? We took leave of him and told him to come back soon. He went away, and we were left like orphans without him. Coming into the school you could sense the emptiness, no games or jokes, and our studies would not go into our heads, just as if we had buried him. A week passed since Lev Nikolayevich had left, another week passed, and still no sign of Lev Nikolayevich. And he did not come back for a long, long time—I cannot remember how many months it was, but to us it seemed an eternity. We asked Pyotr Vasilyevich to write to Lev Nikolayevich to come soon, at once, but Lev Nikolayevich still did not come. We missed him very much, and we even began to have unhappy dreams about him. Once Chernov said:

'No, lads, our studies won't come right without Lev Nikolayevich. Now Vladimir Alexandrovich has slapped me on the cheek and locked Morozov and Kozlov in the dark room where the chalk is. There's only Pyotr Vasilyevich who hasn't touched anyone.'

Kiryushka said, 'I know what, lads, as soon as Lev Nikolayevich comes back let's complain to him; I shall be the first to complain.'

Once we arrived in school early. Pyotr Vasilyevich came and announced to us, 'Lev Nikolayevich has arrived.'

We could not believe it and ran to the house to find out. Alexei Stepanovich came out, laughed and said:

'He's arrived, he's arrived, he's sleeping.'

We were in no mood for study now, and we did not go into school, but started running about in the garden, waiting for Lev Nikolayevich. Soon it was made known that Lev Nikolayevich was coming out. I think Alexei Stepanovich came out and waved his hand to us. You can imagine our joy! We went running off down the garden paths towards Lev Nikolayevich; before we could see him we shouted at the tops of our voices from far away:

'Hallo, Lev Nikolayevich! Hallo Lev Nikolayevich!'

We ran up to the porch. Lev Nikolayevich was standing brushing his hair with two brushes. We surrounded him in a ring, asking him questions, looking him up and down from head to foot, feeling his blouse and trousers.

Some people said to him: 'Lev Nikolayevich, how much older you look!'

He replied in joke: 'Yes, I have grown old, the sand is trickling out of me.'

After that our school was set right again, and the old gaiety reigned.

Once Lev Nikolayevich brought a teacher up to us in school and said:

'This will be your drawing teacher. He is called Gustav Fyodorovich Keller. He doesn't know any Russian; he's a German.'

Then he turned to the German and started talking to him in German. They looked at us and both started to laugh.

We took a liking to Gustav Fyodorovich. He taught us well. And he, on the other hand, learnt to speak Russian from us.

What variety of men did we *not* have in the Yasnaya Polyana school? There were local people, Russians, various gentlemen, teachers, civil servants, various writers and a variety of people from abroad, not Russians at all. They would stare and smile, but they did not speak Russian. They would jabber away about something or other with Lev Nikolayevich and smile again and nod their heads at Lev Nikolayevich, as if in sign of agreement. Lev Nikolayevich would break off the conversation, put a question to one of us pupils and start talking again. Nothing could be understood. Only you could tell from the expressions on their faces: now they would be talking seriously as though they were attacking one another, now they would smile.

In the last year of our studies we had something new nearly every day: the visits of various gentlemen, Russians, teachers, civil servants, writers and foreigners.

How Lev Nikolayevich used to take us home in the evenings

Our school grew and grew and flourished more and more. We found our studies easy and our games carefree. I have said that the teachers were cheerful. Each teacher talked in such a way that we could easily understand. Everything was impressed upon our memories, and we answered questions willingly. Lev Nikolayevich himself was scarcely ever away from us. He became particularly attached to Class I, i.e. the best pupils. The work was serious. He seemed to penetrate to something deep in the heart of the pupil.

Many a time we would linger over our studies until late. Classes 2 and 3 had already dispersed to their homes, but we remained to spend the evening, since Lev Nikolayevich loved to read books with us in the evenings. Our favourite evening book was *Robinson Crusoe*. I was a fluent, clear reader, and the reading was entrusted to me and to Chernov. And when we had been sitting up late with our readings and story-telling and jokes until midnight in bad weather Lev Nikolayevich used to take us to our various homes on his horses.

He would frequently check and scrutinize us keenly to see which books produced an effect upon whom. Amongst my favourite reading were Koltsov's[20] verses 'Why are you sleeping, you peasant lad?' I used to apply these verses to my father, remembering how father had sold the last two poods[21] of flour to make a feast. Or the lines:

> I shall look, I shall go, I shall wonder at
> What reward God sends for men's labouring.

I would learn verses like these by heart.

Lev Nikolayevich had enough time and enthusiasm to do anything with us. We studied, played, made merry, chatted, sat up till midnight and strolled in the woods and the young plantation.

One day we were walking along the road. Lev Nikolayevich

stopped; we too stood and stared. He pointed out, as though it was a serious find, a scrap of rope a few inches long which someone had dropped.

'Someone pick up the rope, it will be useful for something.'

We started laughing and asked, 'What's the good of it?'

'How do you mean what's the good? It would be useful for tying up a sack or tying the wheel to the cross-piece;[22] if you're asked you'll have it ready and won't have to look for a piece.'

No one picked it up. I played the fool for a bit in front of my companions; I picked up the rope and straight away it came in handy for tying up my faulty pocket, which I was losing my lunch out of.

We walked further. Suddenly Kozlov stepped in with a quick question:

'Lev Nikolayevich, is it nice being rich? How do you get rich?'

Lev Nikolayevich turned to him and said:

'When you go to work try to save five kopecks out of your labours each day, and when thirty years have passed count it up and you'll have a lot of money.'

We reached the village and Lev Nikolayevich, like a watchman, escorted us each to his own place, interesting himself in them and peering into the window of each one; in some they were having supper, in some they were going to bed; in others they were already asleep.

When we got to our house a light was burning brightly in it; through the window my father and Kandaurov and Tit Boriskin could be seen sitting there. They were dealing cards, and playing for money. Lev Nikolayevich stared a little harder and said:

'They're playing cards in your place, and there's money on the table! Well, goodbye.'

'Goodbye, Lev Nikolayevich!' And he set off down to his own house, alone and fearless, unafraid of our witch Kopylova.

A competition with the gymnasium pupils. The Evening after it.[23]

One day we were sitting in school working. Lev Nikolayevich came in and announced a piece of news to us.

'Do you know what I've got to tell you?'

We pricked up our ears and wondered what the news was.

'Tomorrow some pupils from the gymnasium at Tula are coming to see us with their teacher and they want to compete with us to see who studies better, us or them.'

The next day we began to get ready. We were overcome with shyness as on the first occasion when he had entered the school, at the thought of standing up for ourselves against such fine young gentlemen. Early the next day we were standing by the blackboard solving the problems which we had been set. Our difficulty was not so much in solving the problems as in making friends with newcomers; it was as if we were two warring nations. They looked upon us as something quite new, and we looked upon them as a rarity. We overcame our fear and they overcame their shamefacedness. We set about solving the same problem which was set for them and for us. The writing out, the division, multiplication, subtraction and fractionizing began. We began to concentrate upon our task as though we had forgotten about our opponents. Our best champions in arithmetic were Romantsev and Kozlov. As soon as they got a grip on it they were the first to solve the problem and they said to Lev Nikolayevich:

'How's this? Have we got the right answer?'

We had got 943½. Lev Nikolayevich went over the working of the problem and said:

'I think it ought to come to that too.'

Lev Nikolayevich turned to the gymnasium teacher.

'We have solved it; we've got the number required.'

'We shall be done too in a moment,' said their teacher.

Their blackboard was covered in writing, and the problem was incorrectly solved. Lev Nikolayevich, without humiliating them, addressed our companions in a kindly way.

'That's the way, that's the way, fine!—You've done well, only just here you've missed a bit out in the fractionizing, but otherwise you were doing fine.'

We made trial of our knowledge in everything that was taught in our school, and yielded in nothing to our young gentlemen from the town, and by the time we said goodbye we were on a pleasant and straightforward footing as equals with our companions. Lev Nikolavevich was pleased with us and with them. Only he said to us when the others had gone:

'That will give them something to think about.'

The evening of that day was a special one for us, like a solemn festival. Everyone was as jolly as could be. We played at lapta[24] with Lev Nikolayevich and ran about until we were ready to drop.

Then we sat on the terrace and chatted and told jokes, which Lev Nikolayevich always had at the ready. He told us folk-tales, frightening ones and funny ones, and sang songs, making the words refer to us. He began with me:

Now then Vas'ka the midget
If you ate enough water-melon
You'd really grow up . . .
Kirill is standing there
Looking out of the window . . .

and so on, about each one.

Lev Nikolayevich was generally a really terrible joker; he would miss no opportunity of a joke and of having a laugh.

He used to call us by various nicknames. He often did this. He used to call Taras Fokanov 'Pussy', and me 'Vas'ka the midget', and Kiryushka 'Singed ears' and so on. Once I asked him:

'And what nickname shall we give you?'

'And don't you know yet what they used to call me when I was little? Haven't I told you?'

'No.'

'They used to tease me by calling me "Levka-the-bubble".'

Bursting out laughing we all asked:

'Why did they nickname you "the bubble"?'

'I was fat and blown out like a melon. So that was the nickname they gave me.'[25]

Our evening went on until just after midnight, as it had before. I said to Lev Nikolayevich:

'How quickly you made up songs about us!'

We began to take our leave, but Lev Nikolayevich stopped us and said:

'Write me some letters.'

Astonished by the novelty and not knowing what to write, we asked:

'What sort of letters and what are we to write?'

'Well, describe what you do at home and how you live.'

When we came back with the letters we had composed, handing them in one after another, he read them through in silence and gave no reply to anyone. He read everything through and then took one letter and began to read it aloud:

'Lev Nikolayevich. We are poor and if you gave me some money I would start to do business and get rich. Danila Kozlov.'

Lev Nikolayevich read the letter through, put it down and said:

'Letters like that are bad, Kozlov. I don't like it.'

Then he took another letter, looked through it in silence and said to me:

'Morozov, and is all this true that you have described to me?'

'Well, you told us to write about what we do and how we live. So I've written the truth, I reckon.'

Lev Nikolayevich smiled at me as though he were expressing gratitude for my letter and mumbled something—I could not make out what.

Writing a composition. Intimacy with Lev Nikolayevich.

We happened to be reading a certain book along with Lev Nikolayevich, I cannot remember the title of the book, but it was very good. Pausing at the full stops I would often put this question to Lev Nikolayevich:

'But Lev Nikolayevich, can you make things up like that yourself?'

'I don't know.'

After reading the book Lev Nikolayevich said to us, to the whole class:

'If you like we'll write something ourselves, we'll invent it.'

And we set about the composition. The task was difficult, we started to think but there was nothing to think about, and we did not know how to begin.

'Well now, let's begin perhaps about some old man, in verse perhaps.'

Again we fail to start. 'How can we write about an old man?' we think.

'Well, like this, then,' said Lev Nikolayevich. 'By the window's an old man,' he began and fell silent.

'Well, who's going on?' said Lev Nikolayevich.

Everyone was silent, searching for a rhyme, but again Lev Nikolayevich dropped a hint as to what we should write next.

'What's he dressed in?'

'In a shabby sheepskin,' said Makarov.

Lev Nikolayevich made a correction. '"In a ragged sheepskin" would be still better. Well, and then?'

'And in the street another man
Coloured eggs is peeling'' I suggested.

The rhyme was a difficult one, and, hesitating over that, we came to an end. We had finished with the one subject, but Lev Nikolayevich had evidently taken it into his head to begin another. He set us to write about proverbs, but for some reason we made nothing of it. Once three of us started to write a composition together, Lev Nikolayevich, Makarov and myself, Morozov. We did everything according to an order. First Lev Nikolayevich would say something, then Makarov, then I would. And it was as if we did not give in to one another, but were equal writers. We wrote a whole page and passed on to the next. Lev Nikolayevich was delighted at our success, and kept on saying:

'How splendid it's turning out! How fine! Heaven grant us to finish it, and get it printed, it will make a book.'

I felt jealous of Lev Nikolayevich being the only one to profit by a book which was the common work of us all, people would read it and say, 'Lev Nikolayevich wrote it.' Not wanting to yield up to him alone what had been our invention too, I staked my claim and said:

'But Lev Nikolayevich, how are you going to have it printed?'

Lev Nikolayevich looked at me and did not understand the question.

'We'll just have it printed.'

'No, Lev Nikolayevich, you take and print all three of us. With our surnames, for instance: Makarov, Morozov, and what's your surname?'

'Tolstoy.'

'Right then, you just put down all three: Makarov, Morozov and Tolstoy.'

Lev Nikolayevich smiled and affirmed: 'So we will print the three.'

Unfortunately I can remember nothing of 'our famous work' as Lev Nikolayevich called it. I have forgotten it all; it has vanished from my memory. And unfortunately our piece of work itself was not brought to fruition. It was destroyed by our schoolfellows in a game of bangers. And for a long, long time Lev Nikolayevich lamented our composition and was annoyed with the mischief-makers. Then I undertook to restore what had been lost and write it down exactly as it had been. I remained behind to spend all night in Lev Nikolayevich's house and set about the job together with Makarov. And the rewriting would not come out right for us. Makarov and I had an argument between ourselves, and we had both forgotten the most essential things. We wrote it, but not so well as it had been, and Lev Nikolayevich always regretted what had been lost. Nevertheless Lev Nikolayevich did not abandon his desire, and he said to me:

'Morozov, write something for me yourself.'

'But what am I to write, Lev Nikolayevich?'

'Write about what you can first remember about yourself, and how old you were. Five or six years old. How you lived, and what in general you can remember about your life.'

'All right, Lev Nikolayevich.'

And I began to write; I wrote for a long time; I racked my brains. Lev Nikolayevich would look over what I had written and say:

'It's good, very, very good!'

I would continue with greater zeal, and again Lev Nikolayevich would look it over and again say:

'It's good, very, very good! Carry on!'

I went on and on racking my brains, and at last I began to be tired of it. It seemed too long to me, and I wanted to get the ending finished off quickly.

I put at the end 'From then on we began to live well' and then I brought it to him and said:

'Lev Nikolayevich, have a look, see if that isn't enough for me to write?'

Lev Nikolayevich had a look and said, 'It's good, it's very, very good!' folded up what I had written and took it away.

'Now I'll get it printed for you.'

In my heart I did not believe this. But soon I read my story in print, 'The life of a soldier's wife' as Lev Nikolayevich called my story.

I rejoiced over the story I had written and had printed. I was promoted, and seemed to stand out as the top pupil of the Yasnaya Polyana school. Certain visitors arrived, people interested in schools and close acquaintances of Lev Nikolayevich, they paid me my due as a young scribbler, showered me with encouraging phrases, and my heart swelled with triumphant pride. Lev Nikolayevich did not treat me as an easily distracted schoolboy, but seriously as a senior. He never praised me or exalted me for any exploits whatsoever, but I had stolen my way into his heart. And although in school in our games, in our conversations and our walks he always behaved in exactly the same way towards all of us, yet I could read it in him that Lev Nikolayevich loved me. As if I were attached to his staff I often stayed behind to spend the night in Lev Nikolayevich's house and slept beside him on his bedroom floor.

He loved singing and playing the piano. And I possessed a good voice. And we used to sing his favourite song with him:

> How happy am I
> Alone with thee
> Thy song is better than the nightingale's,
> And the brook running over the stones
> Draws us on into solitude.

In school we were taught church singing. Several times we drove with Lev Nikolayevich to the church to sing as a choir. Sometimes a choir of twenty to twenty-five persons was assembled. Lev Nikolayevich sang bass.[26] His voice was good and strong. We would set off for the church like this: we would gather at the school in the morning, carts would be sent to the school and we would take our places in these carts with Lev Nikolayevich and be driven off to the church. I sang alto and was a good singer. For singing alto in this way I used to be rewarded by being given the mark of 5+. Sometimes he would put plusses all round the five, like this: + + +
+5+
+ + +
Nothing could have been a higher reward to me.

It was not only for singing that we got marks. I remember that Lev Nikolayevich himself would give us marks very rarely, and then as if in joke and I think only for singing. But the other teachers gave marks for all subjects. But the irascible teacher Vladimir Alexandrovich gave marks more often than anybody. At the beginning of our studies we did not even understand what 'marks' were. I remember that they were given in the middle of our studies. At the end of our studies, however, there were again none.

The closing of the school. Lev Nikolayevich's marriage.

That year our school did not reopen, something in our attitude to it had disintegrated and grown confused. The field work had come to an end, the fields were cleared and the school could have begun, but it was as if a sort of silent strike had been declared; instead of the former seventy pupils only fifteen turned up. Practically nobody came from the distant villages and nearby districts. Many of our Yasnaya Polyana children held off because of their parents. Their fathers said: 'That's enough studying. You've done a bit of study and that'll do. You know how to read and write and that'll do. You're not a little colt to be a-studyin'. Time to be earnin' y'r bread.' One went this way, one another, and they were all dispersed in various directions as labourers 'getting the corn down' as people say. Lev Nikolayevich was annoyed and regretted this, saying, 'They shouldn't have given up, they should have gone on studying.' But Lev Nikolayevich too seemed to have something else in mind. In a little while he went away to Moscow again, and the rumour went round that there he had married a Miss Sofia Andreyevna Behrs, whom I had seen when I was staying with Lev Nikolayevich, and who had praised my voice. 'She's a nice young lady, she gave me tea just as if I was a relation', so I reported on her to my friends. 'God give Lev Nikolayevich a happy life!'

But we were disturbed by the news that Lev Nikolayevich was getting married. We knew that the fun we had had with him before would come to an end. After Lev Nikolayevich's marriage our school still continued for a certain time, but it was not at all the same as it had been before. We had Pyotr Vassilyevich, Ivan Ivanovich and Vladimir Alexandrovich for teachers, but Lev Nikolayevich himself rarely visited us. And the school began to flag. The pupils were gradually dispersing. Within a few months there were only half of the pupils left, or even less. And a short time saw the removal of half of that half that remained as well. The benches were ever more thinly filled. The last pupils were bored and gloomy. The pupils from other villages and districts left. There were only the Yasnaya Polyana pupils left, and only about ten of those.

I do not remember whether our school carried on for as much as a year after Lev Nikolayevich's marriage, but I do remember that our school was closed altogether in 1863. And I never found anything so difficult in my life as parting with the Yasnaya Polyana school and with our teacher Lev Nikolayevich.

After the school had closed we still did not break off relations with Lev Nikolayevich altogether. Three of us: Kiryushka, Ignatka and I, were always dropping in at Lev Nikolayevich's house as we passed to have a chat about something or other. Lev

Nikolayevich was pleased that we did not forget him. He would joke with us as he had in school.

Once we were sitting in Lev Nikolayevich's house, and Lev Nikolayevich, feeling Ignat's cheeks, said:

'Ignat, you seem to have got thinner lately.'

Ignat was fat and thick-set, with high cheek-bones.

'Of course I've got thinner. Work's really begun now all right. You know we get up and we've not got time to turn round ourselves; no sooner started at dawn than sunset is fading. It's ploughing all day long, and when we're asleep at night we're looking up to see if the horses haven't got through into your oats. And if they do that blusterer of yours, Mitrofan Nikolayevich, takes and claps 'em into the pound. And if you drive them out iron hobbles cut their legs to mincemeat.'

Lev Nikolayevich laughed at the word 'blusterer' and said in a serious tone:

'You know, Ignat, I don't know why he drives them into the pound.'

'Well, you ask him. You're not much of a master, you don't even know what's going on in your household. Get away! I reckon you know all right. . . . It's because of the redemption-work.[27] You slave away at the donkey-work all day and drop asleep like you were dead, and that's how he's got you on the hook. Your own work and the redemption-work.'

'Ignat, I shall find out all about this and order Mitrofan not to act so.'

Then Ignat came out with some joke that would make us laugh till our sides ached. He was bold and shrank from nothing.

Suddenly Sofia Andreyevna came out to us and said:

'Lev, dear, what are you up to that's so funny and amusing? Oh, you've got your pupils here! Are you having some fun with them? Let me have a look at them and see what they're like,' and Sofia Andreyevna, putting her glasses to her eyes, examined us.

'Morozov, Kirilla and Ignat! And do you find it great fun to be with Lev Nikolayevich?'

'Ever so,' we replied.

'Oh, Lev, dear, what nice boys!'

'Ignat and I don't see eye to eye,' said Lev Nikolayevich. 'We've been talking about the farming, and he is indignant with me because I let things go wrong.'

But our interviews with Lev Nikolayevich were not long and

not frequent. I will say frankly that our relations with him had begun to grow cooler, and there was something about them which began to smack of triviality. It was not like before, when we used to come flying in through his doors without being announced. That was all wrong now, you had to ask Alexei Stepanovich first, and Alexei Stepanovich would say that the countess was asleep or had not finished dressing yet, or else that the count was busy writing and he could not show us in.

And Lev Nikolayevich began to receive us for a short time only. He would joke for a bit or read some short book, set us an easy problem to do in our heads, and then say:

'Well, goodbye, come again, I am going to do a spot of work.'

At that period Lev Nikolayevich was writing some big book or other.[28]

A year after Lev Nikolayevich's marriage we dropped going to see him altogether.

'Not goin' to see him any more, that's enough, time we were earning our bread now, you can't put back the slice when it's once been cut off,' said Kiryushka about the fact that we could not get on with Lev Nikolayevich as we used to.

My feelings were worse hurt than anybody's. I still wanted to go on and on visiting him, to go on and on living with him.

[Ignat and Morozov are employed by Tolstoy on his farm. They fail in their duties, letting horses go astray. Ignat takes the lead and insists on lying to Tolstoy about this, who, after trying to get the truth out of them, dismisses them. They resolve to get jobs in Tula.]

Conclusion

Ignat was true to his word, and a month later he got me a place in Tula as a postilion; later I lived at the post station as a driver. I spent several years in this way. During this period I met Lev Nikolayevich very rarely, and met my schoolmates only now and again, and then only the ones from Yasnaya Polyana. After schooling I never met the others again, nor my dear friend Chernov, who came from the distant village of Lamintsevo. I would occasionally walk in from Tula to see Lev Nikolayevich. There was no intimacy between us at that time. Lev Nikolayevich was busy with family affairs and with his writings and did not interest himself in us as he had earlier.

Many years passed—twenty-five years after my schooling. Lev Nikolayevich grew old and began to write religious books. By this time I was the father of a large family. And I was again drawn to Lev Nikolayevich. I began to walk over to see him often, and then an intimacy grew up between me and him once more—but a different one—a spiritual intimacy. Again I began to feel that I could not tear myself away from Lev Nikolayevich, that we were like the wax and the wax-end. However, I did not succeed in seeing him as often as I should have wished. Fate wrenched me away from him. Ever since the time when I left Yasnaya Polyana as a boy I have been living in Tula, as if I were a convict serving his term, loaded with fetters and securely held with a chain.

Those are all my memories of my schooldays. Fifty years have passed since then. I am now an old man. But my memories of the school and of Lev Nikolayevich himself are still clear. My memories always cheer me, especially when I am in a tight corner and life is going badly.

At such wearisome moments I retire into myself and start to recall my life. What happened to me? Who was I? I retire further and further back into my memories and stop when I come to the Yasnaya Polyana school and Lev Nikolayevich. My memories sketch it all in to the finest detail. Here am I—a ten-year-old schoolboy, here is the young, gay Lev Nikolayevich, the slides down the steep hill, the romps with Lev Nikolayevich, snowballing with him, the games of lapta, the walks through the woods and fields, the chats on the terrace, our conversations about wizards. . . . And I seem to awaken and feel myself no longer a decrepit old man with a meaningless life, but a ten-year-old schoolboy. And I have never lost and never shall lose my memories of those happy, bright days of my life. My love for Lev Nikolayevich, which was then kindled in me, burns brightly in my heart and illuminates my life.

[5]

Should we teach the peasant children to write, or should they teach us?

First published in the September number of the magazine. The title of this article is somewhat involved in the original. We have ventured to borrow the neat translation of it used by Sir Isaiah Berlin in his essay 'Tolstoy and Enlightenment'.

In the fifth Yasnaya Polyana Booklet, in the section of children's compositions, the editors have printed by mistake 'The story of how a boy was frightened in Tula'. This little story was not composed by a boy but put together by a teacher from a dream which he had had and told the boys. Some readers who follow the Yasnaya Polyana Booklets have expressed doubt as to whether this tale really came from a pupil. I hasten to apologize to readers for this oversight and to observe à propos how impossible imitations are in this genre. This story was detected not because it was better but because it was worse, incomparably worse than *all* compositions by children. All the remaining stories come from the children themselves. Two of them: 'He feeds you with a spoon and pokes you in the eye with the handle' and 'The life of a soldier's wife', which were printed in that number, were composed in the following way.

The principal skill of the teacher in teaching language and the principal exercise whereby we can guide children in their writing of compositions consists in setting subjects, and not so much in setting as in presenting a greater choice, in indicating the scale of the composition and in pointing out opening devices. Many intelligent and talented pupils have written trivia; they would write 'the fire broke out, they began to haul, and I came out into the street' and nothing would emerge, in spite of the fact that the subject of the composition was a rich one and the events described had left a deep impression on the child.[1] They did not understand the main point: why write? and what is good about writing it down? They did not understand art—the beauty of expressing life in words and the absorbing power of that art. As I have written in the second number, I tried many different approaches in setting compositions. According to their inclinations, I set them exact, artistic, touching, funny and epic subjects for essays—it did not work. This is how I inadvertently hit upon the right method.

For a long time now reading Snyegiryov's collection of proverbs has been one of my favourite—not studies—but pleasures. At each proverb I find myself imagining characters from the people and their clashes, suggested by the meaning of the proverb. Amongst my unrealized dreams I have always imagined a series, not so much of stories as of pictures, written around proverbs. Once last winter I became absorbed after dinner in reading Snyegiryov's book and brought the book to school. It was the Russian language lesson.

'Well, then, why doesn't someone write about a proverb?' I said. The best pupils—Fyedka, Syomka and others—pricked up their ears.

'How do you mean, about a proverb? Tell us.' The questions came in showers.

We came across the proverb 'He feeds you with a spoon and pokes you in the eye with the handle'.

'Now, imagine', I said, 'that a peasant took a beggar into his house and then, for reasons of his own, began to reproach him, and it ends up with him 'feeding him with a spoon and poking him in the eye with the handle.'

'But how would you write it?' said Fyedka, and all the others who had been about to prick up their ears suddenly turned away, having come to the conclusion that the task was beyond their powers, and set about their own work which they had begun before.

'Write it yourself,' someone said to me.

They were all busy with their work; I took a pen and an inkwell and began to write.

'Well', I said, 'let's see who will write it best, I will do it too.'

I began the story which was printed in Yasnaya Polyana Booklet no. 4 and wrote the first page. Any unbiased person who possesses a feeling for art and for the common people's way of life, and who reads that first page written by me and the following pages of the story which were written by the pupils themselves will distinguish that page from the others like a fly in the milk; it is so false and artificial and written in such bad language. It should also be noted that in its original form it was still more monstrous and has been much improved, thanks to the pupils' suggestions.

Fyedka kept looking at me from behind his own exercise-book, and, when my eyes met his, smiled, winked and said 'Write away, write away, I'll show you.'

He was obviously interested to see a grown-up writing a composition. Finishing his own composition worse and faster than usual, he climbed on to the back of my armchair and began to read over my shoulder. I could not carry on now; the others came up to us and I read aloud to them what I had written. They did not like it; no one praised it. I felt ashamed, and in order to soothe my literary vanity I began to tell them my plan for what was to follow. As I told it I got carried away and recovered my spirits, and they began to make suggestions to me; someone said that the old man should be a wizard; someone said no, that was no good, let him just be a soldier; no, it would be better if he were to rob them; no, they said, that would not fit the proverb, and so on.

They were all extraordinarily interested. It was evidently new and absorbing for them to be present at the process of composing a story and to participate in it. Their judgments were for the most part unanimous and true both in the construction of the story itself and down to the details and the characterisation. They almost all took part in the composition; but from the very beginning there stood out particularly sharply the positive Syomka, for his clear-cut artistry of description, and Fyedka, for the rightness of his poetical ideas and particularly for the warmth and rapidity of his imagination. Their demands were so unfortuitous and precise that more than once I began by arguing with them and was obliged to give way. I had firmly stuck in my head the demands of correct construction and a right relationship between the meaning of the proverb and the story; they, on the contrary, demanded only artistic truth. I wanted, for instance, to have the peasant who had taken the old man into his home repent of his good deed himself—they considered this to be impossible and created a shrew of a wife.

I said 'At first the peasant felt sorry for the old man, and afterwards he begrudged him bread.'

Fyedka replied that that would be inconsistent, 'He didn't obey his wife from the very beginning, and he won't give in afterwards either.'

'And what sort of man is he according to you?' I asked.

'He's like old Timofei,' said Fyedka, smiling, 'a sort of thin beard and he goes to church and he keeps bees.'

'Kind, but obstinate?' I said.

'Yes,' said Fyedka, '*he's* not going to listen to his wife.'

Some enthusiastic work began at the point where they carried the old man into the cottage. Here they evidently felt for the first time the excitement of fixing an artistic detail by means of language. Syomka distinguished himself particularly in this respect: the truest details came pouring forth one after another. The only thing that one might reproach them with was that these details depicted only the present moment, without any connection with the general feeling of the story. I could not keep up with writing it down and my only request was that they should wait a little and not forget what they had said. It seemed as though Syomka was seeing and describing things which were present before his eyes; the stiff, frozen bark sandals and the mud which flowed from them when they were thawed out, and the dry shells they turned into when the woman threw them into the stove; Fyedka on the other hand saw only those details which called forth in him the feeling with which he regarded a particular character. Fyedka saw the snow which had got inside the old man's foot-rags and the feeling of sympathy with which the peasant said 'Lord! What he went about in!'[2] (Fyedka even demonstrated how the peasant said this, spreading his arms and shaking his head.) He saw the old overcoat put together out of a bundle of rags and the torn shirt which could be seen, the old man's thin body wet with melting snow; he invented the wife who grumblingly, at her husband's command, took off his sandals, and the old man's pitiful groan as he said through his teeth: 'Gently missus, I've got sores there.'[3] Syomka needed predominantly objective images: the sandals, the ragged overcoat, the old man, the woman, almost unconnected with one another; Fyedka needed to call forth the feeling of pity in which he was himself steeped.

He kept rushing ahead and talking about how they would feed the old man, how one night he would fall down, how later in the fields he would teach the boy to read and write, so that I was obliged to ask him not to hurry and not to forget what he had said. His eyes were glistening, almost with tears; his black, thin little hands clenched convulsively; he grew angry with me and was constantly urging me on:

'Have you written that? Have you written that?' he kept asking me.

He behaved towards all the others with despotic wrath, he wanted to speak by himself—and not to speak in the way that people retell stories, but as they write, i.e. to fix the images of his feeling artistically by means of words; he would not permit me, for instance, to rearrange the words; if he said 'I've got sores on my feet' then he would not permit me to say 'There are sores on my feet.' His soul which was touched and agitated at that moment by a feeling of pity, that is of love, enveloped every image in an artistic form and rejected everything which did not correspond to the idea of eternal beauty and harmony. As soon as Syomka got carried away into blurting out disproportionate details about lambs in the stable and so on, Fyedka grew angry and said:

'Hey, I've settled that.'

I had only to drop a hint, for instance, about what the peasant was doing when the wife ran off to see the neighbour and Fyedka's imagination at once produced a picture of lambs bleating in the stable, together with the sighs of the old man and the babbling of the boy Seryozhka; I had only to hint at an artificial and false picture for him to say at once angrily that we did not want that. I proposed, for instance, to describe the peasant's appearance—he did not agree; but on receiving a suggestion that we should describe what the peasant was thinking when his wife ran to the neighbour, he immediately invented this turn of thought:

'Ah, now if you had come across Savoska that's dead and gone he would have torn your hair out long ago.' And he said this in such a weary tone of accustomed seriousness and yet good nature, with his head propped on his hand, that the lads rocked with laughter.

The main characteristic of any art—the sense of measure—was developed in him extraordinarily. A superfluous touch suggested by one of the boys jarred upon him. He took over the construction of the story so despotically, and with a right to that despotism, that soon the boys went home and he was left with Syomka alone, who did not yield to him, although he was working in a different mode.

We worked from seven o'clock till eleven; they felt neither

hunger nor fatigue, and they even grew cross with me when I stopped writing; they took to writing themselves by turns, but soon gave it up, it did not work. It was only then that Fyedka asked me what my name was.[4] We burst out laughing at his not knowing it.

'I know,' he said 'what to call you, but what's your household? Like we've got the Fokanychevs, the Zyabrevs, the Yermilins.'

I told him.

'And are we going to print it?' he asked.

'Yes!'

'Then we ought to put in print "by Makarov, Morozov and Tolstoy".'

He was excited for a long time and could not go to sleep, and I cannot convey the feeling of excitement, joy, fear and almost repentance which I experienced in the course of that evening. I felt that from that day onwards a new world of delights and sufferings had opened for him—the world of art; it seemed as though I had been prying into something which no one ever has the right to see, the birth of the mysterious flower of poetry. I felt both fear and joy, like a treasure-seeker who should see a flower upon a fern; I was joyful because suddenly, quite unexpectedly, the philosopher's stone which I had been seeking in vain for two years was revealed to me—the art of teaching how to express thoughts; I felt fear because that art called forth new demands, a whole world of desires which were not consonant with the environment in which the pupils lived, as it seemed to me in the first moment. There was no mistaking it. It was not chance, but conscious creativity. I beg the reader to read through the first chapter of the story and note the wealth of touches of true creative talent scattered through it; for instance, the touch whereby the woman complains bitterly about her husband to the neighbour, and yet the woman, for whom the author has an obvious lack of sympathy, weeps when the neighbour reminds her of the ruin of her house. For an author writing by intellect and memory alone the shrewish wife is no more than a foil to her husband; she would invite the neighbour out of sheer desire to annoy her husband, but Fyedka's artistic feeling embraces the wife as well—and she too weeps, is afraid, and suffers, in his eyes it is not her fault. And after that the minor point that the neighbour put on a woman's fur coat,[5] I remember that it struck me so much that I asked:

'Why a *woman's* fur coat?' Nobody had led Fyedka up to the idea of saying that the neighbour put a fur coat on.

He said, 'That's right, it's like him.'

When I asked whether we could say that he put a man's fur coat on he said, 'No, better if it's a woman's.'

And this touch is indeed extraordinary. You cannot make out at first why it is a *woman's* fur coat, and yet you feel that this is excellent and that it could not be otherwise. Every word of a work of art, whether it belongs to Goethe or to Fyedka, differs from the non-artistic in that it calls forth a countless multitude of ideas, images and interpretations. The neighbour in a woman's fur coat is bound to be imagined as a puny, narrow-chested peasant, as he obviously ought to be. The woman's fur coat, draped over a bench, the first one he laid his hand on, also conjures up for you the whole life and manners of a peasant on a winter's evening. By way of the fur coat you automatically imagine too that later hour when the peasant is sitting undressed in the light of a wood splinter lamp, and the women coming in and out to get water and clean out the cattle sheds, and all the outward untidiness of peasant life where not a single person clearly possesses any particular garment, and not a single thing has its own definite place. By that single phrase 'he put on a woman's fur coat' the whole character of the environment in which the action is proceeding is established, and that phrase was not uttered by chance, but consciously. I still remember vividly how the words which the peasant says at the point where he has found the paper and cannot read it arose in his imagination: 'Now if my Seryozhka could read he would jump up sharp, grab the paper out of my hands, read it all and tell me who this old man is.' In this way we see the attitude of a working man to the book which he is holding in his sun-browned hands; that good man with his patriarchal, pious inclinations rises up before us in his entirety. You feel that the author must have loved him deeply and then understood him entirely to have placed in his mouth later on the digression about how, 'We've come to such a pass nowadays that people will do you down straight away for no reason at all.' The idea of the dream was put forward by me, but it was Fyedka's idea to have a goat with sores on his feet, and he was particularly pleased with it. And the peasant's reflection at the time when his back started to itch, and the picture of the silence of the night—all this is so far from fortuitous, in all these touches we feel such a conscious artistic power!—I remember too that during the time when the peasant is falling asleep I suggested making him think about his son's future and the future relations of his son and the old man, how the old man would teach Seryozhka to read and write and so on.

Fyedka frowned and said, 'Yes, yes that's all right', but you could see that he did not like the suggestion, and twice he forgot it.

The sense of measure was stronger in him than in any of the writers I knew—that same sense of measure which a few artists acquire by enormous labour and study lived in his unspoilt childish soul in all its original force.

I abandoned my lesson because I was too agitated.

'What's the matter with you, why are you so pale? Could you be unwell?' my companion asked me.

In fact only two or three times in my life had I been so deeply stirred as on that evening, and for a long time I could not account for what I had experienced. Dimly it seemed that I had been guilty of criminal prying through a glass beehive into the work of the bees which is concealed from mortal gaze; it seemed to me that I had corrupted the pure primitive soul of a peasant child. I dimly sensed in myself repentance for some sort of sacrilege. I was reminded of the children who are forced by idle and corrupt old men to prance about and present sensuous scenes in order to rekindle their weary and jaded imaginations, and yet I was overjoyed, as a man should be who has seen things which no one ever saw before.

For a long time I could not account for this impression which I had received, although I felt that this was one of those impressions which educate a man in his mature years, which raise him to a new level of life and force him to renounce the old and devote himself entirely to the new. The next day I could still not believe what I had experienced the day before. It seemed to me so strange that a semi-literate peasant boy should suddenly evince such a conscious artistic power as Goethe, on his sublime summit of development, could not attain. It seemed to me so strange and insulting that I, the author of 'Childhood' who had earned a certain success and recognition for artistic talent from the educated Russian public, that I, in a matter of art, not only could not instruct or help the eleven year old Syomka and Fyedka, but I was only just able—and then only in a happy moment of stimulation—to follow and understand them. This seemed so strange to me that I could not believe what had happened the day before.

On the evening of the next day we set about continuing the story. When I asked Fyedka whether he had thought about the next part of the story and how it would be he waved his arms without replying and simply said:

'I know, I know! Who's going to write?'

We started to continue it, and again on the boys' part the same feeling for artistic truth and measure and the same absorption.

Half-way through the lesson I was obliged to leave them. They went on without me and wrote two pages just as well, with just as much deep feeling and rightness as the first ones. Only these pages were a little poorer in detail, and the details were not always adroitly arranged, and in two places there were repetitions. All this evidently came from the fact that the mechanical process of writing gave them difficulty. It was the same on the third day. During these lessons other boys came up and, since they knew the tone and content of the story, often made suggestions and added their own appropriate touches. Syomka kept going off and coming back. Fyedka by himself conducted the story from beginning to end and edited all the proposed alterations. There could be no doubt about it, nor any idea that this success was the work of chance: we had evidently chanced to hit upon the approach which was more natural and more stimulating than all the previous ones. But all this was too unusual, and I could not believe what was going on before my very eyes. It was as though one more special event was required to demolish all my doubts. I had to go away for a few days, and the story was left unfinished. The manuscript, three large sheets covered in writing, remained in the room of the teacher to whom I had shown it. Before I went away, while I was still engaged in composition, a newly arrived pupil had shown the lads the art of making paper bangers, and the whole school, in the usual way, was going through a phase of bangers, which displaced a snowballing phase which, in its turn, had displaced a phase for carving sticks. The bangers phase continued during my absence. Syomka and Fyedka, who were amongst the singers, used to go into the teacher's room for a practice and spend whole evenings there, and even nights sometimes. In between and during the singing, of course, the bangers were about their business, and all available papers which fell into the boys' hands were turned into bangers. Next day before lessons the banging had become so annoying to the pupils themselves, that of their own accord they followed it with a general persecution of bangers; with shouts and screams the bangers were all gathered up and triumphantly thrust into the stoked-up stove. The bangers phase was at an end, but our manuscript had perished with it. I have never felt any loss so hard as the loss of those three closely-written sheets; I was in despair. Brushing it all aside, I wanted to start a new story, but I could not forget the loss, and involuntarily I was heaping reproaches every minute upon the teacher and the banger-makers. (I cannot but take this opportunity of observing that only as a result of outward disorder and complete freedom for the pupils, which Messrs. Markov in 'The Russian Messenger' and Glebov in the magazine 'Upbringing' no. 4 so kindly jeer at, did I discover without the least difficulty, without any threats or devices, all the details of the complex story of how the manuscript was turned into bangers and they were burnt.) Syomka and Fyedka could see that I was distressed and obviously did not understand why, although they sympathized. At last Fyedka shyly suggested to me that they should write out the same one afresh.

'By yourselves?' I said. 'I am not going to help any more.'

'Syomka and I will stay the night,' said Fyedka.

And indeed after the lesson they came to the house between eight and nine, locked themselves in the study, a fact which afforded me no little pleasure, laughed for a little while, fell silent and until after eleven, when I went up to the door I could only hear them conversing with one another in quiet voices and the scratching of a pen. Only once they had an argument as to what had come first and came to me for a ruling: did he look for the bag before his wife went to the neighbour or afterwards? I told them that that didn't matter. Between eleven and twelve o'clock I knocked at their door and went in. Fyedka, in a new white fur coat trimmed with black, was sitting in the depths of an armchair with one leg crossed upon the other, his shaggy young head propped on his hand and playing with a pair of scissors in the other hand. His large black eyes, shining with an unnatural but serious and adult glitter were staring somewhere into the distance; his irregular lips, pursed as if he were about to whistle, were obviously in the act of forming a word which, his imagination having hit upon it, he was about to utter. Syomka, standing in front of the large writing-table, with a large white fragment of sheepskin on his back (tailors had only just come to the village), with loosened sash and dishevelled head, was writing on the crooked lines, constantly stubbing the pen into the inkwell. I rumpled Syomka's hair and as he looked at me, startled, with puzzled sleepy eyes, his plump high-boned face with its straying hair was so funny that I started to chuckle, but the children did not start laughing. Fyedka, without altering the expression on his face, touched Syomka's sleeve, meaning that he should go on writing:

'Wait a minute you,' he said to me presently (Fyedka talks to me like that when he is absorbed and excited), and he dictated a bit more.

I took the exercise-book from them, and five minutes later when, seated around the little cupboard, they were consuming potatoes and kvass[6] by turns, looking at the silver spoons, which were marvellous in their eyes, they burst out, without knowing why themselves, into ringing childish laughter; the old woman listening to them upstairs also laughed without knowing why.

'What are you laughing for?' said Syomka, 'sit up straight or else you'll be filled up lopsided.'

And as they took off their fur coats and stretched out underneath the writing table to sleep they could not stop their outbursts of childish, peasant, healthy, enchanting laughter. I read through what they had written. It was a new variant of the same thing. Some things were missed out, some new artistic beauties were added. And again the same feeling for beauty, truth and measure. Later one sheet of the lost manuscript was found. In the printed story I combined the two variants, using the page which was found to help my memory. The story was written in early spring, before our teaching year ended. Because of certain circumstances I could not find the time to make any new experiments. In illustration of a proverb only one story was written by two boys, who are the most mediocre in ability and most corrupted (because they are from servants' families). That is 'Glad of a holiday, drunk till dawn', which was printed in the third number. The same phenomena were repeated in the case of these boys and this story as with Syomka and Fyedka and the first story, but with a difference in the level of talent and the level of enthusiasm and participation in the work on my part.

In summer we do not study, have not studied and will not do so. I shall devote a separate article[7] to the reason why summer studies are impossible in our school.

Fyedka and some other boys lived with me for part of the summer. Having had their fill of bathing and playing they thought of doing a little work. I proposed to them that they should write a composition and gave them several subjects. I told them a very gripping story about a theft of money, the story of a certain murder,[8] the story of how a molokan[9] was miraculously converted to orthodoxy, and I also proposed that they should write in the form of an autobiography the story of a boy whose poor and dissolute father was sent to be a soldier[10] and to whom the father returned as a reformed and good man.

I said 'I would write it like this: I remember when I was little, I had a mother, a father and such and such other relations, and what they were like. Then I would write that I remember how my father used to go on the spree, my mother was always crying and he used to beat her; then how they sent him to be a soldier, how she wailed and we began to get on still worse, how the father came back and I didn't seem to recognize him, and he asked whether Matryona was alive here—meaning his wife—and how we rejoiced then and started to prosper.' That is all I said to them at first.

Fyedka was extremely pleased with this subject. He seized a pen and paper straight away and began to write. During the writing I put into his head only the idea of the sister and the idea of the mother's death. He wrote all the rest himself and did not even show it to me, except for the first chapter until it was all finished. When he showed me the first chapter and I began to read it I felt that he was in a state of great excitement and was looking, with bated breath, now at the manuscript following my reading, and now at my face, wishing to detect an expression of approval or disapproval upon it. When I told him that it was very good he quite flared up, but said nothing to me and took the exercise-book over to the desk with a tensely calm step, put it away and slowly went out into the yard. In the yard that day he rushed around wildly with the lads, and, whenever our eyes met, looked at me with such grateful, tender eyes. A day later he had already forgotten about what he had written. I merely invented the title, divided it into chapters and here and there corrected mistakes which he had made simply out of carelessness. This story in its original form is printed in this number under the title 'The life of a soldier's wife.'

I shall not speak of the first chapter, although it has its own inimitable beauties, and although the devil-may-care Gordei is presented in it with extraordinary truth and vigour—Gordei who seems to be ashamed to admit that he is repentant and just thinks it decent to ask the village meeting[11] to look after his son—in spite of that this chapter is incomparably weaker than all the following ones. And the only person responsible for this is I, who could not resist the temptation, when this chapter was being written, of suggesting things to him and telling how I would have written it. If there is a certain vulgarity of approach in the opening, in the description of the characters and of the dwelling, then I alone am responsible for it. If I had left him alone I am sure he would have described the same thing unobtrusively in the course of the action, with greater art, without that mannerism of logically arranged descriptions which is accepted amongst us and has become impossible: first the description of the dramatis personae and even their biographies, then a description of the place and milieu and only then the action begins. And strange to relate all these descriptions, sometimes covering tens of pages, do less to acquaint the reader with the characters than an artistic touch nonchalantly thrown in at a point when the action has already begun between characters who have not been described at all. Thus in the first chapter just Gordei's one phrase 'That's just what I need' when, shrugging his shoulders, he submits to his fate of being a soldier and merely asks for the meeting not to abandon his son—this phrase does more to acquaint the reader with the character than the description which is repeated several times and was concocted by me, of his dress, person and habit of going to the tavern. Just such another impression is produced by the words of the old woman who is always reproving her son when she speaks enviously to her daughter in law in a moment of sorrow: 'That's enough now, Matryona! What can you do about it—it seems it is God's will! After all you are still young, God may yet bring him back to see you again. But at my time of life, I am always ailing . . . in no time at all I shall be dead.'

In the second chapter my influence for vulgarity and corruption is still noticeable, but again the deeply artistic touches in the description of the scenes and the death of the boy redeem the whole piece of work. I suggested that the boy should have thin legs, I suggested the sentimental detail about old Nefed making the little coffin; but the complaints of the mother expressed in one phrase, 'O Lord, when will this brat be dead!' put before the reader all the essence of the situation; and after that the night during which the elder brother is aroused by his mother's tears, and her reply to the grandmother's question as to what was the matter with her in the simple words 'My son is dead' and the grandmother getting up and lighting a lamp and washing the little body—all this is his own; all this is so compressed, so simple and so powerful—not a single word can be discarded, not a single one changed or added. There are but five lines in all, and in those five lines the whole picture of that mournful night is drawn for the reader, and a picture reflected in the imagination of a six- or seven-year-old boy. 'At midnight mother started crying for some reason. Grandmother got up and said, "What's the matter? Christ be with you." Mother said, "My son is dead." Grandmother lit a lamp, washed the boy, dressed him in a shirt, girded him up and placed him beneath the ikons.[12] When dawn came . . .' We can see the boy himself, awakened by the familiar weeping of his mother from his dozing with a kaftan for a cover somewhere upon the stove, following what is being done in the hut with frightened glistening eyes; we can see too that exhausted, suffering soldier's wife who a day before had said, 'Will that brat take long to die?' repentant and so crushed by the thought of that brat's death that she can only say, 'My son is dead', does not know what to do and calls upon the old woman to help her; we can see too that old woman, weary with a lifetime's suffering, bent and thin with bony limbs, unhurriedly and calmly setting about the job with accustomed, work-worn hands; lighting a splint-lamp, fetching water and washing the boy, laying out everything in its place and the boy, when he is washed and girded, under the ikons. And we see those ikons and all that night, sleepless till dawn, as if we had lived it ourselves as the boy who was peeping out from under the kaftan lived it; that night is evoked in all its detail and remains in our imagination.

By the third chapter there is less of my influence. The whole personality of the sister belongs to him. Back in the first chapter he had characterised the relationship of the sister to the family at a single stroke: 'she was working on her own account at her fine clothes, she was preparing to get married'. And this one stroke is enough to give a complete sketch of the girl, who cannot and in fact does not take part in the joys and sorrows of the family. She has her own legitimate interest, her own sole aim which Providence has placed before her, her future marriage and family. Now our dear friend the writer, especially if he is of the sort that wish to edify the common people by presenting them with examples of morality worthy to be imitated, would certainly have raised the question of the sister's participation in the general hardships and sorrow of the family. He would either make her into a shameful example of indifference or else a model of love and self-sacrifice, and we should have an idea, but no living character of the sister. Only a person who has studied life deeply and got to know it could understand that for the sister the question of the family's sorrows and of the father's being recruited as a soldier is quite rightly a secondary question; she has her marriage. And this the artist in the simplicity of his soul can see, even though he is a child. If we described the sister as a most touching and selfless maiden we would not be able to form a picture of her and would not love her as we love her now. As it is I regard that plump-cheeked, rosy girl as so dear and so much alive, running out of an evening to the round-dances in the shoes and red calico kerchief which she bought with the money she has earned, loving her family although she feels oppressed by the poverty and gloom which are so much in contradiction to her temperament. I feel that she is a kind girl simply from the fact that her mother never complained of her and never felt any sorrow on her account. I feel, on the contrary, that she alone with her concern about pretty clothes, her humming of fragments of song and the tales of village scandals which she brings back from her work in the summer or the street in winter, served in that woeful period of loneliness for the soldier's wife as a representative of joy and youth and hope. Not for nothing does he say that the only joy they had was when they gave the sister in marriage; not for nothing does he describe the wedding celebrations with such loving detail; not for nothing does he make the mother say after the wedding, 'Now we are ruined and done for.' Clearly, having parted with the sister they have lost the joy and gaiety which she used to bring into their house. All of this description of the wedding is uncommonly good. There are details at which we cannot help being quite bemused, and when we remember that this was written by an eleven-year-old boy we ask ourselves, 'Could this really not be by chance?' This can be seen by reading between the lines of that condensed and powerful description of a seven-year-old boy, with clever and attentive little eyes, no taller than the table, whom nobody pays any attention to, but who remembers and notices everything. When he wanted a piece of bread, for instance, he did not say that he asked his mother, he said that he bent mother down to him. And this is not said by chance, it is said because he can remember his relationship with his mother at that period of his growth and how his relations with his mother were timid in front of other people and close when they were alone together. He remembers another out of the multitude of observations which he has been able to make during the marriage ceremonies; he has remembered and has noted down just what will pick out the character of these ceremonies for him and for each one of us. When people said it was bitter[13] the sister took Kondrashka *by the ears* and they began to kiss. And then the death of the grandmother and her remembrance of her son before she dies and the special character of the mother's grief—all this is so firm and condensed, and it is all his own.

The father's return was what I had said most about when I was setting the subject of the story. I liked that scene and told it with sentimental vulgarity, but he took a great liking to that very scene, and he begged me:

'Don't say anything! I know myself, I know!' he said to me and began to write, and from that point onwards he wrote the whole story to the end at one sitting.

I shall be very interested to know the opinion of other critics, but I consider I have a duty to utter my own opinion frankly. I have met with nothing like these pages in Russian literature. In the whole of that encounter there is not a single hint that this is touching; it merely relates what went on, but out of all that went on nothing is related except what is essential if the reader is to understand the situation of all the characters. The soldier said only three phrases in his own home. At first he was still plucking up his courage and said 'How d'ye do?' When he had begun to forget the role that he had taken on he said, 'Is this all the family you've got?' And everything came out with the words 'Where's my mother then?' All of them such simple, natural words, and none of the characters is forgotten! The boy was glad and even cried a little, but he is a child and therefore straight away, in spite of the fact that his father was weeping, examined his pack and his pockets. Nor is the sister forgotten. We seem to see that rosy young woman shyly making her way past the people into the hut in her shoes and kissing her father without saying anything. We seem to see the bewildered, happy soldier, kissing everyone in turn, not knowing who they are himself, and when he realizes that the young woman is his daughter, calling her back to him and kissing her, this time not just like any young wench but as the daughter that he once left apparently without regret.

The father was reformed. How many false and clumsy sentences we would have heaped up at this opportunity! But Fyedka simply told how the sister brought vodka and he did not start to drink it. And we can see too the wife, having taken her last twenty-three kopecks out of her bag, out of breath, whispering in the porchway to the young woman to go and fetch some vodka and pouring coppers into her hand. We can see that young woman putting the curtain over her arm with a pint bottle in her hand, clattering with her shoes and wagging her elbows behind her and running to the tavern with the pint bottle in her hand. We see her, blushing, come into the hut, bring out the bottle from under the curtain, and the mother placing it with satisfaction and gaiety on the table, and we see how the soldier's wife felt both hurt and pleased that her husband did not begin to drink. And consider, if he did not start to drink at a moment like that, then he really had reformed. We feel that all the members of the family have become quite different people.

'My father said a prayer and sat down to table. I sat down next to him; my sister sat on the chest and my mother stood beside the table and looked at my father and said "Just fancy, you've got younger—you've no beard." Everybody began to laugh.'

And only when everyone had gone away did the real family conversations begin. Only then is it revealed that the soldier has grown richer and has grown richer in the simplest and most natural way, in just the same way as almost everyone in this world gets rich, i.e. other people's money, official, communal money, as a result of a happy chance got left behind in his hands. Some of the readers of the story have observed that this detail is immoral, and that the idea of the exchequer as milch cow ought to be stamped out and not confirmed in the minds of the common people. But for my part I prize this touch particularly, not to speak of artistic truth. After all, official moneys always do get left behind, why should they not sometimes be left with a homeless soldier like Gordei? In their views about honesty we find a total contradiction between the common people and the upper class. The people's standards are particularly serious and strict about honesty in the closest relationships, for instance to one's family, to the village, to the commune. In dealings with strangers—the public, the state and especially with a foreigner and with the exchequer, the general rules of honesty seem to them only faintly applicable. A peasant who would never lie to his brother, who would endure any hardship whatsoever for his family, who would not take a kopeck more than he deserved from a fellow-villager or a neighbour, that same peasant will flay the skin off a foreigner or a townsman and will lie at every word he says to a gentleman or a civil servant; if he is a soldier he will stab a French prisoner without the slightest qualm of conscience, and if official moneys should fall into his hands he would regard it as a crime against his family not to make use of them. In the upper class, on the contrary, quite the opposite is the case. Our good friend would rather cheat his wife, his brother, a merchant with whom he has done business for decades, his servants, his peasants and his neighbour, and the very same man when abroad is consumed by the constant fear that he may unwittingly cheat somebody and is constantly asking to be shown who else he ought to give money to. That same good friend will skin his company and his regiment to pay for champagne and gloves and will overflow with graciousness towards a captured Frenchman. The same man, with respect to official funds, regards it as the greatest of crimes to make use of these when he has no money (he just *regards* it as that) but in the event he generally fails to hold out and does the thing which he regards as scoundrelly. I am not saying what is best, I am simply saying what, as it seems to me, is the case. I will only observe that honesty is not a principle, that the expression 'honest principles' is nonsense. Honesty is a moral habit; in order to acquire it there is no other way but to begin with the closest relationships. The expression 'honest principles' is in my opinion quite meaningless, there are honest habits, but there are no such things as honest principles.

The words 'honest principles' are only a phrase; as a result these supposedly honest principles, which relate to the remotest circumstances of life—official funds, the state, Europe, humanity, and are not based upon habits of honesty, not developed in the closest relationships of life—for this reason these honest principles or, more properly, phrases about honesty turn out to be untenable in contact with life.

I return to the story. In our opinion what seems at the first moment to be the immoral feature of money taken from public funds possesses, on the contrary, the most endearing and touching character. How often a writer from our circles, who wishes in the simplicity of his soul to present his hero as an ideal of honesty, displays to us all the dirty and depraved interior of his imagination. Here, on the other hand, what the author wants is to make his hero happy; his return home to the family should have been enough for happiness, but it was necessary to remove the poverty which had been weighing upon the family for so many years; where could he obtain riches from? From the impersonal public account. If riches are to be given they must be taken from someone—there was no more proper and reasonable way of finding them.

In the very scene where this money is announced there is a tiny detail, a single word, which seems to strike me afresh every time I read it. It illuminates the whole picture, delineates all the characters and their relationships, and it is but one word, and a word used incorrectly, syntactically wrong—it is the word 'hastened'. A teacher of syntax is bound to say that it is incorrect. 'Hastened' requires a continuation—'hastened to do what?' the teacher is bound to ask. But here it reads simply 'My mother took the money and hastened, she put it away safe'—and this is splendid. I wish that I might say a word like that, and I wish that teachers who give instruction in language would say or write down a sentence like that.

> When we had had supper my sister kissed my father again and went home. Then my father started to rummage in his pack, and my mother and I watched.
>
> Then my mother caught sight of a book in it and said, 'Learned to read have you?'
>
> My father said, 'That I have.' Then my father took out a big bundle and gave it to my mother.
>
> 'What's this?' says Mother.
>
> 'Money,' says Father.
>
> My mother was glad and hastened, she put it away safe. Then my mother came back and says, 'Where did you get it from?'
>
> My father says, 'I was a sergeant and had the army money; I gave it out to the soldiers and there was some left, so I took it.'
>
> My mother was so glad she was running about like mad. The day was over by now, evening was coming on. A lamp was lit. My father took up the book and began to read. I sat beside him and listened, and my mother shone the splint-lamp on to it. And my father read the book for a long time. Then we went to bed. I lay down on the back bench with my father, and my

mother lay down at our feet, and they were talking together for a long time, almost till midnight. Then we went to sleep.

Another scarcely noticeable detail which one does not find at all striking but which leaves a deep impression, about how they went to bed: the father lay down with the son, the mother lay at their feet and for a long time they could not bring themselves to end their conversation. How warmly, I think, the son squeezed up against his father's chest, and how marvellous and joyful a thing for him, as he was dropping asleep or between dozes, to hear still those two voices, one of which he had not heard for so long. One might think that it is all over: the father has returned, they are not poor any more. But Fyedka was not satisfied with this (those imaginary people had evidently established themselves too vividly in his imagination) he still wanted to imagine a picture of how their way of life changed, to show himself clearly that this woman is no longer a lonely, miserable soldier's wife with little children, but that there was now a strong man in the house who would remove from his wife's weary shoulders all the burden of crushing sorrow and poverty and conduct the new life independently, firmly and gaily. And to this end he sketches you just one scene: the healthy soldier cutting firewood with a jagged axe and carrying it into the house. We can see the sharp-eyed boy, who is used to the creaking and groaning of his feeble mother and grandmother, gazing with astonishment, respect and pride at his father's muscular arms in their rolled-up sleeves, at the energetic strokes of the axe, which are accompanied by the chesty grunts of a man at work, and at the block which splinters like matchwood beneath the jagged axe. We have watched this and we are perfectly reassured about the future of the soldier's wife. The dear soul will not come to grief now, I think.

In the morning my mother got up, went up to my father and said:

'Up you get, Gordei! We need firewood for the stove.'

Dad got up, put on his boots and his hat and said, 'Got an axe?'

My mother said, 'Yes, but it's jagged—maybe it won't chop.'

My father took the axe firmly in both hands, went up to the block, set it upright and hit it with all his might and split the block in two; he chopped up the wood and dragged it across into the cottage. Mother set about stoking up the fire; she filled it right up and it gave out a nice glow.

But even this is not enough for the artist. He wants to show you another side of their life too, the poetry of happy family life, and he sketches you the following picture.

When it was glowing nicely my father says, 'Matryona!'

My mother came up and says, 'Well, what is it?'

Father said, 'I'm thinking of buying a cow, five lambs, two horses and a cottage—this one's falling down, you know—so, it'll come to about a hundred and fifty roubles in all.'

My mother seemed to ponder, then she said, 'Then we shall run through all the money.'

Father said, 'We shall work.'

My mother said, 'Well, all right, we'll buy it but I'll tell you what—where do we get the framework?'

My father said, 'Hasn't Kiryukha got one then?'

My mother said, 'That's just it, he hasn't. The Fokanychevs have grabbed it.'

My father thought for a while and said, 'Well, we'll get one from Bryantsev.'

My mother said, 'I'd be surprised if he's got one either.'

My dad says, ''Course he will, he's from the state forest.'

Mum says, 'I'm afraid he'll charge a lot; look out, he's a proper rogue.'

Dad says, 'I'll go and take him some vodka and talk it over with him; and you bake us an egg in the ashes for dinner.'

Then Mum got up a nice bit of dinner, she borrowed something from her folks. Then my father took some vodka and went off to see Bryantsev, and we stayed behind and sat waiting for a long time. I got bored without my father, I began to ask my mother to let me go where father had gone.

Mum said, 'You'll get lost.'

I began to cry and made to leave, but my mother hit me, and I sat down on the stove and began to cry still more. Then I saw my father come into the cottage and say

'What are you crying about?'

My mother said, 'Fyedyushka was going to run off after you, and I hit him.'

My father came up to me and says, 'What are you crying about?'

I began to complain about my mother.

My father went up to my mother and started to beat her,

made out he was anyway, and he keeps on saying, 'Don't you hit Fyedya! Don't you hit Fyedya!'

Mum made out she was crying. And I sat on Dad's knee and was glad. Then Dad sat down to table and put me next to him and shouted out, 'Now Mother, give me and Fyedya our dinners, we're hungry!'

So Mum gave us beef, and we started to eat. We finished dinner, and my mother said, 'Well, what about the frame?'

Dad said, 'Fifty silver roubles.'

Mum said, 'That's nothing.'

Dad says, 'Yes, there's no doubt about it, it's a first-rate frame.'

It may seem very simple, and that very little is said, but their whole family life is placed in perspective for you. You can see that the boy is still a little child, who will cry for a bit and be glad the next minute; you can see that the boy cannot appreciate his mother's love and has deserted her in favour of his virile father who has split the chopping block; you can see that the mother knows that it must be so and is not jealous; you can see this wonderful Gordei with his heart overflowing with happiness. You have noticed that they ate beef, and that charming comedy which they all play in and everyone knows that it is a comedy, but they play it because they are brimming over with happiness. 'Don't you hit Fyedya!' says the father, shaking his fist at her. And the mother, who is used to unfeigned tears, pretends to cry, while smiling happily at the father and son, and the boy, who climbed on to his father's knee, was proud and glad without knowing why himself—proud and glad, perhaps at the fact that they were now happy.

'Then Dad sat down to table and put me next to him and shouted out, "Now, Mother, give me and Fyedka our dinners; we're hungry." '

' "We are hungry" ' and ' "he put me next to him." ' What love and happy pride in love breathe in those words! There is nothing more charming or more heartfelt than this last scene in the whole charming story.

But what is it we are wanting to say by all this? What significance has this story, written by one, perhaps exceptional, boy, in a pedagogical context? People will say to us, 'Perhaps you, the teacher, helped him without yourself noticing it, in the composition of these and other stories, and it is too difficult to find the boundary between what is yours and what is original.' People will say to us, 'Assuming that the story *is* good, this is only one of the genres of literature.' They will say to us, 'Fyedka and the other boys whose compositions you have printed are a happy exception.' They will say to us, 'You are a writer yourself, without yourself realizing it you have helped the pupils in ways which cannot be prescribed as a rule for other teachers who are non-writers.' They will say to us, 'It is impossible to deduce any general rule or theory from all this. It is a phenomenon of some interest and nothing more.'

I will try to convey my deductions in such a way that they answer all these objections which I have supposed.

The instincts for truth, beauty and goodness are independent of the level of development. Beauty, truth and goodness are concepts which express only a harmony of relationships with regard to truth, beauty and goodness. A lie is simply a disharmony of relationships with regard to the actual; there is no such thing as absolute truth. I am not lying when I say that tables turn round at the touch of a finger if I believe it, although it is untrue; but I am lying when I say that I have no money if, according to my own ideas, I have some money. No enormous nose is hideous, but it is hideous on a small face. Hideousness is simply disharmony with regard to beauty. Giving your dinner to a beggar or eating it yourself has nothing bad about it in itself; but to give away or eat that dinner when your mother is dying of hunger is a disharmony of relationships with regard to goodness. When we train, educate, develop, or act in any way you please upon the child we must have and do have one aim unconsciously before us: to attain the greatest possible harmony with regard to truth, beauty and goodness. If time did not pass, if the child in all his aspects were not a living thing, we could attain that harmony without trouble by adding where there seems to us to be a lack and subtracting where there seems to us to be something superfluous. But the child lives, every side of his being strives to develop, one side overtaking another, and generally we assume that the very fact that these sides of his being are advancing is an objective and we promote mere development and not harmony of development. Therein lies the eternal mistake of all pedagogical theories. We see our ideal ahead when it lies behind us. The necessary development of a human being is not a means to the attainment of that ideal of harmony which we carry within ourselves, it is actually an obstacle, set by the Creator, to the attainment of the higher ideal of harmony. This necessary law of advancement is the meaning of the tree of the knowledge of good and evil which our first parent tasted. A healthy child is born into the world completely satisfying those demands of absolute harmony with regard to truth, beauty and goodness which we carry within ourselves; he is close to creatures not endowed with souls—to the plant, to the animal, to nature which constantly represents to us that truth, beauty and goodness which we seek and desire. In all ages and amongst all people the child has been regarded as an image of innocence, sinlessness, goodness, truth and beauty. Man is born perfect—such is the great proposition uttered by Rousseau, and this proposition remains as firm and true as a rock. At birth man represents the model of harmony, truth, beauty and goodness. But every hour of life, every minute of time increases the spaces, the magnitude and the time of those relationships which were in perfect harmony at the moment of his birth, and every step and every hour threatens to destroy that harmony, every succeeding step, every succeeding hour threatens a new destruction and gives no hope of reestablishing the harmony which was destroyed.

For the most part educators lose sight of the fact that the childhood stage is the original image of harmony and take the development of the child, which goes on independently in accordance with immutable laws, to be the objective. Development is erroneously taken to be the objective because the same thing happens to educators as to bad sculptors.

Instead of trying to halt a local exaggerated development or to halt the general development in order to await a new change, which would remove the wrong which has appeared, just as a bad sculptor, instead of scraping off what is superfluous, keeps laying on more and more, in the same way educators seem to be concerned about only one thing, that the process of development should not cease, and if they do think about harmony they always try to attain it by approaching a future image which we know nothing about, moving further away from the image which is in the present and past. However wrong the development of the child may have been, primitive features of harmony always remain in him still. By moderating or at least not encouraging development we may hope to make at least some approach towards correctness and harmony. But we are so sure of ourselves, devoted in so dream-like a way to the false ideal of adult perfection, so impatient with the imperfections which are near to us and so firmly convinced of our power to correct them, so little can we understand and value the primitive beauty of the child, that we rush as quickly as we can to exaggerate, to plaster over those imperfections which leap to our eyes, we correct, we train the child. Sometimes one side has to be brought level with another, sometimes the other has to be brought level with the first. People develop the child further and further, and draw further and further away from the former primitive image which has been destroyed, and the attainment of the imagined image of adult perfection grows more and more impossible. *Our ideal is behind and not in front*. Training corrupts human beings, it does not correct them. The more the child is corrupted the less he needs to be trained and the more he needs freedom.

To teach and train a child is impossible and senseless for the simple reason that the child stands nearer than I do, nearer than any adult does, to that ideal of harmony, of truth, beauty and goodness to which I in my pride wish to elevate him. The recognition of that ideal is stronger in him than in me. All he needs from me is material with which to complete himself in a harmonious and many-sided manner. As soon as I gave him complete freedom and stopped teaching him he wrote a poetical work which has had no equal in Russian literature. And therefore it is my conviction that we must not teach writing and composition, and artistic composition in particular, to children in general and to peasant children especially. All that we can do is to teach them how to set about composition.

If what I have done to attain this end can be called methods then those methods are as follows:

1. Suggest a very large and varied choice of subjects, not inventing them specially for children but suggesting the most serious subjects and the ones which most interest the teacher himself.
2. Give the children compositions by children to read and propose only compositions by children as models, for the compositions of children are always juster, more refined and more moral than the compositions of adults.
3. (Especially important.) When looking over children's compositions never make remarks to the pupils either about the tidiness of the exercise books or about handwriting or spelling or, above all, about the construction of the sentences and logic.

4. Since in writing the difficulty lies not in the length or content of the subject matter, but in the artistic nature of its theme, the step by step approach must apply not to the length or the content or the language but to the mechanics of the job, which consists, firstly, in choosing one out of the large number of thoughts and images which present themselves; secondly, in choosing words in which to clothe it; thirdly, in remembering it and choosing a place for it; fourthly, in remembering what you have written, not repeating yourself, leaving nothing out and knowing how to connect what is to come with what has gone before; fifthly, and finally, in being able to think and write it down at the same time without the one hindering the other. For this purpose I did the following: at first I would undertake some of these aspects of the work myself, gradually handing them over to be tackled by them. At first I would choose for them out of the thoughts and images which presented themselves those which seemed the best to me, remember them, point out a place for them and manipulate what was written so as to save them from repetitions, and I did the writing myself, leaving them to clothe the images and thoughts in words; then I left it to them to choose and manipulate what was written, and finally, as in the writing of a 'A soldier's life', they undertook the actual process of writing as well.

[6]

He feeds you with a spoon and pokes you in the eye with the handle: Makarov, Morozov and Tolstoy

First published in the April number of the supplementary series Yasnaya Polyana Booklets *(May 1862). The real name of 'Syomka' was Makarov; 'Fyedka', as we have mentioned, was Vasily Morozov. The manuscript has not survived. We have used as our text the facsimile reprint in* Tvorcheskie raboty uchenikov Tolstogo v Yasnoi Polyane, *ed. Thomas G. Winner (Brown University Slavic Reprint no. 10).*

There was once a big snowstorm. Then a woman got dressed and went out for water. She was carrying the buckets; she could scarcely drag her feet through the snow, and she could not see anything in front of her. Suddenly she stumbled against something on the doorstep and spilt some water; she was frightened and screamed. And her husband said through the window, 'What are you screaming for?'

And she said, 'Semyon, light a spill and come out right away; Lord knows what we've got lying on the doorstep.'

The man came out, looked it over and said, 'It's a man lying there, he must have got frozen.'

Then the woman said, 'Suppose I go and call for a neighbour; he'll have to be dragged away.'

Then the man said, 'No one would think you wore a cross.'

But the woman ran off to the neighbour's. The neighbour came and said, 'The man must have frozen to death. You mustn't touch him.'

And the neighbour's wife said, 'Perhaps he's just pretending on purpose.'

And the woman said, 'We must tell the elder; he'll report it to the constable.'

And the neighbour said, 'You just touch him and they'll take you to court straight away.'

But Semyon examined the man and felt him and saw that he was alive and said, 'Fine Christians you are—just look at you!'

He clasped the old man round the middle and dragged him into the cottage. And he said to his wife, 'Light a spill.'

The wife went to light a spill and grumbled to herself under her breath, 'He takes all sorts of beggars into the house.'

They laid him on the stove to thaw out; he started to stir and mutter something.

The husband went up to him and started to question him: 'Who are your folks, grandfather? Where are you from?'

But it was impossible to get anything out of the old man. The peasant ordered his wife to take his shoes off for him, and he took off the old man's sheepskin coat himself. The old coat was a poor one and frozen through—the sheepskins were bare of wool and worn thin. As soon as the peasant removed the old man's sheepskin the snow came off it in a shower, and underneath the sheepskin was a soldier's greatcoat, all patched together out of bits and pieces, and underneath the greatcoat was a torn shirt; you could see his body. The peasant took off the greatcoat and was surprised; he thought, 'With what he had on he was bound to get frozen,' and he said to his wife, 'Here, hang his greatcoat and sheepskin on the stove door over the rail; open the oven door so that they dry quicker, and come and take his shoes off.'

Then the woman snorted, snatched the clothes from his hands, and banged the oven door down upon the ground, so that the handle broke off. She went up to the old man and began to take off his shoes and almost wrenched his foot off. Suddenly the old man groaned, and said in such a quiet voice that only the man heard him 'Ouch! gently missus—I've got sores on my feet.'

The peasant shouted at her, 'Gently, you bitch! Oh good Lord, if it wasn't for me she'd be the death of him . . .'

It was all right while the birch-bark sandals were frozen, but when the steam came from them they grew soggy so that dirty water ran over her hands. The woman spat and tossed them over to her husband. The man picked them up and shook his head, saying, 'How come he didn't freeze to death? His feet must be like icicles now! Ah, there are lots and lots of wretched people in this world!'

And he undid the old man's foot-cloths and put them in the drying-box, and threw the soggy sandals into the main stove, and he moved the old man's feet into the middle, took off his own fur coat and put it on him. The old man lying on the stove just grunted 'Oh Lord! O-o-oh!'

The wife put on a kaftan and walked towards the door, and the man said, 'Are you off to the neighbour's again?'

She said, 'I'm going into the yard.'[1]

She slammed the door so that even the lintel shook. But she had deceived her husband; she slammed the yard door, came back and ran out into the street and to her neighbour's. She got to the neighbour's and said, breathless, 'Neighbour, come and talk my old fool round. He's taken in some stinking soldier. He takes them in and expects me to take their shoes off! You ought to see what those sandals were like! It's enough to make you sick, honest!'

And the neighbour said, 'Anyone can see he's gone crazy! How can he do a thing like that? Suppose he dies? You just see, you'll get no good of this.'

And the woman got still more frightened; she even shed tears and said, 'He'll be the ruin of our house; come, neighbour, and talk him round.'

But the neighbour said, 'Blow him! He cursed me properly not long ago and wouldn't listen, and now he'll turn me out of his house altogether. I'm not coming.'

But the woman kept on at him endlessly, and started to kiss his hands. 'Come along, dear neighbour, for God's sake—just think of your poor godson.'

The neighbour put on a woman's fur coat and set off, saying, 'Maybe I'll bring him round somehow, and if I can't I'll give him a piece of my mind and be off.'

Meanwhile the peasant was sitting at table, propping his grey beard on his hand. In the cottage you could just hear the old man moaning, and the boy, Seryozhka, on the shelf above the stove, muttering in his sleep (he was dreaming of a game), 'Catch it, lads, catch the bitch!' and the lambs in the chest[2] calling, 'Baa! baa!' The man remembered about his wife, and thought the storm must have carried her to their neighbour's house again.

'Oh, the wretched woman! One of these days I'll throttle her! She didn't even let the lambs out to go to their mothers. If she'd had to do with Savoska that's dead and gone he would have torn her hair out long ago.'

He sat there and sat there, scratching his head and said 'There we are, perhaps she really does have a feeling that there's trouble brewing. Really there might be something . . . suppose I have a look in the old man's bag to see if there are any papers.' He rose, picked up the old man's bag and began to look at what was in it; he saw that there were two books, a thin one and a thick one.

Then the peasant said, 'The thin one must be a reading-book and this one must be a psalter. Looks like the old man can read.'

He started to turn over the leaves in the thick book and came across a paper with a seal. He was pleased and said, 'This here paper'll be the one all right.'

He turned the paper over and over in his hands, but he could not make it out, and he said, 'Now if my Seryozhka could read he'd jump up sharp, snatch the paper out of my hands, and tell me who this old man is.'

He put the paper back at the same page where he had found it and began to look through the bag once more. He found a rag, unrolled it and found eight half-kopecks, one old quarter-kopeck piece and a medal.

Then the man said, 'Perhaps he's been robbed somewhere. We've come to such a pass nowadays, that as soon as anyone turns up with just a trifle of money he's murdered straight away; you can be done for less than tuppence. Oh Lord above! save us all from evil men!'

He sighed, wrapped everything up again in the rag as it had been before and sat down on the bench. No sooner had he sat down than he heard someone make the door creak. And he said, 'That must be my giddy woman coming.'

The man was about to say, 'Well, then, have you had enough gadding about, you bitch?' Suddenly the neighbour came in. The neighbour entered, sat down on a chest and said 'What's this you're doing against your own household, Semyon? What have you taken on an old man for?'

Semyon just said, 'Ah, you're a godless lot!'

But the neighbour said, 'We'll see about godless. You just see what will happen to you because of him.'

Semyon said, 'Do you want me to throw him out into the street?'

The neighbour said, 'Now look here, mate, you'll have any

amount of suffering on his account. First of all they'll have you up at the local station, after that to the district, from the district they'll send you to the town, and from the town to the Police Court. There they'll write you down on a paper and pack you off to gaol, and there you'll stay till you die. It might be another matter if he had papers, but he might be one of these chaps without a pass.'

But the peasant said, 'Well, what will be will be; even if the tsar himself punishes me, I have said I won't abandon the old man.'

But his wife really started to howl, and said, 'It's no use, neighbour, you won't shift him; he's been like that all his life. Seems he wants to set out with his little children and a beggar's pouch. If only he'd have pity on his son. Oh Lord!'

And the neighbour said, 'But really, you ought to look in his bag and see if there are papers in it, at least we could find out who the man is.'

And the peasant said, 'I found a book in his bag, and in the book there was a paper with a seal; perhaps that's it.'

So the neighbour sent off to his uncle to send Vanyushka to work out the paper. Vanyushka came and began to read the paper, and the peasant said to his wife, 'What are you fidgeting about for? You'd better fetch a candle, it's as black as pitch here.'

But the neighbour said, 'It doesn't matter; he's a young chap, he can read it without.'

They began to read and they discovered that he was a discharged soldier coming from the Caucasus, and he had been in a lot of battles, and had got two medals as a reward from the tsar, and had been wounded three times.

The neighbour said, 'There'll be trouble if he dies, even if he has got papers. Look here, neighbour! Did you hear what happened to a peasant in the village of Yagodnaya? He took in a beggar just the same, and that beggar died. They argued it and argued it in the court, and sent him off to gaol, and so he rotted there for the sake of a beggar. You won't get away with it either.'

Semyon thought a bit and then said, 'Be off out of my place; go away please.'

And the neighbour said to Semyon, 'You'll be no mate of mine after this!' He put on his cap and said, 'Goodbye missus,' and left.

The wife started to cry and say, 'Oh my poor little bairn, Seryozhka! O-o-oh! We're all done for . . . and we're going to wander through the world to beg our bread and our house will be ruined.' And she went on wailing for a long time.

Then Semyon said, 'That's enough of your howling; get the supper, I'm hungry.'

His wife grumbled to herself, 'May you choke on the first morsel.' and went to dish up the soup. Then she carried on as if she was crazy, rattling away with the pot-holder and chucking the logs on. When she stuck the pot-holder into the stove she spilt the soup. She drew out the empty pot and hurled it to the ground so that the fragments were dashed into little bits.

Semyon said, 'You guzzle away! You're like a pig in a trough, but you don't want to dirty your hands.'

Then Semyon got off the bench and went to see if he could find something to eat; he rummaged around and found Seryozhka's porridge in a dish in the oven, and ate it. Then he went up to the old man to see whether he was still alive. And the old man had thawed out and was asleep in a sprawl. Then he went and made up his own bed and lay down under the step; he put on his fur coat, and put his wife's kaftan under his head. He was only just falling asleep when his wife snatched the kaftan from under his head, so that he struck his head against the bench. Then he said, 'God bless my soul, what a curse you are!' and did not swear at her any more than that.

He felt underneath the step to see if there was anything that he could use as a head-rest, and found there the old foot-cloths and put them under his head, and began to fall asleep. Suddenly he had a dream that an old goat came to him, and the goat's feet were covered in sores, and it was something like the old man and something like a goat. The goat said, 'Thank you, Semyon, for saving my life. Because you saved me I will do you a good turn.' He felt so sorry for the goat. And suddenly he saw his wife climb down from the stove, sit astride the goat, seize it by the horns and force its head backwards towards the spine. Semyon felt still more sorry for the goat; he shouted, 'Stop it!' And it seemed Seryozhka started howling and saying, 'Mummy, there's no reason for it, don't beat the goat! I feel sorry for it!' The peasant woke up and said, 'Good Lord, what have I been dreaming of!' He turned over on his side, scratched his back and said, 'It's time I had a steambath or my back will be really itchy. I expect it's even worse for the old man.' And he soon fell asleep again.

In the cottage everything fell quiet; there was only the peasant and his wife snoring, and Seryozhka exclaiming 'Ah!' in his sleep, and cockroaches falling off the sleeping shelf, and the sheep coughing because of the heat, and stamping their hoofs and looking for something to drink. And outside the snow-storm had grown still, it had turned frosty; the moon was shining. The watchman was walking down the street over the snow, scrunching it and rapping on the gates with his truncheon.

In the morning the old man was conscious before anyone else and began to look around him for his foot-cloths and sandals, and wondered whether they were in the stove-drawer. He bent down and began to feel for them; he could not reach, because the stove-drawers were low down. He bent down lower. The hook flew off and the old man fell off the stove, so that the lambs and their mothers scattered and stared. The lambs looked at him and thought someone was teasing them; they grew bolder and started to jump over the old man. Then the peasant awoke and saw the old man lying in the middle of the cottage. He helped him up, sat him on the bench and said, 'What's up, grandfather, did you hurt yourself?'

And the old man said, 'It's nothing. I'm better now.'

The old man felt a bit fresher than the day before. Meanwhile Seryozhka had woken up and was staring at the old man from his bunk and thinking, there was no such person in our house yesterday. Then the old man said, 'Little boy, don't be afraid of me—come here and I'll give you a kopeck.' The old man got the rag out of his bag, picked out a quarter-kopeck and offered it to him. Seryozhka took the quarter-kopeck and kept looking at it. The peasant said, 'Aren't you hungry, grandfather?'

'Give me something then, good man; God will not forget you.'

The peasant cut a slice, put salt on it and gave it to him. And Seryozhka said, 'Grandfather, shall I fetch you some water, or some bread and milk?'

'There's a good boy—bring some in the name of God.'

The old man broke his bread and began to eat. The wife stoked up the stove and went to the pond to wash napkins, and the peasant went off to feed the stock, and dropped in at the neighbour's for a gossip. Meanwhile Seryozhka lost his shyness and hung around by the old man, very glad, and kept giving him things to eat—he fetched him potatoes and showed him where the milk was in the pit and said, 'Help yourself, grandfather.'

But the old man said, 'Thank you my boy, I don't want any. It would be better if your father or mother gave it to me.' Then the wife and husband arrived and began to prepare dinner. The peasant said, 'Akulina, give us some cabbage soup. Come along now, sit down, grandfather.'

The old man could scarcely drag himself round the bench to the table, like a little child. The wife saw that he was sitting next to her husband; she drew in her breath and even ground her teeth and said, 'Let's collect some more beggars, there's plenty of those devils wandering over the face of the earth. You can't shelter them all. You'd do better to buy a new door for the stove.'

But her husband said, 'You broke it yourself; you buy it. Sell some cloth and buy one.'

But the woman said, 'And what'll you do for shirts, devil take you?'

She lost her temper and did not sit down to dinner.

And the peasant said, 'The thicker the lips, the thinner the belly',[3] and they started to abuse one another again. The old man felt embarrassed and he started to leave the table. But Seryozhka dipped a spoon in and carried it to his mouth, saying, 'Eat it, grandfather', and spilt it all over his beard, and it even splashed down inside his shirt. The old man said, 'Oh good grief, there's kindness for you!'

They ate cabbage soup and potatoes. The peasant said, 'Akulina, pour out some milk.'

The old man made as if to go away. But Seryozhka grabbed him by the finger and shouted, 'Grandfather, milk, milk!'

The wife fetched a small cupful, put it in front of Seryozhka and said, 'Stuff yourself, you little devil, burst your sides!' and she bent down to Seryozhka and whispered and threatened him with her finger and said, 'Just you watch it, if you give it to that old devil I'll whip the hide off your back.'

As soon as her back was turned Seryozhka seized the cup, stood on the bench and started to pour it right into the old man's mouth. 'Drink it quick, grandfather, or Mum will beat me.'

Half the milk ended up in his mouth, and half on his beard, his shirt and the ground. The old man only mumbled; his mouth was full. A crumb stuck in his throat; he belched, and felt still more embarrassed. And the peasant roared with laughter and said, 'Well done, Seryozhka, don't forget the old folks.' And Seryozhka burst out laughing at the old man.

Even the wife almost started to laugh, and said to herself,

'He's been well and truly stuffed, he has, the mucky, ragged beggarman.' And she almost burst with laughing.

And the old man rose from the table; he even sighed and sat down to one side of the stove, covered his face with his hands and said nothing.

Summer came. The old man's strength had grown greater. And the peasant said, 'Grandfather, go and guard the horses.'

The old man was glad to be sent to do some work. He took the thin little ABC book, mounted the grey and rode off. Only Seryozhka woke up and shouted out, 'Grandfather, get me down from the sleeping-shelf—I'll fall.' And his mother said:

'See what the little devil's got used to!'

And his father laughed. 'Say goodbye, Seryozhka, your grandfather's gone.' And he got out a kopeck piece of his own and gave it to him and said, 'That's for you. Grandfather left it for you because you gave him milk to drink.'

When Seryozkha snatched at the kopeck piece to put it under the bench it rolled beneath the floor boards with a ringing noise. He jumped up and wanted to run after the old man, but he did not know which way to run and shouted out, 'Grandfather's gone! Grandfather!'

And the peasant was afraid; he thought, 'Heaven knows where he'll run to,' and he said, 'Seryozkha, don't run away; here's that grandfather of yours; he's hiding from you deliberately in the chest.' Seryozhka turned round and rushed to the chest, opened it and looked in; there was nothing but bread in it. And cockroaches were running over the bread. Didn't he just yell at the top of his voice 'Grandfather! grandfather!' And his father felt sorry for him, and said, 'That will do. Shall I tell you where grandfather is?'

'Yes, tell me.'

'He's watching the horses.'

'Dad, take me there.' But his father said:

'Do you know where your mate Vanka watched them? Do you know Puzikov Heights?'

'Yes, I know. Give me a lump of porridge', he said, 'and I'll take it to him.'

He put the lump inside his shirt, took a knife and scampered off as fast as his legs would carry him. His father watched him till he was like a little black gnat in the distance. 'See', he said, 'how used to him he's grown. There's no parting them.'

Seryozhka came running up to Puzikov Heights out of breath.

And grandfather caught sight of him and said, 'Ah, my dear boy!' and kissed him.

Seryozhka got out the porridge, laid it on a handkerchief and said, 'Here, grandfather, cut it up, and carve a whistle for me.'

'Very well, my dear, I will, I will.'

The old man ate the porridge, took the ABC book and began to read. Seryozhka was surprised and said, 'Grandfather, who are you talking to?'

'I am saying prayers.'

Seryozhka made as if to snatch at the book and pull it over to himself. 'What's that? What's that?'

But the old man said, 'That's a sin, Seryozhka, a sin. Don't touch; that's reading. The priest will cut your ear off and you'll cry.'

'Well, I'll hide in the chest, where you were.'

'God will find you out there too and drag you out by the leg.'

'Well, where is he? God, I mean.'

'He's standing here with us right now.' Seryozhka was surprised and fell silent; then he said, 'I know what, I'll do some talking with the print . . .'

'All right then, I'll teach you.'

The old man showed him the big words, sharpened a stick and started to point things out and say, 'Say after me—az, buki[4]—well say it then. Az, Seryozhka, learn it.'

But Seryozhka was afraid even to touch the book; he drew back. The old man gave him the pointer and said, 'Take it.' But Seryozhka was afraid of that too and frowned and said, 'What about that priest, grandfather? Will he cut my ear off?'

And the old man said, 'That's if you're naughty; the priest will take you by the ear like this, and it will hurt.'

Seryozhka learned one line by heart. The sun was low by then. And the old man said, 'Let's go, Seryozhka.'

The old man started to try to catch the horse, but the horse would not let him. Seryozhka shouted, 'Grandfather! grandfather! He'll kill you, and then who shall I learn my ABC from?'

The old man caught the horse, mounted and said, 'Give me your hand.'

And Seryozhka said, 'Don't drop it. . . Az, buki, vedi.' Seryozhka kept repeating them as he rode. Other children came riding by on horses and shouted, 'Hey, Seryozhka, what are you doing?'

But *he* kept on gabbling his ABC. They said, 'What's this?'

And he said, 'I'm learning to read.'

Then they arrived. Seryozhka was still repeating az buki. His father was surprised and said, 'That's it, Seryozhka, well done. I'll buy you a ring-bun; only why did you throw the kopeck away? It's rolled under the floor.'

Seryozhka said, 'That's az and that's buki.'

They had supper and went to bed, and Seryozhka was still babbling, 'Az, buki' and shouted, 'Grandfather, give me the pointer . . . Come and read, Mitka, or the priest will cut your ear off.'

He got up early in the morning and said,'I know what, Dad, shall I teach you to read?'

And his father said, 'All right, teach me.'

And Seryozhka said, 'Say after me: az'.

And the peasant said, 'Vlas.'[5]

Seryozhka just burst out into a roar at his father and shook with laughter. Seryozhka said, 'Say buki'.

And his father said: 'Ruki' [Hands].

Seryozhka said: 'Vedi.'

And his father said, 'Breden' [Drag-net].

And Seryozhka shouted, 'Grandfather, Dad can't talk.'

Autumn came. Semyon had not sent the old man away. One day Semyon went to town to buy corn. And his wife bought white bread and vodka and put on the samovar and invited the neighbour in. And she said to herself, 'What am I to do about that old man? He'll tell my husband everything for sure.' So she said, 'Yemelyanych, what are you lying about like that for? Go and keep an eye on the foal with the white legs; it's a contrary runaway horse; it'll be off somewhere in a minute.'

But grandfather's back was hurting him. He said nothing to her but just groaned aloud, 'Oh Lord above!'

The woman said, 'You eat our bread and you don't want to see to things. Seems you're a man when it comes to eating and a boy when it comes to working.'

The old man just drew on his sheepskin and said, 'I would go, but I haven't the strength today; there's bad weather coming on; my back is aching.'

But the woman got still angrier and said, 'It doesn't ache when you eat, but it aches when you walk.'

The old man started to climb down from the stove; he accidentally brushed against a pot and knocked it over. When the woman saw that she screamed at him still louder, 'Oh you stinking devil! It's quite clear you do it on purpose. I daresay that was why they threw you out of the army, because you were such a lazy scrounger.'

The old man thought, 'I don't want a scene with the woman.' He took his greatcoat and went into the porch to put it on.

Just as he was struggling with his coat in the porch it caught against a samovar in the darkness; the samovar fell over, the tap broke and the water poured out. The old man simply did not know what to do. When the woman heard that the old man had knocked the samovar over she was quite beside herself with fury, and sprang out through the door and started to pick it up. When she shoved his shoulder he banged his head against the lintel of the door. And the woman said, 'Confound you, you damned beggar! You eat our bread and do these things to us on purpose.'

The old man did not go out to the horses, but put on his greatcoat and went back into the cottage. He said nothing to the woman, but fetched his bag and began to pack all his things into it. The books were underneath the ikons. He bent over to get them across the table. The woman started back from before him. The old man found his psalter and put it in the bag, and placed his ABC books beside it. And the woman started to peel some vegetables as if she could not see him, but she was thinking to herself, 'What's he up to; let's be sure he doesn't pinch anything of ours.'

The neighbour arrived and said, 'What's up, grandfather, are you poorly?'

And the old man said, 'What's that?'

'What are you shaking all over for?'

The old man did not start talking to him; he put on his belt,crossed himself, slung his bag upon his back, took the ABC book in his hands and began to pray before the ikons.

And the neighbour said, 'Where are you off to, grandfather?'

The old man said nothing. Then the neighbour said, 'See here, missus, you're going to be in hot water from Semyon over this.'

And the woman said, 'For the sake of a stinking beggar, and he'll beat me too. It makes no odds.'

And the old man bowed to them and said, 'Thank you for all your courtesy,' and he left the cottage.

And the woman jumped up and went into the porch to see

where the old man would go. Seryozhka was playing with some lads in the street. When he saw grandfather he jumped up and said, 'Where are you going, grandfather? Take me with you.'

But the old man took hold of him, kissed him and said, 'Goodbye, my dear, I am going home. Here is the ABC book for you, Seryozhka, it is a present from me.'

Seryozhka burst into tears, grabbed grandfather by the coat and would not let him go. But the woman sprang forward, seized Seryozhka's hand and said, 'Fancy crying about a beggar.' And as she tugged at him she said 'Let him go or you'll be stinking yourself.'

But Seryozhka sobbed and said, 'Why are you going, grandfather?'

And the old man said, 'I am going because they fed me with a spoon and poked me in the eye with the handle.'

The woman pulled Seryozhka away and took him into the cottage, and the old man hobbled along the side of the street. Seryozhka climbed up on to his sleeping-shelf and sobbed all evening without stopping. The woman began to drink vodka with the neighbour. They had a drink, and the neighbour said, 'And what will you say to Semyon when he asks about the old man?'

And the woman said, 'I shall say he has gone to the devil. So long as he doesn't meet him. Who's going to tell him?'

Suddenly they heard someone arriving. The woman hid the vodka bottle. The peasant unharnessed the horse, came into the cottage, looked around and said, 'Where is Amelyanych then? Or hasn't he come home yet?'

And the woman said, 'God knows where he's got to. He lay around and lay around and then went off somewhere . . .'

So the peasant hung his hat on the hook, took his belt off, sat down at the table and said, 'Seryozhka, hey Seryozhka! Come over here and see what I've brought you from town.'

And he took a mug out of his shirt. Seryozhka came up to his father, and he was crying.

Father said, 'What's the matter?'

And he said, 'Grandfather's gone away.'

'Why has he gone away?'

'Mum drove him away.'

And the woman said, 'It was high time he was gone.'

The peasant then asked, 'What did he say when he was leaving?'

'He said he was leaving because you had fed him with a spoon and poked him in the eye with the handle.' And he broke down and cried, and would not take the mug. Semyon lost his temper; he even shook all over, and said, 'You've brought trouble on yourself now, you bitch! You've disgraced my house, damn you!'

And the neighbour began to beg him, 'Leave her alone. Forgive her; she won't do it again.'

And the peasant then shouted, 'Get out of my house! Don't let me catch you here again! No one's going to tell me what's right between me and my own wife.'

The neighbour left. And the peasant sat down to supper. But Seryozhka was so frightened that he would not get down from the stove, and he stopped crying.

The End

[7]

The life of a soldier's wife

This translation is based on a manuscript in the Tolstoy Museum in Moscow, to which we are indebted for a photocopy. The handwriting is neither Morozov's nor Tolstoy's. Probably it is that of a member of Tolstoy's entourage who was given the task of tidying up Morozov's manuscript for the press. Since Morozov's manuscript has disappeared the copy is the nearest available to what he actually wrote. It differs only very slightly from the text published in the Yasnaya Polyana booklet *for September. Tolstoy dates the story '1 July 1862'.*

In 1875 Tolstoy reprinted the story in one of his readers for Russian children. By then his respect for the unerring natural taste of his pupil had been modified, for he cut the story by more than a third of the original length and altered many details.

The farthest back I can remember, I was about six; we were poor and lived on the edge of the village. There were my father, my mother, my grandmother and my sister. I remember, as if in a dream, how my grandmother loved me more than my mother did. She used to go around in an old white robe and a shabby check skirt, and she had an old linen rag round her head. Whenever I started running off anywhere she would say, 'Mind you don't hurt yourself, Fyedya!' My mother was a meek woman. Father often used to wallop her when he came in drunk. She used to weep a few tears and say nothing. She wore a calico kerchief, went barefoot in summer and wore bark sandals in winter.

My father was about thirty; he was of middle height, thickset, with a broad chest. His beard was small; he wore a short blue jacket. On his head he wore a post-driver's cap. I was afraid of him; when I got up to mischief he gave me a good hiding and swore at me. When he began to hit me I would go running straight up to my grandmother; she would protect me.

My sister was always excitable. When something really excited me I always went to my big sister to let off steam.

For as far back as I can remember our cottage had been in a

tumbledown way; we held it up with props. The cottage had been cramped anyway, and when it was propped up it became still worse. Then I remember me and my mate Tarasok climbing up on to a support. Grandmother said to me, 'Don't you climb on the support, you young devils, or you'll knock the cottage down.' Tarasok and I went into the yard birdnesting. I was daring enough for anything; I caught hold of the fence and jumped right over it. Then I caught hold of a stick with both hands and wanted to climb up some more—the stick broke and I went flying head over heels. It just happened there was a shaft lying there. When I fell off I hit my cheek right against the shaft and yelled blue murder. And that mark is still there on my cheek.

The yard was crowded and open at one end and had heaps of rotten straw in it here and there. In the yard there was only one miserable old lop-sided horse. We had no cow; there were two wretched little sheep and one lamb. I always slept with that lamb; he used to make me all greasy. We ate dry bread and drank water; we had no one to do the work; my mother was pregnant and kept complaining about her stomach. Grandmother was always near the stove, and always had a headache. The only one who worked was my sister, and that was not for the family, but on her own account—she was buying herself fine clothes and preparing to get married. As for my father, it went without saying—whatever he earned, he drank.

I remember old Nefed coming to us—he was the village elder—and starting to curse my father for something. I just heard Nefed say: 'Everyone's paid the tax money; you're the only one who hasn't.[1] Look out for yourself, Gordyushka, my lad, the meeting will be called and they'll send you for a soldier.'[2] I heard him mention a pillow.[3] I was sorry they were going to have my father shot. I snatched up my own pillow, put it on the elder's knees and said, 'Here you are, here's a pillow, only don't send my father for a soldier.' Everyone burst out laughing. The elder said, 'You see, Gordei, whatever you earn, you drink, but your son looks after you so, he'll even give up his last pillow for you.' My father threw up his hand and went out into the yard. And grandmother said to the elder, 'That's just what he wants; to leave his family and his house and not think about anything.'

My father was not at all afraid, and I remember that he went on going to the tavern.

A month later the elder called a village meeting. A lot of people came to our yard, and people began to shout something. 'He ought to be sent for a soldier.' My mother was standing beside the people, crying. I went up to her and said, 'Ma, what are you crying about?'

My mother caught me in her arms and started to cry harder, and said, 'You're not sorry for him, and they want to send him for a soldier.'

Then they sent old Yefim to fetch my father. Old Yefim brought him along drunk. I said, 'Ma, what will he do there?'

Mother said to me, 'The soldiers will bayonet him.'

I felt sorry. I took and started to cry. Old Nefed looked at my father and said, 'Well, what's your judgement?'

The people shouted, 'Make him a soldier!'

My father threw up his hand again and said, 'That's just what I need, only don't forget my son.'

Then a cart came up to us; they put my father in the cart and drove off. My mother clung round my father's neck and started to cry. The cart set off gently; my mother and my mother's sister Agafya and old Tatyana walked after the cart, and they were all crying. And I was sitting on my father's knees. So we got as far as the church; my father and the relations prayed, and he made me get out of the cart. We said goodbye; my mother and relations just burst out sobbing and cried all the way.

So we arrived home; grandmother was sitting by the window crying, and my mother flopped down on a bench and went on sobbing right up to dinner-time. Grandmother began to soothe my mother and said, 'That's enough now, Matryona. What can you do about it?'—but she was sighing herself—'It seems it is God's will. After all, you are still young; God may yet bring him back to see you again. But at my time of life I am always ailing, in no time at all I shall be dead.'

My mother said, 'Oh mother! I do feel bad! I do feel bad!' and she burst out sobbing.

And grandmother said, 'Well, what are we to do now? There's no getting him back, you know!'

My sister was sitting crying by the step too; her eyes were red with tears.

So we started a poor sort of life, three times worse than when my father was there—nothing to eat, the sheep were sold to buy bread, and they sold my pretty little lamb; all we had left was the lop-sided mare, and she had broken a leg.

After my father had been sent for a soldier, a month later my mother had a baby. Grandmother went out to fetch a woman.

Then she borrowed some groats from her father-in-law and sent her son to get a priest. Then she stoked up the stove and began to cook porridge. My sister went to collect people for the christening. She fetched the people and a cottage-loaf apiece, and they sat down on the benches. Our relations began to set out the tables and cover them with cloths. Everything was ready and the benches had been fetched. We all sat down in our places; the priest arrived and read from a book. The boy was passed over to him and a tub of water was set down. All of a sudden he plunged the boy into the water.

I thought he wanted to drown him and shouted out, 'Give the boy here!'

But grandmother made as if to hit me and said, 'Don't shout or he'll hit you!'

I fell silent. And he plunged him in three times, and then gave him to Auntie Akulina. My aunt wrapped him up in muslin and gave him to mother.

Then we all sat down to table; grandmother placed the two bowls of porridge on the table and served people with it. Everyone began to eat. When everyone had eaten their fill they got up from the table, thanked grandmother and all left.

I went up to mother and said, 'Ma, what's his name?'

Mother said, 'Same as yours.'[4]

The boy was thin; he had puny little legs and kept on screaming.

Mother said, 'Lord, when will that brat be dead?'

A week passed. Grandmother said, 'Well, thank God, that's the christening over.' But the boy was doing worse and worse all the time.

At midnight mother started crying for some reason. Grandmother got up and said, 'What's the matter? Christ be with you!'

Mother said, 'My son is dead.'

Grandmother lit a lamp, washed the boy, dressed him in a shirt, girded him up and placed him beneath the ikons. When dawn came my grandmother went to old Nefed's and told him. Old Nefed arrived with some planks and began to make a coffin. He made the little coffin and laid the boy in it. Then my mother sat down and began to keen and wail in a thin voice, and went on wailing for a long time. Then old Nefed took the boy and carried him off to be buried.

The only rejoicing we had was when we gave my sister to be married. A husband called Kondrashka was found for her. So they came courting, and brought a loaf of white bread and a lot of vodka, and all sat down at a table, and mother sat down too. Then old Ivan poured some vodka into a glass and brought it to my mother; mother drank it. Then he sliced some bread and gave it to mother.

I was standing by the table, and I did so want a bit of bread. I bent mother down and spoke into her ear. Mother burst out laughing, and old Ivan said, 'What does he want, a bit of bread?' and went and cut me off a big piece. I took the bread and went off into the store-room.

Then old Ivan poured some more out into a glass and took it to my mother. Mother said, 'No, no more for me.'

But old Ivan insisted; mother took it and drank it down. When everyone had gone out, old Ivan said, 'Well, tomorrow we'll begin.'

Mother said, 'All right,' and he went home.

I got up early next morning; I saw my sister dressed up in her new shoes and a nice kerchief and a new fur coat. Then I saw that mother was also dressed up nice and was stoking up the stove, and Kiryushka's mother was washing beef. When the cottage was warmed up a lot of people came to see us, a whole houseful. Then I saw three troikas coming, and the bridegroom Kondrashka in a new kaftan and a tall cap, and he drove right into our yard. Straight away the bridegroom got out of the cart and then came into the cottage. Then they brought my sister out, and the groom took her by the hand. They were made to sit at the table, and the women began to recite the greetings,[5] and went on for a long time reciting them. Then they left the table, said a prayer, went into the yard and went up to the troika. Kondrashka took my sister and made her sit in the cart, and got into the other one himself. When they had all taken their places they crossed themselves and set off.

I went out into the street and watched; they galloped away to the church and disappeared from sight. Then I went into the cottage, and mother gave me a piece of bread. Then I sat down by the window and waited for them to come, and said, 'Mum, when is my sister coming?'

Then I heard someone shout, 'The wedding party's coming!'

I was delighted, and went out to have a look; I saw a lot of people standing by the porch playing a song which went, 'Why were you so long a-coming?' Then they drove into the yard again. The bridegroom got out and helped my sister out, and they went into the cottage.

They were going to sit down at the table, but people were at the table, and I was sitting there with a rolling pin. Then Uncle Gerasim said, 'Get up from the table.'

I felt afraid and wanted to be off. Grandmother said 'You show him the rolling pin and say, "What's this then?" and he'll give you some money.'[6]

Gerasim said, 'I'll hit you with my whip!'

'And I'll hit you with the rolling pin,' I said.

Then Gerasim poured out a glass of vodka and put some money in it and handed it to me. I drank it down and took out the money, and served vodka to everyone; the other people stood up and they sat down.

Then people started to play songs and dance. Mother gave me some beef. Then they served Uncle Gerasim with some vodka. He drank a little and said, 'It's bitter!'[7]

My sister took Kondrashka by the ears and they began to kiss. And they went on playing for a long time. When they had done playing and everyone had gone the bridegroom took my sister home. And mother said, 'Now we are ruined and done for!'

A year passed; we did not have anything to eat at all. So my mother went and begged some flour from the village elder, and each month they used to give us two poods[8] of flour. Half a year later my grandmother began to be very ill, and lay on her bed saying, 'Now I shall never see Gordei', and kept on crying. Then she would say 'God be with him', and said to my mother, 'If he comes—and God grant it—don't quarrel with him.'

A month later my grandmother died; only my mother was left. They laid grandmother out beneath the ikons; my mother sat down beside her and started to cry. I remember my mother crying beside her and saying, 'O my dear mother, who will care for your wretched child now? What am I to do now? How can I take counsel? How shall I live out my life?'[9] And my mother went on crying like this for a long time.

They brought a coffin and started to lay grandmother in it. The priest was sent for. The priest came, recited the dead-mass and she was carried off to be buried. My mother went too and cried all the way. When grandmother had been buried my mother came back, and I saw that she was so pale. Just the two of us remained, mother and I, and for a long time we lived in poverty.

And now six years had passed since the time when my father had been sent for a soldier; I was twelve years old.

One day mother sent me out to feed the lop-sided mare. I

watched over it for a long time. Soldiers were going past. Then I saw a soldier coming who was like my father; he came up to me and said:

'Where are you from?'

I said, 'From Yasnaya.'

'Well now, do you know Matryona Shintyakova?'

I said, 'Yes.'

'Hasn't she got married?'

'No.'

Then I asked, 'And would you have seen my father in the army? His name is Gordei Shintyakov.'

'Yes, I have. We were in the same regiment, and the colonel didn't half beat him.'

As soon as I heard this I felt sorry and began to cry. Then I noticed tears running down the soldier's cheeks; he started crying too. So I took him to our house. He prayed[10] and said, 'How d'ye do?' Then he took his coat off and sat down on the chest and started to look hard at everything. Then he said, 'Well now, is this all the family you've got?'

My mother said, 'That's all.'

At that the soldier began to weep and said, 'Where's my mother then?'

Mother ran up to my father and said, 'Your mother died a long time ago.'

I ran up and started to kiss my father. My father was weeping, but in spite of that I started looking at everything that was in his packs and his pockets. In the pack I found two nice medals and slipped them inside my shirt. Then people arrived and kissed my father. Father stopped crying and looked at the people and just could not recognize them. Then my sister came along and kissed my father. Father said, 'Which is this young woman?'

Mother burst out laughing and sad, 'He's a fine one; he doesn't know his own daughter.'

Father called her over to him again and kissed her again and asked mother how long she had been married.

Mother said, 'A long time now.'

Then all the folk went home, only my sister stayed. Mother started to stoke up the stove and cook an omelette, and sent my sister out for a pint of vodka. The liquor was brought in and put on the table.

Father said, 'What's this?'

My sister said, 'It's vodka for you.'

Father said, 'No, I've stopped drinking now.'

Mother said, 'Now thank Heaven that you've stopped.'

Then the omelette was served up. Father said a prayer and sat down to table. I sat down next to him; my sister sat on the chest, and Mother stood by the table and looked at Father and said, 'Just fancy, you've got younger! You've no beard.'

Everybody began to laugh. When we had had supper my sister kissed Father again and went off home. Then Father began to rummage in his pack, and Mother and I watched. Then Mother caught sight of a book in it and said, 'Learnt to read, have you?'

Father said, 'That I have.'

Then Father took out a big bundle and gave it to Mother.

'What's this?' says Mother.

'Money,' says Father.

My mother was glad, and hastened, she put it away safe. Then my mother came back and said, 'Where did you get it from?'

Father said, 'I was an officer[11] and had the army money. I gave it out to the soldiers and there was some left, so I took it.'

My mother was so glad she was running about like mad. The day was over by now; evening was coming on. A lamp was lit. My father took up the book and began to read. I sat beside him and listened, and Mother shone the lamp on to it. And my father read the book for a long time. Then we went to bed. I lay down on the back bench with my father, and my mother lay at our feet, and they were talking for a long time, almost till midnight. Then we went to sleep.

In the morning my mother got up, went up to my father and said, 'Up you get, Gordei, we need firewood for the stove.' Dad got up, put on his boots and cap and said, 'Got an axe?'

Mother said, 'Yes, but it's jagged, maybe it won't chop.'

My father took the axe firmly in both hands, went up to the block, set it upright and hit it with all his might and split the block in two; he chopped up the wood and brought it into the cottage. Mother set about stoking up the stove; she filled it right up and it gave out a good glow. When it was glowing nicely my father says:

'Matryona!'

My mother came up and said, 'Well, what is it?'

Father said, 'I'm thinking of buying a cow, five lambs, two horses and a cottage—this one's falling down, you know—so it'll come to about a hundred and fifty roubles in all.'

Mother seemed to ponder then she said, 'Then we shall run through the money.'

Father said, 'We shall work.'

My mother said, 'Well, all right, we'll buy it, but I'll tell you what—where do we get the framework?'

Father said, 'Hasn't Kiryukha got one then?'

My mother said, 'That's just it, he hasn't. The Fokanichevs have grabbed it.'

Father thought for a bit and said, 'Well, we'll get one from Bryantsev.'

My mother said, 'I'd be surprised if he's got one either.'

Father said, ' 'Course he will, he's from the state forest.'

Mother said, 'I'm afraid he'll charge a lot. Look out, he's a proper rogue.'

Father said, 'I'll go and take him some vodka and talk it over with him. And you bake us an egg in the ashes for dinner.'

Then Mum got up a nice bit of dinner; she borrowed it from her folks. Then Father took some vodka and went off to see Bryantsev, and we stayed behind and sat waiting for a long time. I got bored without my father. I began to ask my mother to let me go where Father had gone. Mum said, 'You'll get lost.'

I started to cry and made to leave, but my mother hit me, and I sat down on the stove and cried still more. Then I saw my father come into the cottage and say, 'What are you crying about?'

Mother said, 'Fedyushka was going to run off after you, and I hit him.'

Father came up to me and said, 'What are you crying about?'

I began to complain about my mother. My father went up to my mother and started to beat her, made out he was anyway, and he keeps on saying, 'Don't you hit Fedya! Don't you hit Fedya!' Mum made out she was crying. And I sat on Dad's knee and was glad.

Then Dad sat down to table and put me next to him and shouted, 'Now Mother, give me and Fedya our dinners; we're hungry!'

So Mother gave us beef, and we began to eat. We finished dinner, and Mother said, 'Well, what about the frame?'

Father said, 'Fifty silver roubles.'

Mother said, 'That's nothing.'

Father said, 'Yes, there's no doubt about it, it's a first-rate frame.'

The End

[8]

On methods of teaching reading

We have decided to omit from this article all detailed discussion of reading method. It was a subject in which Tolstoy was deeply interested, but the difficulties involved in presenting his views in detail to readers who do not know Russian seem insurmountable. In fact he oscillates between two contradictory positions. sometimes he says that discussion of method is irrelevant, since all real teaching tends to be eclectic anyway, and problems of method are bound to solve themselves if the teacher-pupil relationship is right. More often he claims that he has stumbled upon the natural and easiest method, the method by which children learn in reality irrespective of what method their teachers think they are imposing.

This method was the one which Tolstoy promoted in the controversial experiment sponsored by the Moscow Literacy Committee, and his essay of 1874 'On the Education of the People' (not included in this volume) is in large part devoted to a defence of it and an onslaught on German 'Anschauungsunterricht'.

Reading Method

In the 'schools of literacy' run by ex-soldiers, sextons, etc. the children learned each letter by a traditional name which was a Slavonic word beginning with that letter. A was 'az', B was 'buki' etc. Then the child was taught to read a syllable, e.g. ba—by saying the name of each letter and then putting together the initial sounds, 'buki-az-ba'. Tolstoy's method is essentially the same, except that he renames the letters. For a vowel the children simply utter the vowel sound; for a consonant they add one simple vowel, a Russian -e after the consonant sound.

Tolstoy repeatedly condemns the procedure imported from

Germany, in which the children were asked to utter consonants alone, without any succeeding vowel. Ignoring the distinction between voiced and unvoiced consonants (which exists in Russian), he says that this is impossible. It is in his view contrary to the nature of the Russian language, in which the distinction between 'soft' and 'hard' consonants is of great importance.

Anschauungsunterricht

This was the German name (literally 'visual instruction' or 'instruction from observation') for a practice advocated by German successors of Pestalozzi, and which had many adherents in Russia. The children were considered to be unable to proceed straight away to a meaningful course in reading and writing because their minds were so drastically 'undeveloped', that is to say they lacked basic concepts of qualities and relationships, such as they were bound to encounter in any text. They did not know the meaning, for instance, of 'above' and 'under', 'quickly' and 'slowly', 'loud' and 'soft'. Therefore before and during instruction in reading the teacher must conduct a carefully planned series of demonstrations and interrogations based on simple visual aids and pictures, designed to implant these concepts. Great emphasis was to be placed upon logic and the disciplined repetition in correct sequence of propositions.

The amusing 'Fischbuch' episode is Tolstoy's view of one of these lessons.

I

A great many people at the present time are very seriously engaged in investigating, borrowing or inventing the best method of teaching reading; a great many have already invented and identified this best method. It very often happens that we meet in literature and in life the question: by what method do you teach? It must be admitted, however, that we hear this question mostly either from people who have very little education and who have long been engaged in teaching children as a trade, or from people who are encouraging the education of the people from the vantage point of their study and are even ready to write a little article for the benefit of it and collect a subscription for publishing an ABC book with an improved method, or from people who favour only the one method—their own, or, lastly, from people who do not concern themselves with teaching at all—from the public, who repeat what the majority of people say. People who are seriously engaged in work and who are educated no longer put questions like that.

It seems to be admitted by everyone as an indisputable truth that the objective of the popular school is the teaching of reading and writing, that literacy is the first stage in education and that it is therefore essential to find the best method of teaching it. One person will tell you that the phonetic method is very good, and another assures you that Zolotov's method is the best, and a third knows of a still better method again—the Lancaster one, and so on. Only a lazy man omits to sneer at 'Buki-az-ba'[1] teaching, and everyone is confident that in order to spread education amongst the common people it is only necessary to write down the best method, subscribe three silver roubles apiece, hire a building and a teacher, or even ourselves, out of our superfluity of education, distribute a little portion of it—of a Sunday, in between mass and paying calls—to the unfortunate common people who are perishing in ignorance, and the job is done.

Intelligent, educated and wealthy people are gathered together; a lofty and felicitous idea suddenly occurs to one of them—of doing some good to those awful Russian common people. 'Let's do it!' Everyone agrees, and a society is born having as its object the education of the people—the printing of good cheap books for the people, the foundation of schools, assistance to teachers and so on. A constitution is written, ladies take part, all the formal side of organisational work gone through, and the activity of the society begins. To print good books for the people!—how simple and easy it seems, like all great ideas. There is only one snag: there are no good books for the people—not only in our country but not in Europe either. In order to print such books it is necessary to make them, and not one of the philanthropically minded members would dream of undertaking such work; the society, out of the roubles which have been collected, hands over to somebody or other the task of composing or selecting and translating the best of European popular literature (it is easy to select all this), and the people will be happy and will make rapid strides towards education and the society will be very pleased. As regards the other side of its activities—the schools, the society acts in exactly the same way.

Only very few people, sustained by a spirit of self-sacrifice, devote their precious leisure to teaching the people. (The circumstance that these people have never read a single book of educational theory and have never seen any school other than the one in which they themselves studied is not taken into account.) The others encourage the schools. Again it seems so simple and again there turns out to be an unexpected difficulty, that is that there is no other way of assisting education than to teach oneself and devote oneself entirely to this work.

But philanthropic societies and private persons do not seem to notice this difficulty and continue to engage in popular education in this fashion and to be very satisfied. This phenomenon is in one respect amusing and harmless, since the activities of these societies and persons make no contact with the people; in another respect this phenomenon is dangerous, introducing yet more fog into our as yet indeterminate view of popular education. The causes of this phenomenon may be in part the agitated state of our society and in part the general human tendency to make every honourable idea into a plaything of conceit and idleness. But the fundamental cause lies, as it seems to us, in the great confusion as to what this literacy is, the diffusion of which constitutes the aim of all educators of the people, and which has given rise to such strange discussions amongst us.

Literacy is a concept which exists not only in our country but is recognized all over Europe as the programme of the elementary school for the common people. Lesen und schreiben, lire et écrire, reading and writing. But what is literacy and what has it got in common with the first stage of education? Literacy is the art of making up words out of certain signs and pronouncing them, and of putting the same signs together as words and delineating them. What then have literacy and education in common? Literacy is a certain skill (Ger. *Fertigkeit*); education is knowledge of facts and of their interrelations. But perhaps this skill in spelling out words is essential if we are to introduce a person to the first stage of education, and there is no other means of doing it? We cannot see this at all, and we often do see quite the opposite, provided that in speaking of education we mean not only scholastic education but education in life as well. Amongst people who are at a lower level of education we see that knowing or not knowing how to read and write does not in the least alter their level of education. We see people who know very well all the facts which are essential for agriculture and a large number of relationships of these facts, and who do not know how to read and write; or splendid military organizers, splendid traders, bailiffs, foremen, craftsmen, artisans, contractors and simply people educated by life, with wide knowledge and sound judgment based on that knowledge, who cannot read or write, and, on the other hand, we see people who can read and write and who have not gained any new knowledge as a result of that skill. Anyone who seriously looks into popular education not only in Russia but also in Europe will be bound to conclude that education is acquired by the people quite independently of literacy and that, with rare exceptions in the case of quite outstanding talents, literacy remains a skill which has no application, in the majority of cases even a harmful skill, harmful because nothing in life can remain neutral. If literacy is inapplicable and useless then it will be harmful.

But perhaps a certain level of education, which is higher than those examples of illiterate education which we have cited, is impossible without literacy? This may well be, but we do not know this and we have no reason to postulate this for purposes of educating the coming generation. What is impossible is simply the level of education which *we* have, and we cannot and do not want to imagine any other but this. We have an ideal of a school for teaching reading and writing, which compromises in our opinion the cornerstone of education, and we do not want to know about all those levels of education which exist not below our school, but quite outside it and independently of it.

We say that everyone who cannot read or write is equally uneducated—in our eyes they are barbarians. In order to begin education literacy is needed and by this means we introduce the people willy-nilly to our form of education. It would be very agreeable for me, with the education that I possess, to agree with that opinion; I am even convinced that literacy is an essential condition of a certain level of education; but I cannot be sure that my education is good, that the path which learning is proceeding along is the right one, and above all I cannot disregard three-quarters of the human race which is educated without literacy. If we are set upon educating the common people let us ask them how they educate themselves and what are their favourite instruments for that purpose. If we want to seek out a first principle, a first stage of education, why are we bound to seek it in literacy, and not far deeper? Why come to a stop before one of the infinite number of instruments of education and see in it the alpha and omega of education, when it is only one of the fortuitous insignificant circumstances of education? In Europe they have long been teaching people to read and write, but there is no popular literature, that is to say nowhere does the common people, the class of persons who are exclusively engaged in physical work, read books. It would seem that this phenomenon deserved attention and elucidation, but meanwhile people think they will help matters merely by continuing to teach reading and writing.

All the questions of life are solved remarkably easily and simply in theory and only in the application to the job does it appear that they are not so easily solved, and that they disintegrate into thousands of other questions which are difficult to solve. It seems so simple and easy to educate the people; you just drill them in reading and writing, even if it has to be done by force, give them some good books—and there you are. But in practice it turns out to be quite another thing. The people do not want to learn to read and write. Very good, we can force them. Another difficulty—there are no books. We can commission them. But the books which have been commissioned are bad; and it is impossible to force people to write good books. The chief difficulty, however, is that people do not want to read these books, and no means of forcing them to read them has yet been invented; and the people continue to educate themselves not in the schools of literacy but in their own way. Perhaps the historical moment has not yet come for the people to participate in a common education and they will have to spend another hundred years learning to read and write; perhaps the people are spoiled (as many think); perhaps the people will have to write their own books for themselves; perhaps the best method has not yet been found; it may also be the case that education by means of the book and of literacy is an aristocratic mode of education which is less appropriate for the working class than other educational tools which have been developed in our day. It may be that the main advantage of instruction by means of literacy, which consists in being able to instruct in science without its auxiliary equipment, does not exist for the common people in our day. Perhaps it is easier for a workman to learn botany from the plants, zoology from the animals and arithmetic from the abacus with which he comes into contact, than from a book. Perhaps the workman will find time to listen to an oral account and to look at a museum or an exhibition but will not find the time to read a book. It may even be the case that a bookish mode of learning is definitely repugnant to his way of life and cast of character. Very often we see attention, interest and clear understanding on the part of a working man when an informed person is telling him something and expounding it; but it is hard to imagine that same workman with a book in his calloused hands, penetrating the meaning of a brief popular exposition of some science or other. All these are merely suggestions as to the reasons, which may be quite erroneous, but the fact itself, the nonexistence of popular literature and the resistance of the people to education by means of literacy hold good all over Europe.

Similarly all over Europe we find the view of the class which is conducting the education that the school of literacy is the first stage of education. The origin of a conception which seems so unreasonable will become quite clear as soon as we examine the historical development of education. It was not the lowest but the highest schools which were founded first: the monastic schools to begin with, then secondary schools and then schools for the people. In our country the academy was founded first of all, then the universities, then the gymnasia,[2] then the district schools and then the schools for the common people. From this historical point of view Smaragdov's textbook, which gives the history of mankind in two quires, is just as necessary in the district school as literacy is in the people's school. Literacy is the last educational stage in this organized hierarchy of institutions, or the first stage if you begin from the bottom, and therefore the lower school must merely respond to the requirements which the higher school lays down.[3] But there is another point of view which presents the people's school as an autonomous institution which is not obliged to bear the burden of the faults in the structure of the higher educational institution, but has its own independent goal of educating the common people. The lower we go down this ladder of education which has been established by the state the more we feel the necessity of making education at each stage independent and complete. From the gymnasium there are only one-fifth who do not proceed to the university, from the district school[4] only one-fifth proceeds to the gymnasium, from the people's school one in a thousand proceeds to higher education. Consequently the co-ordination of the people's school with the higher institution is the last objective which it ought to pursue. Yet only by this co-ordination can we explain the view that the schools for the common people are schools of literacy.

The discussion in our literature about the usefulness or harmfulness of literacy, which it was so easy to laugh at, is in our opinion an extremely serious discussion which is destined to elucidate many questions. This discussion, by the way, was never peculiar to our country, nor is it now. Some say that it is harmful for the people to have the opportunity of reading books and magazines which are presented to it by speculators and political parties; they say that literacy removes the working class from its milieu, fosters in it discontent with its position and gives rise to vices and a decline in morality. Others say or imply that education cannot be harmful, but will always be useful. The first are more or less conscientious objectors, the others are theorists. As always happens in arguments, both groups are perfectly right. The argument, as it seems to us, is simply a matter of unclear presentation of the question. The one group perfectly justly attack literacy as a separately developed ability to read and write without any other knowledge (which is what the majority of schools are doing, for what they have learnt by heart is forgotten and literacy alone remains); the others defend literacy when what they mean by it is the first stage of education, and they are wrong only in their incorrect understanding of what literacy is. If the question is put thus: is elementary education useful to the people or is it not? then no one can reply in the negative. But if they ask: is it or is it not useful to train the people to read when they do not know how to read and have no books to read? then I hope that any dispassionate man would reply: I do not know; I do not know this in just the same way as I do not know whether it would be useful to train all the common people to play the violin or to sew shoes. But after taking a closer look at the result of literacy in the form in which it is given to the people, I think that the majority would give an answer against literacy, if we take into account the prolonged coercion, the disproportionate development of the memory, the false idea of the nature of science, the revulsion from further education, the treacherous conceit and opportunities for senseless reading, which are acquired in these schools. In the Yasnaya Polyana school all the pupils who come to us from the schools of literacy constantly fall behind pupils who come from the school of life, and not only do they fall behind, but they fall behind more and more the longer they studied in the school of literacy.

What the aim, and therefore the curriculum, of a school for the people consists in, is something that we not only cannot explain here, but we do not suppose to be explicable at all. A school for the people ought to respond to the people's requirements—this is all that we can positively say on such a question. As to what these requirements consist in, this can only be answered by studying them and by free experiment. But literacy makes up only one small, inconspicuous part of these requirements, and consequently schools of literacy are schools which are possibly very gratifying for their founders but also useless and often harmful for the people, and without even the remotest resemblance to schools for elementary education. For the same reason the question of how to teach literacy rapidly and by what method is a question of little interest in the field of education for the common people. For the same reason those people who for their own amusement concern themselves with schools of literacy would do far better to exchange that occupation for a more interesting one, for the field of education for the people, which does not consist of literacy alone, is not only a different field, but one which absolutely demands direct and stubborn work and study of the common people. However, in so far as literacy is needed by the people, schools of literacy do appear and subsist of their own accord, exactly as many of them as are needed. In our country these schools exist in large numbers because the teachers in them are unable to communicate anything else of what they know besides reading, and the common people have a demand for literacy in a certain proportion of their number for practical purposes—reading a shop-sign, writing down a calculation, reading the psalter over a deceased person for a fee and so on. These schools exist just as tailors' and joiners' workshops do, the common people have a similar opinion of them as of the workshop and the methods of the students are the same; in just the same way the pupil studies intermittently, as best he can, anyhow; in the same way the master uses the pupil for his own needs—for fetching vodka, splitting wood, cleaning out the threshing-floor; the period of instruction is just the same. Just as in the case of a craft, this literacy is never used for further education, but only for practical ends. The sexton or soldier teaches, and a peasant with three sons sends one to learn reading and writing, as he might send one to learn tailoring, and the legitimate interest of both sides is satisfied; but to see in this a certain stage of education and to erect a state school on this basis, supposing that the only defect of that other school was in its method of teaching reading and writing, and to draw pupils into it by cunning or force—this would be either a crime or an error.

But—people will say to me—in a school for the education of the people, as you understand it, the teaching of reading and writing will still constitute one of the principal conditions of education, not only because there is the demand for literacy in the people's attitude to education, but also because the great majority of teachers know only how to read and write, and therefore the question of method in teaching still presents itself as a difficult question and one which requires solution. To this we will reply that in the majority of schools, while our knowledge of the common people and of the educational art remains insufficient, education will indeed begin with instruction in reading and writing, but that the process of learning the printed and handwritten signs appears to us to be very trivial and to have been known long ago. The sextons teach reading in three months by the 'buki-az-ba' method; an intelligent father or brother can teach it by the same means much faster; they say that it is taught yet faster by Zolotov's method or the *Lautiermethode*.[5] But when the teaching has been done, by this, that or the other method, nothing has been gained if they have not been taught to understand what they have read, which constitutes the principal objective in teaching reading. But of this most necessary, difficult and as yet undiscovered method we hear nothing. And therefore the question of what is the most convenient way of teaching reading, although it does require an answer, appears to us to be very trivial, and obstinacy in the search for a method, and the waste of efforts which it is more important to apply to the education which is to follow, seem to us to be a great misunderstanding, arising out of an inexact conception of literacy and education.

II

A teacher from a German seminary, who has been trained in the best method, is teaching by the Fischbuch. Bold and self-assured, he takes his seat in the classroom; his equipment is ready: the little slabs with the letters on, the board with diagrams on and the little book with a representation of a fish. The teacher surveys his pupils and already knows everything: what they ought to understand, what their souls consist of, and a great deal else which he has been taught in the seminary.

He opens the book and points to the fish. 'What is this, dear children?' Please to observe, this is *Anschauungsunterricht* (visual instruction). The poor children are pleased to see this fish, unless word has already reached them from other schools and their elder brothers about what blood is squeezed out of that fish, what moral acrobatics and torment they are to be put through on account of that fish. Be that as it may, they say, 'It's a fish.' 'No,' replies the teacher. (Everything that I am telling is not an invention, not a satire, but a reproduction of facts which I saw, without any exception, in all the best schools of Germany and those English schools which have already borrowed this splendid and superior method.)

'No,' says the teacher, 'What can you see?' The children are silent. Do not forget that they have to sit up straight, each in his place, and not fidget—*Ruhe* and *Gehorsam!* (quiet and obedience).

'What can you see then?'

'A book,' says the stupidest. All the clever ones have already thought a thousand times over of what they can see and know by intuition that they will not guess what the teacher requires, and that they have to say that the fish is not a fish, but something or other which they cannot put a name to.

'Yes, yes', says the teacher, rejoicing, 'very good, a book.' The clever ones take courage, the stupid one himself does not know what he is being praised for.

'And what is in the book?' says the teacher. The perkiest and cleverest one makes a guess and says proudly and joyfully:

'Letters.'

'No, no, not at all,' replies the teacher, sorrowfully even, 'you must think about what you are saying.' Again all the clever ones preserve a gloomy silence and do not even try, but think about the sort of spectacles the teacher has and why he does not take them off but looks over the top of them, and so on.

'So what *is* in the book?' Everyone is silent. 'What is this here?' He points to the fish.

'A fish,' says some bold spirit.

'Yes a fish, but it is not a live fish, is it?'

''No, it's not alive.'

'Very good. Is it dead then?'

'No.'

'Excellent. What sort of fish is it, then?'

'*Ein Bild* [a picture].'

'Right, excellent.'

They all repeat that it is a picture and think that the thing is over. No, they have still to say that it is a picture representing a fish. And in exactly the same way the teacher strives to make the pupils say that this is a picture representing a fish. He imagines that the pupils are reasoning, and it never occurs to him that if he has been ordered to make the pupils say that this is a picture representing a fish, or if he himself wants them to, it would be far simpler openly to make them learn this wise pronouncement by heart.

But the pupils are lucky if the teacher leaves them in peace at that. I myself have seen him making them say that this is not a fish but a thing—*ein Ding*—and then that that thing is—a fish. This, please to notice, is the new *Anschauungsunterricht* combined with reading, this is the art of making children think. But now the *Anschauungsunterricht* is over, the analysis of the word begins. The word 'Fisch' is displayed, made up of letters upon pieces of cardboard. The best and cleverest think that here they will make up ground by grasping the formation and names of the letters straight away, but how wrong they are!

'What does a fish have in front?'

Those who have been cowed are silent, at last the bold spirit says, 'A head.'

'Good, very good. And where is the head? In what?'

'In front.'

'Very good, and what comes after the head?'

'The fish.'

'No, think.' They are to say, 'The body, *Leib*.' And this is said, but by now the pupils are losing all hope and self-confidence and are concentrating all their intellectual powers upon finding out what the teacher wants. 'The head, the body and the end of the fish, the tail. Excellent! All together, "The fish has a head, a body and a tail". This is a fish composed of letters and this is a drawing of a fish.' The fish composed of letters is suddenly divided into three parts: 'f', 'i' and 'sch.' With the complacency of a conjurer who has just sprinkled everybody with flowers instead of wine the teacher moves the 'f' to one side, displays it and says, 'This is the head, 'i'—this is the body, 'sch'—this is the tail," and he repeats 'Fisch, ffff-iiii-schschschsch. This is ffff, this is iiii, this is schschschsch.' And the unhappy children torment themselves and hiss and puff, trying to pronounce a consonant without a vowel, which is a physical impossibility.[6] Without admitting it, the teacher himself uses a semi-vowel, something like a Russian y, after the f. At first the pupils are amused by this hissing, but then they perceive that they are required to memorize these fff-s and shsh-s, and they say shif, shish and fif and cannot recognize the word Fisch at all in ffff-iiii-sssshhhh. The teacher, who knows the best method, will not come to their aid and advise them to remember f for Feder and Faust, sch for Schürze and Schachtel and so on, but demands ssschchch; not only does he not come to their aid but he definitely stops them learning the letters from a picture ABC or from words, such as az, budu, vedat', glagol[7] . . . he stops them from learning syllables *and* from reading things they know without learning syllables; in a word, to use the German expression—*er ignoriert*—he makes a point of not knowing—any methods other than the Fisch, and the fact that a fish is a thing, and so on.

There is the reading method, and for the initial development of thought there is an *Anschauungsunterricht* method (see Danzel's *Entwurf*) both are combined and the children have to pass through the eyes of these needles. Every step is taken to see that there shall be no development in the school other than along this course. Any movement, word or question is forbidden. 'Die Hände fein zusammen! Ruhe und Gehorsam!' (Hands folded! Quiet and obedience!) And there are people who jeer at 'buki-az-ba'[8], who assert that 'buki-az-ba' is a method which destroys the intellectual capacities and who recommend the '*Lautiermethode in Verbindung mit Anschauungsunterricht*' (the phonetic method combined with visual instruction), i.e., they recommend us to have them learn by heart 'a fish is a thing and f is its head, i its body and sch is the fish's tail' but not to have them learn the psalter and the book of hours by heart. English and French educationists proudly utter the word *Anschauungsunterricht* (which is a difficult one for them to pronounce) and say they are introducing it into elementary education. To us this *Anschauungsunterricht,* of which I shall have occasion to speak again in detail, appears perfectly incomprehensible. What is this visual instruction? How can there be any instruction which is *not* visual? All five senses are used in learning, and therefore *Anschauungsunterricht* always has existed and always will exist.

For the European school, which is struggling out of a medieval formalism, the name and idea of visual instruction are understandable as a contrast to the previous method of instruction; even the mistakes, which consist in adhering to the old method and merely introducing external devices, are excusable; but for us, I repeat, the *Anschauungsunterricht* is senseless. To this day, after vainly seeking for this *Anschauungsunterricht* and Pestalozzi's method all over Europe, I have found nothing except that geography should be taught from relief maps if you have any, painting with paints, geometry from drawings, zoology from animals, and so on, which we have all known from birth, which there was no need to invent because it was invented long ago by nature herself, and is consequently well known to anyone who was not trained in the contrary ideas. And these similar methods, and methods for training teachers according to certain methods, are seriously proposed to us, who are starting our schools in the second half of the nineteenth century, unburdened by any historical restraints and errors, with an altogether different consciousness from that which was the foundation of the European schools. Not to mention the falsity of such methods and the violence done to the spirit of the pupils, why should we, whose sextons can teach reading in six months by means of 'buki-az-ba', borrow a *Lautieranschauungsunterrichtsmethode* which requires a year or more of study?

We said in the above that in our opinion every method is good and every method is one-sided; every one is convenient for a particular pupil and for a particular language and nation. For this reason the phonetic method and any other un-Russian method will be worse for us than 'buki-az-ba'. If in Germany, where several generations have already been taught to think according to the special laws defined by the Kants and Schleiermachers, where the best teachers are trained, where the Lautiermethode was begun in the eighteenth century, Lautieranschauungsunterricht still produces such undistinguished results, what then would be the case here, if a particular method was recognized by law, and we had a particular Lesebuch[9] full of moral sayings? What would come of teaching by some newly introduced method which had not been assimilated by the people and the teachers?

I will recount a few recent incidents. This autumn a teacher who had worked in the Yasnaya Polyana school opened his own school in a village where out of forty pupils half had already been taught their 'azes'[10] and syllables and a third could read. Two weeks later general discontent with the school was expressed amongst the peasants. The chief points of the accusation were:

that the teaching was after the German fashion—'a', 'be' and not 'az', 'buki'—that they were being taught fairy-tales and not prayers, and that the school was disorderly. In an interview with the teacher I informed him of the peasants' opinion. The teacher, a man with a university education, explained to me with a contemptuous smile that he was teaching them all over again with 'a, be' instead of 'az, buki' to make it easier for them to compose syllables, that they were reading fairy-tales in order to accustom them to understanding what they read commensurately with their range of ideas and that with his new method he considered it unnecessary to punish the children, and therefore there could be no question of the strict orderliness which the peasants had grown used to, seeing their children spelling out syllables with their pointers.

I visited that school in its third week. The boys were divided into three sections, and the teacher was assiduously going round from one to another. Some of them, the lowest ones, were standing by the table learning by heart from a sheet of cardboard the places where the letters were. I began to question them; more than half of them knew their letters, calling them az, buki, etc., others even knew syllables; one of them could read, but he was learning it all from scratch, ticking off on his fingers and repeating: a, be, ve and imagining that this was something new; others—the middling ones—were spelling out syllables aloud: s, k, a—ska, one of them would set a problem and the others would reply. And they had been doing this for more than a fortnight, whereas one day is quite a long time to allow for this process of discarding the superfluous vowel e. I also found some of them who knew their syllables in the old-fashioned way and were reading. These, just like the first group, were ashamed of their knowledge and renounced it, imagining that nothing would do but to piece letters together: 'be, re, a—bra'. Finally, the third group was reading. These unfortunates were sitting on the floor, each holding in his hand a book which was right in front of his eyes and were repeating aloud, pretending to read them, these two lines:

> Where the sky comes to an end
> Lives a nation without bread.[11]

When they had finished these lines they started again from the beginning, with weary, worried faces, occasionally stealing a glance at me as if they were asking, 'Is it all right?' It is a terrible and improbable thing to relate. Some of these boys were quite well able to read, others did not know how to compose syllables; those who could were holding back out of a feeling of solidarity, those who could not were repeating things by heart and had gone on repeating for three weeks those two lines from an abominable adaptation of Yershov's fairy-tale, which is no good for the common people anyway.

I began to question them about sacred history; nobody knew anything because the teacher, *according to the new method,* did not make them learn things by heart, but told them stories drawn from a short sacred history. I asked questions about numeration; no one knew it, although the teacher, once again according to the new method, had been spending two hours a day demonstrating numeration up to millions on the blackboard to all of them together, but he had not made them learn it by heart. I asked them their prayers, not one of them knew them; they could say 'Our Father' with some errors, as they had learnt it at home. And yet they were splendid boys, full of life, intellect and desire for learning. And—this is the most dreadful thing of all—all this was done according to *my* method. Every device used in my school was to be found here too; learning the letters by having them all write them together in chalk, and making syllables by ear, and a first reading-piece which a child could understand, and oral stories from sacred history and mathematics without memorization. And yet in everything one could sense the device which the teacher knew best, that of learning by heart, which he was avoiding consciously and which was the sole device that he had mastered, and he was applying it against his own will to quite different materials; he was making them learn Yershov's story by heart instead of a prayer, he was making them learn sacred history by heart not out of a book, but from his own bad, lifeless oral account; the same applies to mathematics and composing syllables. And it is impossible to knock into the head of this unhappy teacher with his university education the idea that all the reproaches by *uncouth* peasants are right a thousand times over, that the sexton teaches incomparably better than he does, and that if he wants to teach he can teach reading by the "buki-az-ba" method with rote learning, and by this means he can perform a certain practical service. But this teacher with a university education had, in his own words, studied the method of the Yasnaya Polyana school, which he had for some reason or other seen fit to take as a model.

I saw another example in a district school in one of our capitals.[12] After listening with a sinking heart to the best pupils trumpeting forth in our honour (the water communications of Russia in the highest class, the history of Alexander of Macedon in the middle one) we were already about to depart, together with the friend with whom we were visiting the school, when the state supervisor invited us to take a look at the new method of teaching reading which he had discovered and was preparing to publish.

'I selected eight of the poorest ones,' he said to us, 'and I am carrying out experiments on them and testing my method.'

We went in; eight boys were standing in a huddle.

'To your places!' shouted the supervisor in a voice belonging to the oldest method of all.

The boys stood in a ring and braced up. He was about an hour telling us how this splendid phonetic method had formerly been in use all over the capital, but now there was only one school where it was left, and he wanted to revive it. The boys were still standing there. At last he took a card from the table with m-y-sh on it.

'What is this?' he said, pointing to mysh (English = mouse).

'Byk (bull)' replied the boy.

'What is this?—mer-er.'

The boy said, 'mer-er'.

'And this is y and this is sh, altogether it is mysh. And if we put in "lo" here we get "mylo" (soap).'

The children were barely able to give us these answers, which they had learnt by heart. I tried asking them something new; nobody knew anything except 'mysh' and 'byk'.

'Have they been studying for long?' I asked.

The supervisor has been making experiments for more than a year. The boys are aged from six to nine and they are all real live boys—not dolls but alive.

When I observed to the supervisor that in Germany the phonetic method did not work like that he explained to me that unfortunately the phonetic method had been corrupted in Germany. I tried to assure him of the contrary, but as a proof of his idea he fetched for me out of another room five German reading primers of the thirties and forties which were not composed for the phonetic method. We fell silent and left, and the eight boys remained for the supervisor's experiments. This was in the autumn of 1861.

And that very supervisor may be able to teach those eight boys to read quite well by making them sit stiffly at the table with their ABC books and primers, and perhaps he can even pull their hair in just the same way as the reverend deacon who taught *him* used to pull *his*. How many, many examples of such teaching by new methods are to be found in our time, which is giving birth to such a wealth of schools, not to speak of the Sunday schools, which are riddled with such inconsistencies!

And here are some other, contrasting examples. In a village school which was opened last month I noticed when the instruction was just beginning a healthy hook-nosed lad of about fourteen who was mumbling something to himself and smiling complacently whilst the pupils were repeating their letters. He was not on the roll of scholars. I questioned him—he knew all his letters, occasionally relapsing into buki, rtsy, etc.; as always he was ashamed of this, supposing it to be forbidden and a bad thing. I ask him for syllables—he knew them; I got him to read—he read without forming the syllables, although he did not believe this himself.

'Where did you learn?'

'This summer there was a friend living with me out at the herd-watching, he knew how and he showed me.'

'Have you got an ABC book?'

'Yes.'

'Where did you get it?'

'I bought it.'

'Have you been studying long?'

'Through the summer, like. When he showed me in the fields I took and studied it.'

Once another pupil, at the Yasnaya Polyana school, a boy about ten years old, who had studied before with a sexton, brought me his brother. The brother could read well at seven years old and had learnt in the evenings from his brother in the course of one winter. I know of such examples, and anyone who cares to make some enquiries among the common people will find a great many. What then is the point of our inventing new methods and insisting on abandoning 'buki-az-ba' and approving of all methods but 'buki-az-ba'?

Besides all this the Russian language and the Cyrillic alphabet have one enormous distinction from and advantage over all the European languages and alphabets, from which a special type of teaching of reading ought naturally to flow. The superiority of the Russian alphabet consists in the fact that every sound in it is pronounced, and is pronounced as it is, which we do not find in any other language. 'Che'[13] is pronounced 'ts-kh-e' and not 'she' as in French or 'khe' as in German; 'a' is 'a', and not 'ai', 'e', and 'a' as in English; 'c' is 'c' and 'ts'[14] is 'ts' and not 'ch' and 'k' as in Italian, not to mention those Slavonic languages which do not use the Cyrillic alphabet.

What, then, is the best method of teaching reading in Russian? Neither the newest, phonetic method, nor the oldest one, that of 'azes' syllables and interpretation, nor the vowel method nor Zolotov's method. In a word, there is no best method. The best method for a particular teacher is the method which the teacher knows better than any other. All other methods which the teacher knows or may invent must be aids to teaching which has been started according to the one method. Every nation and every language has a predominant tendency towards some one method. In order to identify this method it is merely necessary to know which method the common people has adopted for the longest time; this method in its broad outlines will be that which is most suited to the people. In our case this is the method of letters, syllables and interpretations, a very imperfect one, like all methods, and therefore capable of being perfected by all the discoveries that the new methods offer us.

Every individual personality, if he is to learn to read as quickly as possible, must be taught quite distinctly from every other, and therefore there must be a special method for everyone. One will find insurmountable difficulty in something which does not hold up the other in the least, and vice versa. One pupil has a good memory, and finds it easier to learn the syllables by heart than to understand that the consonant is pronounced without a vowel sound; another has a bent for tranquil reasoning and will understand the phonetic method, which is the most rational one; a third has a flair, an instinct, and by reading whole words he perceives the law by which words are composed.

The best teacher will be the one that always has a clarification of what is holding up the pupil ready at hand. Clarifying difficulties in this manner will give the teacher a knowledge of the greatest possible number of methods, the ability to invent new methods; he has no one method that he follows, but a conviction that all methods are one-sided and that the best method would be one able to settle all possible difficulties that the pupil might encounter, i.e. no method, but an art or a talent.

Every teacher of reading must thoroughly know and test by his own experience the one method which has been worked out by the common people; he must try to acquaint himself with the greatest possible number of methods, accepting them as auxiliary approaches; regarding every difficulty the pupil has in understanding not as a fault in the pupil but as a fault in his teaching, he must try to develop his own ability to discover new approaches. Every teacher must know that each method that is discovered is only a stair on which we must stand in order to proceed further; he must know that if he himself does not do so then someone else who has mastered this method will use it as a basis for proceeding further, and that since teaching is an art finality and perfection are unattainable—development and the process of approaching perfection are endless.

In one of the following numbers we will present an example of such a development of our approach to teaching reading which has gone on before our very eyes.

[9]
Training and education

First published in the July number of the magazine (which did not in fact appear until September 1862). Written while Tolstoy was taking his kumyss cure in the steppes. This article, with its sweeping condemnation of state and private institutions, was the subject of a worried report from the chief Moscow censor to the new minister of education, Golovin. It was passed after some delay, and it is possible that the text we have is the result of cutting by the censors. Golovin took the view that an attack upon universities would be sure to elicit many replies from outraged academics, and these would be more effective than suppression of the article. He thought attacks upon humbler institutions more dangerous. Perhaps the original form of the article contained more onslaughts on schools.

There are many words which have no precise definition, which overlap one another, but which are nevertheless essential for the communication of ideas. Such are the words 'training', 'education' and even 'tuition'.

Teachers sometimes recognize no distinction between education and training, but are nevertheless unable to express their thoughts without using the words *education, training, tuition* or *instruction*. There must certainly be distinct concepts corresponding to these words. Perhaps there are reasons why we are instinctively unwilling to use these concepts in their exact and real sense; but the concepts do exist separately and have a right to do so. In Germany there exists a clear-cut division of the concepts *Erziehung* (training) and *Unterricht* (instruction). It is admitted that training includes instruction, that instruction is one of the chief means of training, and that all instruction contains an element of training in it *(erziehliges Element)*. But the concept of education, *Bildung,* overlaps either with training or with instruction. The most widespread German definition would be this: training is the education of the best people in accordance with the ideal of human perfection which has been worked out by a particular age. Instruction, including moral development, is a means of attaining this, although not the sole one, another besides instruction being the placing of the subject in conditions which are conducive to the aim of training—discipline and coercion, *Zucht.*

The human spirit, so the Germans say, must be exercised just as the body is by gymnastics. *Der Geist muss gezüchtigt werden.*

Education (Russian *obrazovanie,* German *Bildung*) is, as we have said, in German, amongst the upper classes and even sometimes in pedagogical literature, either confused with instruction and training, or else is admitted to be a social phenomenon with which the science of pedagogy is not concerned. In the French language I do not even know a word corresponding to the concept of education *(obrazovanie): éducation, instruction, civilisation* are quite different concepts. Similarly there is no word in the English language either which corresponds to the concept *obrazovanie.*[1]

German practising teachers sometimes do not even recognize the distinction between training *(vospitanie)* and education *(obrazovanie):* according to their idea both merge into one indivisible whole. In chatting with the celebrated Diesterweg[2] I raised the question of education, training and instruction. Diesterweg reacted with a sharp irony to people who distinguished the one from the other—according to his ideas both are fused together. And yet we were talking of *training, education* and *instruction* and understood one another clearly. He said himself that education includes an element of training which is to be found in all instruction.

What then do these words mean, and how should they be understood?

I shall not repeat the disputes and conversations which I have had with educationists about this subject, nor copy our from books the contradictory opinions which are extant in literature on this subject—it would take too long, and anyone who cares to read through the first article on teaching that he comes across can check the truth of what I said, rather I shall try to explain here the provenance of these concepts, the distinctions between them and the reasons why they are not clearly understood.

According to the educationist training *(vospitanie)* includes instruction *(prepodavanie)*.

The so-called science of pedagogy is concerned with training alone, and regards the human being in the process of education as a creature completely subordinated to the trainer. Only through the latter's mediation does the subject receive impressions of significance for education or training, whether these impressions come through books, oral stories, memorizing assignments or artistic or physical exercises. The whole external world is permitted to act upon the pupil only in so far as the trainer considers proper. The trainer tries to surround his charge with an impassable wall excluding the influence of the world, and to admit through the funnel of his scientific school-training only what he regards as useful. I am not talking about what was or is done amongst what are called backward people, I am not waging a war against windmills, I am talking of how training is regarded and practised amongst the so-called best progressive educators. Everywhere the influence of life is alien to the concerns of the teacher, everywhere a Chinese wall of bookish wisdom is built around the school, through which the educational influences of life are admitted only in so far as the trainers please. The influence of life is not recognized. Such is the view of the science of pedagogy, because it arrogates to itself the right of determining what is necessary for the education of the best human being, and thinks it possible to remove from the trainee every influence external to the training; and this is what training does in practice.

With an attitude like this as the basis it is natural that training and education should be confused with one another, for it is recognized that if there were no training there would be no education. In recent times, when the demand for freedom in education has begun to be dimly felt, the best teachers have become convinced that instruction is the sole means of training, but they mean coercive, compulsory instruction, and therefore they have begun to confuse all three concepts—training, education and instruction.

According to the educational theorist training is the action of one human being upon another and includes three forms of action: 1) the moral or forcible influence of the trainer (a mode of life, punishments); 2) tuition and instruction; and 3) the manipulation of living influences upon the trainee. The error and confusion of concepts proceeds, in our firm opinion, from the fact that pedagogy regards training and not education as its subject-matter and does not see that it is impossible for the trainer to foresee, coordinate and determine all living influences. Every educationist agrees that life exerts its influence both before school and after school, and, in spite of all efforts to expel it, during school time too. This influence is so strong that in most cases all influence of school training is destroyed; but the educationist concludes from this only that the science and art of pedagogy are insufficiently developed, and continues none the less to consider that his aim is the training of people in accordance with a certain model, and not education, i.e. the study of the ways in which people form themselves and co-operation with this free process of formation. I agree that *Unterricht* (teaching or instruction) is a part of *Erziehung* (training, upbringing), but education includes both the one and the other.

Training is not the whole subject-matter of pedagogy but one of the phenomena to which pedagogy cannot fail to devote attention; whereas the subject-matter of pedagogy should and can be nothing other than education. As we firmly believe, education, in the broad sense, consists of the sum of all the influences which develop a human being, and give him or her a broader outlook on the world and new information. Children's games, suffering, parents' punishments, books, work, study forced and unforced, the arts, the sciences, life: all these educate.

General education may be understood to be either the *result* of all the influences which life exerts upon a person (in the sense of the education of a man, we say 'an educated man') or as the influence in itself of all the conditions of life upon a man (in the sense of 'the education of a German, of a Russian peasant, of a serf-owner', we say, 'the man received a bad education' or 'a good one', etc.).[3] It is only with this last that we are concerned. Training is the action of one person upon another with the object of making the trainee acquire certain moral habits. (We say 'he was trained in hypocrisy' or 'to be a robber' or 'to be a kindly man'. The Spartans trained courageous men, the French train one-sided and complacent ones.) Instruction is the transference of information from one person to another (one can be instructed in chess, history, bootmaking). Drilling, a variation upon instruction, is the action of one person upon another with the object of making the pupil acquire certain physical habits (one can be drilled in singing, carpentry, dancing, rowing, declamation). Instruction and drilling are means of education when they are free, and means of training when the drilling is enforced and when the instruction is exclusive (i.e., when the instruction is in only those subjects which the trainer regards as necessary). The truth is clear and declares itself to everyone instinctively. However we may try to combine what is separate and separate the inseparable and adapt our thought to the existing order of things—the truth is obvious.

Training is the coercive, forcible action of one person upon another with the object of educating the sort of person who seems good to us; and education is a free relationship between people which has as its basis the need of the one to acquire knowledge and of the other to impart that which he has already acquired. Instruction, *Unterricht,* is a means both of education and of training. The difference between education and training lies solely in the coercion which training claims as its right. Training is forcible education. Education is free.

Training is the French *éducation,* the English education,[4] the German *Erziehung,* concepts which exist in Europe, *obrazovanie* (education), on the other hand, is a concept which exists only in Russia, and partially in Germany, where there is a word which almost corresponds—*Bildung*. But in France and England this concept and word do not exist at all. *'Civilisation'* means enlightenment, *'instruction'*[5] is a European concept which cannot be translated into Russian, denoting an abundance of school-room knowledge of the sciences or the act of imparting that knowledge, but it is not the same as education (Russian *obrazovanie*) which includes knowledge of the sciences and the arts and physical development.

I have spoken in my first article of the right to use force in educational matters and have tried to show that: 1) force is impossible; 2) it leads to no results or to miserable ones; 3) that this force can have no other basis than caprice (the Circassian teaches people how to steal, the Mohammedan teaches them to murder infidels). There is no such thing as a science of training. Training is the urge to moral despotism erected into a principle. I shall not say that training is the expression of an evil side of human nature, but I will say that it is a phenomenon which proves the underdeveloped state of human thought, and cannot therefore be established as the basis of a rational human activity, of a science.

Training is one man's urge to make another the same as himself (the urge of a poor man to take wealth away from a rich, an old man's feeling of envy upon seeing fresh and powerful youth—the feeling of envy elevated into a principle and a theory). I am convinced that the only reason why a trainer can set about the training of a child with such ardour is that behind that urge lies envy of the child's purity and the desire to make him like the trainer himself, i.e., more corrupt.

I know an avaricious farmer, always making an extra ha'penny by rascally means, who, in reply to my exhortations and inducements to send his splendid twelve-year-old son to my Yasnaya Polyana school, always gives the same answer, stretching his great red muzzle into a self-satisfied smile: 'That's as may be, y'r Lordship, but what I need to do most is to fill him full of my own spirit first.' And he drags him around everywhere with him and boasts that his twelve-year-old son has learnt how to swindle the peasants who bring in his father's wheat. We all know those fathers reared as cadets and in military colleges, who consider that the only good education is one that is soaked in the same spirit as that in which the fathers were themselves reared? And do not professors in the universities and monks in the seminaries inculcate their own spirit in exactly the same way? I do not want to prove what I have already proved once, and which is only too easy to prove: that training, regarded as the deliberate forming of human beings according to certain models, is sterile, illegitimate and impossible. Here I shall confine myself to one question. The right to train does not exist. I do not recognize it, it has not been and will not be recognized by the whole younger generation undergoing training, which is always and everywhere in revolt against the coercion in our training. *How will you prove the existence of this right?* I do not know and am not postulating anything, but you are recognizing and postulating a new right, which in our eyes does not exist, the right of one person to make other people into what he wishes. Prove this right, but not just by saying that abuse of power does in fact exist and has existed for a long time. You are not the plaintiffs, we are; you are the defendants. Several times already, by word of mouth and in print, people have replied to the ideas I expressed in *Yasnaya Polyana* magazine in the same way as people soothe an upset child. They have said to me, 'There's no doubt about it, training as it went on in medieval monasteries is a bad thing, that is not in question, but gymnasia[6] and universities are quite another matter.' Other people again have said, 'There's no doubt about it, this is so, but, taking into consideration, etc.,

etc. such and such circumstances, one has to admit that we can't do anything else.' It seems to me that such a mode of reply reveals not seriousness but feeble thinking. The question is put thus: does one human being have the right to train another or does he not? You cannot reply 'No, but, nevertheless . . .' You must reply yes or no. If yes, then the Jewish synagogue and the deacon's school[7] have just as good a right to exist as all your universities. If no, then your university, as a training institution, is just as illegitimate, unless it is perfect, and everybody admits that it is not. I can see no middle course, and not just in theory, but in reality. To me the gymnasium with its Latin and the university professor with his radicalism or materialism are equally revolting. Neither the gymnasium pupil nor the student has freedom of choice. As far as my observations go even the results of these two varieties of training are equally monstrous. Is it not obvious that the courses of study in our higher educational institutions will seem to our posterity in the twenty-first century just as strange and useless as the medieval schools seem to us now? It is so easy to come to the simple conclusion: if there have been no absolute truths in the history of human knowledge, but one set of errors has continually given place to another, then what basis have we for forcing the younger generation to acquire knowledge which will presumably turn out to be erroneous? People will say and have said: 'If it has always been so, what are you fussing about?—it must be so.' I cannot see this at all. If people have always killed one another it does not in the least follow from that that it always has to be so and that murder ought to be erected into a principle, especially if reasons for these murders were to be found and the possibility of getting on without them were to be demonstratred. Above all, why, if you recognize a general human right to train people, do you censure bad training? The father who has sent his son to a gymnasium indulges in censure, so does religion when it looks at the universities, so does the government, so do the educated classes. We must either recognize that *anyone* has the right, or that no one has—I can see no middle way. Science must decide the question: have we the right to train people or not? Why not tell the truth? As we know, the university does not like priestly education and says that there is nothing worse than a seminary; the clergy do not like university education and say that there is nothing worse than the education given by the universities, that they are simply schools of pride and atheism; parents censure the universities, the universities censure military colleges; the government censures the universities and vice versa. Who is right and who is wrong? Healthy thought in a nation which is alive and not dead cannot, when faced with such questions, concern itself with devising visual aids; it must answer these questions. And whether this thought is called pedagogy or not makes no difference. There are two possible answers: either we can recognize that the right exists for whoever is nearest to us, or whoever we love or fear most, as the majority do (if I am a priest I consider the seminary best; if I am in the army I prefer the military college; if I am a student then I recognize only the universities—we all do this, merely surrounding our prejudices with more or less ingenious arguments and quite failing to notice that all our opponents are doing the same thing), or we cannot admit that the right to train exists for anybody. I have chosen this last course and have tried to show why.

I say that universities, not only the Russian ones but all over Europe, whenever they are not entirely free, have no basis other than arbitrary power, and are just as much enormities as monastic schools. I beg that future critics will not gloss over my arguments: either I am lying or all pedagogy is mistaken—there is no middle way. Accordingly, until the right to train has been proved to exist I shall not believe in it. But nevertheless, even whilst not recognizing the right to train, I cannot fail to recognize the phenomenon itself, the fact of training, and I must explain it. Where did we get training from, and that strange attitude of our society, that inexplicable contradiction, whereby we say: this mother is bad, she has no right to train her own daughter—take her away from her mother; this institution is bad—destroy it; and this one is good, we must support it? What is the cause of the existence of training?

If such an abnormal phenomenon as force in education, or training, has existed for centuries, then the reasons for this phenomenon must be rooted in human nature. I see these reasons in (1) the family, (2) religion, (3) the state and (4) society (in the narrow sense that it has in our country, the civil-service and gentry stratum).

The first reason consists in the fact that a father and mother, whoever they may be, desire to make their children the same as they are themselves, or at least the same as they would like to be. This urge is so natural that one cannot be horrified at it. Until such time as the right of every personality to free development has entered the consciousness of every parent nothing else can be demanded. Besides, the parents will depend more than anyone else upon what their son becomes; so that the urge to train him in their own ways can be called natural, if not right.

The second reason giving rise to the phenomena of training is religion. As soon as a man—a Mohammedan, a Jew or a Christian—firmly believes that a person who does not accept his teaching cannot be saved and is ruining his soul forever, he cannot fail to desire to guide each child, even by force, and train him in his own teaching.

I repeat once again: religion is the sole legitimate and rational basis for training.

The third and most substantial reason for training is the need of governments to train the sort of people they require for certain purposes. This need is the basis for the foundation of military colleges, law schools, engineering and other schools. If there were no servants of government there would be no government; if there were no government there would be no state. No doubt that reason too has indisputable arguments in its favour.

The fourth need, finally, comes from a need of *society,* of that society in the narrow sense which is represented in our country by the gentry, the civil servants and in part by the merchant class. This society needs assistants, copiers and agents.

It is remarkable—I beg the reader, for the sake of being clear about what follows, to pay special attention to this circumstance—it is remarkable that in scholarly writings and literature we constantly meet with attacks upon force in family training (they say the parents are corrupting their children, and yet it seems so natural that a mother and father should want to make their children like themselves), we meet with attacks upon religious training (it seems that a year ago all Europe was groaning over the fate of one little Jew who was forcibly brought up as a Christian; and yet there is nothing more legitimate than the desire to give a child who has come into my care the chance of eternal salvation in the sole religion that I believe in); we meet with attacks upon the training of civil servants and army officers; but how can we expect the government, which is necessary to all of us, not to educate servants for itself and for us? But we do not hear attacks upon education conducted by the educated classes. Privileged society with its universities is always right, and that in spite of the fact that it gives training in ideas which are alien to the people, to the whole mass of the people, and has no justification but pride. Why is this so? I think it is simply because we do not hear the voice which is attacking us, and we do not hear it because it does not speak in print or from the professorial chair. But it is the mighty voice of the people—we must give ear to it.

In our period and our society take any institution you like that is run by the upper classes—from the school for the common people and the shelter for poor children to the girls' boarding school, the gymnasia and the universities—in all these institutions you will find a phenomenon which is incomprehensible but draws nobody's attention. Parents, ranging from peasants and urban artisans to merchants and noblemen, complain that their children are being trained in ideas alien to their milieu. The merchants and the noblemen of the old school say: we don't want gymnasia and universities, which will make our children into atheists and agitators. The peasants and artisans do not want schools, shelters and hostels, they do not want their children to be turned into white-handed drones and clerks instead of ploughmen. Whereas all those engaged in training without exception, from the schools for the people up to the higher educational institutions, are concerned about one thing, to train the children confided to them in such a way that those children will not be like their parents. Some trainers naïvely admit it, others, while not admitting it, believe themselves to be models of what their charges ought to be and the parents models of the grossness, ignorance and vices which the charges ought not to acquire. A schoolmistress, a grotesque creature distorted by life, who supposes that the highest perfection of human nature consists in the art of curtseying, in the wearing of collars and in the French tongue, confidentially informs you that she is a martyr to her duties, that all her work of training is in vain because of the impossibility of removing children entirely from the influence of their parents, that her girls, who have already begun to forget the Russian language and speak bad French, who have begun to forget how they chatted with the cook-girls, messed about in the kitchen and ran about in bare feet, and who have learned, thank Heaven, about Alexander of Macedon and Guadeloupe, forget all this as soon, alas, as they meet the folk from home again and pick up all their trivial habits afresh. The same schoolmistress will not only, without feeling inhibited in front of her pupils, mock at their mothers and all women in general who belong to their milieu, but she even regards it as a service which she is rendering her pupils that she changes their attitude and ideas by irony directed against their former environment. I pass over the artificial material circumstances which must completely alter the pupils' whole attitude. At home all the conveniences of life, water, cakes, good things to eat, a well-cooked dinner, the cleanliness and amenities of the household—all this depends on the work and care of mother and all the family. The more work and care—the more comfort, the less work and care—the less comfort. A simple matter, but more instructive, I venture to think, than the French language and Alexander of Macedon. But in upper-class education life's continual reward for work done is made so remote that not only will dinner be no better or worse, the pillow-slips no cleaner or dirtier, the floors no better or worse swept for the pupil's having bothered about it or not, but she has not even her own cubicle, her own corner, which she could tidy or not as the mood took her, no chance of making herself something to wear out of scraps and ribbons. 'What of it? It's no use flogging a dead horse', nine-tenths of my readers will say, 'Why talk about girls' boarding schools and all that?' No, they are not dead, they are alive and kicking, supported by the right to train. Girls' boarding schools are not a bit more monstrous than gymnasia and universities. Both have the same fundamental principle: one person or a small collection of people are admitted to have the right to make other people into what they want them to be. Girls' boarding schools are not dead horses; thousands of them exist and will exist, because they have the same right to educate as gymnasia and universities which are engaged in training. The distinction is perhaps to be found in the fact that for some reason we do not admit the family's right to train as it thinks fit; we tear a child away from a depraved mother and place her in a hostel, where a corrupted schoolmistress will set her right.

We do not admit the religious right to train, we cry out against seminaries and monastic schools, we do not admit that the government has this right, we are discontented with military colleges, law schools, etc. but our strength fails us when it comes to denying the legitimacy of the institutions in which *society,* i.e., not the people, but the upper class, claims the right to train in *its* way—girls' boarding schools and universities. Universities? Yes, universities. I shall permit myself to analyse even that shrine of highest wisdom. From my point of view not only has it not advanced one step beyond the institute for ladies, but it even contains the root of the trouble, the despotism of the upper classes, against which no hand has yet been raised.

Just as the boarding-school has decided that there is no doing without an instrument known as the pianoforte and the French language, so a certain sage or a company of such sages (if you like, take this company to mean the representatives of European learning, from whom we are supposed to have borrowed the organisation of our universities,even so this company of sages will still be very small in comparison with the mass of future pupils for whom the university is organized) has established a university for the study of all sciences whatsoever at their very highest level, and, do not forget this, has established such institutions in Moscow and Petersburg, in Kazan, in Kiev, in Derpt, in Kharkov, tomorrow others will be established in Saratov and Nikolayev; wherever they choose an institution for the study of all the sciences at the highest level will be established. I doubt whether these sages invented the organisation of this institution. It is easier for the schoolmistress; she has a model—herself. But here the models are too various and complex. But suppose such an organisation invented, suppose (what is still less likely) that we have the men for such institutions. Let us look at the activity of such an institution and its results. I have already spoken of the impossibility of laying down a programme for any educational institution whatsoever, and least of all for a university, which does not prepare pupils for any other institution, but directly for life. I shall simply repeat a proposition with which no unprejudiced people can fail to agree, that it is quite impossible to prove that the division into faculties is necessary.

Like the schoolmistress, the university considers that the first condition of admitting a person to participation in education is to cut him off from his original environment. As a general rule the university takes only pupils who have gone through the seven years temptation of the gymnasium course and who are living in a large city. A small proportion of the free students[8] go through the same gymnasium course, but with the help of private tutors instead of the gymnasium.

Before entering the gymnasium the pupil must complete a course in the district school and the elementary school.

Leaving aside learned references to history and profound comparisons with the state of affairs in the European states, I shall simply try to speak of what is happening before our eyes in Russia.

I hope we are all agreed that the task of our educational institutions is primarily to disseminate education amongst all social classes and not to maintain education in the class which has had exclusive control of it, i.e., we shall not be concerned for the education of the sons of some millionaire or magnate (they will get an education, if not in a Russian, then in a European institution) so much as we shall value giving education to the son of an innkeeper, of a merchant of the third guild, an artisan, a priest, a former domestic serf and so on. I do not speak of the peasant, that dream is so far from being realised. In a word, the university's purpose is to disseminate education amongst the greatest possible number of people. Let us take as an example the son of a minor city merchant or of a minor country gentleman. First of all the boy is sent to learn reading and writing. This study, as we know, consists in memorizing incomprehensible Church Slavonic vocables, which lasts, as we know, for three to four years.[9] The knowledge which he bears away from study of this kind turns out to be inapplicable to life; the moral habits which he bears away from the same source amount to disrespect towards elders and teachers, sometimes pilfering of books and so on, and above all idleness and sloth.

It seems superfluous to demonstrate that a school which takes three years to teach what can be learnt in three months is a school of idleness and sloth. A child who is obliged to sit motionless over a book for six hours, trying all day to learn what he could learn in half an hour, is being artificially initiated into the completest and most pernicious idleness. After such a school nine-tenths of parents, especially the mothers, find their children partly corrupted, physically weakened and alienated, but the need to make them into socially successful men prompts them to send them on to the district school. In that institution the instruction in idleness, deception and hypocrisy and the physical weakening continues with greater force. In the district school you may still see healthy faces, in the gymnasium rarely, in the university almost never. In the district school the subjects of instruction are still less applicable to life than in the first one. Here they begin Alexander of Macedon, Guadeloupe and the supposed explanation of natural phenomena which give the pupil nothing except false pride and contempt for his parents, in which he is supported by the example of his teacher. We all know these pupils, with their deep contempt for all simple uneducated people, based on their hearing from the teacher that the earth is round and air consists of nitrogen and oxygen! After the district school the foolish mother, who is so agreeably mocked at by writers of stories, is still more worried at the physical and moral changes in her child. The gymnasium course begins, with the same methods—examination and coercion, which develop hypocrisy, deception and idleness, and the son of the merchant or minor nobleman, who does not know where to seek a workman or an estate-manager, is now learning by heart French and Latin grammar and the history of Luther, and is straining to write an essay on the virtues of representative government in a style that is alien to him. Besides all this utterly inapplicable wisdom he is learning how to run up debts, deception, how to wheedle money out of his parents, dissolute behaviour and so on, sciences which will attain their final development at the university. Here in the gymnasium we already see the final renunciation of home. Enlightened teachers try to raise him above his natural environment, to this end they let him read Belinsky, Macaulay, Lewis and so on, all this not so that he may show a special bent towards something or other, but so as *to develop him* generally, as they call it. And on the basis of vague ideas and the words corresponding to them—progress, liberalism, materialism, historical development and so on—the gymnasium pupil comes to regard his past with contempt and a sense of alienation. His mentors' object is attained, but his parents, and especially his mother, look with still greater dismay upon their Vanya, emaciated, speaking in an alien tongue, thinking with an alien intelligence, cigarette-smoking, wine-drinking, self-confident and self-complacent as he is. 'The deed is done, and the others are just the same', think the parents, 'no doubt it has to be so', and Vanya is off to the university. The parents dare not say to themselves that they have made a mistake.

At the university, as we have said before, you seldom see anyone with a healthy, fresh face, and you will not see one person who looks back with respect, or even without respect but calmly, upon the environment from which he came and in which he will have to live; he looks upon it with contempt, revulsion and lofty pity. This is how he regards the people from his own milieu, his parents, and this is how he regards the activity which should await him in accordance with his social position. Only three careers, by way of exception, appear to him surrounded by a golden halo: those of the scholar, the writer and the civil servant.

Of the subjects of instruction there is not one which is applicable to life, and they are taught in just the same way as people give instruction in the Psalter and Obodovsky's geography. I except only the experimental subjects, such as chemistry, physiology, anatomy, even astronomy, in which the students are made to work; all the other subjects, such as philosophy, history, law, philology, are learnt by heart, with the sole object of giving an answer at the examination—at any examination, intermediate or final, it is just the same. I can see the lofty contempt of professors who read these lines. They will not even deign to treat me with exasperation, and will not descend from the heights of their greatness to demonstrate to a writer of stories that he understands nothing about this important and mysterious matter. I know this, but I certainly cannot for this reason withhold the conclusions of reason and observation. I certainly cannot recognize, along with the worthy professors, the mysterious rites of education producing invisible effects in the students independently of the form and content of the professors' lectures. I do not recognize all this, just as I do not recognize the equally mysterious educational influence of a classical training, which nobody explains and which it is not considered necessary to argue about. However many universally acknowledged sages and persons of worthy character may assert that the very best thing for the development of a human being is to learn Latin grammar and Greek and Latin verses in the original, when they could be read in translation; I shall not believe this, just as I shall not believe that it is necessary for a human being's development to stand on one leg for three hours. This has to be proved by something more than experience. You can prove anything you like by experience. The sexton with his psalter proves by experience that the best means of teaching reading is to make the pupil learn the psalms; the shoemaker says that the best way of teaching his trade is to make the lads draw water and chop wood and so on for two years. By such a method you will prove anything you like. I say all this simply in order that the defenders of universities should not talk to me about historical significance and mysterious educative influence and the general connection between state educational institutions and cite me as examples the universities of Oxford and Heidelberg, but should allow me to reason by simple common sense and reason thus themselves. I only know that for me, entering a university at the age of sixteen to eighteen, the scope of my activities is already circumscribed by the faculty which I had entered, and quite arbitrarily circumscribed. I arrive at one of lectures prescribed for me by the faculty and I am not only obliged to listen to everything which the professor reads out, but also to memorize it, if not word by word then proposition by proposition. If I do not learn all that the professor will not give me the necessary certificate at the final or intermediate examination. I shall not speak of the abuses, which are repeated hundreds of times over. In order to obtain this certificate I am obliged to humour the professor's favourite obsessions; either I must always sit in the front row and take notes, or look frightened or cheerful at the examination, or have just the same opinions as the professor, or faithfully frequent his evening parties (these are not my inventions, but students' opinions which can be heard at any time at any university). On hearing the lectures I may disagree with the professor's views, I may, on the basis of my reading on the subject, consider that the professor's lectures are bad, just the same I must listen to them, or at any rate learn them.

There exists in the universities a dogma not uttered aloud by the professors, that is the dogma of the papal infallibility of the professor. Not only that, but the education of the students by the professor proceeds, as with all priests, secretly, in camera, and with the uninitiated and students required to show reverence. As soon as a professor is appointed he begins to lecture, and though he may be stupid by nature or have grown so in the execution of his duties, though he may have fallen far behind in the march of science, though he may be a man of unworthy character, he continues to give lectures as long as he lives and the students have no means of expressing their pleasure or displeasure. Not only this, but what a professor says in his lectures remains a secret from everyone except the students. Perhaps it is a result of my ignorance, but I know of no text-books compiled from professors' lectures. If there are such courses then they are in a proportion of one to a hundred.

What does this mean?! A professor teaches a subject in a higher educational institution—let us say the history of Russian law or civil law, suppose he knows this subject on the highest level, suppose he has contrived to combine all the various views on this subject or has chosen one of them, the most modern, and has shown why it is so—why then does he deprive us all, deprive all Europe of the fruits of his wisdom and communicate it only to the students at his lectures? Is he really unaware that good publishers exist who will pay good money for good books, that literary critics exist who evaluate literary works, and that his students would find it much more convenient to read his book at home, lying on their beds, than to take down notes of his lectures? If science changes and is supplemented each year, then new supplementary articles could appear each year. Literature and society would be grateful. Why then do they not print their courses?

I would like to explain this in terms of indifference to literary success, but unfortunately I see that the same priests of science do not decline to publish a light political article, which is sometimes nothing to do with their subject. I fear that the secrecy of university teaching arises from the fact that 90 out of 100 lecture courses would not, if published, stand up to our "undeveloped" literary criticism. Why do you *have* to lecture, rather than place in the students' hands a good book of yours, or of somebody else's, one, two or ten good books?

The rule that at the university the professor must give lectures and that they must be by himself is one of the dogmas of university practice in which I do not believe and which are impossible to prove. 'Oral communication imprints itself more strongly on the mind and so on,' people will say to me; all this is wrong. I know of myself and many other people, who are not an exception, but the general rule, and who understand nothing from oral communication and understand things properly only when they are comfortably reading a book at home. Oral communication would make sense only if the students had the right to make objections, and then the lecture would be a discussion, and not a lesson. Only then would we, the public, no longer have the right to demand of the professors publication of the guides which they have used for thirty years at a time in teaching our children and our brethren. Under the present system lecturing is just an amusing ritual, devoid of significance, and especially amusing because of the solemnity with which it is conducted.

I am no seeker after ways of improving the universities; I am not saying that if we admitted the right of students to make objections at lectures it would be possible to make sense of university teaching. From what I know of professors and students it seems to me that in that case the students would behave like schoolboys and show off their liberal ideas, the professors would be incapable of leading the debates coolly without recourse to authority, and things would be still worse. But in my opinion it does not in the least follow from this that the students must be silent and the professors should have the right to say anything that they think fit; it simply follows from this that the whole organisation of universities rests upon a false foundation.

We can understand a university which lives up to its name, its basic idea, which is a gathering of people for the purpose of mutual education. Such universities, unbeknown to us, arise and exist in various corners of Russia; in the universities themselves, in the student groups, people come together, read, talk amongst themselves, and in the end a rule as to how they are to come together and talk amongst themselves is established. This is a real university. But our universities, in spite of the empty talk about the supposed 'liberalism' of their organisation, are institutions whose organisation differs in no respect from that of institutions for the education of women or military colleges. Just as the military colleges train officers and the law school trains civil servants, so the universities train civil servants and 'men with a university education'. (As everyone knows this is a special rank or title, almost a caste.) The recent university incidents[10] are to be explained, as far as I am concerned, in the simplest fashion: the students were permitted to wear their shirt collars outside and leave their uniforms unbuttoned, there was a move to give up punishing them for non-attendance at lectures, and consequently the whole edifice very nearly collapsed and fell. There is only one means of putting the matter right: to put them in the detention room again if they do not attend lectures, and to revive uniforms. It would be still better, on the model of the English institutions, to punish them for unsatisfactory progress and bad behaviour, and above all to limit the number of students to the number of people required. This would be consistent, and with an organisation like that the universities would give us the sort of people that they used to give us. Universities as institutions for the education of members of society, in the narrow sense of upper-class officialdom, are rational; but once people took it into their heads to make them into institutions for the education of all Russian society it became apparent that they would not do. I cannot understand at all for what reason people recognize that uniforms and disciplines are necessary in military colleges, but in the universities, where the teaching is exactly the same, with examinations and coercion and a syllabus and without any right of the pupils to make objections at lectures or to absent themselves from them—why in the universities people talk about freedom and think they can manage without the methods of the military colleges! Let us not be abashed by the example of the German universities; we cannot follow the example of the Germans; for them every custom and every law is sacred, but for us, fortunately or unfortunately, the opposite is the case.

The whole trouble in university matters, as in general education matters, comes primarily from people who do not reason, but who accept the ideas of the age and therefore suppose that they can serve two masters at once. These are those same people who answer the thoughts which I expressed previously in *Yasnaya Polyana* like this: 'True, the time is past when children might be beaten to make them learn and have things hammered into them by rote—all this is quite right—but you must agree that it is sometimes impossible to do without the birch, and that sometimes you have to make them learn things by heart. You are right, but why go to extremes? and so on.'

How gently these people reason, as it would seem, and yet it is they who have become the enemies of truth and liberty. The only reason why they apparently agree with you is so that, once they have taken possession of your idea, they may betray it, and hack it and trim it to suit themselves. They do not agree at all that freedom is essential; they only say this because they are afraid not to bow down before the idol of our age. They are merely like officials who praise to his face the governor of the province, the man who holds power in his hands. How many thousand times over I prefer my friend the parish priest, who says straightforwardly that it is no use arguing when people may die an unhappy death for want of knowing the Law of God, and therefore it is essential to teach the child the Law of God by no matter what means and save him. He says that force is essential, that study is study, and not amusement. One can argue with him, but one cannot with the gentlemen who serve both despotism and freedom. It is these gentlemen who give rise to that special condition of the universities which we now find and which demands a sort of special art of diplomacy in which, to use Figaro's expression, no one knows who is deceiving whom: the pupils deceive their parents and mentors, the mentors deceive the parents, the pupils and the government, and so on in all possible permutations and combinations. And they tell us that it is quite right that it should be so; they say to you "You are the uninitiated, don't poke your nose into our affairs, this needs a special art and special knowledge—this is a historical development." But it would seem that the matter is very simple; some wish to teach, others wish to learn. Let the former teach as much as they know how to, let the latter learn as much as they wish.

I remember at the very height of the affair concerning Kostomarov's plan for the universities[11] I was defending the plan against a certain professor. With what inimitable ponderous seriousness, almost in a whisper, solemnly, confidentially, the professor said to me: 'But do you know what sort of plan this is? This is not a plan for the new university but a plan for the destruction of universities,' he said, gazing at me in horror. 'But what then? That would be a very good thing,' I replied, *'because the universities are bad.'* The professor would not argue with me any longer, although he was unable to prove to me that the universities are good, and no one is able to prove that.

We are all men, all human, even professors. No workman will tell you that the factory where he gets his crust of bread ought to be destroyed, and this not because he has worked it out, but unthinkingly. The gentlemen who are agitating for greater freedom for the universities are like a man who, after having tried to breed young nightingales in a room and come to the conclusion that nightingales need freedom, let them out of the cage and began to give them their freedom on the end of a leash, and was then surprised to find that the nightingales did not breed with leashes attached to their legs either, but only dislocated their legs and perished.

No-one has ever thought about founding universities on the basis of the people's needs. And this has been impossible, because the people's needs have been and remain unknown. But the universities were founded upon the demand partly of the government, partly of upper-class society, and a ladder of educational institutions preparing for the universities and having nothing in common with the people's needs has already been established. The government needed civil servants, medical men, lawyers and teachers—the universities were founded in order to train them. Now upper-class society needs a certain variety of liberal, and the universities are training such people. The mistake is merely that the people do not need this sort of liberal in the least.

People usually say that the faults of the universities are a result of the faults of the lower institutions. I assert the contrary: the faults of the popular schools, especially of the district schools, are predominantly a result of the falsity of the universities' requirements.

Let us now take a look at the practice of the universities. Out of the fifty students composing the audience at a lecture ten people in the first two rows have notebooks and are writing things down: of those ten six are taking notes to please the professor, in the spirit of servility which has been developed by school and gymnasium, the other four are writing notes out of a sincere desire to note down the whole course, but give up at the fourth lecture, and at the very most two or three of them, i.e., 1/15 or 1/20 of the course, will put the lectures together. It is very difficult not to miss a single lecture. In a mathematical subject, and in any other for that matter, if one lecture is missed the thread is lost. The student falls back on the text-book, and a simple thought naturally occurs to him—he need not take on the useless work of noting down the lectures when one can do the same thing from the textbook or from other people's notes. In a mathematical or any other subject, as every teacher ought to know, no pupil is capable of following the arguments and proofs of the teacher *continually,* no matter what efforts the teacher makes to be detailed, clear, and fascinating. Very often the pupil undergoes a moment of vacancy or distraction; he needs to ask how? why? what went before? The thread is lost, but the professor goes on. The chief concern of the students (and I am speaking now only of the best) is to obtain some notes or a textbook with which they can prepare for the examination. The majority go to the lectures either because they have nothing to do and they have not yet grown bored with them, or in order to please the professor, or, in rare cases, for reasons of fashion, when one out of a hundred professors one has become popular and frequent ing his lectures has become a matter of intellectual dandyism amongst the students. Almost always from the students' point of view the lectures constitute an empty formality which is necessary only for examination purposes. Most of them, through the year, do not work at their own subjects, but at others, the syllabus of which is determined by the voluntary circle which the students happen to join. Usually they regard lectures as soldiers regard drill, and an examination as the latter regard an inspection, i.e., as a tedious necessity. The programme drawn up by a voluntary study circle shows in recent times little variety; it consists for the most part of the following: readings and accounts of readings of old articles by Belinsky and new articles by the Chernyshevskys, Antonoviches, Pisarevs and so on,[12] plus the reading of new books which have enjoyed a brilliant success in

Europe without any connection or relation to the subjects which they are studying: Lewis,[13] Buckle and so on. But the main occupation is reading banned books and copying them out. Feuerbach, Moleschott,[14], Büchner[15] and particularly Herzen and Ogaryov. Everything is copied not according to its value, but according to the degree to which it is banned. I have seen wads of copied books in students' lodgings, incomparably larger than the whole of a four-year course of instruction would be, and amongst these manuscripts thick manuscript volumes of Push-kins's most revolting poems and the most pedestrian and col-ourless poems of Ryleyev.[16] Meetings and discussions about the most various and grandiose subjects form another pastime, for instance, about re-establishing the independence of the Ukraine, about spreading literacy amongst the common people, about playing some trick collectively on a professor or inspector, which they call demanding explanations, about amalgamating two voluntary circles, an aristocratic one and a plebeian one, and so on. All this is sometimes comical, but often it is endearing, touching and poetical, as idle young people often are. But the point is that these are the pastimes which absorb young men—the son of a minor nobleman or of a merchant of the third guild—whose fathers sent them in the hope of making them into assist-ants for themselves, in the one case so that he may help to make their tiny estate productive, in the other so that he may help to carry on the trade more correctly and profitably. The opinions that exist in these circles concerning the professors are as fol-lows: of one professor they say that he is utterly stupid although a hard worker; another has fallen behind the march of science, although he was once capable; a third is venal and promotes only those who satisfy certain demands that he makes; a fourth is the laughing-stock of the human race, who has been reading out his barbarously written notes for thirty years without stopping—and it is a happy university where out of fifty professors there is one who is respected and liked by the students.

Formerly, when there were annual promotion examinations, there occurred every year something which was, if not study of the subject, at least an annual swotting up of notes before the examination. Now this swotting occurs twice, at the transition from the second year to the third year and before the finals. The same lots which used to be cast four times in the duration of the whole course are now cast twice.

Once examinations with their present organisation exist, be they end of year examinations or finals, it makes no difference, the senseless swotting and the lottery and the personal favours and caprices of the professor and the deception by the students absolutely must exist. I do not know what examination experiences the organisers of the universities had, but what common sense shows me, what I have experienced on more than one occasion and what many many people agree with me in asserting, is that examinations cannot serve as a measure of knowledge, but merely serve as an opportunity for exercising the grossly arbitrary power of the professors and for gross deception on the part of the students. I have sat for three examinations in my life: in my first year I was not promoted from the first to the second year of the course by the professor of Russian history who had had a quarrel with my relations just before, in spite of the fact that I had not missed a single lecture and knew my Russian history, and also because of a one[17] in the German language which was given me by the same professor in spite of the fact that I knew the German language incomparably better than any of the students in our year. In the following year I got a 5 in Russian history because, having had an argument with a student friend as to who had the better memory, we had each learned one question by heart and in the examination I happened to get the very same question as I had learnt, as far as I remember it was the biography of Mazeppa. That was in '46. In '48 I sat for the entrance examination at St Petersburg University and literally knew nothing and literally began to prepare myself a week before the examination. I stayed up all night and got a pass mark in civil and criminal law, having prepared for each subject no longer than a week. In the present year, '62, I have known students who graduated after working on their subjects for a week before the examination. Also this year I know that fourth-year students have forged question-slips, I know that a certain professor gave a student 3 instead of 5 because the student ventured to smile. The professor remarked to him: 'We are allowed to smile, but you may not,' and gave him a 3.

I hope no one will take the incidents I have cited to be exceptional. Anyone who knows universities knows that the incidents cited constitute the rule and not the exception, and that it cannot be otherwise. But if anyone should doubt it we can cite millions of cases. Accusers can be found, and with their signatures, in the case of the Ministry of Popular Education just as they were in the case of the Ministry of the Interior and of Justice.[18] What happened in '48[19] is happening in '62 and will happen in '72 while the organisation remains the same. The abolition of uniforms and of promotion examinations does not advance the cause of freedom by a hair's breadth; these are new patches on old clothes, which only destroy the old clothing. You cannot pour new wine into old bottles. I flatter myself with the hope that even the defenders of universities will say 'Yes, this is true, or partly true. But you forget that there are students who follow the lectures lovingly, and for whom examinations are not in the least necessary, and above all you are forgetting the educational influence of the universities.' No, I am not forgetting either; concerning the first, the students who work independently, I would say that they do not need universities with their organisation, they need only textbooks, a library, not lectures to listen to but discussions with leaders. But the universities will scarcely give even this minority knowledge appropriate to their environment, unless they happen to want to be writers or professors. The main thing is, however, that even this minority is subjected to that influence which people call educative, and which I call the corrupting influence of the universities. But this second defence concerning the educative influence of the universities is one of those which are based on faith and must first of all be proved. Who has proved, and how, that the universities do have this educative influence, whence does this mysterious educative influence proceed? There is no contact with the professors; there is no trust and love arising therefrom; there is, in the majority of cases, fear and distrust. The students will learn from the professors nothing new, nothing which they could not learn from books. The educative influence is to be found, we suppose, in the community of young people engaged on the same subject? No doubt, but they are for the most part not engaged upon scholarship, as you think, but upon preparing for examinations, hoodwinking professors, displaying their liberalism and all the things which usually take a hold upon people who are cut off from their background and their family and artificially united by means of a spirit of comradeship which has been elevated into a principle and taken to the point of complacency and arrogance. I am not talking about the exception—students living with their families—they are less subject to the educative, i.e. corrupting, influence of student life, nor am I talking about those rare exceptions, people who are devoted to learning from their youth up, who, because of their persistent labours, are also not fully subject to this influence. And in fact people do prepare themselves for life and for work; every kind of work demands, besides the fact that one gets used to it, orderliness, correctness and above all the ability to live and deal with people. Observe how a peasant's son learns to be a husbandman, how a deacon's son learns how to be a deacon by reciting in the choir, the son of a Kirghiz herdsman to be a herdsman; from a tender age he enters into a direct relationship with life, nature and people, from a tender age he studies fruitfully by working, and he studies with security as to the material side of life, i.e. he is provided with a crust of bread, clothing and shelter, and now observe the student, cut off from home and family, cast into a strange town full of temptations to one of his immature years, without a livelihood (because his parents reckon only for essential expenses and it all goes upon crazes), in a circle of companions whose society serves only to strengthen his faults, without guides, without an aim, having left the old and not arrived at the new. With few exceptions this is the condition of the student. They become what they must become: either officials, of use only to the government, or professor-officials, or writer-officials of use to upper-class society, or people who are pointlessly cut off from their former environment, with their youth ruined and unable to find themselves a place in life, what are called 'men with a university education', developed people, i.e. irritable, sick liberals. The university is our first and principal institution for training. It is the first to claim for itself the right to train and the first to prove, by the results that it gets, the impropriety and impossibility of training. Only from the point of view of upper-class society can the fruits of the university be justified. The university does not prepare the sort of people that mankind needs, but the sort of people that a corrupt society needs.

The course is over. I am supposing my imaginary trainee to be one of the best trainees in all respects. He goes back to his family; they are all strangers to him, father, mother and kindred. He does not believe in their faith, he does not desire what they desire, he does not pray to their God, but to other idols. His father and mother are disappointed, and their son often wishes to merge himself with them in one family, but cannot do so any more. What I am saying is not just a phrase or a fantasy. I know of many students who, after returning to their families, have frequently insulted the beliefs of their parents and have come to disagree with almost all the convictions of their families, about marriage, about honour, about trade. But the deed is done, and the parents console themselves with the thought that times are like that *nowadays,* and such is *modern* education; that their son will make a career for himself, if not in their milieu then at least independently, will find his own means of existence and even help them, and be happy in his own way. Unfortunately in nine cases out of ten the parents are mistaken in this as well. When he has finished his course the student does not know where to lay his head. It is a strange thing, but the knowledge which he has acquired is needed by nobody; nobody will give anything for it. Its sole application is in writing and in teaching, i.e. the science of educating still more unneeded people of the same sort. It is a strange thing! Education is rare in Russia, consequently it ought to sell dearly and be highly prized. But in fact the opposite turns out to be the case. We need engine-drivers, we have few of them, and engine-drivers are recruited from all over Europe and highly paid; why then do men educated in the university fashion (we have few educated men) say that they are needed, and yet not only do we not prize them, but they do not know what to do with themselves? Why is it that a man who has completed a course as a carpenter or a stonemason or plasterer gets 15 to 17 roubles straight away anywhere if he is a journeyman, and 25 roubles a month if he is a master-contractor, and a student is glad to get 10? (I am excluding writing and officialdom and talking about what a student can get for practical activity.) Why do landlords who have remained[20] in control of land which has to be made productive pay 300 to 500 roubles to peasant-bailiffs and will not pay even 200 roubles to students with qualifications in economics and natural science? Why do peasant-contractors on the railways have charge of thousands of workmen, but students do not? Why is it that if a student does get a job with a good salary he does not get it because of knowledge which he acquired at the university, but for knowledge acquired since? Why is it that graduates in law become officers, and mathematicians and scientists become officials? A farm-worker who has lived in clover for a year takes home 50 to 60 roubles, but a student, after a year's subsistence, leaves behind 100 roubles of debts. Why do the common people pay a teacher in a people's school 8, 9 or 10 roubles a month irrespective of whether he is a sexton or a student? Why will a merchant not appoint a student as his manager, or marry his daughter to one or take one into his house, but rather a boy of peasant origin? Because, people will say to me, society does not yet realize the value of education, because a graduate teacher will not beat children, a graduate manager will not deceive the workers and ensnare them with advance payments, a graduate merchant will not give short weight because the fruits of education are not as tangible as the fruits of routine and ignorance. This may well be, I shall reply, although my observations show me the opposite. Either a graduate does not know how to conduct business at all, honestly or dishonestly, or else, if he does know how, he conducts the business merely in accordance with his nature, with that general array of moral habits which life, independently of school, has worked out in him. I know an equal number of honest graduates and honest non-graduates, and of the opposite. But let us even suppose that university education does develop a feeling for fair dealing in a man, and that as a result of this uneducated people prefer other uneducated people to graduates and rate them higher than graduates. Let us suppose that this is so; why then do we, the so-called educated people and people of means, gentlefolk, writers, professors, why can we find no use for graduates otherwise than in the civil service? I am not talking about the civil service since advancement in the service cannot be taken to be a measure of usefulness and knowledge. Everyone knows that the student, the retired officer, the ruined landowner, the foreigner and so on, as soon as they need for any reason to earn a living, go to the capital, and, according to the connections they have and the level of their demands either get a post in the administration or, if they do not get one, consider themselves insulted. For this reason I am not talking about advancement in the service; but I ask why the very same professor as gave the students their education gives 15 roubles a month to a concierge or 20 roubles to a carpenter, but says to a graduate that comes to him that he is very sorry but he cannot give him a job, except by pulling strings amongst civil servants, or he offers him 10 roubles for a job as a copyist or a corrector of the work that he is publishing, i.e., offers him the sort of job in which he is applying nothing more than the knowledge he brought from the district school—the ability to write. But jobs where one can apply the history of Roman law or Greek literature and the integral calculus do not and cannot exist.

Thus in the majority of cases the son who has returned home

to his father after the university does not fulfil his parents' hopes and, in order not to become a burden to the family, has to take a job which requires nothing more than the ability to write, and in which he finds himself competing with all literate Russians. One advantage remains—official rank,[21] but only for the civil service, in which connections and other conditions have much greater significance; another advantage is liberalism, which is applicable to nothing. It seems to me that the proportion of university men occupying well-paid positions outside the civil service must be uncommonly small. Correct statistical information about the activities of ex-students would be important material for the science of education and would, I am convinced, prove mathematically the truth which I am trying to elicit from mere suppositions and such data as we have—the truth that people with a university education are little needed and direct their activities predominantly towards writing and teaching, i.e., repeating the vicious circle of educating more people who are not needed for life.

But I did not foresee one objection, or rather source of objections, which naturally occurs to the majority of my readers: why should the same higher education as turns out to be so fruitful in Europe be inapplicable in our country? European societies are more educated than Russian society, why should Russian society not follow the same road as European nations? This objection would be irrefutable if it were proved, firstly, that the road which the European peoples have followed is the best road, secondly that all humanity is following the same road and, thirdly, that our education is gaining acceptance amongst the common people. All the Orient has been and is educated in quite different ways from those of European man. If it were proved that a young animal, a wolf or a dog, was reared upon meat and was brought by this means to its full development, would I have the right to conclude that when rearing a young horse or hare I cannot develop them to the full otherwise than by means of meat? Could I conclude from these contradictory experiments that, if I reared a young bear, he would need either meat or oats? Experience would show me that he needed both. Even if it seems to me that it is more natural to form meat by means of meat, and if my previous experiments confirm my supposition, I cannot continue to give meat to a colt if he rejects it every time and his organism does not assimilate this food. Exactly the same thing occurs with the education, European in both form and content, which is transplanted to our soil. The organism of the Russian people does not assimilate it, and yet there must be another food sustaining its organism, for it lives. This food seems to us to be no food, no more than grass does to a predatory animal, but nevertheless the historical-physiological process is effected, and this food which we do not recognize is assimilated by the organism of the people, and the vast animal gains in strength and grows.

Summing up what has been said above we arrive at the following propositions:—

1. Education and training are two different concepts.
2. Education is free and therefore legitimate and right; training is coercive and therefore illegitimate and wrong, cannot be justified by reason and therefore cannot be the subject-matter of pedagogy.
3. Training, as a phenomenon, has its beginnings a) in the family; b) in faith; c) in the government; d) in the upper classes.
4. The family, religious and governmental foundations of training are natural and can be justified by necessity; but training by the upper classes has no foundations except pride in human reason and therefore bears the most harmful fruits, such as universities and university education.

Only now, when we have in part elucidated our views on education and training and defined the limits of each of them can we reply to the questions put by Mr Glebov in the magazine *Vospitanie (training)* for 1862 no. 5, the questions which occur first and naturally when making a serious enquiry into educational work:

1. What must the school be if it is not to intervene in training?
2. What is meant by the school's not intervening in matters of training?
3. Is it possible to separate training from teaching, especially elementary teaching, when the training element enters into young minds even in the higher schools?

(We have already explained that the form of the higher educational institution into which the training element enters, does *not* serve as a model for us. Not only do we reject the discipline of the higher educational institutions as much as that of the lower, but we see in them the origin of the whole evil.)

In order to reply to the questions which have been put we shall simply re-arrange them: 1) What is meant by the school's not intervening in training? 2) Is such non-intervention possible? and 3) What must the school be if not concerning itself with training?

In order to avoid misunderstandings I must first explain what I mean by the word school, which I have used in the same sense in the first article of the first number of *Yasnaya Polyana*. By the word school I mean not the building in which people study, not the teachers, not the pupils, not a particular tendency in teaching; by the word school I mean *the conscious action of the educator upon the persons who are educating themselves,* i.e., a particular portion of education, irrespective of how that action is expressed: the teaching of Tsar's Regulations to recruits is a school, the giving of public lectures is a school, a course in Mohammedan religious instruction is a school, the collection of a museum and the opening of it to all who wish to see it is also a school.

I give my answer to the first question. The school's non-intervention in the work of education means the school's non-intervention in the education (formation) of the beliefs, the convictions and the character of the person being educated. And this non-intervention is to be attained by offering the person being educated complete freedom to accept that instruction which accords with his requirements, which he wants, and accepts in so far as he needs and wants it, and to decline that instruction which he does not need or want.

Public lectures and museums are the best examples of schools without intervention in training. Universities are examples of schools with intervention in the matter of training. In these institutions the pupils are bound by a particular course, a syllabus, a combination of selected studies; they are bound by the requirement to take examinations and principally by the offer of rights based on them, i.e., on the examinations, or, to put it more accurately, by deprivation of rights in the event of their not observing the prescribed conditions. (A fourth-year student taking an examination is theatened with a most serious punishment, the loss of ten or twelve years of hardship at the gymnasium or the university and the forfeiture of the advantages for the sake of which he endured twelve years of hardship.) In these institutions everything is arranged in such a manner that the pupil will accept the element of training in education and acquire the beliefs, the principles and the character which the founders of the institution require. The coercive training element, consisting in the exclusive choice of one field of studies and in the threat of punishment, is just as strong and obvious to a serious observer as it is in the institution using corporal punishment, which superficial observers hold up as a contrast to the universities.

On the other hand public lectures, which are continually growing in number in Europe and America, not only do not impose a particular field of study, not only do not demand that one attends them upon pain of punishment, but demand certain other sacrifices from the pupils, by which very fact they demonstrate, in contrast to the former, the complete freedom of choice and approach upon which they are based. That is what is meant by the intervention and non-intervention of the school in training. If I am told that such non-intervention, which is possible for higher institutions and adults, is impossible for lower levels and juveniles, because we see no examples of it—no public lectures for children and so on—I shall reply that if we do not interpret the word 'school' too narrowly, but take it in the definition given above, we shall find plenty of free educational influences without intervention in training for the lower stages of knowledge and the lower age-groups, corresponding to the higher institutions and the public lectures. Such is the learning of reading and writing from one's friends and brothers, such are the traditional children's games, about whose educational influence I intend to insert a special article,[22] such are the public spectacles, the peep-shows and so on, such are pictures and books, such are folk-tales and songs, such are jobs and such, finally, are the efforts of the Yasnaya Polyana school.

The answer to the first question also gives in part the answer to the second: is such non-intervention possible? One cannot prove theoretically that it is possible. The one thing which confirms that it is possible is observation, which proves that altogether untrained people, i.e. those subject only to free educational influences, are fresher, stronger, more powerful, more independent, juster, more humane and, above all, more useful than people who have been trained in any way whatsoever. But perhaps this proposition too requires proof in many people's eyes. I should have a lot more to say about those proofs. I shall cite just one. Why is the generation of trained people not zoologically improved? A stock of animals which are trained improves; the stock of people who are trained deteriorates and grows weaker. Take at random a hundred children from several generations of trained people and a hundred untrained children of the common people and compare them in any way you like: for strength, dexterity, intelligence, receptivity, morality or even in all respects, and you will be struck by the enormous superiority of the children of the untrained generations, and the greater the superiority the lower the age will be, and vice versa. This is a terrible thing to say because of the conclusions which it entails, but it is so. The only way of finally proving the possibility of non-intervention in lower schools to people whose personal experience and inner feelings tell them nothing in favour of such an opinion is by conscientious study of the free influences by means of which the common people are educated, a many-sided discussion of the question and a long series of experiments and reports on them.

What must the school be if not intervening in matters of training? A school, as we have said above, is the conscious action of an educator upon persons being educated. How is he to act so as not to overstep the bounds of education, i.e. of freedom? I reply: the school must have an object, the imparting of information, of knowledge (Fr. instruction) without trying to pass into the moral sphere of principles, belief and character; its object must be learning alone, and not the results of its influence upon the human personality. The school must not try to foresee the consequences produced by learning, but must offer, in conveying it, complete freedom as to how it is applied. The school must not regard one subject or a whole combination of subjects as essential; but it must proffer the knowledge it possesses, leaving the pupils the right to accept it or not. The structure and programme of the school must be based not on a theoretical attitude, but solely on what is possible, i.e. on what the teachers know. I shall explain by an example. I wish to found an educational institution. I do not compose a programme based on my theoretical views and seek teachers on the basis of this programme, but I invite any people who feel a vocation for the communication of knowledge to give such lessons or lectures as they can. It goes without saying that we will be guided by previous experience in the choice of these lessons, i.e., we shall not even try to teach those subjects which are listened to unwillingly, in a Russian village we shall not lecture on the Spanish language, astrology or geography, just as a merchant would not open a shop in that village to sell surgical instruments or crinolines. We cannot foresee the demand for our offer, but our final judge shall be simply experience, and we do not consider that we would have the right to open even one shop in which tar was sold only on condition that for every ten pounds of tar you took off our hands a pound of ginger or pomade. We shall not concern ourselves with the use that the consumers will make of our wares, we believe that they know what they need, and it is enough work for us just to guess their requirements and respond to them. It may well be that we shall find one teacher of zoology, one teacher of medieval history, one of divinity and one of surveying. If these teachers are capable of making their lessons absorbing these lessons will be useful in spite of the apparent inconsistency and fortuitousness. I do not believe in the possibility of a theoretically planned harmonious scheme of subjects, but I do believe that each subject, when the teaching is free, fits harmoniously into the scheme of knowledge of each human being. People will perhaps say that if the programme is thus fortuitous useless and even harmful subjects may come into the course, and that it will be impossible to teach many subjects because the pupils will be insufficiently prepared for them. To that I would reply that, in the first place, there are no harmful or useless subjects for anybody whatsoever, and that there is such a thing as common sense and the demand of the pupils, which, provided the teaching is free, would not admit useless or harmful subjects if there were any; in the second place a bad teacher needs pupils who have been prepared, but for a good one it is easier to start algebra or analytical geometry with a pupil who knows no arithmetic than with a pupil who knows it badly; it is easier to start medieval history with a pupil who has not learnt ancient history by heart. I do not believe that a professor who teaches at the university differentials and integrals or the history of Russian civil law and who cannot teach arithmetic and history in a Russian elementary school is a good professor. I do not see that it is useful, valuable or even possible to teach well just one part of a subject. Above all, however, I am convinced that supply will always respond to demand, and that at every stage of learning there will be a sufficient number of pupils and of teachers.

But how, people will say to me, can an educator not desire to produce a certain training influence by means of his teaching? This urge is a most natural one, it has its origin in a natural requirement inherent in the transfer of knowledge from teacher to taught. This urge simply gives the teacher the strength to tackle his job, it gives him the degree of enthusiasm which he cannot do without. It is impossible to deny the existence of this urge, and I have never thought of doing so; in my eyes its existence only proves all the more strongly that freedom in teaching work is essential. You cannot forbid a man who loves and teaches history to try and convey to his pupils the historical outlook which he has, and which he considers to be profitable and essential for a human being's development, or to convey the method that he thinks best in the study of mathematics or science—on the contrary, the fact that he foresees this end in moral training encourages the teacher. But the point is that the training element in learning cannot be communicated forcibly. I cannot draw the reader's attention sufficiently to this fact. The training element in, let us say, history or mathematics, is communicated only when the teacher passionately knows and loves his subject; only then does that love communicate itself to the pupils and work upon them as moral training. In the contrary case, i.e., when it is decided somewhere that such and such a subject affords moral training and it is laid down that some shall teach it and others listen, the teaching produces completely opposite results, i.e. not only does not give moral training through knowledge, but it produces an aversion to knowledge. People say that knowledge bears in itself an element of moral training *(erziehliges Element)*—this is both true and untrue, and in this proposition lies the fundamental error in the existing paradoxical view of training. Knowledge is knowledge and bears nothing in itself. The element of moral training, however, lies in the teaching of the knowledge, in the teacher's love of his subject and in his loving communication of it, in the teacher's relationship to his pupil. *If you wish to train your pupils morally by means of knowledge love your subject and know it, and the pupils will love both you and the subject, and you will train them; but if you do not love it yourself, then no matter how much you make them study the subject will not produce a moral influence.* And here again the only yardstick, the only salvation is once more the same freedom of the pupils to listen to the teacher or not to listen, to accept or not to accept his moral influence, i.e., it is for them alone to decide whether he knows and loves his subject.

What then will the school be if there is no intervention in training?

The many-sided and extremely varied conscious action of one human being upon another for the purpose of communicating knowledge (Fr. instruction) without forcing the pupil either by direct force or by diplomacy to accept what we want. The school will not, perhaps, be a school as we understand it, with blackboards, benches, and rostra for the teachers or professors—it will perhaps be a peepshow, a theatre, a library, a museum, a discussion group; the scheme of subjects and the programme will perhaps turn out quite differently in each case (I only know of my own experience: the Yasnaya Polyana school with the division of subjects which I described has in the space of half a year, partly because of the demands of the pupils and their parents, partly because of the inadequacy of the teachers' knowledge, quite changed and assumed new forms.)

'But what are we to do? Will there really be no district schools, will there be no gymnasia, will there be no chair of the history of Roman law any more? What will become of the human race?' I hear people say. They will not exist if they are not required by the pupils and if you cannot contrive to make them good. 'But after all children do not always know what they need, children make mistakes and so on,' I hear people say. I do not enter an argument of this kind. This argument would lead us to the question: does man judge man's nature to be good? and so on. I do not know and I am not going to start upon that path; I only say that if we are able to know what to teach then do not stop me from forcibly teaching Russian children the French language, medieval genealogy and the art of theft. I shall justify it all as well as you can. 'So will there be no more gymnasia and Latin? What am I going to do?' I hear again.

Never fear, there will be both Latin and rhetoric, these will exist for a hundred years yet, and will exist simply because 'we have bought the medicine, so we must drink it' (as a certain patient said). It is doubtful whether the idea which I am expressing, perhaps unclearly, unskilfully, unconvincingly, will become commonly accepted even in a hundred years' time; it will take at least a hundred years for all the ready-made institutions—schools, gymnasia, universities—to die out, and then freely formed institutions will grow, having as their basis freedom for the generation that is studying.

Notes

Introduction

I *The historical background*

1. See 'The Historian's Craft'.
2. Hugh Seton-Watson, *The Russian Empire 1801–1917* (Oxford, 1967), p. 477.
3. Article by Tolstoy in *Yasnaya Polyana* magazine, 'A project for a general plan of organisation of schools for the people' (not included in the present volume).
4. Article by Tolstoy in *Yasnaya Polyana* magazine, 'On the activities of society in the field of popular education' (not included in the present volume).
5. Article by Tolstoy in *Yasnaya Polyana* magazine: 'On the free appearance and development of schools amongst the common people'.
6. That is how I came to buy for an English child, some years ago, a translation with the surprising title-page 'The Three Bears' by Leo Tolstoy.
7. But an incident of 1888 is so characteristic that it deserves mention. Tolstoy visited a Moscow elementary school, and applied a few days later for a teaching post there—because he was so disgusted by its methods and atmosphere. One of the governors, a Moscow merchant, paid a visit to the world-famous writer to talk it over. No appointment ensued.

II *The pedagogy of freedom*

8. See the memoirs of Vasily Morozov, chapter 4.
9. *Children's Minds,* Margaret Donaldson (Fontana, 1978), p. 113.
10. 'A critique of the concept of compensatory education', in Basil Bernstein, *Class, Codes and Control,* vol. 1 (Routledge & Kegan Paul 1971), p. 192.
11. Maurice Galton, Brian Simon and Paul Croll, *Inside the Primary Classroom* (Routledge & Kegan Paul, 1980).
12. See in particular 'The voice of poetry in the conversation of mankind', from Michael Oakeshott, *Rationalism in Politics* (Methuen, 1968), p. 162.
13. John Vaizey as quoted in M. I. Finley, *The Use and Abuse of History* (Chatto & Windus, 1975), p. 210.
14. Ernst Gombrich. 'The Tree of Knowledge', *The Listener*, 8 March 1979.
15. For a further discussion of this point see Michael Armstrong, *Closely Observed Children* (Writers & Readers Publishing Cooperative, 1980).

Chapter 1: On the education of the people

1. Boys who graduated successfully from certain state schools in Russia were entitled to enter the state service at certain specified ranks. High rank in the state service

(military or civil) conferred far more social prestige than any private professional status.

2. Free from school attendance.

3. Dialect.

4. Johann Peter Hebel (or Hebbel), 1760–1826, author of popular stories and poems in the Alemannic dialect of German.

5. To make stupid.

6. In English in the original.

7. Tolstoy presumably means that the boys' skill in 'sums' as presented in the book was useless because they could not see how a real-life problem could be turned into an abstract 'sum'.

8. Pleasure gardens.

9. Of teaching reading.

CHAPTER 2: The Yasnaya Polyana school in the months of November and December

I *General sketch of the character of the school. Mechanical and progressive reading. Grammar and writing.*

1. Given incorrectly with a feminine ending.

2. Familiar form.

3. Koltsov: writer of lyrical poems in the folk idiom. His pictures of rural life tend to be gloomy.

4. A common punishment in the nineteenth-century Russian nursery was to make the child kneel in the corner. See, for instance, Tolstoy's 'Childhood'.

5. A fantastic story set in the Ukraine.

6. Originally a strip of forest protected because of its value as an obstacle to Tartar cavalry.

7. A name given in the Caucasus to outlaws or to leaders of the resistance to Russian colonization.

8. A Caucasian chieftain who went over to the Russians. Tolstoy was later to make his story the basis of a work of fiction.

9. A Church Slavonic chant, known by its opening word.

10. A post station where horses were changed, not a railway station.

11. That is, a folk-tale.

12. Has the same effect as *vous* in French.

13. As distinct from the peasant idiom.

14. Collectors of folk-tales in the traditional folk idiom, which differs considerably in style and vocabulary from literary Russian of the nineteenth century.

15. An early-nineteenth-century sentimentalist writer with a simple but elegant style.

16. Pushkin's folk-tales in verse are acknowledged masterpieces in a style which subtly bridges the gap between the popular and literary languages. Yershov's verse fairy-tale 'The little hump-backed horse', though not of equal value, continues to be republished in the Soviet Union.

17. I.e., a quire of printed pages.

18. Russian for 'whom', a sample of a type of spelling irregularity shared by numerous Russian words.

19. A bi-monthly periodical intended for a popular readership.

20. Chichikov's manservant in *Dead Souls,* whose attitude to reading was somewhat

like Joe Gargery's. 'What he liked was not what he was reading about, but rather the reading itself, or, to put it better, the very process of reading, the way a word kept on sort of coming out of the letters, and sometimes the devil alone knew what that word meant.' (*Dead Souls,* vol. 1, chap. 2).

21. Contemporary children's publications, long forgotten by now.

22. In prose this time. Perhaps the least interesting of Pushkin's volume of experimental short stories *Tales by Belkin.*

23. Another of Gogol's early "folksy" Ukrainian stories.

24. A classic translation of the *Iliad* done in the early nineteenth century by a friend of Pushkin in a high style far removed from contemporary Russian speech.

25. A children's story. A Russian translation was published in London with a foreword by the famous exiled writer Herzen.

26. I.e., a turgid pastiche of the Russian folk-tale style.

27. Most Russians would intend a compliment by such a remark. The verse fables of Krylov (an older contemporary of Pushkin) are classics of racy and vigorous Russian wit.

28. Heroic folk-songs, often about ancient Kiev and the struggles against pagan nations of the steppes.

29. The supplements entitled 'Yasnaya Polyana booklets' contained reading-matter for peasant children. Very little was in fact published in the magazine itself in the field of research into popular taste in reading-matter.

30. The usual beginner's text for the pupils of sextons, priests and other old-fashioned, popular instructors.

31. In the pre-revolutionary orthography.

32. Two letters with the same sound. One of them, "yat", was dropped from the Russian alphabet altogether in the 1917 spelling reform.

33. Work.

34. Raspberry.

35. Which was correct. See note 32 above. In some Russian schools children used to learn by heart a list of the words spelt with a 'yat'.

36. In standard Russian words ending in o are invariably neuter.

37. I.e., from what infinitive: it is a verb.

38. A character in the Cyrillic alphabet which modifies consonants, but never appears independently. It is the only written difference between uchitsya—studies (3rd pers. sing. present tense) and uchit'sya—to study (infinitive).

39. We see from Vasily Morozov's memoirs that some boys thought the chief point of learning to write was to earn money as a letter-writer for illiterate clients.

40. See the second part of the article.

II *Sacred history, Russian history, geography.*

41. A modern historian would probably say, 'the Varangian period'—early medieval Russia, when the ruling élite was of Norse origin. M. P. Pogodin (1800–1875) wrote numerous historical works and textbooks for school courses on Russian history.

42. *Not* written questions as in the standard British examination. Tolstoy has in mind a type of oral examination, in which one expounds in public a question drawn from a hat. He describes it in chapters 10 to 12 of his early story 'Youth'. It is not obsolete. A young Frenchwoman described to me some years ago the ordeal of an examination in Greek of this type. According to student legend, the examiners notched the table in triumph whenever a girl was reduced to tears.

43. Top mark. Russian teachers use a 5-point scale in which 5 means excellent and 1 very poor.

44. Rags wrapped round the feet and ankles instead of socks.

45. There is no need to conclude that Tolstoy was going through a fundamentalist phase. On the contrary, he was at his least religious in this period. He was writing under censorship, however, and is prepared to pass the placatory phrase 'truthful as revelation' since for him it has some metaphorical value. If the Bible stories are truthful as art they are in some sense a revelation of human nature.

46. I.e., into popular Russian, not Church Slavonic. A translation of the New Testament into modern Russian was published long before, in 1818, by the officially approved Russian Bible Society. Perhaps it was not, in Tolstoy's view, 'the language of the common people'.

47. Theodor Mommsen (1817–1903), the well-known historian of Rome. His *Römische Geschichte* appeared 1854–56 in three volumes. Max Duncker was a historian and liberal politician whose *Geschichte des Altertums* was still appearing when Tolstoy wrote (nine volumes, 1852–86). Both very serious authors who would take considerable adaptation for children.

48. Alexandra Ishimova's *History of Russia told to children* received a prize of 2,500 roubles in 1852. She also translated Fenimore Cooper and gave lessons to princesses.

49. The pood was a little over 35 pounds. Perhaps he means 'of silver'.

50. The famous victory of Dmitry of the Don over the Tartars in 1378.

51. When a national movement led by Minin and Pozharsky repelled the Poles.

52. The Russian word 'zemlya' means either 'world' or 'land'. Probably the teacher meant to ask 'What is our land like?' and the pupil took the word in its other sense. I have not found a way of rendering this verbal misunderstanding in English.

53. Several parts of the Russian Empire had substantial enclaves of Germans, e.g., the Volga basin.

54. Russified forms of recognizably German names. Presumably local German residents.

55. Scilicet: On the Russian fast days.

56. In Tsarist Russia these were legally recognized estates with different rights and duties.

57. The town of Tula was and is famous for certain lighter metal industries, including the making of samovars. The makers were not, of course, a separate legal class.

58. Instruction by observation. See below, p. 272.

59. In which, it will be recalled, Tolstoy had himself served.

60. Barclay de Tolly, a Russian general of German and Scottish descent. He was replaced as commander by Kutuzov after losing Smolensk to Napoleon.

61. Features of the fortifications at Sevastopol.

62. Used for beating the clothes as they are washed.

63. Peter Parley (1793–1860) was an American author and publisher of numerous children's works.

64. J. N. A. Thierry (1795–1856) French romantic historian whose works on France and England in the Middle Ages enjoyed a long popularity.

65. Mitrofanushka is the name-role in *The Minor,* a comedy by Fonvizin which first appeared in 1783. It is a vigorous satire on provincial backwardness and ignorance.

66. Sophie Rostopchine, countess of Segur, a Franco-Russian lady, author of many popular children's works in French (1799–1874).

III *Drawing and singing.*

67. We have omitted from this article an account of drawing lessons written by Tolstoy's German assistant, Gustav Keller.

68. Aleksandr Andreevich Ivanov (1806–58) an academic painter. One of his best-known works is *The Appearance of the Messiah*.

69. We ask the reader to direct his attention to this hideous picture which is remarkable for the strength of its religious and poetical feeling, and which stands in relation to contemporary Russian painting as Fra Beato Angelico does to the painting of the successors of Michael-Angelo's school. (Note by L.N.T.)

In the popular legend Archbishop Ioann of Novgorod found a devil in a pitcher of water, made the sign of the cross over it, extracted the devil and flew away on its back on a pilgrimage to Jerusalem. This remarkable incident was commemorated in a crude "lubok" woodcut. (A.H.P.)

70. A love poem by Pushkin, among the best known in the Russian language.

71. Of folk songs.

72. Emile-Joseph-Maurice Chevé or Chevet (1804–64), a French doctor who became one of the chief advocates of a method of teaching part-singing, in which the notes of the tonic sol-fa are represented by the figures 1 to 7. For details see the entry in Grove's *Dictionary of Music and Musicians*.

73. Unanimously rejected.

CHAPTER 3: An extract from the reminiscences of a teacher at Yasnaya Polyana school

1. A popular mispronunciation of Nikolayevich.

CHAPTER 4: Extracts from the reminiscences of a pupil at Yasnaya Polyana school

1. Perhaps the reason Morozov mentions the Psalter separately from plain reading and writing is that it would be in Church Slavonic, a language imperfectly understood by Russians.

2. The pood was a little over 35 pounds weight.

3. A neighbouring village where there were shops.

4. A cubicle of lattice-work in which clothes were kept.

5. A kind of small beer made from crusts of bread.

6. A greeting traditionally exchanged between squads of soldiers and their officers in the tsarist army.

7. Perhaps it may seem strange that Morozov had never seen either Lev Nikolayevich or his house before he enrolled in the school. But Morozov remembers this very well and explains it by saying that there were always strict agents and bailiffs on Lev Nikolayevich's estate who forbade the children to enter the home farm. (Note by Alexei Sergeyenko to the 1917 edition.)

8. Again a soldier's form of reply to an officer.

9. Vas'ka is the traditional name of the cat in the animal cycle of Russian folk-tales.

10. Obviously ikons, representing the saints or, in some cases, the Trinity or the Saviour. Nevertheless the term 'gods' in this sense (spelt with a small letter even in the pre-Communist edition) is unusual. Possibly regional usage.

11. I.e., the opening letters of the Russian alphabet.

12. Alabaster.

13. Caesarea.

14. As a matter of fact he was thirty-one.

15. A vulgar variant of Nikolayevich.

16. See above, Note 4 on Chap. 2 p. 331.
17. Normal sleeping place in a peasant hut.
18. The Crimean War. Tolstoy served at Sevastopol.
19. P. V. Morozov, one of Tolstoy's closest assistants. See above, p. 185.
20. See above, Note 3 on Chap. 2 p. 327.
21. See above, Note 2 on p. 330.
22. Of a peasant cart or 'telega'.
23. A gymnasium was a type of secondary school. P. V. Morozov (the *teacher* at the Yasnaya Polyana school) mentions in his memoirs that the headmaster of the Tula Gymnasium for Boys, I. F. Goyarin, "frequently visited our school with his pupils" but does not mention a competition.
24. A traditional Russian game something akin to tennis.
25. The nickname 'Bubble' and the reason for it are confirmed in Tolstoy's 'Remininiscences of childhood' written 1903–6.
26. Alexei Sergeyenko (editor of the *Reminiscences*) believes this to be a mistake, and that Tolstoy's voice was 'much higher'.
27. When animals strayed on to the master's pasture or crops they were impounded until the erring peasant had discharged a stint of extra work for the master in lieu of a money fine. (At least I *think* this is the right interpretation.)
28. *War and Peace*.

CHAPTER 5: Should we teach the peasant children to write, or should they teach us?

1. It is taken for granted here that the burning down of wooden houses, and the practice of pulling down houses to prevent the fire spreading, is perfectly likely to be within a child's direct experience. For Tolstoy the subject 'A conflagration' is an invitation to realism, not fantasy.
2. These words do not occur in the story as we have it. But the peasant does say 'With what he had on he was bound to get frozen' and the opening words are similar. Tolstoy's memory seems to have failed him.
3. Again a slight alteration of the wording.
4. Scilicet surname ('Household' name in the peasant boy's vocabulary.) He would have called Tolstoy so far by his first name and father's name', Lev Nikolayevich. This is still the form in which Soviet children address their teachers.
5. A fur coat is not, of course, necessarily associated with luxury in Russia. Peasants often had coats made of the skins of hares which they shot or trapped themselves. And it is common for Russian *men* to wear fur.
6. A kind of small beer, made from crusts of bread.
7. It was never written.
8. The one alluded to in the first part of 'Yasnaya Polyana school in the months of November and December'?
9. Molokan (lit. milk-drinker) member of a dissenting sect whose doctrines (according to Mackenzie Wallace) bore considerable resemblance to presbyterianism. A native Russian growth, however, unconnected historically with Western protestantism.
10. In the days of serfdom land-owners could send unsatisfactory serfs into the army as a punishment.
11. A meeting of the Village Commune which dealt with periodical distribution of land, choice of conscripts (subject to the master's approval) and other collective responsibilities of the village.

12. The holy ikons which occupied a corner shrine in even a peasant hut.

13. A well-known custom. When the guests at a wedding breakfast make the traditional complaint that their wine is bitter the bride and groom must kiss to make it taste sweeter for them.

CHAPTER 6: He feeds you with a spoon and pokes you in the eye with the handle

1. I.e., to urinate.

2. The chest or 'konnik' served as a seat or sleeping bench as well as a container. It seems to have been used, like a Welsh lambing chair, to lodge unweaned lambs which were being reared in the cottage.

3. This obscure proverb may mean that talk does not make one richer—'Fine words butter no parsnips'.

4. The traditional names of the first two Russian letters.

5. A man's name. Rhymes in Russian with 'az'.

CHAPTER 7: The life of a soldier's wife

1. The village had a communal responsibility for raising the poll-tax. If a man did not pay, his neighbours would have to pay for him.

2. The peasant village assembly (Russ. mir) usually had to decide how to fulfil the periodical quota of army recruits (though the master sometimes intervened). It suited everyone to send a tax-defaulter.

3. An untranslatable play upon words. The boy mistook podushnye (poll-tax) for podushka (pillow).

4. It was not unknown to have two children with the same Christian name in one family. The choice of name was often left to the priest, who might well choose the name of the saint in the church calendar for the child's birthday. Some saints had more than one day.

5. Traditional verses said on the groom's arrival. Quite apart from the church service, the secular celebration was punctuated by numerous traditional formulae, many harking back to more primitive marital customs.

6. A relic of previous marriage customs. The little boy must pretend to defend his sister against the bridegroom who is supposed to be carrying her off by force. He is then offered a symbolical brideprice (the money in the glass of vodka). After Fedka has accepted this the bridegroom's party sit down and are made welcome.

7. A traditional joke at Russian weddings. The bride and bridegroom must then kiss to sweeten the guests' drink.

8. One pood was a little over thirty-five pounds.

9. Traditional keening formulae.

10. I.e., crossed himself before the ikons in one corner of the cottage.

11. Vasily Morozov does not know the difference between an officer and an N.C.O. (Russ. unter-ofitser).

CHAPTER 8: On methods of teaching reading

1. See editors' note, above.

2. Secondary schools resembling the German Gymnasium.

3. An obscure sentence. I think Tolstoy is merely alluding to the notorious fact that

the syllabus and ethos of any school are influenced by the entrance requirements of a higher one.

4. A sort of higher grade school. They were not at all numerous.

5. German for phonetic method.

6. Surely Tolstoy is wrong here. Both 'f' and 'sh' are unvoiced consonants.

7. Russian words beginning with the first four letters of the alphabet. In English it might be apple, book, cat, dog.

8. The traditional Russian routine of naming the letters in a syllable and then combining them. See Editor's Note at the head of this article.

9. German for 'reader'.

10. I.e., the ABC.

11. A rhymed couplet in the original. Yershov's verse tale 'The little humpbacked horse' mentioned below is still part of Russian children's literature.

12. Scilicet, Petersburg or Moscow. Moscow had retained the courtesy title of 'stolitsa' (capital) alongside Petersburg.

13. A single letter, of course, in Russian.

14. We find Tolstoy's examples somewhat eccentric, and difficult to render in English letters. His main idea, however, is clearly that in Russian no combination of letters represents a sound other than the sum of its parts, as is the case, for instance, of 'ch' in English, which is not simply c + h. Therefore, a Russian letter has only one constant value.

CHAPTER 9: Training and education

1. *'Obrazovanie'* corresponds in fact very closely to the English concept 'education', but the Russian word is derived from the verb 'to form' and Tolstoy is sometimes inclined to dwell upon this etymological meaning. Cf. German *Bildung*.

2. Friedrich-Adolf Diesterweg (1790–1866) a German educationist in the Pestalozzi tradition whom Tolstoy met in 1861 during his European tour.

3. The distinction here appears to be between education as a finished effect upon a person and education as a process.

4. It is not. Tolstoy attributes to our English word 'education' a narrower sense than it has.

5. It seems reasonably certain that Tolstoy has in mind the two *French* words thus spelt, and is assuming that the two English words are identical in meaning as in form. His English was by no means as good as his French.

6. In the German sense. A type of secondary school in Russia modelled on the German Gymnasium. Not very unlike a French lycée.

7. I.e., the primitive school in which a village deacon taught reading.

8. Students who may hear lectures but who do not enjoy the full rights, nor submit to the full discipline, of the university. Cf. the *Freihörer* of the German university or the *auditeur libre* of the French.

9. In the old-fashioned Russian system the usual first reader was the Psalter or other scriptural extracts, which were in Church Slavonic, not Russian.

10. Student unrest at the universities of St Petersburg, Moscow, Kiev and Kazan in the autumn of 1861. Some of the students who were rusticated were engaged by Tolstoy as teachers. See Introduction by Alan Pinch.

11. In 1861 Kostomarov, a Petersburg history professor, published a plan for university reform. The universities were to become open institutions offering public lectures for all, including women.

12. I.e., of heroes of the liberal and freethinking tradition, founders of the intelligentsia in the special Russian sense of the word.

13. George Henry Lewis (1817–78) Darwinist and positivist philosopher.

14. A Russian physiologist popular amongst the young materialists of the 1860s.

15. *Not* the playwright, but another materialist writer. Readers of Turgenev's *Fathers and Children* will remember how the father Kirsanov is told to read Büchner's *Kraft und Stoff* instead of Pushkin.

16. Pushkin wrote a certain amount of scabrous and blasphemous verse, often very skilful and witty. Ryleyev—a minor poet executed for treason in 1826. All his best known poems express political dissent.

17. Under the Russian 5 point system of marking 5—excellent, 4—good, 3—fairly good, 2—poor, 1—failure.

18. The early sixties saw a sharp reaction of public opinion in Russia against the civil service as a whole.

19. I.e., when Tolstoy was a university student. He is *not* referring to revolutions.

20. I think Tolstoy uses this verb because he is writing soon after the upheaval of the emancipation of the serfs and accompanying redistribution of land, when some landlords left the land for other pursuits.

21. A graduate entering the civil service did not take the lowest rank.

22. It was never written.

Select Bibliography

The originals of the texts translated are in the following:

L. N. Tolstoy, *Polnoye sobraniye sochinenii* [Complete collected works], vol. 8, ed. N. M. Mendel'son and V. F. Savodnik, Moscow, 1959.

V. S. Morozov, *Vospominaniya o L've Nikolayeviche Tolstom uchenika Yasno-polyanskoi shkoly Vasiliya Stepanovicha Morozova* [Reminiscenses of Lev Nikolayevich Tolstoy by a pupil at Yasnaya Polyana school, Vasily Stepanovich Morozov], 'Posrednik' Press, Moscow, 1917.

Tvorcheskiye raboty uchenikov Tolstogo v Yasnoi Polyane [Creative work by pupils of Tolstoy at Yasnaya Polyana], ed. Thomas G. Winner, Brown University Press, 1974

L. N. Tolstoy v vospominaniyakh sovremennikov [L. N. Tolstoy in the reminiscences of contemporaries], vol. 1, Moscow, 1955.

Of the vast literature on Tolstoy and his times we have found the following particularly useful:

Berlin, Isaiah, 'Tolstoy and Enlightenment', *Encounter* 16, no. 2, February 1961, and in *Russian Thinkers,* The Hogarth Press, 1978.

Besançon, Alain, *Education et société en Russie dans le second tiers du 19è siècle,* Mouton, Paris and The Hague, 1974.

Gusev, N. N., *Lev Nikolayevich Tolstoy, Materialy k biografii s 1855 po 1869 god* [Lev Nikolayevich Tolstoy, materials for a biography 1855–69], Moscow, 1957.

Gusev, N. N., *Khronika zhizni i tvorchestva L. N. Tolstogo* [A chronicle of the life and work of L. N. Tolstoy], Moscow, 1958–60.

Hans, Nicholas, *A History of Russian Educational Policy, 1701–1917,* Russell and Russell, New York, 1964.

Maude, Aylmer, *The Life of Tolstoy,* Oxford University Press, 1953.

Seton-Watson, Hugh, *The Russian Empire 1801–1971,* Clarendon Press, 1967.

Principles for Evaluating Chemicals in the Environment

A Report of the

Committee for the Working Conference on Principles of Protocols for Evaluating Chemicals in the Environment

Environmental Studies Board
National Academy of Sciences–
National Academy of Engineering

and

Committee on Toxicology
National Research Council

NATIONAL ACADEMY OF SCIENCES
WASHINGTON, D.C. 1975

NOTICE: The project that is the subject of this report was approved by the Governing Board of the National Research Council, acting in behalf of the National Academy of Sciences. Such approval reflects the Board's judgment that the project is of national importance and appropriate with respect to both the purposes and resources of the National Research Council.

The members of the committee selected to undertake this project and prepare this report were chosen for recognized scholarly competence and with due consideration for the balance of disciplines appropriate to the project. Responsibility for the detailed aspects of this report rests with that committee.

Each report issuing from a study committee of the National Research Council is reviewed by an independent group of qualified individuals according to procedures established and monitored by the Report Review Committee of the National Academy of Sciences. Distribution of the report is approved, by the President of the Academy, upon satisfactory completion of the review process.

At the request of and funded by the
Environmental Protection Agency
Contract numbers 68-01-0132 and 68-01-0772

Library of Congress Catalog Card No. 74-31482
International Standard Book No. 0-309-02248-7

Available from
Printing and Publishing Office, National Academy of Sciences
2101 Constitution Avenue, N.W., Washington, D.C. 20418

Printed in the United States of America

Preface

The report which follows was in response to two separate contracts between the Environmental Protection Agency and the National Academy of Sciences–National Research Council. The two contracts dealt with complementary aspects of the safety assessment of chemicals—one relating to human health, the other to effects on other systems. Happily, they were essentially contemporaneous, and those responsible for the separate contracts wisely and immediately sensed the rightness of joining forces in a single comprehensive approach. This early good judgment made possible a most remarkable collaboration between the two components in what is, after all, a series of problems with much interaction and in which arbitrary boundaries would have led to serious and needless impediments as well as duplication of effort by the scientific community.

A significant but not exclusive reason for undertaking this exercise has been the anticipation that some form of legislation approximating one of the versions of the "Toxic Substances Control Act" presented to the last Congress might be passed in the present one. The various versions of the Act all require that information on the safety and benefits of chemicals be submitted to the Administrator of EPA to guide him in making a determination as to what restraints, if any, would be placed on the manufacture and use of specific chemicals. The sense of the several acts, present and pending, places on the Administrator the burden of judging the appropriate restrictions to be placed on manufacture and use; for this, he must have information. It is to the acquisition of this information that the present report is directed. Which questions can be usefully asked at the present state of the art and science of safety assessments? Which questions would be useless because present techniques are inadequate or because the information provided would be irrelevant? These issues stand on their own and will have a wide applicability whether or not a "Toxic Substances Control Act" is passed and put into force. This report is accordingly directed to all branches of the relevant governmental agencies involved in safety assessments and also to those industries concerned with the manufacture, distribution, and use of chemical products.

I would like to note here the extraordinary dedication and intense work that the distinguished scientists involved in the preparation of this report gave to its production. The assignment was a very large one; the time allowed was extremely short. Their work at their desks, in the preconference panel meetings, and finally at the Working Conference at which this report was completed, was extremely arduous. The task made a very substantial drain on their time. I thank them warmly. I should also like to thank the staff of the National Academy of Sciences–National Research Council for their able and perceptive backup; without this, satisfactory completion of the task would have been impossible. I especially wish to commend Mr. Ralph Wands of the Advisory Center on Toxicology, Dr. Charles Malone, and Dr. Charles Baummer of the Environmental Studies Board, and Mrs. A.L. Carlson and Miss Betsy Wilmoth for outstanding management of the central office during the San Antonio Working Conference, and Dr. Arthur J. Pallotta for his services as editorial consultant. Finally, I would like to thank Dr. John Buckley of the Office of Research and Monitoring of the Environmental Protection Agency for his wise advice in the scientific planning of this exercise.

NORTON NELSON, *Chairman*
Committee for the
Working Conference on
Principles of Protocols for
Evaluating Chemicals in the Environment

February 1973